Complexities and Challenges of Nuclear India

Complexities and Challenges of Nuclear India

By

Dr. Roshan Khanijo

(Established 1870)

United Service Institution of India
New Delhi

Vij Books India Pvt Ltd
New Delhi (India)

Published by

Vij Books India Pvt Ltd
(Publishers, Distributors & Importers)
2/19, Ansari Road
Delhi – 110 002
Phones: 91-11-43596460, 91-11-47340674
Fax: 91-11-47340674
e-mail: vijbooks@rediffmail.com

I would like to dedicate this book to Reverend Guruji, who has inspired, and taught me that true happiness can be achieved by following one's dreams.

Contents

List of Tables

List of Figures

Preface

India's nuclear journey has always been an area of fascination for me. Whether it was India's criticism of the NPT, or its overt declaration of becoming a Nuclear Weapon State in 1998, the ambiguity and mystery that has surrounded the development of India's nuclear strategy, has become the hallmark of India's nuclear policy. India is one of the few countries, whose leaders clearly understood the implications of the nuclear explosion in 1945. This cataclysmic event had upturned the security paradigms globally and countries were forced to rethink their strategies. Despite spearheading the shift to a "Nuclear Age" by becoming the first country in Asia to construct a nuclear reactor – namely "Apsara", India lost its initial momentum to China. China capitalized this opportunity, provided by the shifting power balance, by becoming a member of the UN Security Council. Moreover, through their systematic modernization process, China now has emerged as a potent force and a key nuclear nation.

Since India adopted the "Civilian Nuclear Programme" quite early, it becomes necessary to analyse the nuclear issue in a holistic manner. I consider it important to examine and understand the complexities and challenges posed, by the military as well as civilian sector. So, through this book, I am making an attempt to examine both. The feasibility of Thorium reactors, the multi-layered Asian threat, the changing global scenario and the efficacy of India's nuclear doctrine and its force structure are some issues which require attention. In the civilian sector tracing the rise and progress of the power plants will provide an insight into the energy domain. As such India is going to face the energy crunch due to its depleting coal reserves. Nuclear energy may just try to narrow this gap. The closed nuclear cycle, adopted by the Indian scientists, which has been programmed to function through the use of thorium, needs to be re-examined in order to evaluate its applicability and efficacy. The feasibility of Thorium reactors has been debated worldwide but Indian scientists, however, have been aiming to formalize the three stage nuclear power generation as soon as possible. The sanctions which had been imposed on India, post the nuclear explosion of 1974, were relaxed subsequently, and the Indian nuclear industry revived its nuclear cooperation with other nations like Russia, France, South Korea etc. This was possible due to the Indo-US nuclear deal, which was a significant event in the civilian nuclear history of India, as it had opened the pathway for international cooperation. The nuclear deal should have ideally brought about a revolution in the nuclear industry in India, however, the question that has actually emerged out of this situation is whether India has been able to capitalize the opportunity or not. Researchers find themselves examining the fact that the Civil Liability Act, aimed at advancement, has ended up putting roadblocks on its progress instead. The Liability act, though beneficial in many ways, has also created many controversies. It has created negative publicity as far as investors are concerned, and foreign vendors remain reluctant to accept the act in totality.

The Fukushima disaster has brought the issues of nuclear safety and security to the forefront. There has been a lot of debate, regarding the emergency preparedness of India's growing nuclear power plants. It has been suggested, that an Independent Regulatory Body that would serve as a watchdog, is essential to ensure the smooth functioning of the nuclear power plants. The need, for such an autonomous body has resurfaced once again due to growing doubts regarding the neutrality of the Atomic Energy Regulatory Body (AERB). Hence; all these issues need to be addressed in entirety. I have made an attempt, therefore, to research and analyse the civilian sector and understand the broad workings of this sector. The shortage of conventional energy sources – especially the depleting coal reserves – in conjunction with the reduced output of thermal power plants, has forced India to examine alternative sources of energy. Nuclear energy has the potential to grow, and help in mitigating the energy crisis that India is facing, provided high nuclear safety and security standards are maintained.

Post the 1962 Sino-Indian conflict, India is concerned about the intentions of China. The intermittent unapologetic border stand-offs and China's modernization of its nuclear weaponry – especially its missile inventory – remains a cause of concern. The nuclear missile race in Asia is causing geostrategic imbalance. Historically, with the disintegration of USSR, India was forced to rethink its strategic calculus. The emergence of China as an economic giant later on has reshaped the global power nexus.

Hence there is a need to reassess the Indian position vis-à-vis this dramatic shift. Therefore, before understanding India's nuclear policies, it is essential to perform a thorough environmental scan.

The environment post the Cold War, is very different, and the key factor now is the emergence of a major power shift, from Europe to Asia. This in turn has transformed the theory of warfare. Now more asymmetric methods of warfare are adopted by countries especially in Asia. Also for nations in Asia "Nuclear Weapon" is the central theme, in their strategic calculus, to maintain their territorial sovereignty. However; West, headed by America, have tried to downplay the importance of nuclear weapons, and their reliance on precession guided conventional weapons is a major policy changer for many Western countries. This difference in the strategic perception needs to be examined and evaluated. Additionally, nuclear deterrence has always been central to Asia. Whether it was direct or extended deterrence, nuclear deterrence has always had the potential to change the power nexus. Hence; any change in the present status quo, could wreak devastating effects on the precarious stability of the Asian subcontinent.

The 21st century has brought another type of warfare to the forefront, the genesis of which lies in the asymmetric warfare adopted by Pakistan. Pakistan has always competed with India, its inherent insecurity often carried due to the baggage of history, has created instability in South Asia. India cannot ignore Pakistan due to the geographical proximity of both the nations. The latter's incessant nuclear competition, its growing nuclear arsenal and the fissile material production units, and its volatile intentions aimed at deploying tactical nuclear weapons, are cumulatively lowering the threshold in Asia. Pakistan's offensive nuclear doctrine and its ever increasing red lines are escalating nuclear brinkmanship. The vindictive role of Non State Actors (NSAs), (trained in Pakistani soil), serve to make South Asia as a whole, (not just India) vulnerable to nuclear terrorism. The dangerous clouds of "Dirty Bombs" loom large in this region and remain a constant source of threat. Moreover, with the increasing number of covert and overt New Nuclear Weapons States (NNWS), nuclear material theft, sabotage and cyber-crimes, are other grave security issues that need to be addressed. Over and above this boiling pot of volatility, the growing bonhomie of Pakistan and China makes India vulnerable to a collusive Sino-Pak threat that India will find it difficult to fend off, without grave losses.

Is India's Nuclear Doctrine good enough to deal with an increasingly offensive Pakistan? Or the debates to change India's No First Use policy, (which is considered as an impediment in India's nuclear strategy as far as China is concerned) justified? Is India's nuclear doctrine compatible with India's force structure? Or are there strategic gaps that India needs to address promptly, to ensure efficient development of its nuclear policy? An attempt has been made to examine and analyse some of these issues through the course of this book.

On the positive side one must remember, that India has also emerged as a major power in Asia. India's economic growth and its immense markets, make India a major attraction for foreign investors. Therefore, India should engage constructively with other nations, and judiciously use its resources, to shape the world to its advantage. India's future will depend on answering all these questions and implementing the resultant requirements satisfactorily. Therefore; a detailed analysis of India's doctrine and policy has become even more essential now than ever. India's compulsions, its challenges and complexities need to be studied in a logical and impartial manner. My attempt through this book has been to analyse the challenges faced by a nuclear India in a holistic way taking into account the shifting global paradigms. The coming years are going to be crucial for India and the policies and strategies adopted by the policy makers will impact India's present and future, and in the bargain impact the geo-politics of this region as well. Through this journey, I have tried to impartially analyse India's position vis-à-vis the nuclear process, in an attempt to examine it, scrutinize it and analyse the bearing it could have on India's future.

Acknowledgements

I would like to thank the United Service Institution of India (USI) for giving me the opportunity to write this book .The supportive academic environment, the international seminars, the illuminating interaction with foreign and Indian think tanks through various bilateral and multilateral platforms has helped me in enhancing and widening my horizons. I would especially like to thank Lieutenant General P K Singh PVSM, AVSM, (Retd), Director USI, for helping me analyse the issue logically in a structured manner by providing me with new insights through discussions and suggestions. I would also like to thank him for providing me with important references, which has helped in organizing and shaping the book.

My Sincere gratitude to Major General YK Gera (Retd), Consultant and Head (Research), Center for Strategic Studies and Simulation (CS3), for the constant encouragement and informative discussions. He has always been there to prod me in the right direction whenever I have encountered a conundrum or a quandary. His support and encouragement has been invaluable.

I would like to thank Major General B.K Sharma, AVSM, SM** (Retd) for his inputs on China. His expertise on Net Assessment and the candid discussions which I had with him, enriched my knowledge.

I would also like to mention that I remain indebted to all my fellow research scholars for their comments, suggestions and opinions that have helped me fine tune the rough edges of the book. The conducive and friendly environment of CS3 is certainly a great motivational factor that helped immensely during the creation of this book. I would like to thank Brig Amar Cheema (Retd), Col N P S Bisht and Capt. Sandeep Dewan for their invaluable inputs on China, and Professor Nirmala Joshi for giving me an insight on Russia.

I would sincerely like to thank all the people whose comments and suggestions in the aftermath of my various presentations have helped me fine tune and improve upon my initial drafts. I would also like to thank Air Marshal T M Asthana PVSM, AVSM, VSM, (Retd) for his constant support. His careful scrutiny of the chapters in this book, and his subsequent suggestions, has been truly invaluable. My sincerest thanks to Lt Gen B S Nagal, PVSM, AVSM, SM (Retd) as well, for his timely comments and recommendations.

I would also like to thank the entire Library staff of USI for their help in providing me with rare books, obscure journals and unique reference materials promptly without a single complaint. Their silent encouragement has been extremely helpful.

Lastly this book would not have been possible without the help of my daughter, Natallia, whose constant encouragement during my weaker moments of frustration and her editorial assistance have truly aided me in completing this book. I am truly indebted to her for all her support. I would like to give my heartfelt gratitude to my husband, Alok, who has always encouraged me to push my limits, and has been my pillar of strength. I would take this opportunity to thank my parents, who provided me with the opening to follow a field of my choice. From them I have learnt how to stay strong during adversities. I would especially like to dedicate this book to my father, and I hope that in some small capacity, I have managed to make him proud.

List of Abbreviations

AAA	Anti-Aircraft Artillery
A2/AD	Anti-Access/Area Denial
ABM	Anti-Ballistic Missile
ADIZ	Air Defence Identification Zone
AQIM	Al-Qaida Islamic Maghreb
ASBM	Anti- Ship Ballistic Missile
BARC	Bhabha Atomic Research Center
BTWC	Biological and Toxic Weapons Convention
CBM	Confidence Building Measures
C&C	Command and Control
CCS	Cabinet Committee on Security
CMC	Central Military Commission
CWC	Chemical Weapons Convention
CCW	Convention on Certain Conventional Weapons
C4ISR	Command, Control, Communications, Computers, Intelligence, Surveillance and Reconnaissance
CD	Conferences on Disarmament
CMD	Credible Minimum Deterrence
CISMOA	Communications and Information Security Memorandum of Agreement

CNWS	Clandestine Nuclear Weapon States
CSC	Convention of Supplementary Compensation
CTBT	Comprehensive Test Ban Treaty
CONUS	Continental US
CSD	Cold Start Doctrine
DIDL	Defence Item Description List
EPZ	Emergency Planning Zone
FMCT	Fissile Missile Cut off Treaty
HADR	Humanitarian Assistance and Disaster Relief
HEU	Highly Enriched Uranium
HNS	Host Nation Support
IAEA	International Atomic Energy Associations
IAEC	Israel Atomic Energy Commission
IOC	Indian Oil Company
IOR	Indian Ocean Region
IW	Information Warfare
ICBMs	Intercontinental Ballistic Missiles
IMF	International Monetary Fund
JeM	Jaish-e-Muhammad
KRL	Kahuta Research Laboratory
LACM	Land Attack Cruise Missiles
LEU	Low Enriched Uranium
LeT	Lashkar-e-toiba
L&T	Larsen & Toubro
LOCA	Loss of Coolant Accident
LSA	Logistic Support Agreement

LWR	Light Water Reactors
MAD	Mutually Assured Destruction
MENWFZ	Middle East Nuclear Weapon Free Zone
MPADS	Man-Portable Air Defense Systems
MTCR	Missile Technology Control Regime
NAM	Non Aligned Movement
NCA	National Command Authority
NATO	North Atlantic Treaty Organisation
NALCO	National Aluminum Company
NDPG	National Defence Programme Guidelines
NFU	No First Use
NDPG	National Defence Program Guidelines
NNWS	New Nuclear Weapon States
NPT	Nuclear Non-Proliferation Treaty
NPCIL	National Power Corporation of India
NTPC	National Thermal Power Cooperation of India
NSA	Non State Actors
NSG	Nuclear Suppliers Group
NSS	Nuclear Security Summit
NTS	Nuclear Threshold State
NWFZ	Nuclear Weapon Free Zone
NWFW	Nuclear Weapon Free World
PAEC	Pakistan Atomic Energy Commission
PNP	Peaceful Nuclear Programme
SUPARCO	Space and Upper Atmosphere Research Commission

PHWR	Pressurised Heavy Water Reactors
PSI	Proliferation Security Initiative
QRMTs	Quick Reaction Medical Teams
RDD	Radioactive Dispersal Device
REACT	Regional East African Counter Terrorism
RMA	Revolution in Military Affairs
ROK	Republic of Korea
SAF	Second Artillery Force
SAC	Second Artillery Corps
SALT	Strategic Arms Limitation Talks
SAM	Surface to Air Missile
SDF	Self Defence Forces
SLOC	Sea lanes of communications
TSCP	Trans-Sahara Counterterrorism Partnership
SLCM	Submarine Launched Cruise Missile
TNS	Threshold Nuclear States
TTBT	Threshold Test Ban Treaty
UAV	Unarmed Aerial Vehicle
WMD	Weapons of Mass Destruction

1   Introduction

"The war of the future, would be one in which man could extinguish millions of lives at one blow, demolish the great cities of the world, wipe out the cultural achievements of the past--and destroy the very structure of a civilization that has been slowly and painfully built up through hundreds of generations."[1]

The Manhattan Project, introduced the world to a "Nuclear Age", and the twin bombing of Hiroshima and Nagasaki was the dreadful result. This atomic bomb, was more than a weapon of terrible destruction, it became a psychological weapon[2]. In a single stroke, the Americans had upset the strategic balance. They further tested a new type of bomb in 1952 the H-bomb, (thousand times more lethal than the nuclear bomb), and established the "second great step of the nuclear Age"[3]. In the past, history had testified to the fact that nations continuously work to create a balance of power, so that the war could be avoided. Hence in the twentieth century the nations in order to regain global strategic stability began coveting this technology, which led to a nuclear cataclysm and brought a Revolution in Military Affairs (RMA). The shadow of this lethal bomb governed the strategic and tactical temperament of countries world over and created "Nuclear Competition". The nations realised that "Atomic wars could be instrument of force without war[4]".This was qualitatively different than anybody had ever anticipated before, and the deterrence theory became more relevant. As deterrence precludes war, therefore nuclear weapons became the means to extend that deterrence and avoid engaging in full-fledged warfare. According to the theory of deterrence, the threat of using nuclear weapons prevents the adversary from using the same weapons due to the level of damage that can be caused for both sides. Hence, a stage of Nash Equilibrium is reached, through which both the sides try to maintain stability and balance. On the other hand the nations were in a rat race to acquire superior technology, resulting in technological innovations and more sophistication of warheads. This growing technological competence has transformed the strategic concepts too and emerging jargon such as "Mutually Assured Deterrence", "Flexible Response" "No First Use" etc, has become a part of the nuclear vocabulary.

It was believed initially that an era of nuclear deterrence would bring peace. The renowned nuclear strategist Bernard Brodie wrote "Thus far the chief purpose of our military establishment has been to win wars. From now on its chief purpose must be to avert them. It can have almost no other useful purpose."[5] The Cold War gave legitimacy to nuclear deterrence. However; The Korean War, the Berlin Blockade and the Cuban missile crisis, amplified the nuclear threat. Despite the escalation, the destructive power of nuclear weapons acted as a moderator and ensured that the then super powers USA and the erstwhile USSR, treaded with caution, thereby creating a stability which lasted many decades.

The era post the Cold War saw the emergence of New Nuclear Weapon States (NNWS) and ultimately the dispersal of nuclear weapons. This altered the strategic space again as more nations were embroiled in this lethal arms race. The Five Permanent nations (P5) of the United Nations were no longer the sole custodians of the nuclear weapon. The rise of NNWS, the Threshold Nuclear States (TNS) and the Clandestine Nuclear Weapon States (CNWS) has lowered the nuclear threshold since then. The primary reason for this nuclear expansion was, that although the Cold War had witnessed a period of nuclear brinkmanship and nuclear détente, it could not contain the nuclear genie. Even the various nuclear disarmament treaties could not prevent the expansion of nuclear weapons and gradually, this nuclear proliferation became widespread. The Asian continent was the most affected as most of the emerging Nuclear Weapon States both covert and overt happened to be from Asia.

The Cold War concept of nuclear deterrence has changed and ideas like Mutually Assured Destruction (MAD) have been diluted. It was widely deliberated that for deterrence to be realistic, it was essential for nuclear weapons to survive the shock or surprise attack.

Hence newer concepts such as survivability, second strike, punitive attack, etc. developed. The doctrinal changes tested the military build-up and the dyad got transformed into a triad. Some nations with geographical and conventional weaknesses as well as financial constraints found it difficult to counter conventional challenges and so (nations like Pakistan for example) opted for offensive nuclear doctrines such as the "First Use", while developing Tactical Nuclear Weapons (TNW) as offensive weapons to be used as counter force in a limited and controlled battlefield situation. They borrowed this concept from the NATO countries, despite the fact that the NATO countries themselves had abandoned it, as they found it unworkable due to difficulties in controlling the escalated threat levels. Nevertheless, this has been revived by Asian nations thus reaffirming the prominence of nuclear weapons in their strategic thought. Along with this, innovative doctrinal concepts are guiding the nuclear inventories and nations are researching to develop the nuances of nuclear weapons and their delivery systems. They are tiresomely working to acquire a technological edge. Modern guidance systems, the revolution in accuracy and sensors, ballistic missile defense, antisubmarine warfare, intelligence surveillance-and-reconnaissance systems, offensive cyber warfare, conventional precision strike, and long range precision strike, in addition to nuclear strike capabilities are significant components of modern day warfare.

The Stability –Instability Paradox

The strategic significance of nuclear weapons in providing nuclear deterrence in Asia has often been debated due to the change in the nature of warfare. The advent of low- intensity warfare or the asymmetric method has led to this stability – instability paradox.

It is often believed that when two nations have nuclear weapons, they try to avoid each other directly, thereby averting the possibility of a direct encounter. However, this does not prevent them from adopting indirect proxy wars, through the state sponsored Non State Actors (NSA). In simpler terms, the characteristic feature of 21st century warfare has been "Terrorism" and nuclear weapons cannot provide strategic stability here. However; there is also a counter argument to this premise which states that the fact that low intensity was maintained during the standoffs and the conflict was not allowed to escalate to a full-fledged nuclear exchange, was simply due to the concept of nuclear deterrence, and so while it may have provided instability at a lower level, it has continued to make South Asia stable at a higher level. The discussions and debates about the nuclear age may continue, but the fact remains that there has emerged a clear divide in the perception of nations regarding the utility of nuclear weapons.

Conventional verses Nuclear Deterrence

Some of the P5 nations, particularly US, France and Great Britain have decreased their reliance on nuclear weapons and for them the utility of nuclear weapons have greatly diminished, this can be primarily due to the diminishing of nuclear threat scenarios in Europe and secondly due to the increased sophistication of their conventional precision guided systems. This in turn has also revived the efficacy of conventional weapons in the western thought process. But for Russia, China and other nuclear nations in Asia, the threat perception is different. This is due to entwined security interests whereby any increase in the nuclear weapons will have a cascading effect in the entire region. China has slowly modernized and increased the range and precision of its nuclear triad. This aggressive posture becomes a threat for everyone, and is also, therefore, creating complications in the bilateral nuclear disarmament negotiations between Russia and US. Russia would prefer a multilateral nuclear disarmament treaty where China is also an active signatory. The future of nuclear disarmament, therefore, rests on a thin string, and a lot depends on the initiatives taken by China. If China remains adamant about its position and refuses to decrease its nuclear weapons on the pretext that the Americans and the Russia should decrease their nuclear arsenal to China's level, then there are chances that the current nuclear stalemate will continue, which can have a potentially damaging effect in Asia. Since most of the New Nuclear Weapon States and Threshold States are in Asia, any belligerence from China will disrupt the strategic balance and lead to an upsurge in the horizontal proliferation of nuclear weapons.

Nuclear deterrence has already become more buoyant in Asia as many nations with a weak conventional arsenal, consider their repertoire of nuclear weapons as a counter measure to maintain strategic balance within the area. In Asia with the rise of China the balance of power is shifting, and in the process, it is also testing the influence of US in Asia. The US alliance system in Asia is at its lowest point. China's Air Defence Identification Zone (ADIZ) and the Senkaku Island standoff in the East China Sea is considered as an aggressive strategy, aimed at testing the extended deterrence in the region. If this continues, then Asia may see the rise of few more New Nuclear Weapon States such as Japan and South Korea.

India's Dilemma

India is also emerging as a major power and the rise of both China and India will test the global system. This economic resurgence will influence military and foreign relations, and may lead to a system of alliances and partnerships. A strategic churning has begun in Asia. Whether it will be in India's favour or not depends on the strategic choices that India adopts, and to understand these choices, it is essential to scrutinize the global environment more thoroughly. The external factors impact the internal dynamics of the nation state and vice versa. Therefore; to get a holistic view of the situation, it is imperative to analyse both situations together. Historically nuclear weapons have played a key role in defining a country's security policy. They have been developed for various reasons and this may vary from being developed for deterrence purposes to being used as a currency to power.

India's tryst with the atomic bomb is as old as the bomb itself. India's first Prime Minister Pt. Nehru understood the implications of a nuclear test early on, and he along with India's eminent physicist, Dr. Homi Jahangir Bhabha charted India's nuclear destiny. For India nuclear weapons were not a choice but necessary deterrence tools and remain so till now. The Sino-Indian conflict of 1962 had scarred India and the nuclear test by China in 1964 aggravated the security risks. Being flanked by a nuclear neighbour was a dangerous proposition because unlike Pakistan who was a member of CENTO, SEATO, India was not a member of any multilateral alliance systems and hence had to rely on its own resources. India was and continues to be a champion of universal nuclear disarmament. India's Rajeev Gandhi Action Plan for Nuclear Weapon Free and Non-Violent

World Order depicts India's thoughts about nuclear disarmament, but India is against discrimination of any kind. Until all nations take the pledge to disarm their nuclear arsenal, a "Nuclear Zero" cannot be achieved and so until global disarmament becomes a possibility India will be forced to maintain its nuclear arsenal.

The Sino-Pak friendship and Chinese support to Pakistan's nuclear programme has resulted in the birth of another nuclear nation in Asia namely Pakistan. Pakistan has always stated that its nuclear policy is in retaliation to India's nuclear programme, whereas India has repeatedly mentioned that it has never considered Pakistan as its nuclear adversary. Pakistan's support to terrorist organizations, its incessant growth of nuclear fissile material production units, its aggressive nuclear doctrine and its persistent efforts to escalate the tension in the region and its progress along the nuclear ladder has made Asia vulnerable to nuclear brinkmanship. The Pakistani strategy of developing Tactical Nuclear Weapons (TNW) has threatened not only India, but the entire Asian continent as well, since the probability of terrorists acquiring nuclear weapons has increased. Terrorists are guided by ideology and with the mushrooming of suicide bombers, geographical barriers have no meaning anymore. Therefore all the states are at risk from this menace, and until the source is targeted this disease cannot be eradicated.

Atom for Peace

Along with the military usage of nuclear material, a parallel concept the "Atom for Peace" programme in the civilian sector was introduced by the American President Dwight D. Eisenhower in his speech to the UN General Assembly in 1953. This got rid of the secrecy that was generally associated with nuclear technology. Today there are nearly thirty countries that are actively involved in the civilian nuclear programme. There are some 435 nuclear power reactors operating in 31 countries plus Taiwan, with a combined capacity of over 370 GWe.[6] In 2011, these reactors provided 2518 billion KWh; about 13.5 per cent of the world's electricity and over 60 power reactors are currently being constructed in 13 countries plus Taiwan which means that 64,978 tonnes of Uranium would be required to achieve the target.[7] Uranium is the common denominator in both the civilian as well as the military equation. This nuclear fissile material is an important component for civilian as well as military reactors. The presence of large stockpiles of uranium is hazardous since the civilian uranium could be diverted for making nuclear weapons. Like the two sides of a coin, nuclear energy can be used either for generating power and enriching human life or for producing nuclear weapons which can annihilate the human race. The choice to create or destroy is a major decision that has global repercussions and every country has a universal moral obligation to think of the greater good, before their own state related issues. It will be the responsibility of every nation to cooperate in providing global nuclear safety and security standards for the world. The transparency, surveillance and monitoring by the International Atomic Energy Associations (IAEA) is an important effort to control the misuse of nuclear materials. The mandates laid by the International associations should be followed universally and without any discrimination. In other words, it is the responsibility of P5 nations as well as declared Nuclear Weapon States to open their civilian and military nuclear power plants for IAEA supervision. This is only possible when nations agree to work together to eliminate nuclear weapons in a phased manner and create a non-violent world order. While such an image is undoubtedly a utopian concept, its applicability depends on the sharp decision making of the major powers, which can set precedents, for other nations to follow.

Complexities and Challenges of Nuclear India

India's nuclear journey began in 1948 when the Atomic Energy Act was passed. The first successful step took place in 1956 when "Apsara" became the first nuclear research reactor to get operationalised in Asia. Since then considerable changes have taken place, not only in India's internal environment but also in the global nuclear environment as a whole. While there have been phenomenal technological advancements in the military sector, the civilian sector has been marred with safety and security dilemmas. This book has been divided into two sections. The first part deals with the civilian nuclear sector and the second part deals with the military use of nuclear weapons. The focus through this book has been to highlight the changing dynamics of the global nuclear structure with special reference to India and its 'Asian Neighbours'. I have therefore; provided a brief overview of the civilian nuclear programme in order to provide a context for the subsequent analysis.

The Civilian Nuclear Challenge

The first part charts the development of the Civilian Nuclear Energy Programme. It begins with the origin of nuclear energy and then attempts to assess the major aspects of the Indian nuclear programme. In the past few years, India's energy requirements have grown exponentially with growing economic resurgence. There has been an imbalance in the demand and supply ratio in the energy sector. The conventional sources of energy have been unable to match the growing demands of the industries. The prospect of nuclear energy as a clean source of energy has emerged as an alternative to the already depleting non – renewable resources such as coal and natural gas. The government has gone all out to harness this resource, but there are challenges and complexities in using nuclear energy as an alternative source for generating electricity. Sub chapters I and II deal with these aspects in detail. At the beginning of its nuclear journey, India had adopted a three stage nuclear programme due to the presence of large resources of thorium. India's first commercial fast breeder reactor, the 500 MWe Prototype Fast Breeder Reactor (PFBR), is scheduled to become critical in September 2014. However, critics world over are apprehensive about this technology. It is essential to analyse the advantages and disadvantages of this technology. Along with the analysis of the reactor, one also needs to analyse the feasibility and constraints that thorium as an alternate fuel, poses.

The Indian government has projected a target of installing about 20 GWe nuclear power plants by the year 2020 and it aims to supply 25 per cent of the total electricity through nuclear power by 2050. In continuing with this ambitious plan it wants to create "Nuclear Energy Parks".[8] All these projections steer us to the most important question that concerns the "Safety and Security" of these nuclear power plants. Hence sub chapter III deals with the "Nuclear Safety and Security". The Atomic Energy Regulatory Board (AERB) is responsible for the regulation, licensing and safety inspection of all the nuclear facilities, but this body is not an Independent Statutory Authority. It comes under the Atomic Energy Commission. After lot of deliberations in April 2011, the government announced that it would set up a new independent and autonomous Nuclear

Regulatory Authority of India that will also subsume the AERB, and that previous safety assessments of Indian plants would be made public.[9]However, until it is implemented, it is essential to test the working and efficiency of the AERB. Apart from this, it is important to know the parameters for safety and what challenges remain if there are any. Nuclear security has become a major challenge today, especially due to the spread of terrorism. The security concerns are extended to the fissile material as well as the power plants that become vulnerable to attacks through nuclear thefts, sabotage, and radiation leaks. These are severe threats that can cripple any nation. India is one of the few countries that has made substantial progress as far as stringent guidelines regarding the monitoring of nuclear accidents are concerned. India's Civil Liability Act is an encouraging effort in this direction; however, while the act has lot of high points, it also has its own share of limitations and problems. India is facing criticism from foreign firms due to this act and they are becoming increasingly reluctant to enter the nuclear foray. This global hesitation is impacting the nuclear leverage that India gained through the Indo-US nuclear deal. After examining the security paradigm, the last sub chapter deals with the need for International Cooperation in order to augment the energy production. The chapter examines importance of the Nuclear Supplier's Group, the Indo-US Civil Nuclear Deal, etc. Moreover, the need for a more intensive international cooperation with developed countries like Russia, France, and South Korea, along with prospect of indigenous projects with the NTPC, NALCO, SAIL etc, are also analysed.

The Nuclear Environment

Nations exist in a dynamic environment that is constantly changing. These changes in the global environment directly impact the performance, growth and wellbeing of each nation in some way or the other. Moreover, the increased global interdependence due to a universal resource crunch has brought in the elements of both competition and cooperation. In order to reduce confrontation and augment cooperation, it is essential to know and understand the changing roles of global players. Hence the strategic planning begins with identifying these relations. For a nation, it is essential to understand the external and internal environment together, in order to establish linkages, which will make it easier to formulate national and larger strategic objectives. Therefore, in this book, an attempt has been made to perform a global scan of the nuclear environment. The start point is a short nuclear history, (which tries to examining the changing nuclear environment) and subsequently it presents the characteristic features of the global nuclear scenario in the 21st century. Thus, the analysis of the threat environment starts with the second chapter - The Global Nuclear Threat. This begins with sub chapters that covers a short history of the nuclear environment, the traditional nuclear players, the Cold War era and the emergence of New World Order (where nuclear power is no longer under the sole custody of the traditional P5 Nations.) The 21st Century has seen the emergence of New Nuclear Weapon States and Threshold Nuclear States. The second sub chapter highlights the challenges faced by the Nuclear Weapon States (especially US and erstwhile USSR) and the Threshold States, their nuclear arms build-up in the Cold War era, the dilution of this rivalry with the breaking up of the Soviet Union, a short period of Russia's isolation and introspection, the rise of China and strategic shift in the Asia Pacific region, and the subtle confrontation and competition between US and China to gain supremacy in South China Sea. The nuclear proliferation and the conflict between the New Nuclear Weapon States especially the belligerence of North Korea, the flagrant build-up of its nuclear arsenal and its refusal to abide international commitments and subsequently flouting rules on nuclear testing are serious causes of concern. It has had an impact on India as well, because North Korea is known for proliferating nuclear weapons technology. North Korea's alleged transfer of missile technology to Pakistan is one of the reasons for the arms race in Asia. If on one hand the environment in East Asia may become tense due to the rivalry between North and South Korea, on the other hand in West Asia the instability stems from the rivalry between Iran and Israel. Iran's alleged nuclear programme is a major irritant for Israel. Iran's interim nuclear deal in November 2013 is considered an achievement by the world community, however; few nations like Israel and Saudi Arabia consider this deal a smokescreen, behind which Iran will continue its nuclear weapons programme.

Nuclear terrorism is another area where the role of non-state actors has been criticized. They have drastically increased the threat factor and contributed in making the global environment vulnerable to nuclear weapon theft, sabotage and radioactive dispersal in the form of "Dirty Bombs". Out of all the security threats, India is most vulnerable to terrorism, primarily due to Pakistan's continued covert aid to terrorist organizations. Pakistan is not only helping these organizations through financial aid and technical expertise, but it is also providing them with space in their territory to organize and plan such militant activities (It is their grand strategy to bleed India through thousand cuts).So nuclear terrorism is a global threat. It cannot be addressed by one country hence a collective effort is required to tackle this problem, therefore, the last sub chapter in this section deals with Nuclear disarmament. India has been a pioneer in the movement for nuclear disarmament, and the Rajeev Gandhi action plan for a nuclear weapons free zone is an effort to achieve "Nuclear Zero". The world community also had started debating nuclear disarmament in various Conferences on Disarmament (CD). Several treaties aimed at addressing different nuclear problems have been formulated. The Nuclear Non-Proliferation Treaty (NPT), Comprehensive Test Ban Treaty (CTBT), Proliferation Security Initiative (PSI), and Nuclear Security Summit (NSS) are treaties and summits which have attempted to deal with diverse nuclear subjects and situations in a major way. However, in spite of all these treaties, the world has witnessed an upsurge in the horizontal proliferation of nuclear weapons and technology; this highlights the fact that these treaties have their own limitations. Hence it is essential to understand the shortcomings that have emerged in these treaties and suggest alternate ways whereby they can be universally accepted. It is difficult to achieve the utopian concept of "Nuclear Weapon Free World", however, a more realistic nuclear disarmament approach – where the nations can discuss methods to achieve a global nuclear minimum and maximum can be worked out.

The Asian Challenge

After examining the global nuclear environment, it is essential to understand the strategic challenges that India face from its immediate neighbours, which is to work out the specifics of this nuclear threat. India's nuclear threat within Asia stems from its nuclear neighbours – namely China and Pakistan – and the collusive threat that stems from both these countries. Also Asia may face the nuclear challenge from North Korea as well as Iran. Therefore; the Fourth chapter deals with situation in East Asia and West Asia and the all-important Asian Challenge from Pakistan and China, where an attempt has been made to examine the nuclear arsenal of these two countries in detail (since any change in their strategy is going to impact the dynamics in India). It is important to question why nuclear weapons play such an important role in Asia. Whether it is the Threshold States, Covert Nuclear States or Overt Nuclear Weapon States, all of them consider nuclear weapons important for their nation's defence and view them as integral parts of their strategic planning. This is because the nations understand the value of deterrence that these weapons provide. Nuclear weapons can change the power dynamics of a region completely. A weak nation can become strong enough to threaten a strong one due to these weapons. Thus the nuclear weapons become a shield for both the strong as well as not so strong nations, because the scale of the possible damage prevents any responsible nation from taking action. Asia has thus revived the concept of nuclear deterrence and both types of deterrence – namely direct and extended deterrence – is visible here. This has provided a sort of stability at a higher level since the sheer magnitude of the risk has become the cause for the absence of a full-fledged war, but at the lower level the instability continues. It can be said that nowhere in the world is the stability – instability dilemma as apparent as it is in Asia. One can only hope that nations understand the lethality of nuclear weapons and attempt not to escalate the low intensity warfare up to a level where it would become difficult to control. This brings forth another question regarding the applicability of the deterrence principle. For deterrence to work, it is essential that nations should have a credible nuclear deterrence doctrine. This can be achieved when one evaluates its adversary's nuclear strength and strategizes the security paradigms accordingly. Thus the sub chapter on China analyses the Second Artillery Corps, (SAC) "The Strategic Force" of China. This book attempts to examine the logic underlying China's development of nuclear weapons, their nuclear Doctrine, implications of the NFU, and most importantly the change in the nature of warfare which according to Chinese military doctrines has become region centric. Their punch line is "local war under conditions of informationalisation". This is a veiled threat to China's neighbours. President Xi Jinping's statement in 2013 states "We will stick to the road of peaceful development, but will never give up our legitimate rights and will never sacrifice our national core interests. No country should presume that we will trade our core interests or that we will allow harm to be done to our sovereignty, security or development interests."[10] This statement has not helped either, because it has created yet another controversy regarding the definition of Chinese core interests. Apart from Tibet and Taiwan, certain thinkers have debated about the fact that has China included the controversial South China Sea region too as its core interest? The rise of China is also associated with its belligerent attitude that stems from its confidence in its military modernisation process. This is a process that started in the 1990s and has given her the capabilities to become a truly global power.

The SAC has adopted a dual deterrence and dual operations strategy whereby nuclear and conventional weapons are meshed together in its military strategy for an enhanced force. China has increased its second strike capabilities by modernizing and diversifying its nuclear weapons and by developing its nuclear triad. Thus, the modernisation of its missile brigade, and the aggressive trends of its force structure highlight the Chinese psyche.

Pakistan, unlike China openly believes in the "First use" of nuclear weapons and these weapons have always been an intrinsic part of their military strategy. Religious ideology fused with military strength has been an important part of Pakistan's politics. Their friendship with China has provided them with the requisite nuclear technology and since then they have increased their uranium and plutonium stockpiles drastically. Their indulgence in the development of Tactical Nuclear Weapons (TNWs) is a provocative strategy which will increase the threat level not only for India but also for Pakistan, because the utility of TNWs depend on its deployment at the field level that means delegating the authority to the local field commanders. In time of war during communication breakdown their use can precipitate the situation, also accidental use or theft of TNWs is other issue which requires expansive security arrangements. Questions are already being asked regarding the safety and security of Pakistan's nuclear weapons and the TNWs will only increase the need for responsibility. Pakistan is further trying to diversify its nuclear arsenal by developing its nuclear platforms at sea. By planning to nuclearize surface ship and submarines, it is diversifying its nuclear strategy from land to sea.

India had developed its nuclear weapon for deterrence purposes. That is why it is based on the principle of Credible Minimum Deterrence (CMD). But one needs to analyse whether the Indian force structure is competent enough to counter Chinese obstinacy. 2013 has seen several border stand-offs between the two countries. Moreover, with Pakistan increasing its nuclear weapons stockpile, the threat is redoubled since India might not be able to sustain a two front war. In such a scenario, what are the strategic gaps in the modernization procedures and what is the status of India's triad? These are but few questions that need to be answered. Therefore, the last sub chapter in this section "India's Nuclear Challenge", tries to objectively analyse the effectiveness of the Indian command and control system, the efficacy of the nuclear doctrine, the strategic vulnerabilities that arise due to delayed demand and supply, the problems concerning defence indigenization and so forth.

Future Prospects

It is easier to trace the road where the vulnerabilities are known because then they can be effectively addressed, through strategic planning. The last chapter thus tries to summarize the situation and chart the road map towards an effective strategic deterrence. In today's world, it is a fact that it is difficult for a single country to independently address the nuclear menace, whether the issue is related with nuclear terrorism, nuclear proliferation or nationalist belligerence. One needs to build up strategic capabilities, both as an independent nation as well as in partnership with those nations whose interests coalesce. This balance is the essence of efficient strategic planning, which can help in dealing with the changing global dynamics. Competition and cooperation are two sides of the same coin. It is the art of utilizing both these facets at an opportune moment, so that rich dividends could be achieved, by the countries of the nuclear world. But to avail this opportunity, India needs to become economically and militarily strong and it needs to utilize the window of opportunity prudently.

The possibility of a nuclear free world in the near future is remote and nuclear arms control is a more feasible option. But for the arms control to work, it is essential to understand the post-Cold War environment, since it is only through a comprehensive understanding that the situation can be managed. What is required now is a cooperative effort, through which this nuclear environment can be effectively managed. Thus through the last chapter - "Future prospects " the endeavour has been to suggest options whereby a uniform nuclear goal can become a reality, which through applied cooperation can culminate into the larger utopian goal of a "Nuclear Weapon Free World"

Endnotes

1   President Truman in his last "State of the Union" message to Congress, on 07 January 1953, as quoted by Bernard Brodie in "Nuclear Weapons :Strategic or Tactical? Foreign Affairs, January 1954

2   Ward Wilson, (2013) , *"Five Myth About Nuclear Weapons"*, New York, Houghton Mifflin Harcourt

3   Gaddis John Lewis, Phillip H Gordon, Ernest R May and Jonathan Rosenberg, eds, *(*1982.), *Cold War Statesman Confront the bomb Nuclear Diplomacy since 1945,* Oxford University Press,

4   Ibid

5   Bernard Brodie, (1946), *"The Absolute Weapon"*, New York: Harcourt

6   "Plans For New Reactors Worldwide", *World Nuclear Association, (Updated March 2013)* at http://www.world-nuclear.org/info/current-and-future-generation/plans-for-new-reactors-worldwide/

7   Ibid

8   Nuclear Power in India, World Nuclear Association , (Updated December 2013) at http://www.world-nuclear.org/info/Country-Profiles/Countries-G-N/India/

9   Ibid

10 *"China's declaration of key interests misinterpreted"*, 26 August 2013, www.China.Org.CN

2   Nuclear Journey

The Indian nuclear programme was envisioned even before India achieved her independence. As early as 26th June 1946, Pt. Jawaharlal Nehru had said: "As long as the world is constituted as it is, every country will have to devise and use the latest scientific devices for its protection. I have no doubt India will develop her scientific researches and I hope Indian scientists will use the atomic force for constructive purposes. But if India is threatened, she will inevitably try to defend herself by all means at her disposal."[1] This was how the foundation of India's nuclear programme was laid by its first Prime Minister. He had the requisite forethought to perceive that the path towards a prosperous India depended on the timely development of science and technology. Pt Nehru was supported by an eminent physicist, Dr Homi Jahangir Bhabha, who went on to formulate India's Atomic Energy Programme and is therefore remembered as the architect of India's nuclear programme. Although the Atomic Energy Act was passed by the constituent assembly in 1948, the planning of the construction of nuclear reactors began only after 1955, when Dr Bhabha as the President of the UN Conference on the Peaceful use of Atomic Energy persuaded Canada, France and UK to assist India in its power programme.[2] APSARA was the first nuclear research reactor in Asia and it became operational in 1956. India's nuclear programme has been ambiguous right from the beginning. While Prime Minister Nehru voiced his support for the "Civilian Nuclear Programme", he was against the use of nuclear energy for destructive purposes such as the creation of Atom Bombs. On July 24, 1957, Nehru said in the Lok Sabha "We have declared quite clearly that we are not interested in making atom bombs, even if we have the capacity to do so and that in no event will we use nuclear energy for destructive purposes...I hope that will be the policy of all future governments". A country's foreign policy is shaped by her political leaders and they in turn should frame these policies based on national interests, mainly the geo-political and strategic interests. The foreign policy adopted under Pt. Nehru involved the complete elimination of nuclear weapons or in other words the policy of total Global Nuclear Disarmament.

In India the period from 1947 to 1970 was marked by nuclear uncertainty and ambiguity. The various Prime Ministers that succeeded Pt. Nehru continued his policies in spite of the fact that the world was rapidly changing. Nations had begun to covet the nuclear bomb and the reasons for acquiring the capability varied from simply "status" (prestige) to "security" (deterrent) and finally to "scientific research"(nuclear energy for generating electricity). The volatility of the nuclear bomb and the subsequent Cold War era had challenged the prevalent security systems. Soon the arms race was transformed from conventional to nuclear. The era of conflict and confrontation had begun. The world became vulnerable to the growing dangers of the strategic instability inherent in the proliferation of nuclear weapons. The newly independent states were exposed to a bipolar world. However nuclear explosions by Great Britain, France and China changed the threat perception. China's nuclear explosion in 1964 had far reaching effects especially for India as it changed the power balance in Asia. Although India's APSARA was the first nuclear research reactor in Asia, China was the first country to successfully test its atomic bomb on 16 October 1964, using highly enriched Uranium which was produced at the Lanzhou facility and thirty two months later on 17 June 1967, China progressed even further and tested its first thermonuclear device[3]. This achievement is remarkable considering the fact that the time span between the two events, which is detonation of fission and fusion bombs was substantially lesser than what it was for the other Nuclear Weapon States. By way of comparison, 86 months passed between the United States' first atomic test and its first hydrogen bomb test; for the USSR, it was 75 months; for the UK, 66 months; and for France, 105 months[4]. Although India's nuclear programme had a good start, it lost the momentum due to its ambiguous approach, a lack of political will and the inability to understand the changing scenarios. In hindsight our leaders were short sighted and did not comprehend the necessity of enforcing a long term nuclear policy. This negligent planning denied India the opportunity to become a member of the United Nations Permanent Security Council. She also had to contend with the nuclear hegemony of the five nuclear states in the form of the Nuclear Non Proliferation Treaty (NPT). The pressure to sign the NPT, and the various stringent measures adopted by the Nuclear Weapon States (NWS), had made India's road to an independent nuclear power state, that much harder. However; the resilience of India's nuclear scientists, the ground level preparations, the accumulation of Uranium along with the changed threat perception and political compulsions, had a cumulative effect on the erstwhile Prime Minister Mrs. Indira Gandhi. The result was India's first peaceful nuclear explosion in Pokhran in 1974. The intentions behind the test was debated both by the politicians and the scientists, some scientists believed that "A bomb is a bomb and there is nothing peaceful about it" however; in the interest of national security, they were somewhat in unison. From 1985 onwards efforts were made to develop an indigenous missile and delivery system. The 1998 nuclear explosion was the culmination of India's nuclear journey which started in 1948. Finally in 1998 the government overtly declared India a Nuclear Weapon State with a well-defined nuclear doctrine. The nuclear doctrine with its complexities and challenges depicts the vision of nuclear India. The onus now lies on the current political leaders to change and adapt the vision according to the new emerging world order, where Asia is going to play a major role.

Nuclear Energy - An Introduction

The major energy sources, responsible for rapid industrial development, have been the fossil fuels mainly coal, oil and natural gas. However, with increased technological advancement and imminent resource depletion, questions regarding the sustainability of these erstwhile conventional natural resources have been raised. The depletion of coal and other finite resources has been a major cause of concern and the side effects caused by the increased carbon dioxide and monoxide emissions have cumulatively forced scientists to search for alternatives, to sidestep the impending Greenhouse effect. This led to increased speculation, and, thus began the process of exploring alternatives, mainly the renewable sources of energy, namely solar, wind and hydropower. However, these renewable sources were conditional, and could not solve the long term energy needs; hence attempts were made to solve this problem through the sustainable nuclear energy. The journey of nuclear energy started with the discovery of atom by Democritus in the 5th BC. This discovery was just the tip of the iceberg which had to wait for 24 centuries to achieve its true potential and see the light of day. Thompson's discovery of the Electron in 1897 was the required breakthrough which caused an unprecedented revolution in the history of mankind, as this tiny fragment of matter became responsible for fuelling an entire energy source, the "Nuclear Source". The progress in the nuclear field has been very rapid and it was commemorated by several important milestones such as the discovery of Radium, Uranium, Plutonium, Neutron, and the most important the "Radioactivity". The sources of nuclear energy have been the processes of fission, fusion and the radioactivity. On one hand when these were used for an evil cause, the result was the development of the Atomic bomb, on the other hand when scientist harnessed the nuclear energy for the benefit of mankind, the outcome was the nuclear power, generating electricity. Apart from generating electricity nuclear reactors have been employed to power civilian ice breakers in the Arctic region, floating nuclear power plants, provide electricity to coastal areas in Russia, nuclear batteries, supply electrical power for remote locations like the light house, and the day is not far when nuclear energy generated electricity may charge electric powered public transportation like the subways, busses and trolleys. The military is also using the nuclear power for the propulsions of submarines and surface ships.

The concept of civilian nuclear energy started in 1953 when an alternative purpose to the atoms destructive power was proposed by President Eisenhower. He recommended the famous "Atom for Peace[5]" programme whereby nuclear energy was to be used for the constructive purposes of generating electricity. Since then, an increasing number of countries have adopted this model or the productive use of nuclear energy. The first nuclear reactor to successfully produce electricity was the small experimental breeder reactor (EBR-1) in USA[6], which was invented in the year 1951. Russia was quick to parry the US dominion with the creation of the world's first nuclear powered generator, which was commissioned in

Obninsk in 1954[7]. The Cold War was responsible for some of the most rapid transitions in military technology. However, the US gradually reasserted its hegemony by not only constructing the first fully commercial Pressurized Water Reactor (PWR) of 250 MWs but also inventing a Boiling Water Reactor (BWR) with a similar potential level of 250 MWs. The model of the Canadian Reactor CANDU invented in 1962 was based on a diverse principle deviating from the normative theory by using natural Uranium as fuel and heavy water as a moderator and coolant. The Indian nuclear power plants were quick to follow and they based their systems on this model. There are now over 430 commercial nuclear power reactors operating in 31 countries, with a total capacity of 372,000 MWs and they collectively generate approximately 15 per cent of the world's electricity and as of now there are only eight countries known to possess nuclear weapon capability, however, statistics state that a total of 56 countries operate a shocking number of about 240 research reactors in totality[8].

Figure: 1 Nuclear Electricity Production

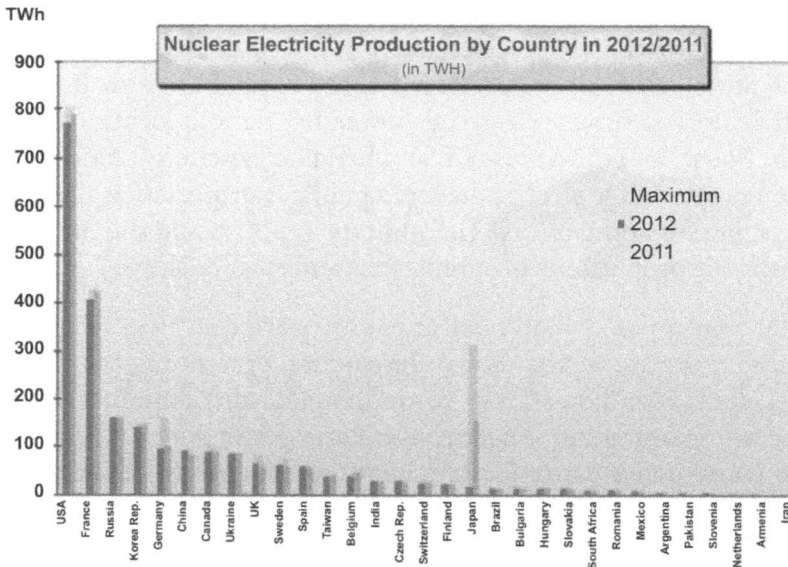

Sources: IAEA-PRIS, MSC, 2013

Nuclear Energy Infrastructure in India

Energy Requirements

The sources providing the energy particularly for the Indian power sector are diverse and varied. The energy requirements are met through a mix of sources ranging from thermal (being the largest), hydroelectric power, nuclear energy along with other sources such as wind, solar energy, compressed natural gas and diesel and the peripheral renewable resources. According to the working group of the 12th plan, the electricity board functional at the time of Independence could only provide electricity to 1500 villages in the country, but the scenario has changed significantly since then and as per the census of 2001 it has consequently been possible to extend the production and provision of electricity to about 5, 38,296 villages out of a total of 5.93,732, which is a healthy 90.8per cent of villages, simultaneously the Installed generation capacity in the utility sector had increased to about 1, 81,500 MW by the end of August 2011[9].

The consumption of electricity has increased manifold due to its enhanced accessibility as well as escalating mass awareness. This has caused a potential strain to the limited non-renewable resources, for despite the increased exploration of alternative means of fuelling and generating power, the next five decades will continue to be largely dominated by coal as a major energy source, simply due to its feasibility as raw material. As of August 2011, the electricity produced from coal was still 55 per cent (99,503MW) compared to other resources like Hydro 21 per cent (38,206MW), gas 10 per cent (17,706MW), nuclear 2 per cent (4780MW), Diesel 1 per cent (1200MW) and rest is 11 percent that is 20,162MW[10].

However the issues regarding the sustainability of a non-renewable resource in the future and the derivative side effects in the form of environmental problems will exhort energy planners to consider other non-carbon resource options, mainly nuclear. Efforts are being made worldwide to harness power from the renewable resources like solar, wind, gas etc. While this endeavour is being pursued, a simultaneous development has been the exploration of nuclear energy (due to its status as one of the cleanest supply options available to countries today). The technology currently being adopted by the nuclear scientists in India is a "closed fuel cycle", where the nuclear spent fuel is being reprocessed in order to minimize the nuclear waste

The Nuclear Fuel Cycle

The nuclear cycle starts with the mining of the Uranium ore. Various minerals like Pitchblende, Uranite, and Carnotite etc contain Uranium. Through the process of milling Uranium ore is separated from its crude material form and is often called as "yellowcake", which is then chemically treated to make it suitable as an input material for Uranium enrichment plants where it is enriched and is sent to nuclear reactors, mostly as Uranium dioxide as fuel, here the Uranium 235 undergoes fission and releases energy which is used to generate electricity.[11]

Figure: 2 The Uranium Cycle

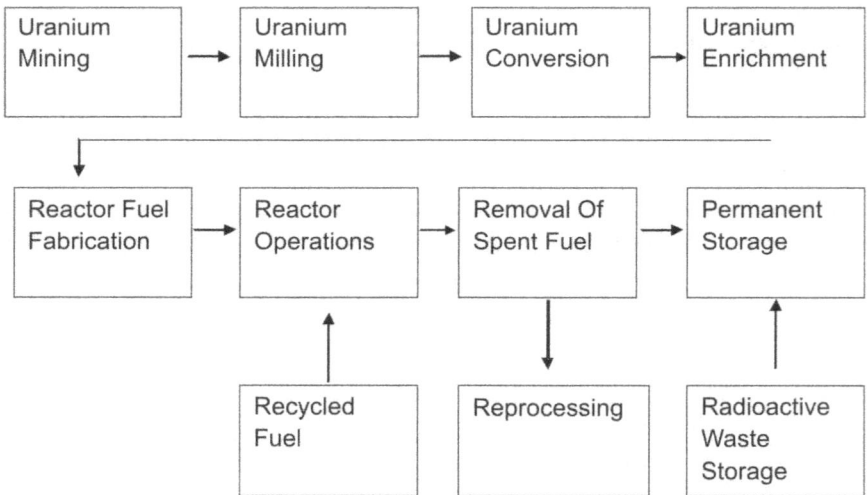

Source: Compiled from Canadian Environmental Assessment Agency on Nuclear Fuel Waste Management

Underpinning Principle

Scientific and technological advancement requires constant investment in infrastructure. In order to become truly indigenous and self-reliant a country must attempt to use every available resource within the country before resorting to imports, as it increases cost efficiency while also providing long term availability options. The inherent intensive potency of the Uranium atom (U_{253}) makes it the best base for nuclear experiments. However; in the past, the use of Uranium as a fuel, in operating nuclear reactors, has raised problems for India. India has limited reserves of natural Uranium, as a result India was dependent on other nations for the import of Uranium and due to sanctions imposed on India because of the nuclear test in 1998, Uranium was not easily accessible hence the civilian nuclear energy programme got hindered.. However; with the Indo-US nuclear deal, India can now import Uranium from various nations. Countries like Australia who were reluctant in the past have now come forward to supply the same.

Initially in order to make India independent in this energy sector, the visionary Dr Bhabha formulated "A Three Stage Nuclear Programme" for India. The rationale behind Dr Bhabha's objective was, India has modest Uranium reserves (102,600 tonnes) and has to depend on other countries for its import, in 2013, 40 per cent of Uranium requirements were imported[12].India has 319,000 tons of thorium[13] (found in the monazite sands of coastal south India). Dr Bhabha's plan for nuclear self-reliance involved a step by step process which through infrastructural developments and economic investments would replace Uranium atoms with Thorium, thereby enhancing the energy output while simultaneously making India self-reliant. The various stages of Dr Bhabha's "Nuclear Programme" are:-

- Pressurized Heavy Water Reactors

- Fast Breeder Reactors

- Thorium Based Reactors

The First Stage of the "Nuclear Programme" is the "**Pressurized Natural Uranium fuelled Heavy Water Reactors[14] (PHWRS)"**

This is the base stage of the three tier programme. Its objective is twofold, to produce power and to generate plutonium for the second stage[15] . During this phase, the nuclear fuel is the fissile isotope of $Uranium_{235}$ obtained from conversion and enrichment. The subsequent atoms of U235 captures a moving neutron and splits into two ,a chain reaction is created ,a moderator is required to control the speed of the emitted neutron hence a coolant[16] is required and as the name suggests, Pressurized Heavy Water is used to control the heat produced by fission. PHWR was, for that reason, a natural choice for implementing the first stage

The Second Stage: **"Fast breeder Reactors using Plutonium based fuel[17]"**-This stage has started at Kalpakkam where Fast Breeder Test Reactor was started. In FBRs, plutonium-239 undergoes fission to produce energy, while the Uranium-238 present in the mixed oxide fuel transmutes to additional plutonium-239, thus, the stage II FBRs are designed to "breed" more fuel than they consume[18]. Once the inventory of plutonium-239 is built up thorium can be introduced as a blanket material in the reactor and transmuted to Uranium-233 for use in the third stage[19]. The Uranium in the first stage, that yield 29 EJ of energy in the once-through fuel cycle, can be made to yield between 65 and 128 times more energy through multiple cycles in fast breeder reactors.[20] The work on FBR is going on and India`s first 500-MW Prototype Fast Breeder Reactor (PFBR), being set up at Kalpakkam will become critical by 2014.

The Third Stage: "**Thorium based reactors**"

A Stage III reactor or an advanced nuclear power system involves a self-sustaining series of thorium-232-Uranium-233 fuelled reactors. In the thorium cycle, the 232Th absorbs a neutron in either FBR or thermal reactors to become 233Th.This emits an electron and an anti-neutrino (v) to become 233Pa which further emits another electron and anti-neutrino by a second β− decay to become 233U[21], the fuel: :

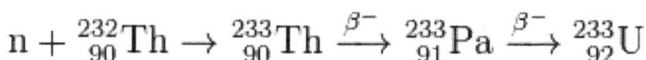

$$n + {}^{232}_{90}\text{Th} \rightarrow {}^{233}_{90}\text{Th} \xrightarrow{\beta^-} {}^{233}_{91}\text{Pa} \xrightarrow{\beta^-} {}^{233}_{92}\text{U}$$

This would be a thermal breeder reactor, which in principle can be refuelled - after its initial fuel charge - using only naturally occurring thorium. Advanced heavy water reactors are required to burn the U-233 and Pu-239 with thorium. The thorium will produce around 75 per cent of the power, with the spent fuel being reprocessed to recycle fissile materials .According to the three stage programme, Indian nuclear energy could grow to about 10 GW through PHWRs fuelled by domestic Uranium, and the growth above that would have to come from FBRs (till about 50GW) and the third stage is to be deployed only after this capacity has been achieved."[22] The actual use of a Thorium reactor commercially will still take time. Since there is a long waiting period before the implementation and utilization of thorium in this way, a parallel approach has emerged which is looking at reactor designs that allow the direct use of thorium in place of the entire conversion process which would be cost effective as well as infrastructurally feasible.[23] Various reactors which are considered for this purpose are the Accelerator Driven Systems (ADS), Advanced Heavy Water Reactor (AHWR) and Compact High Temperature Reactor.

Nuclear Infrastructure

India was the first country in Asia to construct a nuclear reactor, namely "APSARA" which became operational in 1956. Although it was a simple reactor having a large pool of pure water as its moderator, it was a commemorative symbol of India's determination to advance rapidly on the path of science and technology. This enlightening first step, however, was met with lukewarm political acceptance and the lackadaisical planning, coupled with infrastructural and financial constraints were some of the major reasons why India's radical first step was met with mediocre progress for a while. Still despite the policy induced confusion post the creation of APSARA, India has constructed 20 operational nuclear reactors, the journey so far has been slow but steady, as per NPCL the gross generation of Nuclear power in 2006-2007 was 18634MUs, by 2009-2010 it became 18803MUs and up to 2013-14 it became 35333 MUs[24], however; with new technologies and FBRs coming up it has the potential to grow phenomenally. Qualitatively also India has progressed, from acquiring Generation I reactors initially, to a relatively advanced Generation III and IV reactors now, example being the modernized Kaiga power plant which became operational in Jan 2011. Further NPCIL intends to set up five "Nuclear Energy Parks", each with a capacity of up to eight new-generation reactors of 1,000 MWe, six reactors of 1600 MWe or simply 10,000 MWe at a single location[25]. By 2032, 40-45 GWe would be provided from these five, as NPCIL says it is confident of being able to start work by 2012 on at least four new reactors at all four sites designated for imported plants.[26].

In October 2010, India drew up an ambitious plan to reach a nuclear power capacity of 63,000 MW by 2032[27] and former NPCIL Director, Mr. S K Jain, said "Out of the total target of 63,000 MW, about 40,000 MW will be generated through Light Water Reactors (LWR) with international cooperation"[28]. In 2009 India was ranked 9th in the world in terms of operational nuclear power reactors, but India now envisages increasing the contribution of nuclear power to overall electricity generation capacity from 2.8 per cent to 9 per cent within 25 years[29]. As of 2012 the total number of nuclear plant all across India are 20.

Table: 1 Nuclear Power Plant Capacity

Plant	Unit	Type	Capacity (MWe)	Date of commercial operation
TARAPUR ATOMIC POWER STATION (TAPS), Maharashtra	1	BWR	160	October 28, 1969
TARAPUR ATOMIC POWER STATION (TAPS), Maharashtra	2	BWR	160	October 28, 1969
TARAPUR ATOMIC POWER STATION (TAPS), Maharashtra	3	PHWR	540	August 18, 2006
TARAPUR ATOMIC POWER STATION (TAPS), Maharashtra	4	PHWR	540	September 12, 2005
RAJASTHAN ATOMIC POWER STATION (RAPS), Rajasthan	1	PHWR	100	December 16,1973
RAJASTHAN ATOMIC POWER STATION (RAPS), Rajasthan	2	PHWR	200	April 1,1981
RAJASTHAN ATOMIC POWER STATION (RAPS), Rajasthan	3	PHWR	220	June 1, 2000

Plant	Unit	Type	Ca-pacity (MWe)	Date of commercial operation
RAJASTHAN ATOMIC POWER STATION (RAPS), Rajasthan	4	PHWR	220	December 23, 2000
RAJASTHAN ATOMIC POWER STATION (RAPS), Rajasthan	5	PHWR	220	February 4, 2010
RAJASTHAN ATOMIC POWER STATION (RAPS), Rajasthan	6	PHWR	220	March 31, 2010
MADRAS ATOMIC POWER STATION (MAPS), Tamil Nadu	1	PHWR	220	January 27,1984
MADRAS ATOMIC POWER STATION (MAPS), Tamil Nadu	2	PHWR	220	March 21,1986
KAIGA GENERATING STATION, Karnataka	1	PHWR	220	November 16, 2000
KAIGA GENERATING STATION, Karnataka	2	PHWR	220	March 16, 2000
KAIGA GENERATING STATION, Karnataka	3	PHWR	220	May 6, 2007
KAIGA GENERATING STATION, Karnataka	4	PHWR	220	January 20, 2011
NARORA ATOMIC POWER STATION (NAPS) , Uttar Pradesh	1	PHWR	220	January 1,1991
NARORA ATOMIC POWER STATION (NAPS) , Uttar Pradesh	2	PHWR	220	July 1,1992

Plant	Unit	Type	Ca-pacity (MWe)	Date of commercial operation
KAKRAPAR ATOMIC POWER STATION (KAPS), Gujarat	1	PHWR	220	May 6, 1993
KAKRAPAR ATOMIC POWER STATION (KAPS), Gujarat	2	PHWR	220	September 1,1995

Source: NPCIL

Recently in November 2013 the commercial operation of Kudankulam nuclear reactor in Tamil Nadu got started .With this the total number of nuclear power plants as of January 2014 is twenty one. According to NPCIL the projects under construction are Unit 7and 8 of Rajasthan Atomic Power Plant which is expected to become operational by June 2016 and the Unit -3 and 4 of Kakrapara plant by 2015[30].

Complexities in Nuclear Power Generation

India has a flourishing and largely indigenous nuclear power programme yet the power generated by the nuclear power plants till now has been minimal. The causes for the slow growth have been varied, with the reasons ranging from the unavailability of resources and infrastructure (scarcity of Uranium, Nuclear Supplier Group's (NSG) sanctions), to the slow progress of the development of Fast Breeder Reactors. Questions have also been raised regarding the feasibility of thorium as fuel for the nuclear cycle. The NSG predicament has been resolved and therefore now India is able to access and acquire Uranium through sanctioned imports. However, the other technical and infrastructural challenges need to be resolved, only then the Department of Atomic Energy's plan, to increase its power production and generation from a mere 4780MWe in 2012 to 63000 MWe by 2032 can be achieved.

Fast breeder Reactors - Its significance and complications

Dr Kakodkar states that "Our Uranium reserves what we have as per the present state of exploration will be able to support 10,000 MWe generating capacity, which is not large, but it is the starting point for setting up fast reactors.[31] When the same Uranium, which will support 10,000 MWe generating capacity in the PHWRs, comes out as spent fuel and we process that spent fuel into plutonium and residual Uranium, and use it in the fast reactors, we will be able to go to electricity capacity which will be as large 5,00,000 MWe[32]. This is due to the breeding potential of the fast reactors, using the plutonium-Uranium cycle that is the importance of the fast - breeder reactors under Indian conditions, compared to other countries[33]".

India is one of the two countries currently constructing commercial scale breeder reactors (the other is Russia). The work to build an indigenous FBTR had started in the 1960s but it took four decades for the plan to come to fruition and the first FBR became critical in 1985 at Kalpakkam. According to Dr P.R. Vasudeva Rao, Director Indira Gandhi Centre for Atomic Research (IGCAR) India's first commercial Fast Breeder Reactor the 500 MWe Prototype Fast Breeder Reactor (PFBR), at Kalpakkam is almost ready and it would go critical by September 2014.[34]Along with this four more are planned. While on one hand the invention of an indigenous FBTR is a cause of celebration and commemoration, on the other hand the same FBTR also becomes a reason to exercise extreme caution due to the hazardous mishaps associated with it. Since the installation of the reactor two major incidents have already taken place which is a cause of concern. In the month of May 1987, the guide tube, which guides the fuel into the reactor during the loading of the fuel, got bent and could not be removed and the heads of nickel and stainless steel assemblies in the reactor core were also twisted[35]. Using remote cutting machines, the guide tube was cut into two pieces and removed and specially designed grippers were required to extract the sub-assemblies and it took two years for the reactor to resume operations after this mishap[36]. The second averted disaster occurred in 2002 when a potential radioactive sodium leak was checked and contained. The functioning of any FBTR requires liquid sodium to be used as a coolant in order to prevent overheating and explosion. While sodium is an excellent medium for heat transfer and moderation, the pipes that carry sodium, need to be maintained at a temperature of 600°c to prevent it from solidifying. Sodium as an element is also highly reactive when compounded with water or air, therefore as a precaution, a sodium coolant loop needs to be isolated in order to prevent accidental sodium leaks. This is also one of the reasons that deter countries from producing and pursuing FBTR programmes'. In 2002, 75 kg of radioactive sodium had leaked inside the purification cabin due to a manufacturing defect in the imported sodium valve.[37] Although the leak was contained and there was no radioactive release into the atmosphere, the disastrous potential of such a mishap cannot be overlooked. Scientists need to work on a viable solution to avoid any such infrastructure related accidents in the future in order to maintain safe and secure nuclear power as a constant source of reliable energy.[38] Over and above the security hazards that the FBRs seem to pose, the reactor's performance world over has also been relatively mediocre. It took 15 years for the FBR's functionality to achieve a stage of 50 plus days of continuous operation at full power[39] and additionally its functional output in the first 20 years of its life has been rather dismal as well, with the reactor operating only for 36,000 hours, implying that the availability factor is only about 20 per cent[40]. This is one of the major reasons why France, the U.S. and the U.K. have not actively persisted with their breeder reactor programmes.

Some of the main objections to the FBR programme have been regarding its economic viability. The French government found the FBRs too expensive to build and maintain. Therefore, the economic feasibility and the reactors long term practicality appear to be questionable. Secondly the electricity generated by the FBRs did not prove to be cost effective when compared with thermal nuclear reactors. Thirdly the so called advantages of reprocessing the fuel turned out to be very expensive as the cost of plutonium (which is required as an addendum to U_{233}) is several times higher than that of natural Uranium. Lastly with the Indo-US treaty coming through, India will officially be able to import a LWRs and Low Enriched Uranium (LEU). Some schools of thought believe that this development can work to our advantage as India is already the largest producer of PHW therefore the FBR should be abandoned in favour of PHWRs and LWRs. Conversely, on a more optimistic note if the scientists are able to rectify the above mentioned problems of infrastructural loopholes as well as long term viability, then, the situation would be quite different as Mr. Ramalingam, Director IGCAR Reactor Operation and Maintenance Group states "India's grid will be powered by energy from a chain of fast reactors, the FBTR will be remembered as the mother of fast reactors in India and the harbinger of India's energy security and economic sovereignty[41]," India is already constructing higher capacity reactors and Dr Kakodkar, Chairman Atomic Energy Commission and Secretary, Department of Atomic Energy has mentioned that the FBR will be developed in two directions "One direction is to go for higher capacity reactors, may be developing 1,000 MWe reactors, the other direction is to use the reactor design and its associated fuel cycle, which will have a shorter doubling time because we get into a higher and higher generating capacity through the breeding process.[42] The faster the breeding, quicker will be the rise in the Fast Breeder Reactor's capacity and so we should pursue both the directions: one is the higher reactor unit size, and the other, the fuel cycle, which has a shorter doubling time and in this, we have drawn the entire road map including R&D activities, the development that should be done and, the new energy systems to be built."[43]

The Feasibility and Constraints of Thorium as an Alternative fuel

The research regarding the viability of Thorium as an alternative fuel has been going on for a long time now and scientists have found that Thorium happens to be beneficial in numerous ways as well. For instance, Thorium atoms complement Uranium atoms and ensure long term sustainability of nuclear power through a constant cycle of transmutation. The Thorium cycle emits a relatively lesser quantity of plutonium and Minor Actinides thereby minimizing the radio toxicity associated with the spent fuel.[44] The absorption capacity of a cross-section of thermal neutrons for 232Th is nearly three times that of 238U and therefore, a fissile atom with improved capabilities is created (233U) unlike 238U which transforms into 239Pu[45]. As a result, Thorium is more 'fertile' than 238U and is also consequently a storehouse of greater nuclear energy potentialities in thermal reactors. Another major reason often used for advocating the use of Thorium as an alternate fuel is that Thorium dioxide is chemically more stable than Uranium Dioxide and therefore has a higher capacity for radiation resistance[46]. ThO2 is relatively inert and can resist quick oxidization, unlike UO2, which oxidizes easily, as a result consequently, the long term interim storage and permanent disposal in repository becomes much easier[47].

In spite of the several advantages listed above, one must remember that generating sufficient power from Thorium is a very complicated process and Indian scientists will have to enhance infrastructural capabilities as well as remove the security obstacles, impediments and hazards before they can think of using thorium in a commercial way. In India according to the Fast Breeder Reactor model, the use of thorium in the nuclear cycle is usually introduced in the third or the last stage. However due to the scarcity of Uranium and the abundance of Thorium, parallel approaches have emerged whereby Thorium can be used as an alternative fuel in place of Uranium. Scientists are looking at various reactor designs which can allow for a more direct use of Thorium. However; there are disadvantages in using Thorium as an alternative to Uranium$_{235,}$ they being:-

Firstly the most abundant naturally existing isotope of Thorium is Thorium$_{232}$ and like Uranium$_{238,}$ it is fertile and possesses fission possibilities but lacks true fission capabilities, hence It needs to be converted to a fissile isotope and the process used is neutron bombardment. Post the neutron absorption it converts to an unstable isotope which is Thorium$_{233}$[48]. This isotope is energetically volatile and therefore decays quickly transforming into Protactinium$_{233}$ within a short span of 22 minutes and it is this Protactinium that eventually converts into the fissile and useful Uranium$_{233}$ and this complex process requires advanced infrastructural development[49]. This is an operational drawback and in order to correct and rectify it, specific reactors are required. Some examples are the Accelerator Driven Systems (ADS), the Advanced Heavy Water Reactor (AHWR) and the Compact High Temperature Reactor which was essentially the alternative options considered[50]. A Molten Salt Rector (MSR) is also one of the most neutron-efficient designs available At present Indian scientists have approved the AHWR design as the most feasible,(economically as well as operationally) and the preparations for the construction of the AHWR have also begun. The research reactors which attempted this model are KAMINI, CIRUS, and DHRUVA and they have already initiated the use of Thorium and thorium oxide J rods and the ThO2 Pellets which are required for the neutron flux, (which is the flattening of initial core after start-up) are also currently being used in the PHWRs of KAPS, KGS and RAPS[51].

Secondly the biggest problem that scientists face is the fact that the thorium cycle uses and produces $Thorium_{232}$ which has a half-life of 73.6 years, moreover post the neutron absorption and bombardment, the daughter products created emit high intensity gamma rays as result of which there is a significant build-up of heavy radiation doses in the separated U233 sectors[52]. Dealing with this radioactive excess requires automated reprocessing and re-fabrication in heavily shielded hot cells, which increase the cost of the fuel cycle activities, while this stability is useful in preventing radiation leaks or chemical reactions, they do not dissolve easily in concentrated nitric acid unlike UO_2 or (U, Pu)O2 fuels, therefore; in the case of the addition of small quantities of HF, a corrosion of stainless steel equipment and piping takes place in the reprocessing plants.[53] Scientists must keep these details in mind before investing commercially and advocating the utilization of thorium fuels and fuel cycles. It is essential that the experimental stage undergoes minute observation and analysis to prevent security hazards because the currently existing databases documenting the experience of using thorium as fuel and documenting the thorium fuel cycles are very limited in the world. Moreover to complicate matters further most of the Thorium Breeder Reactor models in France, USA, etc. are being discontinued due to their Economic as well as Technical unfeasibility.

Expansion of Nuclear Energy – Government Projections: Its Practicality and Limitations.

The two major factors which currently maintain the power balance in the Indian Power Sector are industrialization and environmental concern. The path to safe progress lies in balancing the economic development and its consequent environmental extraction and depletion. The challenge for India now will be to rework and renovate its energy mix in order to prevent the exhaustion of non-renewable resources. In the year 1947-1948, the Installed capacity was 1362MW and per capita consumption was 16.3KW, however, as in the year 2013ti was 223344MW and provisional per capita consumption was 917.2KWh[54]. The demand for power has increased enormously and the constant depletion of finite coal resources and inevitable environmental hazards have forced scientists and policy makers to look at the only other clean sustainable resource alternative which is available and that is nuclear energy .Keeping this aspect in mind the Department of Atomic Energy has projected some revisions:

1. The target is to install about 20 GWe nuclear power plants by the year 2020. This target includes 2.5 GWe of Oxide fuelled FBRs and 8 GWe of LWRs.

2. R&D for using metal fuel in FBRs will be completed by the year 2020.

3. All the plutonium produced in PHWRs and in LWRs will be used for fuelling FBRs.

Thus the total capacity would increase to 20,000 MWe by the year 2020

Table: 2 Total installed capcity
(As in July 2008)

Name	MWe	Capacity Mwe
17 Reactors at 6 sites in Tarapur, Rawalbhatta, ,Kakrapara, Kaiga Kalpakkam,Narora	4120	4120
3 PHWRs under construction at Kaiga4(220MWe),RAPPS 5&6(220MWe)	660	4780
2LWRs under construction at Kudankulam(2x100MWe)	2000	6780
PFBR under construction at Kalpakkam(1x500MWE)	500	7280
Project plant till 2020 PHWR(8X700MWe) FBR(4X500MWe) LWR(6x1000MWe) AHWR(1X300MWe)	13900	21180
Total by 2020		21180Mwe

Source DAE

The growth rates projected by the DAE are not very pragmatic and it remains to be seen whether or not the targets will be achieved on time. As of now the nuclear capacity is 4560MWe, and it is a little over optimistic to assume that by 2032 this capacity will increase to 63,000 MWe. The reasons for the implausibility of the target is that it requires construction of new mega power plants, and for that one needs substantial financial aid as well as infrastructural support. Apart from that although the NSG waiver has made the import of nuclear fissile material easier, the economic difficulties in facilitating these imports cannot be overlooked. Over and above the obvious infrastructural and economic constraints, there are political, technical and environmental complexities which need to be resolved and it is only upon the successful resolution of these challenges in an impartial and practical manner that the DAE can hope to achieve its goal.

Challenges in Nuclear Expansion

Infrastructural delays, Manufacturing Problems and Cost Estimates-The DAE projections are mostly based on the completion of the nuclear reactors which are still under construction. The development and progress of Indian nuclear reactors has been constantly marred by infrastructural delays and manufacturing defects, not to mention the escalating costs because of cost inflation which occurs due to these delays. The construction work for the Tarapur Atomic Power Station (TAPS) began in 1964 the completion took place only in 1969, a year later than schedule[55]. The Rajasthan Atomic Power Station (RAPS) 1 & 2 have already suffered component failures, and such infrastructural carelessness could cause serious problems in the successful progression of our nuclear programme, also all the original coolant tubes in RAPS2 supplied by Canada were replaced[56]. This added cost impacted our already constrained nuclear budget. The most recent testament to the obstruction of nuclear progress would be the Madras Atomic Power Station (MAPS) whose operation dates have been revised five times already and the operational costs have escalated from 600 million Rs to 1188 million Rs . The PFBR also has already been delayed by a year and it remains to be seen whether the NPCL is efficient enough to complete the projects on time.

1. Political Delays

Delays are just the beginning of the list of complexities that most nuclear plants face. The construction of every new nuclear power plant faces opposition in some form or the other, sometimes the resistance comes from NGOs, and sometimes the contention stems from the various environmental awareness groups. Occasionally the local people, spurred on by the support of the NGOs rebel against the construction and a lot of obstructions have also been raised by obscure political decisions. An example of local opposition is the Kudankulam Nuclear Power Project and the Jaitapur Nuclear Power Project. There have also been instances where some of the NGOs opposing the nuclear power plant constructions have been funded by foreign countries. The Indian Prime minister Dr Manmohan Singh while commenting on this kind of aberrant NGO obstruction has said that "You know what's happening in Kudankulam. The atomic energy programme has gone into difficulties because these NGOs [non-governmental organizations,] mostly I think based in the United States; don't appreciate the need for our country to increase the energy supply." He further stated that "But there are controversies. There are NGOs, often funded from the United States and the Scandinavian countries, which are not fully appreciative of the development challenges that our country faces—".[57] These protests not only delay the implementation of the projects but they also pose political hindrances because state governments become reluctant to start the programme that would possibly antagonize the locals as well as the other ethnic and social groups residing in the state.

2. Fast Breeder Reactors

India's nuclear power generation, as described earlier, follows the three stage development programme. Out of the three India has successfully managed to master just the first stage and the second stage dealing with FBRs has still not reached the operational stage. The PFBR is still under construction and to put things in perspective, most of the countries that began researching and installing the FBRs have abandoned the model as they consider it to be expensive, unsafe and technically not feasible. India has no commercial experience in operating the FBR, and yet scientists are relying heavily on its technology. The commercial success as well as long-term viability of this model is yet to be tested.

3. Light Water Reactors (LWR)

DAE's plan to import the LWR is criticised by some on the grounds that it is neither economically beneficial nor technologically feasible as it will slow down India's indigenous nuclear programme. The cost efficiency is an important factor that needs to be taken into consideration before investing in new technology, and in the case of the LWR this switch seems to be unnecessary as it provides minimal cost relief, with the added complication of a dubious lack of infrastructural support. India as of now possesses ample experience with the operational nature of the PHWR as India is the largest producer of Heavy water, and it would be an ineffectual endeavour to completely renovate the current reactor system without the prospect of any major conceivable benefit. In the words of Dr Gopalakrishnan "...It should be noted that Indian PHWRs are the most efficient plutonium producers ,far superior to the high burn – up LWR's which DAE is planning to import... we have the inherent indigenous ability to further extend the PHWR design to 1000 MWe rating[58]". The LWR would be impractical because:

- We would have to import the LWR at a high cost along with its supplementary and auxiliary components.

- Considering the fact that we do not possess the requisite infrastructure to create LWRs, sustaining them would be almost impossible without constant foreign technological aid.

4. Availability of Plutonium

There will be an immense scarcity of Plutonium for the targeted breeder reactors as India does not have enough reprocessing plants. Constructing new reprocessing plants will take many years and although the Indo-US nuclear deal will help, but the increased dependence on foreign technology will hinder India's plan for indigenisation.

5. Exaggerated Targets

India's atomic energy department has had a history of projecting plausible targets which are seldom met. Physicist Raju states "The DAE has been unable to meet targets even over the very short run. For example in 2003, Kakodkar predicted that about four years from now, DAE will reach an installed capacity of 6800MWe and six years later, nuclear capacity is only 4120MWe[59]". Even the projections given by the first secretary of DAE was wrong, as stated by Physicist Raju and Ramana "---Homi Bhabha predicted that India would produce 18-20,000 MWe of nuclear power by 1987; when 1987 came around, India's nuclear power production capacity was stuck at 512 MWe – less than 3 per cent of Bhabha's projection[60]". These examples are reason enough to learn to be realistic and predict achievable targets.

There are a lot of teething problems. While the principle of resorting to nuclear power is admirable and there is no doubt that the percentage of electricity generated from nuclear energy would increase, attaining this increase in the allotted time and simultaneously accomplishing the statistics and targets planned by the DAE seems to be improbable and impractical; unless the requisite action is taken to correct the political, economic and infrastructural loopholes mentioned. It would be prudent to simultaneously explore alternative renewable resources for fuel because India is going to rely on the thermal power sector for another two decades at the very least, until the nuclear goals are realized.

Atomic Energy Regulations and an Independent AERB

An Atomic Energy Committee was formed in the year 1945, with the aim and principle of formulating the nuclear energy programme. The Atomic Energy Act was passed in 1948 and an Atomic Energy Commission (AEC) was set up with Dr. H. J. Bhabha as its first Chairman. The founding principle and main objective of the AEC was to successfully set up an operational nuclear reactor for experimental purposes. With the rapid growth of the nuclear science and the consequent alterations in the application of nuclear and radiation technologies, the scope of nuclear energy and its capability has increased and therefore a full - fledged department was created to cater to the growing needs of this sector.

The Department of Atomic Energy (DAE)

DAE was set-up on 3rd August, 1954 under the direct charge of the Prime Minister through a Presidential Order. The DAE was instituted for the designing, planning, construction and operation of nuclear power/research reactors and the related supplementary nuclear fuel cycle technologies. Their responsibilities and functions involved the exploration, mining and processing of nuclear minerals, production of heavy water, nuclear fuel fabrication, fuel reprocessing and nuclear waste management.[61]

Atomic Energy Regulatory Board (AERB)

With the increase in the number of nuclear power plants, there was a need to assess the safety and security standards of these plants, so that a potentially disaster free environment could be created. The rising concerns led to the necessity of forming a subsidiary body which would solely work towards regulating the security and reliability of the reactors and plants. As a result in 1983, the Department of Atomic Energy (DAE) established the Atomic Energy Regulatory Board (AERB) whose main function was to lay down the obligatory safety standards to be met by each reactor/plant while simultaneously framing rules and regulations for the civilian nuclear operations as well. However; currently, the AERB's jurisdiction is restricted to the civilian side of the nuclear programme because the strategic and military nuclear facilities have been kept off limits since 2000.[62] Even within this limited gambit, the AERB's functioning is often debated due to its political and infrastructural dependence on its parent body the DAE. A few examples of the AERBs contingency would be:

- The AERB is economically supported by the Department of Atomic Energy (DAE).

- All the technical and infrastructural assistance in terms of manpower and testing facilities are being provided by the DAE.

- The AERB is policy bound to report to the Atomic Energy Commission (AEC).

This structural deformity dilutes the role and authority of the AERB and subsequently raises questions regarding its neutrality and transparency. When a regulatory organization is so deeply steeped with political associations, its authority to enforce stringent action on prohibited practices is diminished. Dr Gopalakrishnan, the former Chairman of the AERB, has said "I think people like us have to really get after the AERB to make sure that they operate independently. There are various signals of when somebody starts operating independently. You can see minutes of their safety meetings, reviews etc. on their websites or we will insist they should put it there basically, transparency[63]." Post Fukushima the concern and awareness regarding the safety and security of nuclear plants in India has increased, however, people residing near the nuclear power plants are still ignorant of the potential hazards and the requisite action necessary in case of a nuclear accident. An increasing list of nuclear mishaps such as 1) the dome collapse at Kaiga, 2) the near meltdown of the core in Narora, 3) The flooding at the KAPS and 4) The radioactive heavy water spill at the MAPS are causes for concern. This makes it necessary for the government to institute a truly independent nuclear safety regulatory body, which can serve as a watchdog on behalf of the public[64]. The nuclear safety convention which India is also a member of, clearly states that "Each contracting body shall take the appropriate steps to ensure an effective separation between the functions of the regulatory body and those of any other body or organization concerned with the promotion or utilization of nuclear energy[65]" According to reports in 2012 the Comptroller and Auditor General of India (CAG) performed a thorough investigation of the AERB, its functioning and its autonomous status. He submitted the results of his inquiry in the 'Activities of Atomic Energy Regulatory Board' which was an eye opener for political authorities, civil researchers as well as the common people. The document brought to our attention a list of the many lacunas in AERB's functioning and the disconcerting hazards that could follow on the pursuance of such a weak lackadaisical body. The major concern presented by the document was the fact that the AERB failed to develop stringent and enforceable safety policies, standards, codes and guidelines. The absence of such a policy at the macro level hampered the micro level planning and functioning of radiation safety.

Limitations of AERB and a need for an Independent AERB

A few limitations and compulsions of the AERB which need to be rectified before it can become a fully functional autonomous body are:

- The increasing reliance on nuclear energy and the rapid rate with which the nuclear power plants are constructed makes it essential to establish an independent AERB, which is free from the shackles of DAE and the draconian official secrets act.

- In order to ensure stringent nuclear safety, AERB should be given the authority to not only frame and revise the rules and regulations, but also to impose heavy penalties in case of operational deficiencies .This can only happen when the AERB becomes truly autonomous and it is freed from political associations.

- AERB members should not be on the DAE payroll. This will ensure more transparency in their functioning and will bring more neutrality to their observations. The safety evaluations will become more mandatory in nature.

- They should have independent testing facilities along with highly professional technical staff with regular advanced training, both in-house as well as from reputed foreign institutions.

- The impartial regulatory reviews could be achieved only from those regulatory advisors who are not affiliated to the Department of Atomic Energy or to its subsidiary departments as. Gopalakrishnan, former Chairman of AERB, has rightly noted that: '...the nuclear regulator (AERB) does not have the comprehensive scientific and technological capabilities or in-depth experience required to carry out much of the safety analyses and evaluations needed[66].'

- Almost 95 per cent of the members in AERB's review and advisory committees are retired employees of the Department of Atomic Energy, either coming from one of their research institutes like the Bhabha Atomic Research Center (BARC) or a power generation company like the Nuclear Power Corporation of India Ltd.

- These members who have worked for 30 to 40 years in the Department of Atomic Energy (DAE) organizations before retiring, and who still continue to enjoy all the retirement benefits from the DAE, including family medical support in their old age, cannot be expected to be informed judicious and impartial judges. The loyalty of most such review committee members is likely to remain with the DAE and this loyalty might blind their vision regarding nuclear safety offences being committed.

- The process for license approval, along with the monitoring and renewal of radiation facilities were found to be weak, and therefore as a result a number of radiation units were found operating without a valid license.

- 91 per cent of the x ray facilities had not been registered. Out of 57,443 X-ray units only 5,270 has been registered[67], 85 per cent of the industrial radiography and radiotherapy units had not been inspected by the AERB. Such carelessness could possibly expose the populace of that area to radiation hazards as well as mishaps.

- One of the reasons for such imprudent inspection could be inadequate manpower. As of 2013 the manpower in AERB had increased from 286 to 310 (251 scientific and technical and 59 supporting staff)[68]which is still not adequate considering the increase in number of radiation facilities being opened every year.

- There is also a decisive lack of organized tabulated information on the basis of which regular inspections can be conducted and the radioactive sources procured by medical and research institutions can be investigated.

- An example of this infrastructural loophole is the Mayapuri incident where scrap dealers came in close contact with radioactive Cobalt 60 resulting in death and severe radiation induced injuries. The International Atomic Energy Agency (IAEA) rated the Mayapuri incident as the most serious case of radiation exposure since 2006[69].

- The AERB should have an authentic system whereby the radioactive materials should be traced continually from the time of their import (at various ports) to the time of their delivery to various medical and research institutions along with the plans for their safe disposal.

- Even the Supreme Court's directions, which were to set up a Directorate of Radiation Safety in each state[70], have not been complied with. Out of 28 states only Kerala, Mizoram and Bihar have followed the dictate and set up the DRS.

- As mentioned earlier, due to manpower limitations, there are possibilities of having inadequate certified radiation safety officers to conduct regular physical inspections at several radiation sites in the country.

- Most of the inspection officers do not have the necessary skills required to do the job. In order to rectify this issue planning systematic training programmes in order to enhance their capabilities in dealing with nuclear facilities, is a must.[71]

- In the on–site and off–site emergency preparedness for nuclear and radiation safety exercises, the AERB had a token role. They did not scrutinize the process physically themselves, they merely reviewed the drill reports. They did not possess the requisite autonomy and independence to personally supervise the drill and take the requisite corrective measures. The CAG report states "No specific codes on emergency preparedness plans for radiation facilities such as industrial radiography, radiotherapy and gamma chambers etc had been brought out although the hazard potential of these were rated as high[72]"

- One suggestion has been that all the civilian nuclear programmes should be placed under the IAEA as it will make our installations more secure and safe. This in turn will boost our chances to become a major civilian nuclear power which will augment our prospects for nuclear exports.

- Another problem most often noted has been the fact that there is no legislative feature in India whereby the decommissioning of the old nuclear plants can be done in a smooth manner. The NPPs which have been running for 30 years do not have a decommissioning plan. There is no mandate stating the process of the proper disposal of nuclear waste along with the shutting down of an erstwhile functioning radioactive power plant. Apart from the few codes and safety manuals that exist, there is no streamlined procedure or method.

- There is a lack of educational infrastructure as far as nuclear science and nuclear engineering are concerned. In order to produce well trained nuclear scientists/engineers/regulators it is essential that the government of India includes nuclear science at post graduate level and also increase the number of seats in different universities and premier technological institutions.

Nuclear Safety and Security

The worldwide generation of electricity by nuclear power plants is projected to increase from about 2.7 trillion kilowatt hours in 2006 to approximately 3.8 trillion kilowatt hours in 2030 and the predicted sector with the quickest and largest growth will be Asia (with an average annual rate of 7.8 per cent from 2006 to 2030,).[73] In India according to government projections and statistics, the electricity that will be generated through nuclear energy, (moving away from conventional sources of thermal energy), will increase to a massive 26 per cent by 2052. It is for this very reason that India has developed an extensive civilian nuclear infrastructure. The Nuclear Power Corporation of India Limited (NPCL) was created in 1987 "with the objective of operating atomic power stations and implementing the atomic power projects for generation of electricity in pursuance of the schemes and programmes of government of India under the Atomic Energy Act, 1962"[74]. As an operator it is the responsibility of the corporation to maintain the highest standards of safety and security. The nuclear accidents in Chernobyl, The Three Mile Island in the US and the recent Fukushima incident in Japan have revealed only too clearly to the world, the dangers of nuclear energy, especially in the case of careless neglect of nuclear safety and security standards. Nuclear safety should be the foremost priority of any government. Appropriate structural and procedural modifications should be made so that national regulatory bodies are in sync with the International bodies mainly the IAEA and possess the requisite power to enforce stringent nuclear safety laws. In India, sadly the treatment of nuclear safety and security has been complicated and politicized. Initially the investigation of the safety issues and standards were carried out by DAE's safety review committees (DAE-SRC), however in 1983 the AERB was created and as a consequence the DAE-SRC became a part of the AERB-SRC. The primary responsibility for ensuring the safety of a Nuclear Power Plant (NPP) should lie with the licensee (in India's case as of now it is the NPCL) however, the establishment of a strong AERB would ensure that the licensee performs its duties according to the laid down system of codes and guides.

The IAEA in 2006 provides some standard definitions in order to avoid the miscarriage of justice:-

Nuclear Safety "The achievement of proper operating conditions, prevention of accidents or mitigation of accident consequences, resulting in protection of site personnel, the public and the environment from under radiation hazards"

Nuclear security "All preventive measures taken to minimize the residual risk of unauthorized transfer of nuclear material and/ or sabotage, which could lead to release of radioactivity and /or adverse impact on the safety of the plant ,plant personnel, public and environment".

Former AERB Chairman Mr. Bajaj states that safety reviews are carried out at multi-tiered levels:

(a) Individual engineers and working groups

(b) Safety committees

(c) Advisory committees

(d) AERB board

All these committees include experts in all the relevant fields and higher level committees include outside experts from academia, national R&D institutes and government bodies.[75]

Though the programme encompasses all the issues but the main concern is how much of it is practically implemented and since AERB is not an independent body there will always be questions raised on it being impartial. Most of the accidents which have taken place in the world so far have been due to design/equipment malfunctioning ,nature's furry or human errors. India though has been lucky as no major incident has taken place but with the nuclear infrastructural expansion many loose ends needs to be tied up. The accidents are rated on the International Nuclear Event Scale (INES).at seven levels based on the severity of the accident. Below Zero scale means no safety significance and various other levels are depicted below

Table: 3 International Nuclear Event Scale

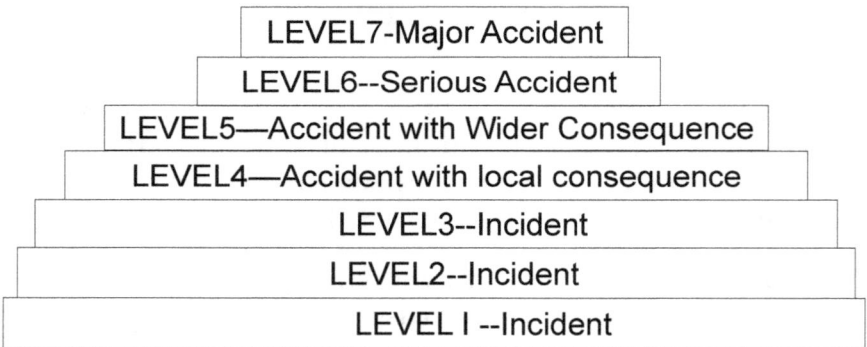

LEVEL7-Major Accident
LEVEL6--Serious Accident
LEVEL5—Accident with Wider Consequence
LEVEL4—Accident with local consequence
LEVEL3--Incident
LEVEL2--Incident
LEVEL I --Incident

Source: International Nuclear Event Scale Established in 1990 at http://mens-news.com/2011/04/japan-raises-nuclear-severity-to-highest-level-same-as-chernobyl/

In India most of the accidents have been incidents except for the Narora fire accident in 1993. However; post Fukushima questions were asked about the capability of nuclear power plants to withstand natural calamities, accidents, management skills, emergency planning and preparedness in any eventuality.

Parameters required for Safety

In order to attain nuclear safety certain parameters need to be adhered to both at pre and post construction levels:-

- The "Defense–in Depth" concept must be followed .This relates to a multi-layered safety system .Giving a nuclear reactor a minimum of four to five layers of protection e.g. If the cladding is made of Zirconium then this can prevent the release of fission products, If the reactor pressure vessel is thick it can prevent cracking and embrittlement and so forth

- Research should be done to see the viability of multiple plant design / one plant design. Both have their advantages and disadvantages. In the former case construction and training costs go up and in the latter if there is a design flaw it will be there in subsequent nuclear reactors as a result they all would have to be taken off line until the defect is rectified.

- Similarly it should be decided in advance whether passive or active safety component would be adopted. In passive safety, active operator involvement is not required and it relies on gravity and convection to enhance the plant safety, whereas active safety incorporates multiple engineered safety features like a double walled containment[76].

- Nuclear power plants should not be constructed in the tectonic fault area In India the tectonic fault line is in the Makran fault in the western side. They should be in Zone 1 or Zone 2 unlike Narora which is in Zone 4[77].

- Nuclear reactors should not be constructed in tsunami prone areas; if reactors are there then measures like building very tall seawalls to block the waves, uninterrupted power systems and diesel generators should be ensured.

Nuclear Waste Management

Like any industry the nuclear industry also produces waste materials; however the difference is that in nuclear power plants radioactive materials emit radiations, which are more difficult to dispose and are more lethal to biosphere than any industrial waste .Right from Uranium mining to fuel fabrication and ultimately to reprocessing of the spent fuel, the radioactive waste is released in various degrees and forms. According to the level of radiation they emit, the radioactive waste can be divided into three parts.

1. Low and intermediate level wastes (LIL) - These radioactive materials are short lived and produce low levels of radiations. In case of liquid waste it is few micro curie/l to mill curie/l and generally has less than 30 years half-life, it gets significantly reduced due to radioactive decay, thus following the 'delay and decay' principles and volume wise 90 per cent of radioactive waste is Low Level[78] (LL)

2. High Level Waste (HLW) - High level radioactive liquid waste (HLW) containing most (99 per cent) of the radioactivity in the entire fuel cycle is produced during reprocessing of spent fuel[79]. In addition, hull waste i.e., the hollow clad tubes, is generated as solid HLW after the spent fuel is dissolved for the purpose of reprocessing.[80]

Various solid, liquid and gaseous waste products are first treated according to their level of radioactivity and then disposed of. Mostly the high level waste after the process of verification which is conducted in hot cells are encapsulated in suitable containers and over packs and stored for dissipation of radioactive decay heat and surveillance for a period of about 30 years and mostly in deep geological repositories[81]

The legal body which is responsible to monitor this are :- Atomic Energy's Safe Disposal of Radioactive Wastes Rules, 1987, which established the requirements for the disposal of radioactive waste in the country, Working of the Mines, Minerals and Handling of Prescribed Substances Rules, 1984,Radiation Protection, Rules 2004. The Atomic Energy Regulatory Board, the regulator, is supposed to ensure that the above rules are observed. The question that arises is whether the AERB is monitoring and the rules are being followed. The level of safety required at the disposal site is equally significant in order to prevent nuclear theft and sabotage. Often the ministry of Environment which is responsible for checks against contamination of such hazardous elements overlook the radioactive waste as there is no special mention of the latter in the hazardous waste rules; hence one can say that there is no single agency to take responsibility for any radioactive material found at a scrap market in India[82]. Thus better coordination between different state agencies and the central authority is required for ensuring smooth management of nuclear waste material.

Challenges and Recommendations

For a holistic approach the first thing is to prevent a disaster. According to Dr Abani, Senior Specialist, Disaster Management of India "the golden rule to reactor safety are the 3Cs first controlling the reactor power secondly cooling the fuel and thirdly containing the release of radioactivity under all conditions and if all this fails then last is the containment"[83]. This requires Planning, monitoring and constant assessments.

The factors which can cause an accident can vary from -:

- Machine/system Failure. Loss of Coolant Accident (LOCA) occurs when adequate cooling is not provided to the reactor. In such cases the reactor gets over heated and may even melt down in extreme cases, releasing harmful radiations in the atmosphere. The Three Mile Island accident was a LOCA.

- Human error.

- Natural calamity to sabotage or terrorist activities.

Large safety margins in nuclear designs, "Defense in Depth" and a mix of active and passive safety measures should be adopted. In order to withstand natural hazards one needs to ensure structural integrity and use of near defect free equipment. Procuring Generation III or Generation IV nuclear reactors is essential because of its various inherent advantages. The advanced generators use water for coolant at very high temperature and pressure which improves nuclear efficiency to 45 per cent as against 35 per cent achieved from old reactors. Some Pebble Bed reactor are helium-cooled, graphite-moderated as "The use of helium and graphite allows the reactor to burn the fuel efficiently and to operate at much higher temperatures than conventional light water reactors." [84].

The other challenge is to find highly skilled workers both for construction purposes as well as for running the plants e.g. the nuclear reactor operators. Engineers and radiation safety physicists are highly skilled professionals who are available only after many years of training .Their shortage may hinder /compromise the safety standards of a nuclear plant.

Secondly compliance of regulatory requirements, mitigation, preparedness in any eventuality and proper response requires co-operation and coordination of various agencies at different levels since most of the power plants are in different states, a lot of responsibility lies on the state authorities and they in turn need to coordinate at the district level and then at the local people.[85] In case of an emergency, a detailed plan has been given by the National Disaster Management Authority of India where the emergencies have been classified as:

- In-Plant Emergencies confined to the plant area the responsibility rests with the NPCIL.

- On-Site Emergency. If it spreads to area beyond the plant but till the distance of 1.6 km which is also known as the exclusive zone.

- Off-Site Emergency is beyond the exclusive zone. It comprises the Sterilized Zone of 5 km, Emergency Planning Zone (EPZ) of 17 km and also beyond in to the Public Domain.

The problem lies in its implementation since various agencies like the fire fighters, medical, police, defence etc are involved, even a small lapse from any of these agency would nullify the efforts .In order to prevent this, specialized trainers are required to not only train first responders but also to conduct mock drills and emergency exercises so that the preparedness of the unit could be assessed.

India has inadequate medical facilities. There is no network of hospitals which can handle radiation induced injuries on a large scale. Not only doctors but medicines (radio- protective prophylaxis) like Iodine prophylaxis along with monitoring equipment, protective gear, decontamination agents etc should be made available in large numbers and at a short notice. The so called Quick Reaction Medical Teams (QRMTs) comprising of doctors, nurses and paramedical staff should be made available quickly in any nuclear eventuality.[86]Unlike floods and tsunami where people can go back to their houses once the water recedes, in nuclear disasters people are displaced for a longer period of time if there area is affected and there is always a possibility of them not coming back to their homes as happened in Chernobyl where even after 25 years people are not able to come back to their homes. Therefore; it is very important for state and centre governments to ensure that all the gaps are filled as far as nuclear safety and security are concerned and all emergencies are addressed before India's ambitious goal of generating 25 per cent of its electricity from nuclear energy by 2050 is implemented.

Nuclear Security

Nuclear security can be understood in two ways

- Nuclear fissile material.
- Nuclear power plant.

In case of former one need to ensure that nuclear fissile material is not diverted to other countries for military use, as dual use of nuclear fissile material plutonium is apparent. India has an excellent track record as far as non-proliferation of fissile material is concerned. However, it is the latter part which India needs to assess. The security in nuclear power plants is a complex procedure. The challenge is not only to secure the plant but also to secure the radioactive waste storage and disposal units from potential saboteurs. It is difficult to provide a full proof security because various methods of attack could be used by the attackers. The major concern is if an insider helps the terrorist it could be fatal. A Mumbai kind of commando attack or cyber threats also could not be ruled out.

Design Basis Threat (DBT) Assessment

According to IAEA the DBT can be effective in countering the terrorist attack. This entails different security measures for different threats. For example "The insider threat" could be prevented by taking simple actions like detailed background check of workers and an ongoing process of watching any abnormal behaviour. Secondly in sensitive areas instead of single access two people should be made to do the inspection.

Simple In – built structural barriers with guards to protect and inspect the ID cards is the basic mechanism of any NPP. However advanced security measures require:

- Advanced intelligence gathering mechanisms.

- Synergy between various security stakeholders especially between guards and operators

- For onsite guards, training should be an ongoing process especially the simulated attack scenarios.

- Mock drills should ensure that emergency response force comprising Intelligence analysts, operators and guards be provided at a short notice.

- Incentives for workers who highlight security lapses so that a healthy security work culture is instilled.

- To provide Defense-in Depth security system; there should be multiple layered security arrangements so that it is difficult for an attacker to access the main area

- A greater synergy between the safety and security teams with emphasis on mock drills.

- Training is the most important aspect. A well trained, alert and motivated security officer can lessen security lapses.

The Civil Nuclear Liability Act

Nuclear energy is bound to play a significant role in future, and hence it has become essential that stringent guidelines be laid down in order to prevent callousness or indifference in the safety aspect of nuclear power generation. It is with this thought in mind that a liability frame work for nuclear damage has finally been passed in the parliament. So far the Indian experience in the field of civil nuclear power generation has been quite satisfactory as the country has not yet witnessed any potent nuclear mishap. The reason for this exemplary safety record has been two fold

(a) Partly due to the fact that the operators adhered to safety and security rules as the number of NPP were less

(b) Partly because these operators belonged to the public sector undertakings.

With the inevitable globalization and privatization of the Indian nuclear sector, it has become essential to establish a legal framework with enforceable penalties for nuclear irresponsibility. A legally binding framework would ensure the requisite caution required while manning the nuclear plants, as well as provide method and procedure for the assured provision of financial assistance to victims in the case of a nuclear accident.

The 1963 Vienna Convention on Civil Liability[87] for nuclear damage was the first law of its kind which had 38 contracting parties. This law, however, was amended in 1997 and it came into force in 2003. In 1988 the Vienna Convention and the Paris Convention was formed. Approximately 30 countries in the world operate a massive number of about 436 civilian nuclear power plants, and nearly 22 countries are a part of either the Vienna convention or the Paris convention. However; considering that Nuclear Liability is such a complex and essential issue, some countries, such as Canada, China, Japan, Korea, Switzerland and South Korea, have established their own national laws in order to tackle emergency situations as well as deal with the offenders in a severe manner to avoid repetition. India also feels that a strict and obligatory liability law is absolutely essential and it should contain clauses regarding the aspects of financial security, operator and suppliers liability, along with proper claim filing procedures.[88]

Highpoints of the Bill

- It fixes liability for nuclear damage and stipulates procedures for compensating the victims and it defines and specifies very clearly namely nuclear incidents, nuclear damage, nuclear fuel, material and nuclear installations[89].

- It specifies the person to be held liable for nuclear damage, the financial limit of the liability and the procedure for claiming compensation.[90]

- All non-central government operators need to take insurance or provide financial security to cover their liability

- In the case of public sector facilities, a liability of 300 million SDR would be borne by the government.

- A penalty fine has been specified for the agencies/ facilities which do not comply with the provisions of the bill.[91]

Limitations and Suggestions

- There should be strict liability, which means that in the case of a nuclear accident, the nuclear operator of the installation facility is held liable irrespective of whether or not the fault / damage is proved.

- The total liability in the bill has been 300 million SDR[92] (Special Drawing Rights) most of which has been borne by the government. The limit of the liability borne by the operator has been a mere Rs.500 Crores.

- Currently all the nuclear power plants are owned by NPCIL (Government owned company) and, therefore, the responsibility lays with the government .However; upon privatization of the nuclear power sector in the future, the liability columns need to be redefined accordingly.

- The Atomic Energy Act of 1962 also needs to be amended accordingly in order to allow private sector operators to operate independently.

- The total liability amount of Rs. 300 SDR is not sufficient to provide compensation in the case of a major nuclear accident.

- Unlike conventional sources, while nuclear mishaps are less frequent, they are more potent and the amount of damage inflected in these accidents are huge with lakhs of people getting affected.

- A clear example of the scale of such mishaps was the Chernobyl nuclear accident, where more than six lakh people were affected.

- In the Bhopal gas incident itself, the Supreme Court had asked the Union Carbide to provide a compensation amount of nearly 470 million dollars[93]. In many countries like the USA ,Russia, Germany, Japan etc the total liability has been unlimited

- This limited liability amount should be increased if required.

- The operator's liability amount is also very low at Rs 500 crores (109 USD).

- As of now it is inconsequential as the operators are government owned, (NPCIL) however; once the private operators enter the nuclear arena, the amount should be redefined otherwise the government will have to pay for the excess damage and the private sector would lose its sense of accountability or responsibility.

- Also insurance or financial security is required by all operators to cover the liability and therefore higher insurance cover, corresponds with higher electricity cost.

Figure: 3 Operator's Liability in Major Countries[94]

Liability of the operator and the government in the top 10 nuclear power generating countries, and India.

Country	Total generation (MW(e))	Operator's Liability (USD million)	State Compensation (USD million)	Total Liability* (USD million)
United States	1,00,683	11,900	Unlimited	Unlimited
France	63,130	861	300	1,161
Japan	46,823	Unlimited	Unlimited	Unlimited
Russia	22,693	No amount specified	Unlimited	Unlimited
Germany	20,480	Unlimited	2,500	Unlimited
South Korea	17,705	474	Unlimited	Unlimited
Ukraine	13,107	237	Unlimited	Unlimited
Canada	12,569	71	Unlimited	Unlimited

Country	Total generation (MW(e))	Operator's Liability (USD million)	State Compensation (USD million)	Total Liability* (USD million)
United Kingdom	10,137	228	50	278
Sweden	9,041	474	198	672
India**	**4,189**	**109**	**345**	**454**

Sources: 31 PRS. * Values have been converted into USD in source document as of December 2009. ** The values for India have been taken from the Bill and calculated at current exchange rates.

- The bill should have provided more than 300 SDR as a liability cap in order to ensure the utilization of the funds available under the convention of Supplementary compensation of 1997. This convention had created an international fund which could be used only if the liability due to nuclear damage is higher than SDR 300[95].

- The examination of the damages and the compensation required would be done by the government and this could cause a miscarriage of justice, as in most cases, the government is the sole party liable to pay the compensation.

- There will be a clash of interests between the required action and the more viable option.

- Hence the evaluation should be done by an independent body, like a judiciary or else a separate autonomous body should be established to assess the damage impartially.

- The time limit provided to the claimants to claim their damages is a short span of ten years which needs to be increased. Most of the other countries investing in nuclear power, such as South Korea and Netherlands have established a more reasonable time limit of 30 years. The reason behind this extension is that nuclear radiation damages and side effects take time to appear and at times, when it affects the genetic makeup of a person, the nuclear diseases may not be seen immediately but might appear in future generations.

International Cooperation

US, India and Nuclear Supplier's Group (NSG)

U.S, India Civil Nuclear Agreement or Indo-US nuclear deal.

The foundation for US civilian nuclear support to India can be traced back to the joint statements[96] issued by the erstwhile US President, Mr. George Bush and the Indian Prime Minster Mr. Manmohan Singh in 2005. Under this agreement, the US agreed to cooperate with India as far as civilian nuclear energy was concerned and in return India agreed to place all its civilian nuclear plants under the IAEA safeguards. However; this would have hampered the military secrecy act and, therefore, India was forced to separate its civilian and military nuclear facilities. After three years of relentless deliberations, on 1st Oct 2008, the US senate passed the treaty and allowed India to purchase nuclear fuel and technology from US. This treaty is a significant milestone in two ways

a) It strengthened the Indo-US relations.

b) The US approached the powerful nuclear cartel NSG to grant a waiver whereby India could do nuclear business with its members.

The NSG which is composed by 46 members[97], granted India the waiver on 06 Sep 2008 and India was free to trade with any of its members. These two remarkable agreements will go a long way in fulfilling the governments' dream of generating 20,000mw of nuclear power by 2020. There were several reasons for the US to consider and accept this agreement such as:

- US recognized India's strong commitment to nuclear non-proliferation despite the fact that India has not yet signed the Nuclear Non Proliferation Treaty (NPT).

- Secondly after the end of the Cold War, the geostrategic situation for the US changed. Russia was no longer an active threat post the disintegration of the USSR but China was emerging as a potential economic competitor.

- The US got involved in the wars with Iraq and Afghanistan which impacted its economy, and US wanted to diversify its economy through multilateral investments in developing nations.

- Simultaneously, in Asia, China was emerging as a major economic as well as military power to be reckoned with. It challenged the American role in the Asia-Pacific region. This led to a subtle shift in the perception of the US strategists who through its "Asia Rebalancing Policy" desired India to be the pivot in Asia.

- They tried to think of India out of the Indo-Pak prism and formulated different polices for India and Pakistan; and India became strategically and financially important. One reason may have been that the US thought that their interests would be served best by backing an upcoming economy, and by supporting India's nuclear energy programme, they could also provide opportunities for their MNCs.

- However; the major concern for the nuclear vendors was that India should cap the third party liability or have a liability clause introduced in line with the Convention of Supplementary Compensation (CSC)[98] for nuclear damage, to ensure that the American vendors could not be sued in the case of a nuclear accident or nuclear sabotage by terrorists. CSC is an international treaty which was created in 1997, through US efforts, and although India has signed the treaty as its 14th member in 2010, the nuances of the agreement still have to be ratified.

- Currently, India's Civil Nuclear liability Act 2010 allows the nuclear operators to sue the suppliers in the case of an accident due to technical defects in the plant.

- It remains to be seen whether the Indian government continues its hard-core stand on nuclear liability or whether it succumbs to US pressure.

India and the Nuclear Supplier's Group (NSG)

The NSG was established in 1974[99], with seven founding members, namely Canada, West Germany, France, Japan, United Kingdom, United States of America and the erstwhile Soviet Union. Currently the membership numbers have grown to reach 46. The NSG was created with the sole purpose of reducing nuclear proliferation, by controlling the export of nuclear supplies and by imposing nuclear safeguarding options based on the IAEA mandates while transferring resources or technology for peaceful purposes. The NSG has established very comprehensive guidelines for nuclear control and transfer[100],they being- Firstly the trigger list needs to be placed under effective physical protection to prevent unauthorized use[101]. As far as safeguarding is concerned, the NSG states that the suppliers should ensure that the transfer of the trigger list items, or potentially hazardous nuclear related technology to a non-nuclear state should be done only when they comply with the IAEA safeguard standards on the peaceful and safe use of all the sources and fissionable materials in its current and future activities[102]. There are also paragraphs regarding the special control which needs to be exercised on sensitive exports, where the recipients have to meet certain criteria. The first essential norm is that the recipient must be a member of the Nuclear Non Proliferation Treaty[103] and should be in full compliance of this treaty and the caution it exercises, and secondly the potential recipient must be committed to following and enforcing the IAEA Safety standards and adhering to their International Safety Conventions. There is also a section which is solely engaged with providing the in-depth definition of technology, production, the use of nuclear supplies in the public domain etc in order to remove the ambiguities and confusion that might stem from loopholes in the definition of nuclear structures. The control section deals with the varying levels of control which is to be exercised during the transfer of nuclear material, equipment or technology. These are basic guidelines from a well-defined NSG charter which ensures supplier responsibility and consequently nuclear temperance by laying down regulations to authorize the transfer of items or related technology, which is identified in the trigger list, only when they are satisfied that the transfers would not contribute to the proliferation of nuclear weapons or other nuclear explosive devices or be diverted to acts of nuclear terrorism.

Initially the NSG was unable to comply with India's request for the transfer of nuclear material as India was not a member of the NPT and its nuclear facilities were also not under IAEA safeguard. However after the US-India civilian accord, US was able to persuade the NSG waiver, as India had complied with one of its major requests which was to place the civil nuclear facilities under the IAEA safeguard and surveillance. India is the only country who without being a member of NPT has been given the clearance to do nuclear business with the NSG members. India has been trying to become a member of several other supplier groups also apart from the NSG, such as the Wassenaar Arrangement (WA), the Australia Group (AG) and the Missile Technology Control Regime and the United States supports India's bid for membership in the four multilateral export control regimes. Currently India is facing a few major challenges as far as its membership with the NSG is concerned, firstly the emergence of custom unions, which are now taking shape in Africa, the Gulf Cooperation Council of six Arab countries, and between some Eurasian countries are creating problems. These members want to know that if one member of a Customs Union is an NSG member, would the others also be considered bound by export control obligations and restrictions on dual-use and trigger-list items?[104] Secondly the procedural rule which states that all the decisions are to be taken by consensus might pose obstructions as China which is also a NSG member may not approve of it .Thirdly Israel and Pakistan both are currently not a member of NPT and so they want the same concession to be given to them as was given to India in the Indo-U.S. treaty. The US, during strategic diplomatic conversations with Israel, debated the complication it might create especially the ire of Arab countries if concessions were given to Israel. Pakistan's case is quite different as it has been blamed for proliferating nuclear technology, but with China's assistance, it has been trying to tide over the current opposition to its favour. These are the issues which make the NSG reluctant to amend its guidelines and induct new members. The China-Pakistan tango, inconvenient as it is for the Indian strategic analysts will continue to create problems for India at present.[105] Many scholars have questioned the relevance of India joining the NSG as a full-fledged member when she already has the waiver for free trade with its members. India's research in the FBR is currently at an advanced stage and its nuclear power generation through PHWRs is phenomenal. In a nutshell, these scholars argue, India already possesses the requisite technology and the knowhow to generate power through nuclear power plants. However; despite these progressive arguments the fact of the matter remains that for all the technical skill and Uranium imports India requires the support of NSG. India's acceptance into the NSG will provide her with several benefits such as the unhindered import of Uranium, mega 1000MWe capacity nuclear reactors and the LWR which would aid India immensely in meeting the high nuclear standards and deadlines set by the government. Secondly, while the NSG so far has the largest number of members (46 members) it is also paradoxically, the hardest supplier group to get into as it has very stringent guidelines for member induction. The members of the NSG are also the members of three other organizations, namely, the MTCR (34members), the AG (40members) and the WA (40 members) and hence once India is a member of the NSG, it would become much easier to apply for membership in the sister organizations thereby increasing the gambit of nuclear development. It is not merely a one sided bargain because India can also contribute on nuclear technology especially the PHWR. Therefore; it is in the interest of both the parties to accommodate each other for the resultant mutual benefit.

International Cooperation with Developed Countries and Additional Indigenous Projects

India's atomic energy market is estimated to be around $150bn[106] (£97bn), this was possible due to the NSG waiver and also due to the current nuclear expansion policy of the Indian government. This has aroused the interest of several developed countries to venture into India's nuclear business market. Countries like Russia, France, Canada, UK and South Korea have all signed nuclear agreements with India. A major breakthrough was achieved in case of South Korea and Russia.

Russia

India's nuclear collaboration with Russia dates back to 1988 when the then PM Rajeev Gandhi and the erstwhile Russian president, Mikhail

Gorbachev had signed an agreement regarding the construction of two nuclear reactors. Since then after some initial disagreements, the nuclear relationship between the two countries has grown tremendously. The Inter-Governmental Agreement[107] (IGA) was signed between the two countries in 2008 for the construction of four nuclear reactors in Kudankulam. The construction of two 1000 MWs nuclear power plants in Kudankulam is going to be completed soon. So far, the maximum capacity and power that India could achieve with a nuclear power plant was 540MWs. This mega plant of 1000MWs would be a first of its kind in our nuclear system which would be a major achievement for the Indian nuclear Industry and an agreement on the protocol for the financing of the Kudankulam units 3 & 4 was also signed on 7thJuly 2012[108]. The most beneficial aspect of this deal according to the NPCL is the fact that Russia is going to finance up to 83 per cent of this project, which basically means that a credit amount of up to USD 3400 million would be given by Russian government[109] in terms of works, value and supplies. This credit is payable in 14 years, which is a year post the commissioning of the project and the Russians have also given India the unconditional right to reprocess spent nuclear fuel. This Indo-Russian deal is going to have a long term effect on the nuclear Industry of India. It holds the potential of going beyond the mere setting up of power stations, and moving towards the establishment of research and development programmes along with a joint facility for nuclear fuel fabrication.

France

On 30th September 2008[110], France became the first country to sign a civil nuclear agreement with India after the NSG waiver. This nuclear agreement provided the novel impetus required for stronger bilateral relations between both the countries. The ministry of External Affairs has stated "As responsible States with advanced nuclear technologies, France and India intend to develop a multiform civil nuclear cooperation covering a wide range of activities including nuclear power projects, R&D, nuclear safety, waste management, education and training[111]". This is a significant move on the path of nuclear progress because France achieves 70 per cent of its power requirements through nuclear energy and this would be a major motivating factor for the Indian Industries. Also the DAE and the Commissariat A L'energie Atomique,or, Et Aux Energies Alternatives(CEA) (France's atomic energy commission), signed an agreement for the mutual exchange of information regarding nuclear science and technology. The French company Areva has been given the contract for supplying the nuclear reactor for the Jaitapur plant in Maharashtra[112]. France is the second country after Russia which allows India to reprocess the spent nuclear fuel from French nuclear reactors. France not only assures India a lifetime's supply of nuclear fuel for these reactors, it also possesses the sources to provide the requisite enrichment and reprocessing technologies[113] .

South Korea

The India-Republic of Korea (ROK) civil nuclear cooperation agreement was signed on the 25th of July 2011. When President Pratibha Patel visited South Korea, it became the ninth country to sign a deal regarding the mutual co-operation in civil nuclear Programme[114] This agreement will help the Korean government gain an entrée into the Indian nuclear power sector. A Memorandum Of Understanding (MOU) was signed by the two countries for technical exchange of Data and experience and KEPCO, the Korean company interested in exporting APR-1400 (Advanced Pressurized Water Reactor)[115] would now find it easier to enter the Indian markets. The Indian reasons underlying this collaboration with Korea have been

- Firstly due to the fact that Indo-Japanese deal was undergoing lot of problems post Fukushima and also the western nations were finding it difficult to enter the energy sector as most of the critical components in the nuclear design were licensed by Japan hence for any transfer of technology the Japanese consent was required, which in turn was delaying the procedure.

- Secondly Korea already possesses twenty years of practical nuclear experience as 35 per cent of her electricity comes through nuclear sources[116].

- Thirdly the IAEA had provided India with positive feedbacks regarding the safety of the nuclear reactors.[117]

- Also the Korean nuclear reactors were more cost efficient

when compared to its western counter parts.

- Lastly, a politically cordial relationship based on economic cooperation would greatly help India in increasing its sphere of influence towards East Asia

Additional Indigenous Projects and Export Opportunities

Apart from the various nuclear alliances being negotiated with developed countries, one of the most promising features so far, has been the interest shown by several nuclear giants such as the NTPC, NALCO etc, in foraying into possible joint ventures with NIPCL and the Indian nuclear power sector. Another significant chapter is the entrance of the industrial giant L&T[118] which is working towards the construction of nuclear machinery. It would be the first step on India's path towards nuclear self-reliance and indigenization. In a press release[119], the National Power Corporation of India (NPCIL) and power generation giant, National Thermal Power Cooperation of India (NTPC) have signed a Joint Venture Agreement (JAV) for the establishment of a Joint Venture Company with the aim of setting up several Nuclear power projects in India where the NTPC would have a 49 per cent share in the JAV. NTPC is proposing to finance the construction of a 2000MW nuclear power plant which could take India miles ahead on the path to nuclear self-reliance[120].

The National Aluminium Company (NALCO), in a bid to diversify[121] and increase its business interests is planning to join the NPCIL as a joint venture to build nuclear power plants in India. They have already selected the Kakrapara Unit 3 & 4 with 700 MWs as their first potential joint venture, the construction of which is estimated to be completed by 2015[122]. It has also offered to buy Uranium assets in Africa.

The Indian Oil Company (IOC) and Oil and Gas (ONGC), are also in negotiations with the AEC to become minority partners with NIPCL The Indian Railway is willing to finance the construction of two 500 PHWR on its land, while the Steel Authority of India Limited (**SAIL**) and the NPCIL are discussing a joint venture to build a 700 MWs PHWR plant[123]. The site will be chosen by NPCIL, which is currently believed to be in Gujarat in western India. Presently there is no provision for the private sector to independently operate the nuclear power plants, however the government has announced that it is working on an amendment to the law which allow the participation of the private sector, provided it is without direct foreign investment[124]. NPICL and Larsen & Toubro (L&T), India's leading engineering, manufacturing & construction companies have laid the foundation stone for their world class steel manufacturing & heavy forging plant. This will help India to develop the critical components and infrastructure required for the smooth function of our nuclear power plants. The press release from L&T stated "The state-of-the-art facility will be one of the best of its kind in the world. It will have the capability to produce ingots weighing up to 600 MT each, and a heavy forge shop equipped with a forging press which will be amongst the largest in the world. The facility will supply finished forgings for nuclear reactors, pressurizers & steam generators[125]." This will boost Indian industry's capabilities in manufacturing equipment for nuclear, thermal and hydrocarbon plants. This infrastructural development in India has come at an appropriate time as there is a lot more emphasis being laid on the utilization of nuclear energy as an alternate fuel due to the rapid depletion of thermal resources. Therefore, the market for such forging will continue to grow and this will begin a new era in the privatization of the nuclear industry and hopefully more industries will follow suit.

Export Opportunities

India was the first country in Asia to build a nuclear power plant, "Apsara", but the greatest paradox is that after so many years, India is still at the nuclear equipment import stage. The reasons for this slow growth may vary from political negligence, to economic, infrastructural and technical constraints as mentioned earlier. However things have started changing after 2008, when the US-India nuclear trade agreement was signed and subsequently the NSG waiver was given to India. Dr S Banerjee Chairman of DAE commented when he was interviewed by RIA Novosti's correspondent in India, Yevgeny Bezeka "The first point here is that India wants to become a donor country and not just a recipient. Since India has its own technology for the entire fuel cycle, it will be appropriate that India would become a donor country... India has strength of making zirconium alloy of any specification. Competence in fuel design of Indian scientists and engineers for different types of reactors is no less. So we can be a donor country[126]." The fact that there are joint facilities for nuclear fuel fabrication, and also that India is currently the largest producer of Heavy water and is ready to export PHWS of 220MWs or 540MWs shows that India is finally determined to capture the lost opportunities on the path to nuclear self-reliance. India's closed cycle nuclear technology will be more commercially feasible in comparison to the open cycle one due to the efficient reprocessing of fissile material, and the minimization of the nuclear waste volume.

India is one of the biggest producer of Heavy Water[127]. The Heavy Water Board (HWB) is in the process of attaining two export projects,

- The first for US-based Linde Electronics and Specialty Gases, where 11,000kg of heavy water is being supplied to the firm USA for use as raw material in the manufacture of deuterated compounds.[128]

- The second Export order was executed for supply of 15,000 kg heavy water to KHNP, Republic of South Korea for makeup requirement for their 700 MWe PHWR. Many research institutions in France, US and UK approached HWB, for supply of heavy water, for non-nuclear applications[129].

- Apart from this, the Board of Radiation and Isotope Technology (BRIT) is also believed to have exported the 'Gamma Chamber 5000', to the National Institute for Physics and Nuclear Engineering in Bucharest, Romania[130]. A Hyderabad-based Nuclear Fuel Complex (NFC) has also recently successfully executed an order from the IAEA for the manufacture, supply and commission of the fuel element end-cap welding unit to the Turkish Atomic Energy Authority.[131] Slowly but surely, India is now making her presence felt in the world market by moving away from being mere recipients to becoming active providers of nuclear expertise.

Recommendations

1. Stress should be laid on PHWRs and LWRs –India's niche areas, rather than on FBRs. As FBR has technical glitches which needs to be worked out and it will still take India a decade to have commercially successful FBRs.

2. An independent Atomic Energy Regulatory Board (AERB) is required as the watchdog of Nuclear Safety and Security.

3. Every state needs to have a Directorate of Radiation Safety (DRS).The states which do not comply with the same should be penalized.

4. There are inadequate certified radiation safety officers; stress should be laid to have adequate number of trained inspectors.

5. The manpower in AERB is just 301 personnel including 251 scientific and technical and 59 supporting staff. This number needs to be increased to at least 500 considering the increase in the number of nuclear power plants in future.

6. There should be specific codes on emergency preparedness and plans for radiation facilities such as industrial radiography, radiotherapy and gamma chambers etc.

7. Legislation should be there for decommissioning old nuclear power plants. Certain NPPs which have been running for 30 years, needs to be decommissioned.

8. In order to produce well trained nuclear scientists/engineers/regulators it is essential that the government of India introduce nuclear science as a subject at post graduate level

9. The "Defense – in Depth" nuclear safety, concept must be followed. (Giving a nuclear reactor a minimum of four to five layers of protection.)--Procuring Generation III or Generation IV nuclear reactors should be recommended.

10. Highly skilled workers are required, both for construction purposes as well as for running the plants e.g. the nuclear reactor operators, engineers and radiation safety physicists

are professionals who are available only after many years of training. Hence the increase in NPP should be in proportionate to the available resources ,otherwise the safety standards would be compromised

11. Specialised trainers are required during emergency drills, to not only train the "First Responders", but also conduct mock drills and emergency exercises so that the preparedness of the unit could be assessed impartially.

12. Medical facilities both in terms of radiation specialist and radio-protective prophylaxis-Iodine prophylaxis along with monitoring equipment, protective gear, and decontamination agents should be made available in all the plant areas.

13. Quick Reaction Medical Teams (QRMTs) comprising of doctors, nurses and paramedical staff should be made available quickly in any nuclear eventualities. Hence all the power plants should cater to this facility.

14. Advanced intelligence gathering mechanisms are required for nuclear safety of the plants and the fissile material

15. Synergy between various security stakeholders especially between guards and operators is required.

16. Training and mock drills should be done regularly and shortcomings should be reported and rectified impartially.

17. The Atomic Energy Act of 1962 also needs to be amended accordingly in order to allow private sector operators to operate independently.

18. An independent authority should be made responsible for assessing compensations because the examination of the damages and the compensation required during a nuclear accident if done by the government, could cause a miscarriage of justice, as in most cases, the government is the sole party liable to pay the compensation.

19. The time limit provided to the claimants to claim their damages is a short span of ten years which needs to be increased.

20. There should be Strict Liability, which means that in the case of a nuclear accident, the nuclear operator of the installation facility is held liable irrespective of whether or not the fault / damage is proved.

21. The total liability in the bill should be more than 300 million SDR to avail the international compensation facility.

22. Lastly, since India has its own technology for the entire fuel cycle, it will be appropriate that India should become a donor country rather than being recipient. Hence India should work to remove various political, economic, infrastructural and technical glitches as mentioned earlier.

Conclusion

India's nuclear journey has been slow but remarkable in many ways. India was one of the few countries where its leaders understood the importance of Science and Technology (especially the nuclear energy) very early. India was quick to initiate its nuclear energy programme, but due to lack of will and financial constraints it lost the focus. Indo-US treaty gave the required boost and created avenues to improvise and build the nuclear infrastructure at a much faster rate. The giant leap projected in producing power from nuclear energy from a mere 1.9 per cent to 9 per cent in 25 years is possible provided infrastructural, legal, political and economic delays are rectified.

Indian scientists had planned a "Closed Fuel Cycle" The first stage of building and generating power from PHWRS has been successfully completed .But as discussed in previous chapters there were operational constraints in completing the second and third stage that is the FBRs and the Thorium reactors. But the process is on and with the advancement of technology especially the AHWR, a revolution in the nuclear energy production is expected. However; this will happen only if the scientists are able to mitigate those problems. A more holistic approach needs to be adopted; enthusiasm and positivity are important drivers but equally important are realistic assessment of goals and capabilities.

With the growth of nuclear energy comes the responsibility of ensuring a safe and secure environment. One has to deal with not only terrorist issues but Fukushima tragedy has made us realize that laxity in security standards cannot be taken lightly. Disaster management is equally important. Regular drills and synergy between the centre and the states is an essential parameter and here the role of AERB is very important. AERB needs to be the ears and eyes of common man and they need to overview the safety and security arrangements in an unbiased and impartial manner. The inherent structural weaknesses of AERB need to be addressed. It is essential that various suggestions mentioned in previous chapters should be considered to prevent a nuclear disaster. Various parameters should be considered before constructing a nuclear plant. A proper planning and constant monitoring is the key for obtaining a nuclear accident free environment.

The Civil Nuclear Liability Act is in the right direction .It gives power to the people and the Strict Liability term should be adhered to .It is essential that Atomic Energy Act of 1962 should be amended to allow the entry of private sector in this field and also to redefine the Nuclear Liability Act accordingly. A via media needs to be discussed so that both the parties the supplier and the user are satisfied and the full potential of the Indo-US nuclear deal could be utilized.

NSG is an important organization and its waiver has given the required boost to the Indian energy sector and it is for the diplomats to ensure that India not only becomes its full member but also becomes member of its sister organizations. Thus India needs to create opportunities through its economic resurgence and make use of the favourable environment .India through its bilateral treaties with countries like France Russia and South Korea has already opened its atomic energy market, but it needs to expedite its indigenous projects .Indian industrial giants like SAIL, NALCO, ONGC, L&T etc are capable of producing "State of the Art" facilities which will improve India's indigenous nuclear power production capabilities, What is required is to have laws which will encourage private sector to invest more in this sector and truly transform the country's potential from a mere recipient state dependent on imports to a full-fledged indigenous nuclear power nation with recognizable export capabilities to reckon with.

Endnotes

1   Ramana M V, " India's Changing Nuclear Policy", Peace Magazine, Jan-Feb 1998.

2   Sarma,N, and Banerjee B, (2008), "Nuclear Power in India: A Critical History", New Delhi, Rupa & Co

3   Declaration of the Government of the People's Republic of China], *Renmin Ribao*, 16 October 1964, via: http://news.xinhuanet.com.

4   Charles H. Murphy, "Mainland China's Evolving Nuclear Deterrent," *Bulletin of the Atomic Scientists*, January 1972

5   "Atom for Peace", Eisenhower President Library Museum at, http://www. eisenhower.archives.gov/research/online_documents/atoms_for_peace.html

6   "Fifty Years Ago: Atomic ReactorEBR1 Produced First Electricity", American Nuclear Society Nuclear News, November 2001

7   Nuclear Power In Russia, World Nuclear Association, Retrieved 26 June 2006 at http://www.world-nuclear.org/info/Country-Profiles/Countries-O-S/Russia--Nuclear-Power/

8   World Nuclear Association ,at www.world-nuclear.org/

9   Report of the Working Group on Power For Twelfth Plan(2012-2017), Government of India, Ministry of Power,(2012),New Delhi

10   Ibid

11   Ferguson D Charles, (2011), Nuclear Energy: What Everyone Needs to Know, New York, Oxford University Press

12   Nuclear Power in India, world Nuclear Association ,updated 30 July 2014 atwww.world-nuclear.org/info/country-profiles/countries-g-n/India

13   Ibid

14   Shaping the third stage of Indian Nuclear Power Programme, Department of atomic Energy, Government of India, atdae.nic.in/writeraddata/.pdf

15   "India's baseline plan for Nuclear energy self-sufficiency", at large.standford. edu/course/2014/ph241/parekh1/docs/67057.pdf

16   What is Uranium? How does it work?, World Nuclear Association, Updated March 2014 at http://www.world-nuclear.org/info/Nuclear-fuel-cycle/introduction/what-is-Uranium--How-Does-it-Work-/

17   See n, 14, Department of Atomic Energy

18 Dr Jain S. K, "Nuclear Power – An Alternative" at http://www.npcil.nic.in/pdf/ nuclear%20power-%20an%20alternative.pdf

19 Ibid

20 Bucher R.G "India's Baseline plan for nuclear energy self-sufficiency stage", Prepared for: National Nuclear Security Administration Office of International Regimes and Agreements,2009

21 Nuclear reaction with Thorium, Thorium fuel Cycle at http://en.wikipedia.org/wiki/Thorium_fuel_cycle

22 See n, 20, Bucher R G

23 Subramanian T.S, "Total self-sufficiency in PHWR programme", Frontline, Volume 24 - Issue 08 retrieved 11 April 2012

24 Nuclear Power Generation(2006-2007 to 2013-2014),Nuclear Power Cooperation of India Limited at http://npcil.nic.in/main/AllProjectOperationDisplay.aspx

25 "Nuclear Power in India", World Nuclear Association (Updated December 2013) at www.**world-nuclear**.org/info/Country-Profiles/Countries-G-N/**India**/

26 Ibid

27 "India Plans 63000MW Nuclear Power Capacity by 2032", The Economic Times, 22 February 2012

28 "India eying 63,000MW Nuclear Power Capacity by 2032",NPCIL,The Economic Times,11 October 2010

29 The Fast Breeder Reactor Almost Ready, The Hindu,Updated:26 July 2013

30 Project Under Construction, NPCIL at http://www.npcil.nic.in/main/ProjectConstructionStatus.aspx

31 Kakodkar, "Fast Breeder Reactor More Important for India", The Hindu, 24 November 2004

32 Ibid

33 Ibid

34 "The Fast Breeder Reactor Almost Ready," The Hindu, Updated: July 26, 2013

35 "A creditable Performance at Kalpakkam" ,The Hindu, at http://www.thehindu.com/2005/10/19/stories/2005101903111300.htm

36 Ibid

37 Ibid

38 Ibid

39 Ramana M V , "India and the Fast Breeder Reactors", Science and Global Security, 2009, at http://www.princeton.edu/~ramana/IndiaFastBreederReactors-Jun09.pdf

40 Ibid

41 "India's symbol of self-reliance FBTR completes 20-years", The Outlook India .com, Chennai, 18 Oct 2005

42 Dr Kakodkar, Chairman Atomic Energy Commission and Secretary, Department of Atomic Energy, in an interview in The Hindu, Mumbai ,24 November 2004.

43 Ibid

44 "Thorium Fuel Cycle Potential Benefits and Challenges", IAEA-TEC,DOC-1450,May 2005,at www-pub.iaea.org/mtcd/publications/pdf/te_1450_web.pdf

45 Ibid

46 Ibid

47 Ibid

48 Ibid

49 Ibid

50 Bucher, R.G. (January 2009), *India's Baseline Plan for Nuclear Energy self-sufficiency stage* (pdf), Argonne National Laboratory, retrieved 26 March 2012

51 See n,44,Thorium Fuel Cycle

52 Ibid

53 Ibid

54 Growth Electricity Sector In India from 1047-2013,Central Electricity Authority, Ministry of Power, Government of India, July 2013

55 Sarma N & Banerjee B, (2008), Nuclear Power in India: A critical History, Rupa &co, New Delhi

56 "Safety Evaluation of Indian Nuclear Power Plant PHRWs at RAPs-2", at

http://wwwnpcil.nic.in/pdf/A2pdf

57 "India PM Manmohan Singh Blames Anti-Nuclear Protests on US NGOs", BBC News India,24 February,2012

58 Gopalakrishnan A, "Abandon the Import of Nuclear Reactor", DNA,05 April 2011

59 Raju S, "India's Atomic Energy Program: Claims and Reality" at www.rupe_ india.org/48/atomic.html

60 Raju S, Ramana M V , "Strange Love",14 May 2011,at www.openthemagazine. com/article/nation/strange-love

61 Department of Atomic Energy at http://dae.nic.in/

62 Ramana M.V, and Ashwin Kumar, "Safety First? Kaiga and Other Nuclear Stories", 2010, Economic and Political Weekly, Vol -XLV No. 7, 13.February 2010

63 Gopalakrishnan   A,   "Complete   Independence   of   AERB   an Imperative",Newsweek,25 March 2011

64 Gopalakrishnan A, "Issues of nuclear safety",   Frontline, retrieved 12 November ,2012

65 IAEA Information Circular, Convention On Nuclear Safety, INFCIR/449,05 July 1994

66 Gopalakrishnan A, "The Nuclear Safety Question", DiaNuke.org,20 Dec 2011 at www.dianuke.org/the-nuclear-safety-question-dr-a-gopalakrishnan

67 "91 per cent X-ray Unit in the Country Without Registration", Business Standard,20 October 2013

68 AERB Annual Report, 2012-1013 at http://www.aerb.gov.in/AERBPortal/ pages/English/annrpt/annrptBody_publications.action

69 Dastidar Avishek G, "AERB Clueless About Machines", Hindustan Times, 29 April ,2010

70 Directorate of Radiation Safety, State Health Society, Bihar at www. statehealthsocietybihar.org/drs.html

71 Chaitinya Ravi , "The Nuclear Safety culture in India ,Past Present and Future", Institute Of Peace And Conflict Studies ,Special Report at http:// www.ipcs.org/special-report/nuclear/the-nuclear-safety-culture-in-india-past-present-and-future-90.html

72 CAG Report Summary, PRS Legislative Research,23 August 2013 ,at http://www.prsindia.org/administrator/uploads/general/1345806440_CAG%20Report%20on%20AERB.pdf

73 "International Energy Outlook .2009", EIA at .http://www.eia.doe.gov/oiaf/ieo/electricity. html

74 Batra Ankush Paul Nelson, "Safety Safeguards and Security in Indian Civil Nuclear Facilities, Nuclear Security Sciences and Policy Institute,05 April 2012

75 Mr. Bajaj in Indian Nuclear Summit Mumbai 2009

76 Ferguson D Charles, (2011), Nuclear Energy: What Everyone Needs to Know, New York, Oxford University Press

77 "Narora Atomic Plant can withstand Quakes", NPCIL, The Economic Times, 17 March 2011

78 Wattal P K, " Indian programme on radioactive waste management", *Sadhana* Vol. 38, Part 5, October 2013, Indian Academy of Sciences ,at http://www.ias.ac.in/sadhana/Pdf2013Oct/6.pdf

79 Ibid

80 Ibid

81 Ibid

82 Kumar Amit, "Dealing with Radioactive Waste", 25 May 2012, Anaylisis Observer Research Foundation at http://orfonline.org/cms/sites/orfonline/modules/analysis/AnalysisDetail.html?cmaid=19081&mmacmaid=19082

83 Abani M C Dr., "Emergency Preparedness in Indian Nuclear Power Reactors", Lecture at Indian Nuclear Summit, 29 September 2011

84 Philip Proefrock, Alternative Nuclear Power: Pebble Bed Reactor, at http://www.ecogeek.org/component/content/article/3657-alternative-nuclear-power-pebble-bed-reactor

85 See n, 83,Emergency Preparedness

86 See n ,76, Ferguson Charles

87 Vienna Convention on Civil Liability For Nuclear Damage, IAEA Information Circular, at https://www.iaea.org/Publications/Documents/Infcircs/1996/inf500.shtml

88 Development on Nuclear Energy Sector in India, 2010, IDSA, Task Force

Report

89 Civil Liability for Nuclear Damage Bill, PRS Legislative Research, at http://www.prsindia.org/billtrack/the-civil-liability-for-nuclear-damage-bill-2010-1042/

90 Ibid

91 Ibid

92 The Civil Liability for Nuclear Damage Act,2010,The Gazette of India, Ministry of Law and Justice, New Delhi,22 September 2010

93 Union Carbide/Dow Lawsuit, Business Human Rights Resource Center at http://business-humanrights.org/en/union-carbidedow-lawsuit-re-bhopal?page=5

94 Civil Liability for Nuclear Damage Bill, PRS Legislative Research, at http://www.prsindia.org/uploads/media/Nuclear/Final%20Brief%20-%20civil%20liability%20for%20nuclear%20damage%20bill.pdf

95 Convention on Supplementary Compensation for Nuclear Damage, Information Circular, INFCI567,22 July 1998

96 Civil Nuclear Cooperation, Ministry Of External Affairs, Government of India, at http://www.mea.gov.in/in-focus-topic.htm?24/Civil+Nuclear+Cooperation

97 NSG Text at www.nuclearsuppliergroup.org

98 See n, 95, Convention on Supplementary Compensation

99 NSG Text at www.nuclearsuppliergroup.org/en/hist

100 Ibid

101 Ibid

102 Ibid

103 Ibid

104 Dikshet Sandeep, " India's quest for NSG membership in trouble" The Hindu, 03 July 2012

105 ibid

106 Varadarajan Siddharth, "India Russia Nuclear Talks hit Liability Snag," The Hindu ,Updated 30 July 2012

107 Yardley Jim, "India Passes Nuclear Deal, New York Times.30 August 2010

108 India Signs Protocol with Russian Federation, Press Release No-

07/2012,DAE,Government of India

109 Cabinet Nod for two more Nuclear Plants at Kudankulam, The Outlook, 20 March 2013 at http://www.outlookindia.com/news/article/Cabinet-Nod-for-Two-More-NPlants-at-Kudankulam/793043

110 "India-France Ink Landmark Nuclear Deal", at www.rediff.com/news/2008/sept/30ndeal3.htm

111 "India, France Civil Energy Nuclear Energy Pact Enters into Force", DNA 14 July 2010

112 Committed to Jaitapur Nuclear Power Plant, India tells France, The Times of India, 10 January 2013

113 "French Parliament ratifies Indo-French nuclear deal ", The Hindu Nov 27, 2009

114 India Signs Civil Nuclear Deal with South Korea, indiatoday in, 25 July 2011 at http://indiatoday.intoday.in/story/india-south-korea-civil-nuclear-deal/1/146085.html

115 Baruah Pranamita, "India-ROK Nuclear Cooperation: Is It a Win- Win situation?", Institute for Peace and Conflict Studies, Article No 3439, 16 August 2011

116 For further information see India-Republic of Korea(ROK) relations, MEA Brief at mea.gov.in/portal/foreignrelation/ROK_short_brief_Jan2013/pdf

117 Baruah Pranamita, "India-ROK Nuclear Cooperation: Is it a Win-Win Situation?" Institute of peace and conflict Studies August 16, 2011 at http://www.ipcs.org/article/india/india-rok-nuclear-cooperation-is-it-a-win-win-situation-3439.html

118 "Nuclear Power In India", World Nuclear Association, at www.world-nuclear.org/info/country_profiles/countriesG-N/India

119 Ibid

120 Ibid

121 Ibid

122 Ibid

123 Ibid

124 Ibid

125 "NPCIL,L&T Flag Off Venture for Special Steels and Ultra heavy Forgings",

Business Standard,09 June 2010

126 "Russia has an Advantage; It has the Reactor ,Others can Only Show Papers", Intell-Briefs,15 March 2010,

127 "India Largest Producer of Heavy water", Deccan Herald,20 April 2012

128 Department of Atomic Energy ,Annual Report (2011-2012), at http://dae.nic.in/writereaddata/ar2012_0.pdf

129 Ibid

130 Board of Radiation and Isotope Technology, Annual Report 92011-2012, at http://www.britatom.gov.in/docs/pdf/ar_eng_11_12.pdf

131 "Indian Firm Cash on Global-N-Market Deals", *The Hindu Business line*, 07 June 2010

3   The Global Nuclear Challenge

In this day and age, with the drastic increase in conventional and nuclear armament, there is a need to contextualise and reinterpret the global scenario in order to avoid catastrophic nuclear fallouts. There is concomitantly, a need to prevent the military mistakes of the past which have not altogether been addressed satisfactorily. One must constantly remember that now more than ever, the use of nuclear weapons will cause global repercussions. There is therefore a need to reassess and rethink this global power balance. The measures include identifying potential threats, to understand nation-states and the intricate nature of their competition and complexities; dealing with emerging trends, the challenges of the future, and ultimately developing long term strategies to counter and if possible to eliminate this powerful nuclear threat.

The Global Players

The advent of the atomic age brought along with it a revolution of a different kind. Nations coveted the nuclear bomb for prestige, power and security. It also changed the global security scenario and the power balance was immediately threatened, as the arms race was inimically transformed into a volatile impasse due to nuclear weapons being preferred over conventional weapons. The 1950s saw nations worldwide, adopting an aggressive nuclear weapons policy both in terms of quality as well as quantity. True to its label, the Cold War became an uninhibited calculated display of strategic ability, as demonstrated by the United States' detonation of the Hydrogen bomb in 1951 which was immediately followed by the Soviet Union's retaliation in 1953. Each time one of these countries increased its arsenal or acquired a new weapon the other was quick to follow suit with a more potent weapon. This desire to outmanoeuvre the adversary by maintaining a larger, stronger and technically more lethal nuclear arsenal resulted in a mad arms race. The world was polarised into two opposing geographical, strategic and economic superpowers. Following this hostile display, other countries began to engage with nuclear technology due to a plethora of reasons primarily, increased threat levels, and an attempt to gain prestige in an increasingly bipolar world. After gaining preliminary success, a handful of Nuclear Weapon States made an attempt to monopolise nuclear technology. This move was resented by potential Nuclear Weapon States and consequently there was a constant tussle between the nuclear and the non-nuclear states. Over time a few nations broke from this rigid control by conducting their own tests and subsequently declaring themselves Nuclear Weapon States thus avoiding the clandestine amassing of weapons that had been practiced hitherto. Due to this proliferation of nuclear technology, the potential challengers who coveted nuclear armament could be predominantly grouped into three sets of nations namely: the Nuclear Weapon States, the Covert or Threshold Nuclear Weapon States and the Non State Actors.

The Prevalent Environment: An Exposition of the Distinctive Characteristics of Nuclear Weapon States (NWS) with Special Reference to Superpowers.

One of the major reasons for acquirement of nuclear technology by Nuclear Weapon States (NWS) was to enhance prestige and become global powers to be reckoned with. The constant nuclear testing and sustained universal increase in the quantity and quality of nuclear weapons, was testimony to their scheme of augmenting and reinforcing their nuclear status. Both the superpowers had played a key role in this liberal proliferation of nuclear technology. Whether it was the help provided by the US to Great Britain and France, or conversely the Sino-USSR treaty, the end result was a tremendous global arms race.

The Cold War Era

The Cold War era from 1945 to 1990 saw dramatic swings in the world scenario. The early phase (1945-55), was primarily about the formation of coalitions and power conglomerates. On the western front, the Marshall plan united Europe under the strategic concept of NATO while the Soviet Union did the same in the east. The power split was not limited to military ideology only but socio political state structuring as well. While the West fluctuated between socialism and capitalism, Eastern Europe was dominated by the communist ideology and unified by the Soviet Union under Warsaw Pact - a mutual defence treaty between eight communist states of Central and Eastern Europe. Additionally, this transitional period was also marked by intense confrontation between the two superpowers as each of them tried to establish their strategic boundaries in order to create new bipolar power houses. The culminating effect of all this instability was a series of near war like situations. The communist conquest of China, The Berlin Blockade, the Korean War, and the polarisation of Europe can be seen as a few examples of what appeared to be a volatile path towards an imminent apocalypse.

The second phase from 1955-65, was one of assessment, evaluation and recruitment. It was a stasis during which the super powers tested their post war boundaries. On the one hand, communists forayed into new areas such as Latin America and South East Asia leading to their eventual formation of a stronghold in Cuba and Vietnam. On the other hand, the United States tried to counter communism through every means possible. They used almost all the resources available to attack the communists by spreading propaganda, using economic warfare and sabotage while simultaneously assisting a whole host of anti-communist movements. They also resorted to hard core military strategies by stationing a fleet in the Taiwan Strait, signing a security pact with Japan and stationing troops in South Korea. All this strategic military assimilation eventually drew to an impasse as the stakes kept getting higher and the resources began running low. Based on the need for alternatives, the super powers began debating the possibility of dialogue in an attempt to lower the danger levels of a high risk nuclear world. The Cuban Missile crisis made them realise the possible dangers of nuclear fallout. When they realised that despite the simultaneous expansion, neither of their core areas were truly threatened, they cautiously began working towards normalising relations. A preliminary step on this road towards nuclear threat reduction was the Limited Test Ban Treaty and with this treaty, a new era of arms control began.

After this relatively minimal first step, the next two decades from 1965 to 1985 saw a drastic change in policy. There was a marked improvement in relations of these erstwhile hostile superpowers. Since both the countries had to suffer setbacks, (US in Vietnam and Soviet Union in Afghanistan) they realised, that direct confrontation undermined their special status and diminished their accumulated resources. Instead, they decided to adopt a new war strategy, namely, proxy wars. By increasing the potential geostrategic effect of the threat, they concomitantly increased the potential collateral damage thereby increasing the number of parties with vested interests. The canvas thus became much wider and included countries from the Middle East and South Asia. They also adopted a dual policy with respect to the international power balance. On the one hand, they increased the scope of the imminent threat, thereby ensuring that their allies were roped into fighting for what appeared to be global causes; while on the other hand, they also began limiting potential threats that could upstage delicate bipolar balance by reducing the external power nexus and working towards arms control. Several bilateral treaties such as the ABM Treaty and the SALT Treaty were signed in an attempt to limit and control the rapidly spiralling arms race.

Another major shift in the power balance of the world was seen during the final period, from 1985 to 2000. The democratization of the Soviet political system by Mikhail Gorbachev, through the implementation of his political liberalization policies (Glasnost/ Perestroika) led to a series of break downs. The first to collapse was the alliance of Eastern Europe-the Warsaw Pact, and then the eventual collapse of the Soviet Union in 1991 and subsequently the emergence of 15 new nation states. This territorial dismemberment of Soviet Union greatly undermined its economic condition and dented its status as the Superpower. Soon a unipolar world came into existence and the Continental US became the sole arbiter of power, unchallenged and solitary. This; however, was a temporary cusp in the changing political scenario as the fall of the USSR, provided several opportunities for hitherto suppressed nations to enter the fray. The unipolar domination was eventually challenged by the emergence of a New World Order where economics, religious fundamentalism and newly emerging Non State Actors, played a major role in altering the power dynamics from Europe to Asia.

Post-Cold War "New World Order"

The emergence of a New World Order saw the political action shift from Europe to Asia. "The world saw the birth of new nation-states in Central Asia, allowed democratization to proceed in many states previously ruled by Marxist dictators, and led to significant progress in resolving several Third World conflicts that had become prolonged during the Cold War."[1] New challenges such as religious militancy, terrorism, economic conflict, and severe competition over scarce resources emerged and they could not be immediately suppressed. Not even by the United States which had by now emerged as the sole super power in terms of politico-military might. Technological inventions such as television, computer and telephone, increased reach and improved connectivity. The result was that there was plethora of information readily available and easily accessible. The state's monopoly over information was challenged as well-informed citizens made accountability a hallmark of political decisions. Economically, finance and trade became important parameters for judging the growth and development of a nation. Developed nations tried to control economic turbulence through financial institutions. Developing nations, in an attempt to outdo each other strove to form trade blocks. In short, nations all around the world became interdependent economically, culturally and socially.

Escalation of Nuclear Weapons

Once the nuclear genie was out of the lamp, it became difficult to contain it, and the super powers could not limit the dissemination of nuclear technology. Like the butterfly effect, within a few years, the nuclear club increased from two Nuclear Weapon States to eight. In 1963 a Nuclear Test Ban treaty was proposed, but by then the stakes had increased. In 1964 China conducted its first nuclear explosion. While China announced its intentions overtly, this act of rebellion was followed covertly by Israel. Israel preferred to remain ambiguous on the nuclear status because it suited its national interests. Almost immediately after the explosion, the US President in office at the time, President Johnson said "The nations that do not seek nuclear weapons can be sure that, if they need our strong support against some threat of nuclear blackmail then they will have it[2]." This guarantee against nuclear attack was for the sole purpose of preventing further proliferation of nuclear armament in the future. However, due to lack of clarity in the documents, which were supposed to define how the guarantees' might work, made the nonnuclear states very vulnerable to the nuclear threat. On one hand the NWS were increasing their arsenal quantitatively and qualitatively by developing new miniaturised weapons, on the other hand they were also trying to curtail the possibility of more countries obtaining nuclear technology, by pressurising them to join the Nuclear Non Proliferation Treaty (NPT) .The nuclear weapon arsenal during the eight decades can be seen in the table given below:-

Table: 4 Nuclear Weapons of P-5 Nations

Year	USA	USSR/Russia	UK	France	China	Total
1945	6					6
1950	369	5				
1960	20,434	1,605	30			22,069
1970	26,119	11,643	280	36	75	38,153
1980	23,764	30,062	350	250	280	54,706
1990	21,211	33,417	300	505	430	55,863
2000	10,615	10,201	185	470	400	21,871

Source:- Robert. S. Noris of the Natural Resources Defence Council and Hans M Kristenen of the Nautilus Institute. 2002, Bulletin of Atomic Scientists.

The non-nuclear nations which were surrounded by NWS were apprehensive about the repercussions of a possible nuclear attack. There was a sense of urgency to restore the balance that had been hitherto maintained. India likewise, found itself on the cusp of a geostrategic imbalance and due to emerging security concerns decided to become a Nuclear Weapon State in 1998. This was immediately followed by Pakistan and subsequently North Korea. Though the burgeoning of Nuclear Weapon States has continued, nevertheless, the superpowers simultaneously in a move to curtail this process signed number of treaties in an attempt to regain control over the spread of nuclear technology. Various international treaties like the Limited Test Ban Treaty (1963), NPT (1968), Strategic Arms

Limitation Talks (SALTI-1972), Anti-Ballistic Missile Treaty (1972), Threshold Test Ban Treaty (1974), Strategic Arms Reduction Treaty II (1993), Comprehensive Test Ban Treaty ((1996) and so on were responsible for gradually curtailing the global nuclear weapons arsenal from an all-time high of 65,057 in 1986 to 20,150 in 2002[3]

The Emergence of Three Groups

Post the major political upheaval it appears that in the new world order, there are primarily three main groups who at a given point of time can threaten the global balance. These three groups are interrelated and a change in the position of any one can potentially affect the others thus altering the power balance .These three groups are:

1. Nuclear Weapon States (NWS)

2. Nuclear Threshold States.(NTS)

3. Non State Actors (NSA)

1. Nuclear Weapon States- Their Nuclear Development Programme

The late 19th and 20th centuries have been the age of atomic revolution. The inventions in the nuclear field have significantly changed the future. Science held the key to the future of the human world. The discovery of Uranium by the German Martin Klaproth in 1789, followed by other inventions like Rontgen's ionizing radiation (1895), Pierre and Marie Curie's phenomenon of "Radioactivity" (1896), etc were all instrumental in setting the base for the fundamental research into the nuclear technology. The discovery of nuclear fission made the possibility of an atom bomb a reality. By the end of 1940, remarkable progress had been made by several groups of scientists residing in America and Europe and they consequently became the pioneers of nuclear technology.

United States of America

The first systematic plan towards the realization of the nuclear bomb was made in the US under "The Manhattan Project[4]". This project made significant progress under Colonel Leslie Groves and Dr

Oppenheimer. The first successful atomic explosion took place in July 1945, at Alamogordo in New Mexico which had a yield of 20 to 22 Kilotons of TNT[5]. However; Japan's aggressive posture during World War II and its refusal to comply with the demands of USA, Great Britain and Russia, led to the bombing of the Japanese cities and ultimately its unconditional surrender. The United States was the first state to demonstrate the lethal nature of the nuclear weapon. On the 6th of August 1945 they detonated a Uranium bomb on Hiroshima and on the 9th of August 1945 Nagasaki was bombarded by a Plutonium bomb. This unfortunate and heinous act ended the World War II. Millions of people died, 75,000 were killed, and nearly the same number of people, were injured. There were a plethora of side effects that followed. The genetic abnormalities that began appearing in the next generation reinforced the scientists' observations, regarding the horrendous evil nature of the nuclear bomb. Politically and strategically the war had rearranged the balance of power once again. Historically, post-World War II and with the decimation of Europe and Asia, the United States became the dominant leader of the "free market" or the capitalist world. The simultaneous rise of communism became an intimidating ideology, and its patriarch the Soviet Union, therefore became a natural adversary. Despite the horrors of the bomb, in the subsequent years the Americans continued experimenting, the resultant was another bomb, mightier than the Uranium bomb, the A-bomb or the Hydrogen bomb, which was detonated in 1952 and that weapon yielded an equivalent of 10 megatons of TNT[6] . This power lust without considering the consequences provoked new hostilities and introduced a new era. This era defined new nuclear jargons like MAD (Mutually Assured Destruction), First Strike etc, which started a nuclear arms race that was only marginally diluted with the collapse of Soviet Union.

Soviet Union

The American bomb had changed and rearranged the global power nexus. Historically it has been proven that nation's endeavour, has always been to maintain the balance of power, and whenever this balance has been altered, it has led to war , where the consequences had always been the loss of life and social structures . Signed as early as the 17th century, the Treaty of Utrecht can be seen as a classic example of how statesman ensured that the balance of power in Europe was maintained and restored ,through the non-violent signing of this treaty. Post World War II, the advent of nuclear technology had dramatically enhanced the power of "The United States of America". In the eyes of its rival, the Soviet Union, the propagator of the communist cause, the "status quo" had been changed. The Russians though had a suspicion about this bomb, and the Russians had already started their research in nuclear physics as early as 1918, when a special office (Department Number one) was being established with the Academy of Sciences Committee to explore the potential usage of radioactive materials[7]. In 1933, the first Soviet conference on nuclear Physics was held in Leningrad[8]. However it was only after Hiroshima that the Soviet leaders decided to mobilize their scientists, and work overtime to meet the new challenge. By 1946 scientists, led by Igor Kurchatov, had successfully completed the important procedure of sustaining an indigenised Uranium chain reaction. For the first time in Eurasia, a Soviet 100MW Reactor was commissioned,[9] and on 29 Aug 1949 the first Soviet Union conducted its first nuclear fission test yielding 22 KT[10]. Thus with a series of nuclear experiments, their long cherished dream of achieving technological parity with the Unites States was achieved. The rivalry between the two nations, however, did not end here, because the erstwhile president of USA President Truman retaliated by declaring that the US would build an even more destructive "super bomb", the Hydrogen bomb. Stalin's Soviet Union immediately followed suit, continuing the nuclear race and they claim that the first Soviet test of a hydrogen bomb, took place on August 12, 1953, however; Americans believed that it was a fission test and actual fusion test took place on 22 November 1955[11]. The ideological war had now taken on new, grim, realistic contours. Thus a new chapter was to be added to the history of the world, an era of "Cold War". Conflict and confrontation had begun .The newly independent states were exposed to a bipolar world. The alliances, the Non Aligned Movement (NAM) and the emergence of new Nuclear Weapon States changed the face of the world and the strategic future of nation –states.

United Kingdom

In the meantime, the medium power states like UK and France aspired to gain nuclear weapons for prestige, and also for the super power status. The British Empire was declining with the diminishing of the Edwardian twilight, and the rise of the new independent nation-States further curtailed its power and prestige. It became one of many nations in the world, no longer an imperialist stronghold. However, the British scientists were pursuing the bomb as early as 1940, but the war and the independence struggles of various colonies interrupted its progress. Prior to the war, the British scientists had shared scientific knowledge with the Americans, but post World War II, the Americans were reluctant to reciprocate[12]. In fact, the Atomic Energy Act of 1946 is a classic example of American unwillingness to aid and abet the spread of nuclear technology. Moreover their turbulent relationship with the Americans and the Soviet Union, especially after the nuclear explosion in 1949, gave the British politicians the impetus to hasten the nuclear programme, and they resumed the same under the British scientist William Perry. He formed a group of scientists who subsequently tested the bomb. However the British government had to face the dilemma of nuclear sites that were appropriate for testing, as there was no extensive uninhabited area suitable for atmospheric nuclear testing[13]. They had to look overseas and their choice was between Australia and USA. Britain's first nuclear test named "Hurricane" was successfully completed on 30 Oct 1952 and a 25 Kiloton yield nuclear bomb was detonated 90 feet underwater in the oceans of Australia[14]. In the period from 1952-1957 a total of 12 tests were conducted. The fusion weapons were developed during 1954 to 1958 and erstwhile Prime Minister Macmillan named the device test in 1957 the "Hydrogen Test". Britain produced about 790 warheads from 1953 to 1992 and an additional 44 test devices or test weapons, but despite this surge, this stockpile was merely one per cent of the entire American stockpile which had been assessed at 70,000 warheads[15]. Since then, they have maintained a relatively limited but potent nuclear force.

France

Many of the key scientists in the 20th century belonged to France. Henri Becquerel, Marie and Pierre Curie, Frederic and Irene Joliot-Curie made important contributions in the field. The French physicists had already acquired Uranium and Heavy Water technology. The German invasion and its subsequent occupation of France, however, temporarily stopped its nuclear programme. The scientists therefore migrated to England and to Canada. Post World War II, the reconstruction of France began and the Atomic Energy Commission (commissariat a l Energie Atomique, or CAE) was created under the leadership of Raoul Dautry. Two major events hastened the nuclear programme. The first was the independence of the French colony of Indonesia in 1954. This lowered their esteem and reduced their power politically, and therefore acquiring the bomb was considered essential to establish the lost French grandeur .Secondly, the Suez crisis of 1956 made the French realise that they could not always rely on their allies and that they needed to be militarily independent. The first French nuclear test took place in 1960 in Algeria and almost four years later, the nuclear weapon was delivered to the Strategic Air Force for service on a Mirage IVA aircraft[16]. It took the French scientists eight years to detonate a Hydrogen bomb, however a two-stage thermonuclear device was detonated on 24 Aug 1968 and subsequently they operationalized their first MIRV in 1985.

China

Chinese nuclear history has been remarkable and exemplary. It can be seen as one of grit and determination. Unlike the western nations, China did not have a scientific, technical or nuclear background. For the longest time they lacked trained nuclear scientists, infrastructure for testing and most importantly finance to fund their nuclear programme. Working their way up to becoming a nuclear stronghold and a power worth reckoning with, has not been easy for China. Post their independence, however, the Chinese leaders, Mao and Deng Xiaoping understood the importance of creating and possessing a nuclear bomb. China coveted the bomb, like many other nations, for prestige and security. Initially China's principal adversary was the US. Their eventual disagreements over the Korean and Vietnamese wars did not make their relationship any less strenuous. Politically and militarily, the Americans supported the nationalist Kuomintang in Taiwan. In the 50s and 60s the Americans deployed nuclear weapons in Taiwan. The fact that the United States threatened to use nuclear weapons against China on several occasions during and after the Korean War facilitated and reinforced the Chinese resolve, to develop nuclear weapons, primarily for the purpose of deterrence. Their biggest nuclear support during this period was the USSR. The Soviet Union, in an attempt to form an allied defence against American interference, designed and built the Chinese fledgling nuclear industry. Hundreds of Chinese scientists were trained in USSR. Liu Xiyao, Vice Chairman of the Second Ministry said "Without Soviet industrial help, it would have been impossible for us to have achieved such rapid success in making the atomic and Hydrogen bombs[17]". However by 1958 the Sino-Russian relationship had started deteriorating and by 1960 the Russians withdrew their assistance for the nuclear programme. It would not be accurate to lay the entire foundation of the Chinese nuclear programme at the hands of the Russians. Many of the Chinese scientists were also trained in the West and were later lured back to the mainland. These scientists also contributed immensely in the preparation and development of the bomb. China's nuclear plan was delayed by few years due to the withdrawal of Soviet support, but on 16 October 1964, China successfully detonated its first 22KT yield nuclear device. Since then their nuclear programme has progressed at an alarming pace; in fact China's progress and tenacity in developing a Hydrogen bomb was admirable. They conducted their first thermonuclear test in on 17 June 1967. A bomb of 3.3MT yield was dropped by an H-6 aircraft bomber[18]. From 1964 to 1993 China had conducted 39 known nuclear tests and during the same time they developed nearly 700 war heads of all types.

India as a NWS

India's nuclear history dates back to 1948, when Atomic Energy Commission was established. India had implemented a three stage nuclear programme which had been formulated by Dr Homi Bhabha. The politicians and the diplomats had advocated the peaceful aspects of nuclear energy, but the ambiguity in India's nuclear approach was evident right from the Nehruvian era. The Sino-Indian war and China's nuclear explosion in 1964 exposed India's vulnerabilities to a nuclear threat. India conducted its first "peaceful nuclear explosion" in 1974 and then a series of tests in 1998. The later test was claimed to be a thermonuclear test but this has been debated by some analysts. The successful completion of these tests helped India to reinstate its position as an emerging power, and finally ending its nuclear ambiguity, by declaring itself a NWS. The compulsion behind India's nuclear programme was based on two major aspects. The first reason was the geo-strategic imbalance that was created after China's first nuclear test, and the second was the nuclear hegemony of the NWS which refused to admit emergent developing nations into the nuclear group. With nuclear China and a hostile Pakistan, India's geopolitical compulsions were evident. Moreover, having witnessed three major wars, the Sino-Pak alliance threatened the balance of power in South Asia. Nuclear balance was supposed to bring stability. "Nuclear Deterrence" as a strategy of conflict management was widely believed to bring back the lost balance in Asia. The policy of "Deterrence" was one of the pillars of the Cold War and was adopted by both the super powers. It had been successfully used by NWS to establish political, economic and military successes. Strategic superiority was politically useful and provided the host nation with bargaining leverage on a wide range of issues. Various alternate measures such as Credible Deterrence, Mutual Assured Deterrence (MAD) etc were devised to deal with issues of nuclear imbalance. Various nuclear doctrines, including the Indian doctrine, laid stress on deterrence and their applicability in political scenarios. It is often said that due to this gradual insistence on deterrence, the world has managed to deter a nuclear war for so long. The aspect of nuclear discrimination adopted by the NWS was observable in various global disarmament treaties. The enforcement of the NPT, the Zangger Committee, the Nuclear Suppliers Group (NSG), the Australia Group, and the Wassenaar Arrangement, were measures to curtail the nuclear development programme of NNWS. India had championed the cause of total nuclear disarmament but she was disillusioned by the unequal standards that were propagated and especially the continued vertical proliferation of the NWS. After the demise of the Cold War, the major nuclear powers did not make the appropriate efforts required for global nuclear disarmament and as a result the global nuclear threat took new dimensions. New nations were emerging with their covert nuclear programmes and the threat perception in Asia had intensified which exposed India to new challenges. In order to balance the instability that seemed to be emerging with nuclear proliferation, India was actually left with no choice but to take the nuclear road.

Pakistan

The Pakistani nuclear programme was designed, in retaliation to India's peaceful nuclear explosion of 1974. The erstwhile Prime minister Mr Bhutto had said "If India builds the bomb, we will eat grass and leaves for a thousand years, even go hungry, but we will get one of our own. The Christians have the bomb, the Jews have the bomb and now the Hindus have the bomb. Why not the Muslims too have the bomb?[19]". This depicts the Islamic propaganda, the smokescreen in the name of religion, which was used cleverly by Mr Bhutto, to incite the Islamic nations into funding Pakistan's nuclear programme. The Pakistan Atomic Energy Commission (PAEC) was formed in 1956 with Dr Nazir Ahmad was its first chairman. However, systematic progress in this field began only under PM Bhutto with his Project 706. The goal of this project was to develop the Atomic bomb using Uranium technology. *Time magazine* had called the Project-706 as Pakistan's equivalent of the United States Manhattan Project[20]. Multiple production sites and research sites operated secretly, however some sources state that the project was disbanded on 11 March 1983 when the PAEC conducted the cold test of a miniature nuclear device[21]. Eventually, under Dr Abdul Qadeer Khan, a German-trained metallurgical engineer and nuclear weapon technologist, Kahuta Research Laboratory (KRL) was built and finally, a few weeks after India's nuclear test, Pakistan detonated nuclear devices in the Chagai hills of Baluchistan on 28 May 1998. A second test, codename Chagai II, was conducted on May 30 1998. Pakistan thus became the 7th country in the world to successfully conduct nuclear tests and develop nuclear weapons technology.

North Korea

The North Korean nuclear programme began as early as in the 1950s with the help of the erstwhile Soviet Union. In 1967 they constructed their first research reactor at Yongbyon. By the early 90s they had started producing fissile material, and soon had enough material to make two bombs. Foreseeing a potential threat, the United States attempted to wean Korea off its nuclear programme with promises of economic assistance and Korea agreed to dismantle all its nuclear facilities and stop the production of Plutonium. But this was merely a verbal assurance which was not followed through and by 2002; U.S discovered that North Korea was running a clandestine Uranium enrichment programme. The EU, U.S., Japan and South Korea stopped shipments of heavy fuel oil in an attempt to curb the covert nuclear mission. North Korea, however, responded by restarting its nuclear reactor and reprocessing plant[22] and as a result, in 2006 North Korea declared that she had conducted her first nuclear test. By April 2009, reports surfaced that North Korea had progressed in acquiring the nuclear technology, this opinion was shared at that time by IAEA Director General Mohamed El Baradei[23] On May 25, 2009, North Korea conducted another test most probably at the same site as that of her first test at Mantapsan, Kilju County, in the north eastern part of North Korea. Following the success of these two, another test was conducted on 11 February 2013 and it is believed that this experiment used low yield nuclear material in order to test a "miniaturized and lighter nuclear device with greater explosive force". There has been a gradual progression in both North Korea's nuclear explosions, as well as her missile build up. On February 12 2013, The Comprehensive Test Ban Treaty Organization (CTBTO) detects seismic activity near North Korea's nuclear test site. The South Korean Defence Ministry estimated the yield at 6-7 kiloton. [24] Similarly the missile range has also increased from the Nodong missile's 1000 km to the claimed 6000 kms of the Taepodong 2 missile. On 12 Dec 2012 North Korea successfully launched the Uncha-3 rocket[25], the multi-stage satellite launcher. This test is just an extension of their pursuit of developing indigenous nuclear weapon technology and in doing so they continue to defy UN Resolutions and sanctions.

2 . Nuclear Threshold States.

There are quite a few countries in Asia, like Japan and South Korea, who have the capacity and the technology to build nuclear weapons, but due to various domestic and international pressures, have refused to take the nuclear path. It has also been observed that nations like Israel, already have a nuclear weapons programme running, and yet officially they continue to maintain nuclear opacity. Similarly Iran is also believed to have progressed in its nuclear programme, despite its contrary claims, and it is a matter of time before its nuclear prowess gets proven. All these countries can declare themselves as Nuclear

COMPLEXITIES AND CHALLENGES OF NUCLEAR INDIA

Weapon States, if the global conditions become unfavourable and their national interests are threatened. Subsequent paragraphs discuss those situations.

Israel

Israel's ambiguous posture is reflected in its policy of neither refuting nor accepting the fact, that it possesses the nuclear technology required to make the bomb. On the contrary they maintain that Israel would not be the first country to nuclearize Middle East. However, various declassified official documents from the US have given ample proof, that Israel has possessed the bomb, since as early as 1975. Hence it can be stated that Israel's nuclear history has been a very chequered one, marred by hidden agendas. In1952, the Israel Atomic Energy Commission (IAEC) was formed and in 1956, during the Suez Canal crisis, Israelis provided strategic help to France, which enabled them to get the French support for their nuclear programme. Thus with the French help they constructed their nuclear complex at Dimona. This complex has the facility to produce not only nuclear weapons, but can also reprocess nuclear fuel. Initially due to adverse public opinion, the French, for a short period of time, withdrew their support, only to restart it clandestinely; as a result the reactor though delayed became critical by 1964. The proof of Israel's nuclear capabilities came to light when American U-2 over flights captured the construction of the reactor and initially this construction was denied by the Israeli officials, but later on Mr David Ben-Gurion, stated in December 1960, that the Dimona complex was a nuclear research centre built for peaceful purposes[26]. At that time, the US government did nothing to stop them, as they realised that it was too late to do so and moreover, their internal compulsions and their relations with Israel compelled them to ignore Israel's nuclear programme. During the 1973 Yom Kippur War, Israel had a number of sophisticated nuclear bombs deployed, and at one time had considered using them also[27]. Carl Duckett, head of the CIA's Office of Science and Technology, had estimated in 1974 that Israel, at the time, had between ten and twenty nuclear weapons. In 1986, the London Sunday Times had published descriptions and photographs of Israeli nuclear warheads, which were given to them by Mr Mordechai Vanunu, a dismissed Israeli nuclear technician[28].

There were also speculations that an underground nuclear facility existed at Dimona. By 1990, the US intelligence community had estimated about 60-80 nuclear warheads including warheads for its mobile Jericho-1 and Jericho-2 missiles and other nuclear tactical weapons[29]. Since then they have continued to modernise and vertically proliferate their nuclear weapons. They have used the "bomb in the basement" nuclear jargon which has worked well for them, since on one hand, it had worked as a deterrent to the Arab world and on the other hand they had not violated the American non-proliferation requirements[30]. However, whether they continue with their covert posture, once the nuclear dynamics in West Asia change, still remains to be seen. If Iran's attempt to overtly become a nuclear power state succeeds, then there is no certainty that Israel will continue to deny their nuclear status. They might be forced to declare their assets to re-ascertain their geo-strategic position. As of now Israel's problems have been amplified, because they believe that Iran's nuclear deal of 2013, Iran has most probably decided to follow the Israeli path of nuclear ambiguity and this will infringe upon the strategic security calculus of Israel.

Japan

Post the Second World War, after the bombing of Hiroshima and Nagasaki, nuclear issues became a taboo in Japan. The inherent animosity towards nuclear weapons was understandable due to the apparent destruction of the twin cities. In Article 9 of the constitution *"the Japanese people forever renounce war as a sovereign right of the nation and the threat or use of force as means of settling international disputes.[31]"* They became staunch followers of nuclear non-proliferation, and the erstwhile PM Eisaku Sato, declared his famous guiding principles, which state that firstly, Japan will promote the use of nuclear power for peaceful purposes, secondly, that it will work for global nuclear disarmament, and thirdly, that they will rely on U.S nuclear deterrence for protection from nuclear attacks.[32] He was instrumental in making Japan a part of the NPT. Post Sato, things have gradually changed. Although the guiding principle still remains the same – the three non-nuclear principles of non-possession, nonproduction, and non-introduction of nuclear weapons – however, few thinkers and politicians have questioned this principle in lieu of the changing security environment. For example, in 1999, the Deputy Vice Minister of Defence Shingo Nishimura, in May 2002, the Deputy Chief Cabinet Secretary Shinzo Abe and later on the controversial Chief Cabinet Secretary Yasuo Fukuda, had all voiced their views in favour of changing their nuclear policy and keeping the option of harbouring nuclear weapons open. Even the academia and professional writers such as Kyoto University professor Terumasa Nakanishi and literary critic Kazuya Fukuda had become sceptical about Japan's non-nuclear policy.

Considering the changed security environment in Asia –Pacific, with ever-increasing focus on the nuclear escapades of North Korea in the Korean peninsula, and increased Chinese maritime activities, it has been stated in various Japanese white papers that Japan, as a sovereign nation, has an inherent right to self-defence. The 2010 National Defence Programme Guidelines (NDPG) introduced the concept of "Dynamic Defence Forces" which consists of readiness[33], mobility and the flexible manoeuvrability of Japan's Self Defence Forces (SDF) in its South – West Island chains for the first time. This was a move aimed at countering China's maritime challenge. At present, Japan does not possess any Weapons of Mass Destruction (WMD), but they have the technology required to produce in a short time, basic nuclear weapons and the concomitant delivery system, Their Space programme is of dual nature, the solid fuelled M5 rocket system, includes technologies, that could be used to produce conventional as well as nuclear Intercontinental Ballistic Missiles (ICBMs). Thus, its latent nuclear weapons capability, while dormant for now, can change, should there be a shift in the power dynamics, and also, if the perceived threat perception in their geostrategic location is altered. The United States will play a major role in preventing Japan from taking the nuclear path. So far, the promise of US nuclear cover has tempered their ambition, and Japan has continued with its non- nuclear approach. However, if there is any shift in the US strategy concerning the Asia – Pacific region, and if North Korea becomes aggressive and poses a threat, then Japan might decide to add nuclear weapons to their current conventional weapon arsenal.

South Korea

South Korea's nuclear ambitions can be traced back to 1970, when under Nixon's doctrine; America withdrew 26000 troops from South Korea. Erstwhile President Park Chung Hee, had authorised a clandestine nuclear weapons programme[34]. The government had established a weapons' exploitation Committee, and the reprocessing facility for the same, was to be supplied by the French government. However, due to US pressure, this plan was effectively stopped. US also pressurised the South Korean Government to sign the NPT which they did and also ratified it, on 23 April 1975[35]. However, rumours of South Korea's nuclear programme was palpable when in 1982 the Korean scientist at Korean Atomic Research Institute tried to extract several milligrams of Plutonium and in 2002, nearly 200 milligrams of Uranium was enriched to weapon grade [36].This was however denied by the South Korean government. The accusations were also brought under IAEA considerations, as it was alleged that the Korean government had failed to report the matter, but the Board of Governors decided to not make a formal finding of noncompliance as it was believed that these experiments produced very small amount of weapon grade fissile material[37].Since then they have been contemplating the possibility of constructing an indigenous reprocessing plant, but due to political compulsions, they have had to relinquish this option. The twin compulsions that prevent them from going ahead with the plant are: firstly inescapable American pressure and secondly the denuclearization agreement signed by them, (which categorically states that North and South Korea would not develop reprocessing or Uranium enrichment capabilities). Although North Korea has violated the spirit of the agreement, but the South Koreans due to the American extended nuclear deterrence, is reluctant to adopt the nuclear program. Moreover, Korea is highly dependent on the import of Uranium for its nuclear power industry. It cannot afford to displease the nuclear supplier cartels as more than 30 per cent of the power in the country, is generated through nuclear energy. Another important reason, as mentioned earlier, is the country's dependence on the Americans for its security, including the extended deterrence which is paramount to South Korea's security calculations. Recently in 2012 South Korean Defence Minister Kim Kwan-jin and his American counterpart,

Leon Panetta, reached an agreement whereby they agreed to develop joint deterrence strategies tailored to specific types of threats posed by North Korea's nuclear missiles and other conventional weapons, this they target to achieve by 2014 through the "Extended Deterrence Policy Committee".[38] Americans have further promised South Korea that they would provide them with a nuclear umbrella in case they are attacked by nuclear weapons, and additionally, the need for customised deterrence strategies has also been discussed. In such a protected environment, the South Korean government would not risk becoming an overt nuclear power, but if the situation in Asia Pacific changes, then South Korea may be forced to rethink its nuclear policy.

Iran

The Iranian nuclear programme was launched in the 1950s with the help of Americans as part of the "Atoms for Peace Programme".[39] In 1967, the Tehran Nuclear Research Center (TNRC) was established. However, the progress in this field was slow due to the opposition from their erstwhile leader Ayatollah Khomeini. After his death, however, in 1989, the programme was revived. Iran began its pursuit of developing nuclear weapons and restarted their research programmes by developing several research sites – two Uranium mines, a research reactor, and Uranium processing facilities that include three known Uranium enrichment plants which were developed.[40] By 1990, the Russians had started helping Iran, by providing them with Russian nuclear experts and the requisite technical information. Moreover, they also helped them in the construction of a nuclear plant at Bushehr, which eventually became operational in 2011. However; according to the 2011, IAEA Report on Iran, the IAEA has serious concerns regarding possible military dimensions to Iran's nuclear programme and the information indicates that Iran has carried out activities relevant to the development of a nuclear explosive device and it also states that prior to the end of 2003, these activities took place under a structured programme, and that some activities may still be going[41].

On 16th November, 2012 the IAEA released a report showing continued expansion in Iranian Uranium enrichment capabilities. At Fordow, 2784 IR-1 centrifuges (16 cascades of 174 each) have been installed, though only 4 cascades are operating and another 4 are fully equipped, vacuum-tested, and ready to begin operating.[42] It is believed that Iran has produced approximately 233 kg of near-20 per cent enriched Uranium, an increase of 43 kg since August 2012 IAEA report.[43] However Iran's 2013 interim nuclear deal has been hailed as a landmark, as it puts restrictions on Iran's Uranium enrichment plans. The details of which are given in subsequent chapters. Nevertheless countries like Israel still believe that Iran already have the ability to test and develop nuclear weapons.

3. Non State Actors (NSA)

The term Non State Actors, refers to any entity that is not actually a state, but whose activities influence state functioning, at both the national as well as international levels. The scope of these organisations vary from inter to intra state organisations. Based on their nature and purposes, they can be defined as civilian welfare NSAs like the civil societies, women's group, human rights associations, trade unions etc, or the violent militarily NSAs such as the various armed groups, terrorist groups, Al Qaida and other rebel groups. In this chapter the violent NSAs and the way they affect the nuclear balance shall be analysed. NSAs can be defined as any armed group that uses violence for its purposes, and whose activities are against the humanitarian law. These militant NSAs will be subject to and punishable by the state laws. The Security Council Resolution in 1540(2004),which deliberates :"All states ,in accordance with their national procedures, shall adopt and enforce appropriate effective laws which prohibit any non-state actor to manufacture, acquire, possess, develop, transport, transfer or use nuclear, chemical or biological weapons and their means of delivery, in particular for terrorist purposes ,as well as attempts to engage in any of the foreign activities participate in them as an accomplice assists or finance them."

It further states that "Non-state-actors; individual or entity, not acting under the lawful authority of any state in conducting activities which come within the scope of this resolution", or in simpler terms any group lacking state authority if it deals with these weapons of mass destruction will be considered as a non-state actor[44]

Rise of Violent Non State Actors (VNSAs)

The Westphalia treaty of 1648 had made the nation –state a pivot, or a central actor around which all activities and entities revolved. This system ensured peace and stability in Europe for a long period. At that time, the NSA's had been marginalised and their role was negligible. However, post-Cold War, the global politics have changed, emergence of week nation-state systems and rise of fundamentalism have enhanced their activities significantly. Some of the reasons for the sudden meteoric rise of the NSAs are:-

(a) A weak sovereign nation-state system; when the state is unable to address the grievances of its citizens, then the legitimacy of the state is challenged by these NSAs and subsequently there is a rise in their number and they then attempt to take the law in their own hands.

(b) The use of NSAs as a tool by the superpowers to wage their "proxy wars". This was quiet evident when the Americans supported the "Taliban" in order to fight the Russians in Afghanistan.

(c) Quite often, the state where these NSA's are trained, tries to create instability in the neighbouring states, by using these NSAs to cause mayhem. Lashkar-e-toiba (LeT), Jaish-e-Muhammad (JeM) etc are classic example of NSA's which are being used by Pakistan against India.

(d) The heterogeneous nature of the state post decolonisation has increased the tension and conflicts amongst the varied ethnic and religious groups. The economic disparity has further fuelled class wars resulting in the rise of anarchic, anti – establishment insurgent movements.

(e) Globalisation and technological advancements, especially through the internet, has acted as a force multiplier and facilitator for the NSAs.

With time these NSAs have become increasingly violent, and have had global ramifications and this has in turn, changed the nature of contemporary warfare. Civil wars, transnational crimes, terrorism, and insurgency have changed the structure of warfare. This shift from traditional to asymmetric warfare has been a defining characteristic of the 21st century. These highly organised networks of violent NSAs, usually target the busy high profile regions of the state in urban areas, such as the markets, stations, airports etc. These areas become easy targets since firstly, they provide the NSAs uncomplicated manoeuvrability and secondly their lethal attacks in such crowded areas, helps fulfil their motto of total destruction (instead of intimidation), and in doing so they highlight the vulnerabilities of the state in protecting its citizens. The Oklahoma City Bombing, 9/11, the Tokyo subway attack, 26/11 Mumbai attacks are few examples of the large scale destruction that these organizations are capable of. Globalisation and the technological revolution have worked to their advantage. Cyber access and technological proficiency has made them more menacing since their arsenal is more sophisticatedly miniaturised and their "hub and spoke" structure (a leaderless resistance) of often small dispensed autonomous entities, has had a filtration effect and therefore they have become much more difficult to destroy. Their "inhuman hatred, all-consuming ill-will and raging fanaticism"[45]has made the new terrorist groups more violent. They have "radically different value systems, mechanisms of legitimisation, justification, concepts of morality and Manichean world views."[46] The use of religion by the Islamist groups has made the zealot Muslims an easy prey to the so called human bombs alias "Suicide Bombers". If they were to acquire nuclear weapons then the potential lethality they are capable of unleashing is beyond imagination. Thus, this form of terrorism which deals with nuclear technology, along with the dirty bomb, is the most pressing issue at the moment and is therefore the most dangerous challenge that the global community need to address.

Nuclear Predicaments or Flashpoints

Historically it can be said that the uneven presence of nuclear weapons has led to the increase in nuclear threats. In a scenario where the geo-strategic nuclear balance is unequal, the threatened countries, having inferior conventional capabilities often try to counter such disastrous threats through taking the nuclear road. In this age of proliferation, the nuclear threat can stem from several sources and is not limited to three groups mentioned earlier. The threatened state could also be attacked by the intra and inter activities of all these three groups. The inter NWS rivalry can be seen in the case of the Cuban missile crisis where the erstwhile superpowers, US and USSR were at the verge of using their nuclear weapons. US- China flash points in Asia –Pacific, Indo-Pak conflict in Asia etc are other such examples. The US-Iran (NWS versus Nuclear Threshold State) verbal war in Asia is an example of intra-group rivalry. The 9/11 twin tower blasts or the 26/11 Mumbai blasts depicted that no country in the world is safe from a NSA threat. The NSAs have repeatedly proved that they are capable of successfully breaching the internal security of nations' world over. The Cold War itself has witnessed a world, where some 47 identifiable incidents took place where nuclear weapons were used as a threat both against the NWS as well as against the NNWSs. From a total of 47 incidents, an Asian country was involved directly or indirectly in 30 incidents.[47]

Table 5: Incidents Involving Threat of Use of Nuclear Weapons

Ser No.	Incident	By Whom	Date
1	Iran	USA	1946
2	US aircraft shot down by Yugoslavia	USA	Nov 1946
3	Inauguration of President in Uruguay	USA	Feb 1947
4	Security of Berlin	USA	Jan 1948
5	Security of Berlin	USA	April 1948
6	Security of Berlin	USA	June 1948
7	Korean War: Security of Europe	USA	July 1950
8	Korean War : Entry of Chinese troops	USA	Nov 1950
9	Korean War : To compel Chinese acceptance of a ceasefire	USA	April/May 1953
10	Security of Japan/South Korea	USA	Aug 1953

Ser No.	Incident	By Whom	Date
11	Guatemala accepts Soviet Bloc Support	USA	May 1954
12	Vietnam Siege of Dien Bien Phu	USA	July 1954
13	China –Taiwan conflict: Tachen Island	USA	Aug 1954
14	Quemoy	USA	1955
15	Suez Crisis	USA	Oct 1956
16	Suez Crisis: To compel Withdrawal of British and French troops from Suez	USSR	Oct 1956
17	In connection with the Berlin Crisis	USSR	Oct 1956
18	Political Crisis in Lebanon	USA	July 1958
19	Political Crisis in Jordan	USA	July 1958
20	China-Taiwan Conflict: Quemoy and Matsu	USA	July 1958
21	Security of Berlin	USA	May 1959
22	Laos	USA	1961
23	Security of Berlin	USA	June 1961
24	Berlin Crisis	USSR	1961
25	Emplacement of Missile in Cuba	USSR	Sept 1962
26	Soviet emplacement of Missile in Cuba	USA	Oct 1962
27	Withdrawal of US Missile from Turkey	USA	April 1963
28	Confrontation between Indonesia and Malaysia	UK	April 1963
29	China's Nuclear Weapon Programme	USSR	1964
30	To compel the termination of Israel's offensive on the Golan Heights	USSR	1969

Ser No.	Incident	By Whom	Date
31	Pueblo seize by North Korea	USA	Jan 1968
32	Vietnam: Siege of Khe Sanh	USA	1968
33	To compel termination of Chinese initiated incident on Sino-Soviet border	USSR	1969
34	Vietnam War	USA	1969-72
35	Indo-Pak War 1971	USA	Dec 1971
36	Bangladesh War	USA	Dec 1971
37	Vietnam negotiations	USA	1972
38	Arab-Israel War	Israel	Oct 1973
39	Arab-Israel War	USA	OCT 1973
40	Arab-Israel War	USSR	OCT 1973
41	Security of Iran	USA	1980
42	South Atlantic War	UK	May 1982
43	West Asia	USA	Jan 1991
44	Kashmir Crisis	Pakistan	1990
45	Gulf War	USA	Jan 1991
46	Indo-Pakistan	Pakistan	1994
47	In connection with Taiwan (elections)	China	March 1996

Source: As quoted by Air Commodore Jasjit Singh in Nuclear India Primary Sources: Data based on Barry Blechman(*Force Without War*) and other documents; Daniel Elsberg, Interview with *New York Conservative Press*,1980;Richard Nixon, *Time Magazine*, July 29,1985;IDSA data base.

The Nuclear Challenge by Nuclear Weapon States - Inter Group Rivalry

After the Second World War the world was polarised into two power blocks: the US led NATO forces and the Soviet Union and its Warsaw allies. Along with them there was a small group of countries who aligned with neither, and became the Non –Aligned countries. These countries, however, were militarily and economically weak and as a result they did not have a major impact. The dissolution of the Soviet Union led to the emergence of new states in central Asia, and the power then revolved around the US. However, an emerging China and a resurgent Russia, have tried to rebalance the power structure. China's phenomenal economic growth has made it a financial power house and a direct competitor to the US in many fields. As a result the animosity between the two has grown immensely, aided by their opposing ideological stances. The Russians are also trying to reinvent themselves after a tumultuous period post the Soviet disintegration. It is still an equal rival with the US as far as nuclear weapons are concerned. In such a precarious world order, the constant tussle between these powers speak ill for the world as a whole, since there is always a possibility that the nuclear threat might escalate,

Possible Nuclear Threat Situation

(a) US-Russia confrontation

Though a situation which involves direct confrontation between USA and Russia is very remote, the fact remains that even after five decades, the nuclear arsenal between the two countries accounts for more than 90 per cent of the total arsenal currently present in the world. The statistics are pretty grim and it makes one question the ability or willingness of the two nations to opt for disarmament.

Figure: 4 Global Nuclear Weapons Inventories, 2014

Country	Deployed Strategic	Non - Strategic	Non - deployed warheads	Total Inventory	Growth trends
USA	1,922	200	5.384	7,506	Decrease
Russia	2.484	2000	4,000	8,484	Decrease
UK	160	-	65	225	Decrease
France	290	-	10	300	Decrease (slight)
China	-	-	250	250	Decrease (slight)
India	80-100	-	-	80-100	Growth
Pakistan	-	-	90-110	90-110	Growth
Israel	-	-	80-200	80-200	Growth (slight)
North Korea	-	-	<10	<10	Growth
Total Nuclear weapons in the world: 17,105					

CHART: Global Nuclear Weapons Inventories, 2014[48]

The world today has approximately 17,105 nuclear weapons, a large percentage of which (15,990 nuclear weapons) are still with these two countries. The growth trend has decreased but very marginally. The major reason for this is the constant competition, between the two countries, who in an attempt to maintain the nuclear balance do not allow the other country to dominate the nuclear scene and continue amassing weapons as security. If US conducted its first subcritical nuclear test in 1997, the erstwhile Soviets followed it up immediately, by conducting their own test in 1998[49]. The subcritical test had dual benefits, since it could be used for studying the properties of Plutonium, as well as for developing new generation nuclear weapons. This duality made the nuclear arms race more challenging for the rest of the NWS. Both the countries' refusal to stop these tests weakened the disarmament accomplishments and took the arms race to another level. However; once the US had mastered this technology, they tried to dissuade other nations from conducting these tests by proposing to discontinue them. In spite of an overt statement of discontinuation, media reports state that US has resumed these tests under the garb of a new concept , the "POLLUX" a first "scaled subcritical experiment " with Plutonium-239, and Pollux will be the closest thing to a full scale nuclear test[50] .If the US has resumed these tests; the Russians cannot be far behind. There have been reports in the Russian media regarding the same which have come from Nezavisimaya Gazeta, the Russian paper, which printed an article by Vladimir Mukhin, titled "Nuclear Umbrella for the Arctic"[51]. The article states that the nuclear test site at Novaya Zemlya has been reinstated and nuclear tests have recommenced. The old maxim, might is right is reflected in the fact that the superpowers can resume their tests whenever they choose without paying attention to world opinion. These double standards have weakened the world system as a whole since there seem to be different principles for different countries. The solution to an apocalyptic nuclear world can be as simple as pressurising the nuclear powers to abandon their sub-critical tests for a greater cause, that is global peace and harmony. But the ground realities remain quite different, and the complexities of international co–operation begin exactly when the benefits of a few nations, are valued over larger universal interests.

b) US-China conflict in Asia –Pacific

The Asia-Pacific region, as was predicted earlier, has emerged as the centre of the global power play. The events in this region are challenging global security. The importance of the Asia-Pacific region can be seen from the fact, that demographically it encompasses nearly half of the world's population, economically it has a fifth of world GDP, 1/3 of world export, half of the world's maritime tonnage. The volume of oil that transits through the Malacca strait to the South China Sea is more than six times the amount of oil that transits through the Suez Canal and seventeen times more than the amount that passes through the Panama Canal. Thus this region has emerged as the new global economic hub. There is a constant tussle amongst major powers to influence the littoral states, through the use of both, hard as well as soft power. The subtle reason for this tussle between the major powers may vary from maintaining the independence of the Sea lanes of communications in case of US to the control of these by the Chinese in South China Sea. The convergence as well as divergence of interests between US and China makes their power play unpredictable and dangerous. Some other reasons which challenge global peace in this region are: the unequal power balance between – declared Nuclear Power States, undeclared Nuclear Capable States with unresolved border issues and violent Non State Actors (the rampant spread of drug cartels and the pirates). The conflict between Japan and China over the Senkaku Island has further increased the vulnerability of all the countries in the region. The focal points may swing from the East and South China Sea, to the Indian Ocean in future, but the truth is that the conflict will remain until a balance is established between the key players who have a tremendous stakes in this region, mainly China and USA in the Asia-Pacific and India, China and the USA in the Indian Ocean. The differing perceptions of US and China, the two major powers in Asia-Pacific region, are the main bone of contention in South China Sea. The United States is the traditional formidable power in this region, and it sees the economic and military rise of China as a cause of concern and a threat, whereas China feels that the activities of the US in the Asia-Pacific region is intended on encircling China. The conflict is the outcome of these perceptions. Both the powers have inherent strengths and weaknesses. The challenge lies in analysing them objectively and coming to a workable solution whereby the balance of power is regained without confrontation.

Figure: 5 Security Challenges in Asia –Pacific

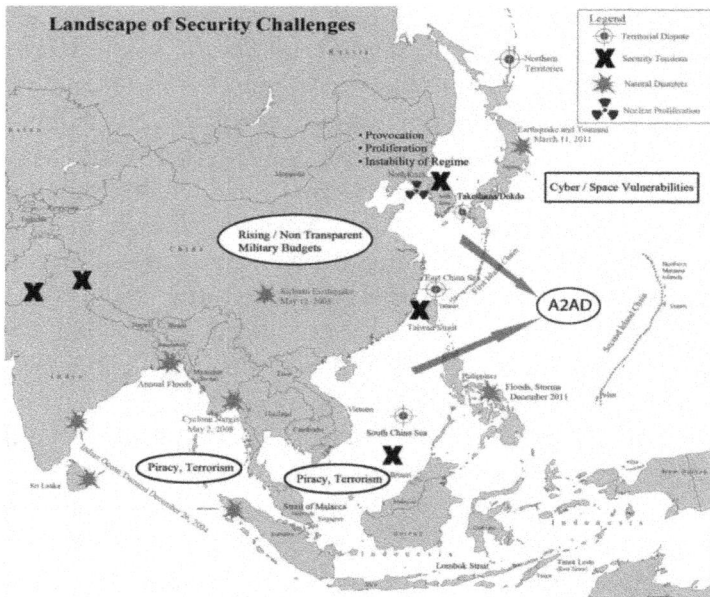

Source: Map Resources, formatted by CSIS

US Role in Asia-Pacific

1 . US Strategy

US engagement with Asia-Pacific dates back to 1784 when "Empress of China" made its first voyage from New York to bring tea and Chinaware from Canton and to export ginseng from western Pennsylvania[52] . Today, nearly 60 per cent of US exports go to countries in the Asia Pacific region. After the decline of British Empire, it was the unsaid role of the United States to maintain the balance of power in the Asia- Pacific region and to prevent the rise of any power that could jeopardise the maritime domain of US[53]. The rise of China both economically and militarily and its ambition to dominate aggressively in the South and East China sea region through the Chinese policy of Anti-Access/Area Denial (A2AD) tends to challenge this balance. Under President Obama, the policy of "Asia Rebalancing/Pivot Strategy" clearly articulates the American interest in this region. The US wants to maintain the status quo and create a better balance in the region. Hillary Clinton's article in November 2011 in Foreign Policy titled "America's Pacific Century" clearly lays down the policies which would be adopted by the Americans .The thrust area according to her being reinforcing bilateral relations with the traditional allies , keeping a substantial military presence, improving relations with emerging powers, expanding commerce and investments with special emphasis on building relationship with multilateral regional institutions like the ASEAN and the East Asia Summit and ultimately the universal goal of promoting peace through democracy and human rights. There has been a relative decline in America's economic and military power and they have tried to counterbalance this perception by declaring their "Asia Rebalancing/ Pivot Strategy". They have the Host Nation Support (HNS) policy with Japan and South Korea by which they can successfully retain the forward area force structure. For example, "The United States government and the government of Japan reached a new five-year Special Measures Agreement that outlines Japan's direct contributions to the U.S.-Japan Alliance through Host Nation Support, thus this represents a strategic contribution to Japan's defense and to regional peace and stability[54]. They also reached an understanding to maintain overall Host Nation Support funding at current levels for the next five years, bearing in mind the Japan FY2010 budget of 188.1 billion yen. They have also emphasised that greater responsibility should be shouldered by the traditional partners like Japan, South Korea and Australia. Though the military support in terms of stationing American troops in the bases would continue, a lot more stress is being laid on increasing training, intelligence, logistics and missile defence of the allied partners, thereby enhancing military cooperation and interoperability. The American Strategy in this region needs to be evaluated in the context of two key areas: namely South East Asia and East Asia. Obama government has continued the policy of strengthening the relationship with its traditional partners, defeating aggression and prevailing over the adversary through deterrence and economic sanctions in East Asia. The South East Asian region, which had been neglected during the Bush administration, has recently become a priority. Kurt Campbell, Assistant Secretary of State for Foreign Affairs states "we are diversifying our strategic and military approach, we will keep a strong commitment in North East Asia, but we will focus more of our attention in southeast Asia"[55] The Americans know that adequate forces are required for this to counter Chinese policy of A2AD, and also to sustain low intensity missions like piracy and Humanitarian Assistance and Disaster Relief (HADR).

The US policy, thus far, has been aimed at maintaining forces that are forward deployed, can monitor various choke points and SLOCS, aided by a naval presence on all the seas so that it can intervene at key points. This can be best explained from Homer Lea's "Policy of Triangles". The two major bases fulfilling this strategy are Guam and Diego Garcia in the Pacific and Indian Ocean respectively. The diagram below depicts that the more number of triangles it manages to form strategically, the stronger it becomes in its control of the SLOCs. For example the "Guam-Japan-South Korea "or the Guan-Taiwan-Japan" etc [56].The formal arrangements with its allies, as observed above, is the spirit of several treaties that have been signed such as the US–Japan Treaty of Mutual Cooperation and Security (1960), South Korea the recent "Strategic Alliance 2015 Plan", Philippines it is "Mutual Defence Treaty between the Republic of Philippine and the United States of America". Thailand being a non NATO ally has annual Cobra Gold exercises. These exercises in the pacific also involve the navies from Indonesia, Singapore, South Korea, Malaysia and Japan, which along with US participation work together towards building bridges, improving operation ability and providing greater leverage to control the SLOCS. Apart from these measures, the US has also initiated a number of trilateral dialogues such as the "US-Japan-Australia" or the "US-Japan-South Korea" talks to enhance communication between the alliances with the aim of enabling a quick unified response in the case of a future conflict.

Figure: 6 Strategic Triangles

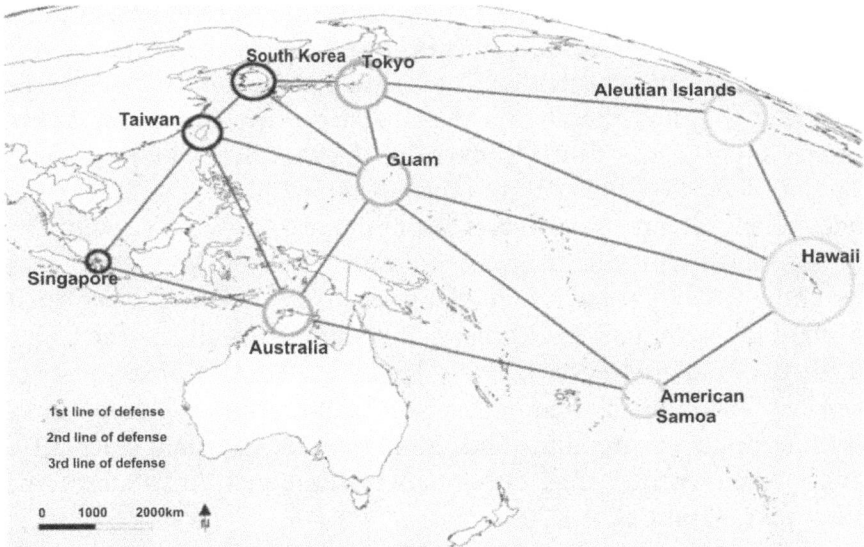

Source : 2012 Deltenre Damien, Université Catholique de Louvain (Belgium)

US Limitations

The major handicaps for the US are: a) their geographical location, or the "Distance Factor" and b) the financial cuts in its defence budgets. Looking at the geographical inconvenience, both Guam and Diego Garcia are at a considerable distance from the Korean peninsula, the former being 3,207.66 Km and the latter 6050 miles. This brings in operational challenges in terms of effective communication and mobilisation. The US Marines can sustain a fight for a month or two, but in a situation involving long tactical conflict, US armies would require immediately deployable precision weapons, minesweepers etc. This tactical armament is currently available in Continental US (CONUS), but due to the distance, they would require a few weeks of warning before the necessary backup could be delivered[57]. Secondly, apart from Japan, South Korea and Australia there are very few countries which can afford HNS for US troops and moreover the political systems of several countries, do not approve of foreign troops stationed on their soil. Thirdly, the ballistic missiles tested by China have improved in their range and precision, especially the Anti-Ship Ballistic Missile (ASBM), DF-21 (which is a major potential threat to the aircraft carrier) and the numbers might increase drastically by 2020. By then, US would be retiring a number of its nuclear powered submarines, due to resource crunches, the replacements might be difficult to arrange, and hence US may be faced by the dual threat of a depleted force in the coming years, which might consequently undermine the confidence of its allies. In such a scenario, China might take advantage of this weakness and become more aggressive. This is one of the reasons why the countries in the Asia- pacific region choose to remain neutral. While they may welcome US military presence, not one of them would like to overtly declare loyalties. Lastly, a threat can also be conjectured for China if the two major allies of the US – Japan and South Korea – were to work as a team in an attempt to create a counterforce against China. Japan's military expenditure has increased considerably since 2010 and subsequently, it has developed phenomenal Anti-Submarine Warfare capabilities.

In spite of all its limitations though, it must be said, that US through its bilateral and regional alliances, continue to maintain a strategic balance in this region. Its forward deployment forces and its superior military force can mitigate to a large extent, the Chinese A2/ AD threat. Additionally, its Asia Pacific Rebalancing /Pivot Strategy, is a reactivation of its "Guam Doctrine"[58] of the seventies. It promises to honour treaty obligations and provide military help but at the same time, it also pushes its allies to shoulder greater responsibility in the Asia –Pacific region. Recent economic realities have forced US to create multiple pivots and in the bargain, reconsider and pursue not only the interest of its allies but also its own changing interests.

China and the Asia Pacific-Region

China knows that, with its 9,000-mile long coastline, it possesses the capability to become a formidable sea power. Historically, the Treaty of Nanking had exposed the military weaknesses of Imperial China, especially in terms of a lack of sea power. This strategic vulnerability was also exposed by the fast developing maritime powers of the western world and Japan. Since then, China has constantly tried to develop and modernise its navy to deal with the new challenge. "The Science of Military Strategy" published by PLA's Academy of Military Science is a window to the PLA's strategic thought .It highlights that in the mid-50s China considered the South eastern coastal area of China as the main strategic road because China believed that there existed a possibility of its strategic encirclement by foreign forces which was mainly led by the United States .There was an apprehension that like in the past a strategic offensive could be launched against China. In order to overcome this threat perception, China started modernization of its PLA Navy. There was a change at the conceptual level also and Chinese white papers have highlighted the principle of "Local War Doctrine" in which the coastal defense was later replaced by modern strategies such as "Offshore Defense" or "Near Sea Defense".

Chinese Strategy

The primary objective of Chinese maritime strategy remains centred on the principle of A2/AD. This was originally developed by the Soviets, in their "Layered Defence", which was a linear combat approach employed to strategically counter the US. The PLA has modified it to suit their needs by trying to develop the thresholds in terms of "Island Chains". For this strategy to work effectively, the controversial first and second island chains have become very important for the Chinese. This is mainly due to their efficiency in terms of "anti-access" or their ability to deny the US forces an access point to infiltrate the Chinese mainland. The reasons why this chain becomes so essential for China is because, the first Island Chain is in the South China Sea which makes it an important geostrategic pivot, however one must remember it is incredibly controversial, since some of the areas claimed by the Chinese are contested entities. Other Asian countries like Vietnam, Philippine, Brunei etc continue to assert their sovereignty over these Islands. Hence the Chinese claim has been refuted and challenged by them. China's aggressiveness in this area will perforce make these nations align with the US as no country in this region has the capability to counter China. An overt alliance will not be in the interest of China hence China needs to tread with caution .Secondly, this region is of utmost economic importance to China, since the bulk of Chinese trade takes place through this sea route. It is important for them to control the area, so that they can control these Sea Lanes of Communications in times of conflict.

Figure: 7 Disputed Claims in South China Sea

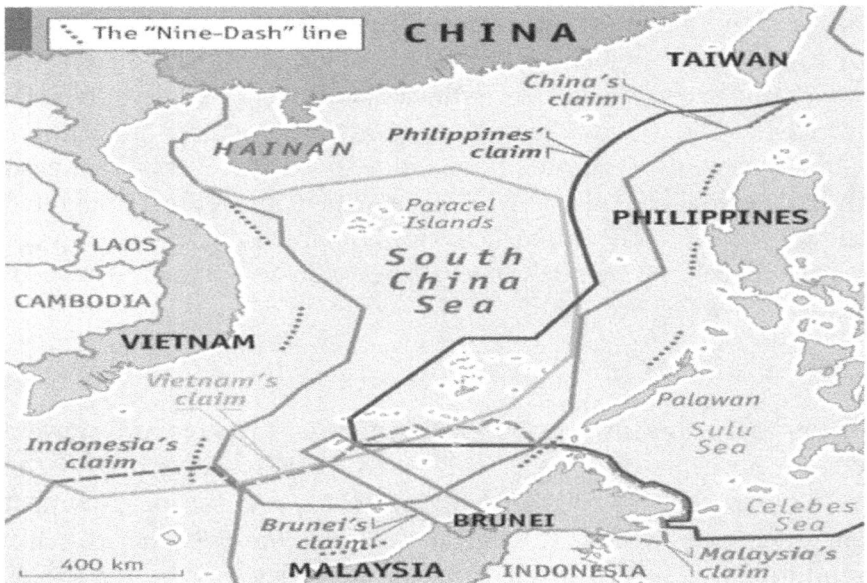

Source:www.economist.com

The traditional Chinese trade route, passes from the Indian Ocean to the South China Sea, through the Strait of Malacca and Sunda. The Chinese are currently trying to find alternate routes through land since their strategists believe that during a conflict, the choke points in this area could be blocked by their adversaries, thus targeting and hindering China's economy. For now, however apart from these land routes and diversified oil markets, a fair amount of trade continues to pass through this area. The Chinese economy has grown at a phenomenal pace. They managed to sustain growth during the global slump as well as after the euro crisis. China, therefore, has emerged as the second largest economy of the world, next only to USA and if the Organisation for Economic Co-operation and Development (OECD) predictions is to be considered, it will surpass USA in another few years. These instances have renewed the confidence of the Chinese leadership and they are bound to become more assertive in international affairs from now on. According to the power transition theory, a rising power is bound to challenge the system which favours the hegemon[59]. This is exactly what is happening in the Asia – Pacific region. China has emerged as a rising power and is reasserting its claim and challenging USA in the South China Sea region. This aggressive posture is backed by its improved military strength. As of 2013, its navel arsenal consists amongst other weapons: 70 Submarines, 4 SSBN, Destroyers 15, 54 Frigates, 216 Patrol and Coastal Combatants,53 Minesweeper, AmphibiousLPD-3, Landing Ship-85,Landing Craft-152 and Logistics and Support 212[60] ,making them the largest and most lethal force in Asia. Moreover there have also been technological advancements such as the newly acquired Aircraft Carrier, the DF-21, the Anti-Ship Missile and several cruise missiles which have led to major improvements in their surveillance capabilities. In 2007, China shot old weather satellites, displaying their anti-satellite capability. All these recent activities and improvements make it a major power that needs to be reckoned with.

Chinese Limitations

Although it has progressed both qualitatively and quantitatively in terms of military capability, the operational ability of the same is yet to be tested. The American policy of rebalancing Asia is considered as US tactics of intimidation by many Chinese strategists, as it leads to encirclement of China .On the other side the Chinese claim of first island chain has been questioned by many Southeast Asian nations. The US forward deployment force, strategically placed in the various bases mentioned, provides them with flexibility, mobile military options, and a lesser degree of vulnerability from A2/AD threats. 80 per cent of China's oil continues to be sourced from the Middle

East, via the Indian Ocean and then into the South China Sea. Such a trade route could be subjected to different modes of attack and various choke points in the middle could be used by the adversary to block the trade routes thus chocking its economy. China has a fair number of disputes with the Asian nations in the South and East China Sea region; hence an attitude of excessive aggression could have a negative impact on its trade with ASEAN countries, and also provide the US with an opportunity to frequently intervene in the Asia –Pacific region. Sooner or later the Chinese government will have to adopt a conciliatory tone, respect international law and keep the SLOCs open, if it wants their economy to continue to flourish.

Consequence for India

India is not directly involved in the conflict; however, India's perception of the situation will significantly determine what role India chooses to play in Asia. Currently, India can interact with nations having similar views by signing joint bilateral treaties, especially with countries like Vietnam, Japan, South Korea and Philippines. Joint naval exercises and defence deals with friendly countries in the region can enhance its role as an Asian player and also give a boost to the look East policy. Nations in this region especially Japan along with US desires India to play a more definitive and positive role, hence it is important for India to have clarity and strategic forethought as far as its role in this region is concerned. It has become quite evident, that in future it will be extremely difficult for any one nation to deal with China; hence it is important to manoeuvre the strategic space through partnerships and alliances.

India, with its economic growth and naval strength has the potential to play a major role in Asia and in coming years the Asian politics would be impacted by the decisions of these two nations.

Conflict arising between the Nuclear Threshold States

1 . The Korean Conflict

The conflict in the Korean peninsula is the aftermath of World War II. Prior to 1945, Korea was ruled by many dynasties, including Japan and China. By the end of 1945 with the defeat and surrender of Japan, Northern Korea was occupied by the Soviets. However;

the 38th parallel divided the Korean peninsula into North and South Korea[61]. The former was initially administered by the Soviets, and then followed up by Chinese forces, thus ensuring that it evolved into a communist country, with Kim Il-Sung as its leader; while the southern part was controlled by the United States. South Korea adopted a democratic form of government, and Mr Syngman Rhee[62] became its first democratically elected president. This division of the Korean peninsula has been a cause of conflict in the past. For the initial period, both the leaders wanted to unite the two Koreas, but each wanted their own political system to prevail. China and USA on their part aided their respective sides, and by ensuring that neither side succeeds, indirectly maintained their divided identity. For China North Korea is its strategic buffer, hence it has always supported the North Koreans. In the future, if there is ever a possibility of unification, China will always try to ensure that the unified Korea remains inclined towards them as allies. This makes the unification that much more difficult and violent, as was visible in the Korean war of 1950. In 1953 a Korean Armistice Agreement[63] was signed between the two fighting factions and a Demilitarised Zone (a 2.5 mile buffer zone) near the 38th parallel was created. Since then North Korea is overtly supported by the Chinese in terms of military, food and economic aid.

North Korean Aggression

Since the armistice numerous incursions have been made by North Korea on the pretext of uniting the country .The axe murder incident, the unearthing of four incursion tunnels leading to South Korea, 2010 sinking of the South Korean corvette ROKS *Cheonan* (the alleged torpedo fired from the North Korean submarine killing 46 sailors), firing artillery shells on Yeonpyeong island,(killing two military personnel and two civilians) are some examples of the intrusions made by North Koreans which have caused mistrust and created tensions between the two countries thereby making the Korean peninsula volatile and unstable. The North Korean reckless missile development programme along with their ambitions of developing nuclear missiles has caused wariness and accelerated the arms race in this region. North Korea was a party to the NPT but withdrew from it in 2003[64]. A nuclear North Korea has far reaching consequences; it has the potential to nuclearize East Asia and place the region on a volatile threshold. The North Koreans have already completed three nuclear tests in 2006, 2009, and the most recent one in 2013 has been universally condemned[65]. Considering the nuclear activities of North Korea, the Americans had been able to restrain South Korea from taking the nuclear road, however; South Korea who till now has restrained from developing nuclear missiles would not hesitate in developing nuclear weapons if her territorial integrity was threatened by the North Koreans and secondly if there was any change in the posture of the American extended nuclear deterrence policy to South

North Korea Missile Development

North Korea has developed its missile technology for various reasons. They claim that security is the primary concern, but there are other secondary considerations as well, such as, developing it as a political tool, strengthening its bargaining power, starting diplomatic dialogues, diverting attention from internal problems and finally as a means of improving their battered economy through arms proliferation – which involves exporting weapon and nuclear technology. These secondary considerations are explosive in nature and therefore pose a major cause for concern. North Korea's missile programme is based on the Soviet Scud missile technology. It began with a very basic tactical FROG – Series (dual purpose), but later on it received the long range Scud B missile[66] from Egypt. The first modified missile based on this Scud Series was named Hwasong-5. Gradually the potential target line for North Korea shifted from South Korea, to Japan and American bases, and as a result they refocused their development programme towards advanced medium and long range missiles. North Korean Missile Inventory includes Hwasong – 5 and 6 which are short range missiles, developed from Scud – B – C type Russian missiles, and deployed in areas near the Demilitarised Zone to enable it to hit potential targets in South Korea.

Figure: 8 North Korean Missile Range

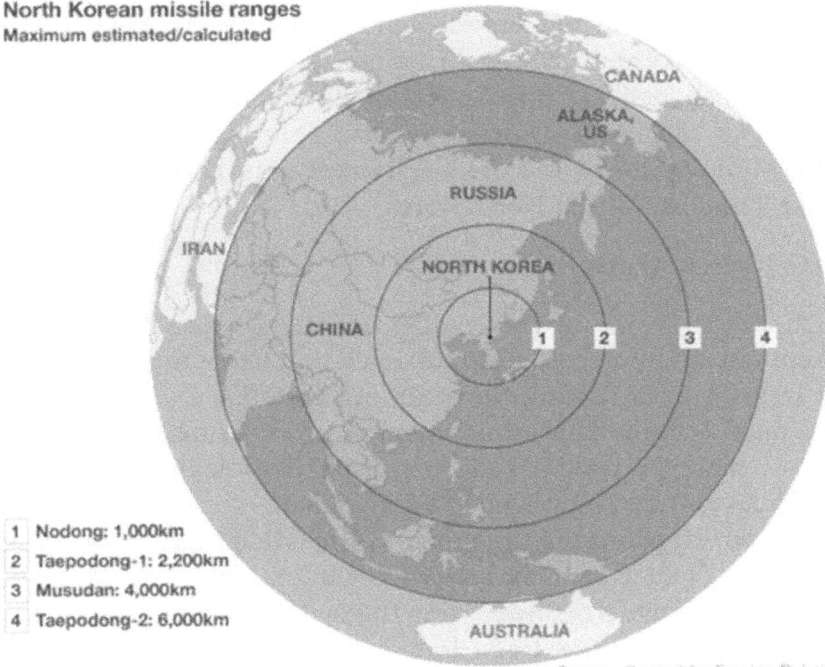

North Korean missile ranges
Maximum estimated/calculated

1 Nodong: 1,000km
2 Taepodong-1: 2,200km
3 Musudan: 4,000km
4 Taepodong-2: 6,000km

Source: Council for Foreign Relations

In the late 1980s they developed their Nodong missile with Japan as its likely target Since all the North Korean Missiles are not very accurate, its "circular error probable" is 2 to 4 km[67] and hence the probability of it not hitting the military target is quiet high yet at the same time, one cannot rule out the possibility that it might cause a lot of collateral damage. Taepodong-X or Musudan is an IRBM and its likely targets are Okinawa, Japan and US bases in the Pacific. The Taepodong 2, domestic ICBM attempt failed in 2006. In 2009, a second nuclear test was conducted and a space booster variant was launched, however this time also, the satellite failed while the missile flew several kilometers before falling. After a failed attempt, the second attempt of the Uncha-3 rocket to launch a satellite had been successful. On 12 December 2012, the satellite successfully entered the orbit. Chae Yeon-seok, a rocket expert at South Korea's state-run Korea Aerospace Research Institute said "North Korea will now turn its attention to developing bigger rockets with heavier payloads; its ultimate aim will be putting a nuclear warhead on the tip[68]." Moreover, despite universal disapproval, they went ahead and performed another nuclear test on the 12th of Feb 2013. They claim to have detonated a "miniaturized and lighter nuclear device with greater explosive force"[69] thus bringing them closer to developing a long range ballistic missile. These developments have had a detrimental effect in the Korean peninsula and East Asia. In Japan Prime Minister Shinzo Abe, of Liberal Democratic Party has asserted to take a tougher line on North Korea.

North Korean Arms Export

North Korea is one of the leading countries when it comes to surreptitiously exporting ballistic missiles. In 2009 the Korean Mining and Development Trading Corporation (KOMID) was declared by the United Nations as a primary company which deals with arms export – mainly exporting ballistic missile technology, components and equipment and North Korea's major share of its hard currency comes from exporting this to countries in the Middle East[70], primarily Egypt, Iran, United Arab Emirates (UAE) and Yemen where the main system of exchange is oil. Apart from this faction, other countries like Pakistan, Libya, Nigeria, Cuba and Syria have also completed arms deals with North Korea. Amongst these, Pakistan's Ghauri[71] MRBM is based on North Korea's Nodong missile. In April 1998, the US had imposed sanctions against Pakistani and North Korean entities for their role in transferring Missile Technology Control Regime Category I ballistic missile-related technology[72]. Pakistan on her part has been allegedly helping North Korea with nuclear technology and there have also been rumours of Pakistan additionally providing them with the opportunity of testing missiles off shore. Similarly Iran has been one of the earliest buyers of these missiles. They have bought the Hwasong series and Nodong missiles and later on possibly Taepodong[73] which were renamed as Shahab missiles (1,2 and 3). A section of strategic academicians believe that North Korea's satellite launch was possible mainly due to Iranian support. Jeffrey Lewis, a proliferation expert at the Monterey Institute of International Studies, believes that the Iranians are assisting the North Koreans with missile development as he states that "The Iranians were doing innovation and change, taking things apart and putting them back together, and it now, to me, looks like the Iranians are better at this than the North Koreans[74]," further he states that "And so the North Koreans have gone from being a technology supplier to possibly the recipient of technologies and services back from the Iranians." Thus both the countries appear to be allied together in their development of long range missiles.

Another danger that must be kept in mind, apart from these strategic concerns, is the lack of safety and security of nuclear materials .Since North Korea has refused IAEA inspectors from inspecting its nuclear plants the possibility of nuclear accidents cannot be ruled out. According to the survey conducted by the Nuclear Threat Initiative (NTI) North Korea was placed last in the list of nuclear safety ratings where 32 countries nuclear safety and security standards were assessed.[75] Also there remains the potential threat of terrorist groups gaining access to the weapons or fissile material. But one must maintain caution before taking stringent action against North Korea, since enforcing too many restrictions may push them off the brink .Some views suggest that the imposed sanctions may prove to be counter - productive, as it might bring economic hardship and in desperation, North Korea may resort to selling nuclear materials or weapon designs to other countries. This has been clearly evinced in the past when North Korea did not hesitate to share her missile technology with Asian countries.

South Korea

After the Second World War, the US took the task of supporting South Korea and Soviet Union aided the North. The division was to be on a temporary basis with a view to ultimately unite the two warring factions but the ideological and political differences of the two nations beginning from their time of inception, continues even today, thus making the dream of a united Korea difficult to implement if not impossible. The UN supervised general elections in South Korea in 1948[76], saw the emergence of Mr. Syngman Rhee, as the first president of a Democratic Republic of Korea. Since then it has witnessed eight republics and alternated between democracy and military rule, but with the election of the sixth republic, the country stabilized into a liberal democracy.

US - South Korean Military Alliance

During the Korean War when North Korea occupied key South Korean cities, the UN Security Council Resolution 82, authorized the intervention of UN forces comprising mainly American forces to intervene and reclaim the areas and formation of the "Demilitarized Zone". Since then South Korea has developed a military alliance with the Americans. The Mutual Defense Treaty[77] was signed in 1953 and US has 37000 troops currently stationed in South Korea. Stability in the peninsula has been maintained so far, mainly due to US presence and support. The subsequent governments have used this stability and ensured the implementation of various economic reforms which have resulted in South Korea becoming a major economic power in Asia. The policy makers gradually thought of weaning US troops from South Korea as they believed that by 1980, the country had become economically, politically and militarily capable to cope with the threats from North Korea. Their defense spending increased from $17.1billion in 2000 to $28.6 billion in 2011 with a peak of $30.1billion in 2007[78]. By 2008 the US troops stationed in South Korea had decreased from 37,000 to 28,500[79], however it has not been completely abolished, the US "Nuclear Umbrella" or "Extended Deterrence" still continues. In Dec 2012, the Pentagon Press Secretary George Little had reported that forty U.S. and South Korean officials participated in an extended deterrence exercise, which looked at deterrence methods in response to a nuclear threat scenario[80]. Furthermore Army Maj. Cathy Wilkinson, a Pentagon Press Office spokesperson has stated that the exercise supports the development of a tailored bilateral deterrence strategy against North Korean nuclear and weapons of mass destruction threats, and demonstrates "unwavering" U.S. commitment to South Korea and the main idea was to maintain credible and effective deterrence in the Korean peninsula[81]. After North Korea conducted its third underground nuclear test in February, 2013 the United States military had flown two of its most advanced bombers in an "extended deterrence mission" all the way from Missouri to the Korean peninsula, where they dropped inert dummy bombs, in a move clearly aimed at warning North Korea against further provocations.[82] The sortie by the two B-2 Spirit stealth bombers "demonstrates the United States' ability to conduct long range, precision strikes quickly and at will."[83]

The initiatives taken by the Korean leadership, especially its president could possibly change the security calculus of the Korean peninsula. If the new president of South Korea, President Park Geun-hye, adopts a liberal policy, and softens the hard-line approach which her predecessor President Lee Myung-bak had taken, she might be able to improve the relation between the two nations. She has already indicated that humanitarian assistance and economic proposals are points to be considered, but only if North Korea changes its attitude, and takes concrete steps towards considering a denuclearization policy and concomitant economic reforms. However any drastic improvement in the relation of the two nations at the moment, seem bleak. Secondly the most probable situation for South Korea is in continuing its close military ties with US, because the possibility of the relations between the two Korean countries improving at the moment is limited, as is evident by the aggressive posture adopted by the North Korean leaders and the continuation of their nuclear missile programme, in spite of sanctions imposed by various nations.

However; if relations between the two Korean nations do improve, or the Americans are unable to provide the extended deterrence as assured to South Koreans, then the latter might be forced to pursue its defence programme independently and consequently, there might be a major shift in the power balance in East Asia. In such a situation, South Korea would leave no stone unturned in trying to develop its independent missile and covert nuclear programme. South Korea has often depicted a desire to develop their reprocessing plant[84] and they had made their displeasure apparent, when during the renegotiation of the civilian nuclear agreement , their long drawn demand to reprocess spent fuel was not accepted, especially after US has allowed Japan that facility. South Korea might also try to increase their economic ties with China in an attempt to keep their options open. The commercial transactions of Korea depict this trend since even today China is their largest trading partner. If they do eventually adopt a pro-China policy due to military and economic compulsions, then they would probably steer away from the Taiwan imbroglio and this in turn might force the Americans to re-examine their strategic calculations to avoid the balance of power shifting in favour of the Chinese. However, this possibility is the least probable amongst the list of possibilities mentioned above since the Americans would not risk abandoning South Korea. Their need for an anchor in the Asia – Pacific region will ensure that they continue the extended deterrence and maintain the status quo in the same region.

US-South Korea Japan Trilateral Dialogue

In June 2012 the three countries namely US, Japan and South Korea met in Singapore during Shangri-La Dialogue .They agreed to formalize a defense trilateral agreement and conducted a joint naval exercise in the Yellow Sea[85]. Before the bilateral intelligence sharing agreement could be finalized the Dokdo/Takishima conflict put a break to the US initiative of beginning and maintaining a cordial relation between the two Asian countries. With the change in leadership, a possible solution to the Dokdo/Takishima conflict could become a significant move. This would help both the countries, in facilitating an exchange of defense related information and tackling common security challenges, namely North Korea's nuclear missile development and China's military modernization. A small beginning has been made which can be seen from the meeting of the finance ministers of both countries. They met in Tokyo during the IMF talks in Oct 2012 to enhance cooperation in economic and financial issues however, episodes like Japanese Prime Minister Shinzo Abe's visit to the war-related Yasukuni Shrine, should be avoided, since it can reopen wounds from past events, and jeopardize the fragile trust building process between the two nations and could also culminate in creating adverse public opinion.

India's Concern about North Korean Missile Development Programme

India does not face a primary threat from North Korea, since there is an absence of any direct dispute between the two countries, due to the geographical distance separating them; however, North Korea's track record in missile proliferation is still a cause of concern for India and this threat, stems primarily from three accounts: Firstly there have been instances when North Korea has been transferring banned missile technology to Pakistan – as is evident in Pakistan's Shaheen 1A missiles which is considered to be a copy of North Korean's Taepodong-I missile. At present Pakistan does not possess ICBM capabilities but India's concern is that North Korea might supply them with the same in exchange for Pakistan's economic and nuclear aid, especially in developing nuclear weapons based on Plutonium. North Korea has the capability, their missiles such as the BM-25 Musdan, have ranges of 4000km and recent reports have also confirmed that the Unha-3 rocket gives North Korea the ability to fire rocket at more than 10,000km(6200miles)range[86]. The successful operational capabilities of these missiles are though highly debatable. Secondly, there is always the remote possibility that other nations like Iran, Iraq, and Egypt in West Asia might be tempted to acquire this technology. This would pose an unwanted additional threat since India is already surrounded by nuclear missiles on its North-eastern and Western borders. This will further destabilize the West Asian region and impact the smooth flow of oil which will impact India's economy. Thirdly her support to terrorist organizations and the possibility of the fissile material and missile falling into the hands of terrorist organizations is a major concern for not only India, but also for the entire world community. (Two organizations, Hamas and Hezbollah, have already demonstrated the ability to obtain and use weapons like Fajr-5 missiles with ranges of 75 km – against Israel)[87] Lastly, one cannot neglect mentioning the prospect of internal instability and violence within the region which can be caused by the explosion of dirty bombs.

2. Iran Israel Conflict

History

Iran and Israel collectively are part of one of the two oldest civilizations in Asia. They enjoyed a friendly and mutually beneficial relationship in the 1970's, but the Islamic Revolution in Iran made them adversaries. After the 1979 revolution, their interests converged once again for a short period due to common geopolitical interests, such as their fear of Pan Arabism, Soviet influence in the Middle East and a common enemy in Iraq. These common threats brought both the countries together and they formed a de-facto alliance. Moderate Iranian leaders like President Hashmei Rafsanjani (1989-1997)(was pragmatic in domestic and Foreign Policy) and President Mohammed Khatami (1997-2005) adopted a language which aimed to end Iran's opposition to Israel's existence and tried to build Arab-Israel Peace process[88]. However; post 2005 there have been several incidents and factors which have ultimately culminated in the weakening of this relationship. After the election of 2005, Mahmoud Ahmadinejad became the President. The radical approach adopted by the ruler of Iran, the rise of the Revolutionary Guards and the principality in Iran, became causes for the start of a Cold War between the two countries which now has the potential to develop into a full-fledged war. Secondly, the converging geopolitical interests were no longer present. Post the Iraq war and the death of President Saddam Hussein, Iraq was no longer a threat and Iran emerged as a powerful nation with aspirations to become a regional power. Iran's anti-Israel rhetoric and its financial support to organizations operating in Israel's periphery became a cause for concern.

All these activities made the two countries hostile to each other and the fact that Israel is a covert nuclear power and Iran is on the verge of becoming one too makes Middle East volatile and unstable[89]
.

Israel Concern

The relationship between the two countries post 2005 has deteriorated to the extent that Israel blames Iran for every regional conflict. Though Iran and Israel do not have any territorial disputes, and their areas of interest are also different – for instance the Israeli interest lies in the Levant and Iran is more interested in the Persian Gulf – there is still a fierce competition to gain regional supremacy between the two countries. Initially the volatile environment had been created by the Iranians, during the reign of the erstwhile President Ahmadinejad, who had adopted a hard-line approach towards Israel, but with the change of guard and the more liberal President Hassan Rouhani coming to power, Iran has taken many positive steps towards collaboration. The signing of an interim nuclear deal in 2013 is one of them. However; times change, and the tables have turned. The Israelis have started taking a more conservative outlook instead and have criticized the Iranian nuclear deal and the relaxation of sanctions.

- **Iran's Political Aspirations**

Iran desires to play a major role in the Middle East. The financial support and arms supplied by Iran to organizations like Hamas in Gaza, and Hezbollah in Lebanon, in addition to the parallel training and covert activities of the Revolutionary Guard in the periphery of Israel is a grave cause of concern for the Israelis. The 2005 war between Israel and Hezbollah was perceived as a proxy war between Iran and Israel. The situation in Middle East has further deteriorated with the fall of pro US leaders like Hosni Mubarak in Egypt, the 2011 Arab spring, the widespread protest by majority of Shi'a Muslims in Arab states like Bahrain and the support of Iran to the Muslim Brotherhood. These are the activities which Israel considers a threat to the stability of the region.

- **Iran's Ideological Warfare**

Iran's political aspirations have been camouflaged by their radical Muslim Ideology. The rise of Revolutionary Guards is a direct culmination of the hard-line approach adopted by the politicians. Anti-Zionist and anti US rhetoric had become the means for making Iran more acceptable in the Arab world. Moreover, by supporting the Palestinian Liberation Organizations, Iran had tried to emerge as a crusader for Islamist rule in the Middle East. However, post the 2013 nuclear deal this radical ideology has lost some of its sheen and Iran has attempted to have a more progressive foreign policy; starting with improving US-Iran relationship, with additional focus on the co-operation that is necessary in terms of addressing the nuclear deadlock . However, the Israelis still view this fragile agreement with scepticism and distrust.

- **Iran Missile programme**

There was a time when Israel exported arms to Iran, and benefitted from the arms sale that took place, but all that has changed now. According to Ronen Bergman, Israel sold Iran US$75 million worth of arms from stocks of Israel Military Industries[90] The Israelis have now become apprehensive about Iran's rapidly expanding missile capabilities – especially with respect to the short and medium range ballistic missiles that they have acquired over the years. Iran exports most of its short range missiles to the Hezbollah and Hamas, which are based in Lebanon and in the Gaza strip. This has increased the vulnerability of the Israeli people as was seen during the Hezbollah war of 2005, and the Gaza war, where the long-range rocket, Fajr-5 reached Tel Aviv and Jerusalem[91]. Along with these small range missiles, Iran also have medium and long range missiles which can directly target Israel and this is a cause of concern for the Israelis.

- **Iran's Nuclear Programme**

Israeli leaders believe that nuclear weapons would provide Iran with an upper hand in terms of the anti-Zionist propaganda. It would enable Iran's allies such as the Hezbollah to become more aggressive. Currently, their activities are limited due to a fear of Israeli retaliation, however once Iran becomes a nuclear capable state, and declares its status overtly, Israel's freedom of action would be compromised.

There are no clear cut red lines; hence the possibility of accidental use of conventional and nuclear arms increases. Secondly Arab resistance to Iran would dissipate due to fear of Iran's retaliatory capabilities.[92] Such a development would also erode US supremacy in the Middle East, while simultaneously increasing the proliferation of weapons. If Iran was to succeed with their nuclear agenda, then Saudi Arabia, UAE and the rest of the Middle East would follow suit, thus questioning the validity and the applicability of the NPT.

Israeli Strategy

Israel's Strategic community is clearly divided as far as punitive actions against Iran are concerned. Their policies swing from an extreme military airstrike to thwart Iran's nuclear programme to a more covert policy of espionage and cyber-attacks. Both have their merits as well as flaws.

- **Israel Military Air Strike**

The hardliners in Israel along with the Prime Minister Netanyahu consider a nuclear, armed Iran, an existential threat. Though the officials do not discuss the military option overtly, they always state that in dealing with Iran, "all the options are on the table". Israelis are considered masters of operational security, especially taking into consideration their strategy of "surprise attacks". The Israeli Air Force has achieved great success in the past as was seen in Operation Focus of 1987, and the destruction of the Iraqi nuclear programme at Osiraka in Operation Opera in 1981. The operation Orchard completely destroyed the Syrian nuclear facility in 2007. Thus Israel's air force is a formidable challenge to overcome. More so as they are constantly upgrading their infrastructure, for example, very recently, in 2010 they have signed a deal for the F-35 Stealth Fighter Aircraft with the US[93]. Some believe that their F-16 and F-15, global positioning systems or mainly the long range early warning X-band radar system (controlled by US in Negev base) can detect targets thousands of miles away[94]. Additionally, their Laser guided munitions are an added asset and the combination of this technical expertise makes them a formidable force. They also possess the Guided Bomb Unit (GBU) which is a 27 2000lb class weapon carrying 550 lb high explosive that can penetrate six feet of reinforced concrete and can be laser guided all these can help in penetrating the Iranian Defence.[95] They have also conducted long range exercises over the Mediterranean Sea. However, as time has elapsed, and Iran has improved her missile capabilities there are few strategists who believe a hard-line military approach would be effective. The Israelis themselves are now having doubts about the operational feasibility of such an approach. They may still consider it, but only if the US actively participated in this strategy and reinforced their military strength. Currently however, the US is reluctant to engage directly in the region and does not approve of this approach, as they still believe that sanctions are a more feasible option and with Iran signing the nuclear deal this possibility further fades away.

Feasibility of Air Strike

In an air strike it is important to consider a few parameters such as the distance of the adversary, the number of targets one needs to hit – both in terms for counter value as well as counter force – its missile capabilities, and in the case of Iran the role that Non State Actors such as the Hezbollah and Hamas can play. The NSAs will play especially important role, since their presence will make the war, a two front war for Iran. All these factors make it very difficult for Israel to go through with this strategy. An Israeli attack is only possible through the strategic use of the Air Force but Israel does not have an ally in the region. As a result, they will first have to use the hostile airspace of Jordan, Iraq or Saudi Arabia. Secondly, the distance is large so they require an immense number of aircrafts to operate over long ranges with precise targeting capabilities. They would also require the support of aerial re-fullers to refuel them. Only by the conglomeration of these factors can they successfully neutralize the adversary's air defense system. Another important factor is that in Israel's previous combat, the target was Iraq and Syria's single nuclear installations, whereas Iran's nuclear target are spread out and camouflaged in the mountains. They will require 12 tankers equivalent per mission if they want to just hit Esfahan, Natanz and Arak and this can be possible considering they have mastered the "buddy refuelling" operation [96] but it would require no margin for operational failure. Despite that, they cannot guarantee that they will hit Fordow which is supposed to be built inside a mountain 295 feet deep. Iran's other Uranium mines are all dispersed, which makes it that much harder to destroy them with a planned strategic attack. Thus Israeli air attacks cannot destroy the Iranian nuclear programme. At best they might damage the installations, and thereby delay the process by a few years. However, this seems unlikely as well since Iran's missiles are varied and widespread. Therefore any attack on their installations would incite a counter attack and severe retaliation from Iran. Iran's medium and long range missiles, especially the Shahab 3 and Shahab 3B become a major threat since the latter can survive ABM and can be used for precision attacks against high value targets. In a war like situation, Hezbollah and Hamas groups can also target Israel through their missiles from Gaza and Lebanon. Iran has also threatened to block off the Strait of Hormuz[97], and since a majority of the oil transits from there such a decision could have a drastic effect on the world economy and the Israelis would be held accountable. Such a scenario would trap Israel from all sides and many believe that Israel is not ready to pay such a heavy price.

Figure 9: Iran's Nuclear Installations

Source:http://www.ynetnews.com/articles/0,7340,L-4209836,00.html

Alternative Options: Cyber and Sabotage

The protagonists of this theory are the retired heads of Mossad, Mr. Meir Dagan and Mr. Ephraim. Earlier they had both denounced the military option stating it would be counterproductive. They believe "sabotage and diplomacy have done much to set back Iran's nuclear ambitions and can do more yet"[98]. The assassination of nuclear scientists, cyber-attacks and blasts at a munitions base are more potent ways of delaying Iran's nuclear programme instead of an overt military option. It is believed that the computer worm known as "Stuxnet" was used to attack Iran's Uranium enrichment centrifuges this made the machines to spin out of control and self-destruct, slowing the Iranian programme's progress[99].Various nuclear scientist like Mr. Mosoud Alimohammadi, Majid Shahriari,Darioush Rezaeinejad , Mostafa Ahamadi-Roshan were all killed in bizarre accidents and this "black ops" campaign to disrupt Iranian nuclear programme has been going on for quite some time[100].

Apart from this Israel may be clandestinely supporting several anti- revolutionary groups like the Mujahedin Khalq Organization (MKO) and the Green Movement with an aim to overthrow the revolutionary leaders. Israel's proxy war in supporting Kurds and Baluch rebels mainly Kurdish Free Life Party of Kurdistan (PJAK) and Baluch rebel Jundullah[101] is another way of creating unrest. Thus, Israel may be pursuing the last two options actively and keeping all other actions including the military option open to intimidate the adversary.

- **Sanctions and Iran's Nuclear Deal its implications for Israel**

The US and European Union believed that the sanctions imposed on Iran by the international community have impacted their fiscal situation. Iranian currency was devalued by 40 per cent, there was a shortage of foreign currency especially dollars and on the social aspect there was scarcity of food as imports had been hit because no new contracts are being signed by the European Union[102]. This wedged the economic condition of Iran, hence they believe that Iran has agreed to go in for a six month interim nuclear deal with major nuclear powers (P5+Germany) in November 2013, whereby some economic sanctions will be eased out and Iran on its part will curb its nuclear activity that is its Uranium enrichment programme. The highlight of the deal is Iran has committed to halt enrichment above 5 percent, to neutralize its stockpile of near 20 percent Uranium, halt progress on its enrichment capacity and halt on the growth of its 3 to 5 per cent stockpile[103] . US believes that this will limit Iran's existing stockpiles of enriched Uranium, as according to the deal Iran will have to curb the number and capabilities of the centrifuges used to enrich Uranium and thus it will be successful in limiting Iran's ability to "produce weapons-grade Plutonium". However the Israeli government called this deal a historic mistake".[104] They believe that Iran has achieved what it wanted – economic sanctions have been relaxed, and they also continue to use the centrifuges. Additionally, their Arak nuclear reactors have not been dismantled, so strategically, it is actually a victory for Iran. Mr. Yair Lapid, Israel's Minister of finance and part of Netanyahu's coalition government stated "I want to clarify that Israel will not let Iran develop nuclear military capability."[105]

Iranian Hostility

Though Iran and Israel do not have any border problems, the emergence of Iran as a contending power in the Middle East and its aggressive anti-Israel policy has created ripples in the region. Iran's nuclear programme is the biggest challenge for Israel. Their attempt to become a successful nuclear weapons state stems from an innate hostility between the two. There are various reasons for this hostility:

- **Ideology and Geostrategic factor**

Iran views Israel as an adversary especially due to the repeated efforts made to destabilize the Iranian nuclear programme. Initially they were hostile to the US since they believed that there was US involvement in the overthrowing of Iran' elected government in 1953. They believe that it will be difficult for US to accept the Islamic revolution and hence the US will continue to instigate unrest and violence through Israel. However, post the Iraq war, and the overthrowing of the Taliban, there has been an immense power shift. There is an absence of a major rival left within the region to threaten Iran. Therefore, they aspire to become an unopposed major power and consequently view Israel as a direct threat that could prevent them from achieving their goals. The rise of the Hezbollah and Hamas and their role in Syria has made Iran a key player in this region. The Iranian interim nuclear deal of 2013 is further bound to change the relationship between US and Iran in a positive way. Post withdrawal from Afghanistan, the Americans will try to avoid overt conflict in any other region and they will harbour a desire to have a more neutral relationship, if not a very friendly one, with Iran. They would also like to involve Iran in solving the Syrian problem. This could further create a wedge between Iran and Israel as the inherent power dynamics would shift in Iran's favour in the future.

- **Israel cyber war and sabotage**

Iran blames Israel for the various cyber-attacks that have been launcher against their nuclear installations and oil plants. Iran also believes that Israel is responsible for surreptitiously killing her nuclear scientists'.

- **Israel responsible for the Sanctions**

Iran believes that Israel would not allow them to develop their nuclear programme peacefully. They blame Israel for the sanctions imposed on them by the world community. While such sanctions are extremely detrimental to their economy, Iran is nevertheless determined to continue their peaceful nuclear programme regardless of the opposition.

- **Israel's covert threat to destroy Iran's nuclear installations**

As discussed above, Israel has made attempts to delay Iran's nuclear progress. In retaliation, Iran has developed its missile system in a way that counters any attack from Israel. They are also trying to encircle Israel with the help of their allies.

Iran's strength

Iran's regional influence has grown after they started supporting various Palestinian organizations in their struggle for their homeland. Israel's relations with Turkey have been strained and Turkey now regards Iran as an important economic and regional balancer against Israel. After the Egyptian uprising, Iran sent two of their warships beyond the Persian Gulf and into the Suez Canal[106] for the first time, demonstrating their growing military strength and the improvements in their naval capability. Iran's nuclear and missile development programme has emboldened them and added more strategic power to their decisions and actions. Iran's "Air–Defense" system has also improved tremendously, and their arsenal now comprises of fighter aircrafts, SAMs and Anti-Aircraft Artillery (AAA) as well and is a mix of Russian and Chinese systems like S-175,HQ-2-CSA-1,MIM-23 Hawk [107]etc. They also have UAV (Unarmed Aerial Vehicle) ababil, Mohajer, Scan Eagle etc. This along with their previous success in the proxy war against Israel has further amplified the Iranian conviction that they can dominate and deal with any power in Middle East. The support provided by them to the Muslim Brotherhood was part of the policy they adopted in an attempt to expand the Islamist ideology and remove the Western influence that was infiltrating the region. The Arab Spring provided them with an opportunity to increase their influence subtly, as the Middle Eastern nations were too involved in their own domestic problems, to bother about emerging powers.

Figure: 10 Iran's Missile Arsenal

Designation	Propellant	Range	IOC	Inventory
Shahab-1	Liquid	300 km	1995	50-300
Shahab-2	Liquid	500 km		50-150
Qiam-1	Liquid	500 km+	2010?	
Shahab-3	Liquid	1,300 km	2002	300
Shahab-4	Liquid	3,218-4,000 km	2008-2009+	16-35 ?
Samen	Solid	800 -1,000 km	2008	replacing Scuds-B/C
Sejjil	Solid	2,000-2,510 km	2009+	>50 -<90 estimated
Ashura	Solid	3,000 km	2010+	
IRIS	liquid / solid	Cancelled	2005	
X-55 LACM	jet engine	3,000 km	2001	12
Karrar UCAV	jet engine	1,000 km	2010?	
Shahab-5	Liquid	5,500 km	R & D	0
Shahab-6	Liquid	10,000 km		0

Source: Compiled from Missile Arsenal at http://www.iranintelligence.com/arsenal

Iran's missile inventory is given above. Apart from these, they also possess short range solid fuel missile such as Fajr, Nazeat, and Zelzal[108]. Additionally, they have also acquired the liquid fuel based Shahab series - 1, 2 and 3 missiles which are believed to have been reverse engineered from the Russian Scud-B missiles.

Strategic Outcome and India's concern

India has friendly relation with Iran and Iran is also strategically important to India, as it provides India an access to approach

Afghanistan. A friendly Iran is leverage against Pakistan. Iran's interim nuclear deal of 2013, has also removed the dilemma of imposing sanctions on Iran and it should also remove a sense of insecurity amongst the nations of the Middle East. A good starting point can be Iran's involvement in creating a Middle East Nuclear Weapon Free Zone (MENWFZ). However, if things change and Iran follows the covert Israeli nuclear path then it has the potentiality to create instability in the Middle East, as after the Arab Spring, most of the nations have a precarious internal situation and this is the perfect ground for the growth of Non State Actors who will ultimately cause chaos and spread terror.

Also there is always a possibility that other nations in the region might try to rival Iran and the region would subsequently become a battleground for an ever increasing arms race. The process has already started as there have been reports in the media about Saudi Arabia contemplating developing /acquiring nuclear weapons from Pakistan[109]. Pakistan is economically dependent on Saudi Arabia and the latter on Pakistan for its internal security, hence both countries have a symbiotic relationship and they can be hand in gloves over this issue. Saudi Arabia is already upgrading its existing Patriot PAC2 batteries to the PAC-3 configuration[110]. The other countries in this region have already started calculating their security conditions. The gulf countries dependence on the Americans –the U.S-GCC missile defense cooperation is seen as a strategic imperative and the March 2012 launch of the U.S.-GCC Strategic Cooperation Forum or SCF is an important indicator of American commitment to Gulf security.[111] Countries like UAE and Kuwait are already working on acquiring BMDs. UAE is procuring two THAAD batteries and it has already acquired Patriot PAC-3 batteries, similarly Kuwait has also upgraded its existing batteries to PAC-3.[112] Israel already has potent multi-layered missile defense systems like its Iron Dome, Arrow, and David's Sling.[113] Thus the mantra is to have advanced, interoperable systems to intercept and destroy attacking missiles. All these will create an arms race in the Middle East, and major powers like US .China and Russia will exploit the security situation to enhance their arms industry. All this may not be good for India as any standoffs in the gulf will impact import of oil, (in the first quarter of 2014 Indian oil imports with Iran rose to 7,3 percent compared to 5.4 per cent last year[114]) and ultimately the Indian economy will suffer. Hence a stable Middle East is in India's interest.

C) Nuclear Terrorism and the Non State Actors.

"The gravest threat faced by the world is of an extremist group getting hold of nuclear weapons or materials."[115]

The major test for the 21st century has been terrorism. The increase in the number of Nuclear Weapon States has made nuclear terrorism a reality, as a result Nuclear Terrorism has become a major challenge in the world today .The threat is trans- national and needs no boundaries. The acquisition of nuclear weapons/ bombs has become a preferred goal for most terrorist organizations. The increase in the number and usage of suicide bombers reflects that these groups are not bothered by the lethality of the methods adopted but the ideology and narrow political gains are their desired objectives. The year 2011 was significant because a number of key terrorists were killed, Osama bin Laden, Atiya Abdul Rahman, (Al-Qaida's second-in command after bin Laden's death), Ilyas Kashmiri, Harun Fazul were few of them[116], but this did not slow down or stop the activities of terrorist organizations. The core had been attacked but new splinter groups emerged. These splinter groups have now spread all across the world and have found easy targets especially in Asia and Africa. The Arab spring had weakened the domestic dynamics of many States, making them a safe haven for terrorist activities. The violent methods adopted by these NSAs are a cause of grave concern for the host nations. The fact remains that in most of the New Nuclear Weapon States, and those states which have civilian nuclear programmes the safety and security standards are not standardized hence the nuclear weapons and fissile material are vulnerable to sabotage and theft.

The African conundrum

The new al-Qaida affiliates such as the AQIM (Al-Qaida Islamic Maghreb) and the Al-Shabaab continue to attack the government. This is possible since they have managed to acquire loose munitions from the Libyan stock, post Libya's collapse. And there was a severe threat looming over the African countries, mainly due to the possibility of terrorists obtaining Man-Portable Air Defense Systems (MPADS) which would have impacted the internal security of many East African nations[117]. The governments of Algeria, Mali, Mauritania, and Niger have tried to tackle the issue collectively by forming regional organizations like the Trans-Sahara Counterterrorism Partnership (TSCTP). Furthermore, the countries of East Africa like Somalia, Sudan, and Kenya have also formed a regional organization called the Partnership for Regional East African Counter Terrorism (PREACT) and this is designed to build the counterterrorism capacity and capability of member countries to thwart short-term terrorist threats and address longer-term vulnerabilities ".[118]

Un-abated terror in Asia

Various Shia and Sunni terrorist organization like the Hamas, Hezbollah, Kataib Hizballah (KH), Asaib Ahl al-Haq (AAH), Kurdistan Workers' Party (PKK) Jaysh Rijal al-Tariqah alNaqshabandiyah (JRTN) etc are often sponsored by the state, and they continue to destabilize the neighbouring nations in the Middle East. In South Asia, Pakistan and Afghanistan are major bases for terrorist organizations like the Al-Qaida, Lashkar-e-Tayyiba (LeT), Tehrik-e-Taliban Pakistan, Jamat-ud-Dawa (JD) and the Haqqani Network[119]. The Indian Mujahedeen continues its attack on the major cities in India. The Lashkar-e-Tayyiba (LeT) is the central core of militant groups like HuM, JeM, HuJI in Pakistan and Bangladesh.

Countries involved with terrorist organisations

These terrorist organisations can carry on their heinous work mainly because they are able to fund, recruit, train, and mastermind different terrorist activities due to the physical place provided by several nations in their territory. This is possible because most of the states are either suffering from weak governance or malicious political agendas which use the name of religious or ethical ideologies to gain support for these activities. The geographical locations of these groups are varied and diverse spanning the continents of Asia, Africa and Latin America, which makes this threat a global concern.

Table: 6 Terrorist Organisations'

S No	Countries/ Regions	Terrorist Organisations
1	Somalia	Al-Shabaab
2	The Trans-Sahara	AQIM
3	Mali.	AQIM
4	The Southern Philippines	Jemaah Islamiya fugitives and AbuSayyaf Group
5	Iraq	Al-Qaida in Iraq (AQI)
6	Lebanon	Hezbollah
7	Yemen	AQIM
8	Afghanistan	The Taliban, the Haqqani Network, Hezb-e-Islami Gulbuddin, al-Qa'ida (AQ), Lashkar-e-Tayyiba
9	Pakistan	Al-Qaida,the Haqqani Network, the Quetta Shura, and Lashkar-e-Tayyiba
10	Colombia	Revolutionary Armed Forces of Colombia (FARC).
11	Venezuela.	National Liberation Army (ELN) and FARC

Source: Compiled from Country Report on Terrorism 2013, US Department of State

The Nuclear Threat

The UN secretary-General has labelled nuclear terrorism as "one of the most serious threats of our time". US President Obama has been equally blunt in stating that "There is no graver danger to global security than the threat of nuclear terrorism, and no more immediate task for the international community than to address that threat."[120] Terrorist intent to acquire and use nuclear weapons to achieve their desired goals is a major cause for concern. The fact that the number of countries having nuclear weapons in the world has increased substantially, has consequently amplified the nuclear threat all over the world. The IAEA Illicit Nuclear Trafficking database notes 1266 incidents reported by 99 countries over last 12 years and 18 incidents involving HEU /Plutonium trafficking[121]. For example in 2009 in Baghdad, Iraq, on 25th October, two vehicle were bombed in Green Zone, when 155 people died and 500 people were injured[122], similarly in 2010 in Moscow, Russia, a suicide bombing in the Metro, killed 38 people and injured 100.

The Atom for Peace programme has further increased the threat as can be seen by the substantial increase in the number of countries involved in the civilian nuclear programme and most of these plants are not adequately safeguarded against nuclear material theft. As of January 21, 2014 there are now over 430 commercial nuclear power reactors operating in 31 countries, with over 370,000 MWe of total capacity and about 70 more reactors are under construction.[123] There are about 56 countries, operating a total of about 240 research reactors, and a further 180 nuclear reactors power some 150 ships and submarines[124]. The nuclear inventory has grown at an alarming rate, which in turn has increased the nuclear threat. According to the IAEA sources the total inventory can be shown as follows:

Inventories – facilities and materials potential targets[125]

- 17 ,000 nuclear weapons

- 3.000 tons civil and military HEU and Pu

- 480 research reactors (160 with HEU)

- 100 fuel cycle facilities

- 430 operating nuclear power plants

- 100.000 Cat I and II radioactive sources

- 1.000.000 Cat III radioactive sources

The presence of such large inventories of nuclear material mainly –Highly Enriched Uranium (HEU) and Plutonium makes it vulnerable to theft .These radioactive sources and radioactively contaminated material, can be easily attained by the terrorist organizations if the states do not have a secure and safe nuclear arrangement. Therefore the world community is basically concerned about six major vulnerabilities namely:-

1. Nuclear weapon Theft.

2. Theft of Nuclear material to make an explosive nuclear device.

3. Theft of Radioactive material to make "Dirty Bombs".

4. Sabotage of nuclear facility or transport and transit routes.

5. Kidnapping and bribing nuclear scientists

6. Cyber-attacks to acquire and damage plant safety.

Nuclear Weapon Theft - The Nuclear device

Questions have often been asked regarding whether these organisations have the ability to construct a crude nuclear device, since that process entails a high ratio and intensity of explosives. Fissile material like HEU or Plutonium is used to create nuclear bombs. Nuclear plants therefore become easy targets, especially the spent fuel since it is often kept outside the core area and the chances of security lapses are consequently much higher than anywhere else. Nations should therefore, make special security arrangements to safeguard these nuclear plants. Most of these terrorist organisations motivate their members in the name of ideology/religion and often lure them and their families with lucrative economic deals. Usually NSAs are fairly large in number and dispersed in a vast geographical area as described previously. It is difficult to tackle them as they are mostly trained and supported economically and militarily by neighbouring states to ensure their own narrow political gains. The strategies adopted by them vary from deceit, force, stealth to suicide bombing. Their main aim is to create terror and the targets are usually critical places, major infrastructural regions, and populous places like railway stations, market places etc where the destruction and damage become colossal. It is often stated that the creation of a crude nuclear device is a possibility, since terrorists often use hi-tech information and the procedure to develop these are easily available, but there are certain constraints which prevent them from doing so as well. These constraints are discussed below.

Nuclear implosion and Gun design

To have a sophisticated nuclear implosion is very difficult to achieve since it requires nuclear, chemical and engineering expertise; however a simpler crude gun based nuclear device can be achieved. The former requires less fissile material 5 kg of Plutonium or 15 kg of HEU for a basic design—but the design and manufacture of such a device is very complicated, requiring precise processing and shaping of the fissile core and precise firing of the high explosive lenses.[126] The gun type assembly though simpler to design and produce, requires a relatively larger amount of HEU. At the very least, a minimum of 50 kg of HEU (90 per cent U-235) as opposed to the earlier 15 kg.

As is evident, it is not easy to acquire large inventories of fissile material, however; due to the presence of large amounts of "loose nukes" (the huge stockpiles of Uranium and Plutonium available)[127], due to an upsurge in their utility in the military and the civilian sector, have made the task little easier. The global Inventory of HEU used in the military for making weapons   is 1850 tonnes and in the civilian sector it is 50 tonnes similarly for Plutonium the global inventory in the military section is 260 tonnes and the civilian is 230 tonnes.

Nuclear Material theft

There is no unified system for accounting for these nuclear materials. Moreover, the safety and security of these materials vary from country to country. The nuclear warheads and the centralized storage of the five permanent members are considered to be the safest; however other sources especially in Pakistan and North Korea are causes of concern. Also, "A terrorist with enough technical knowledge and means could drain a spent fuel pool, triggering a cladding fire that could result in the release of large amounts of radioactive material."[128] The civilian nuclear programme which uses and produces irradiated low enriched Uranium and Plutonium that is consequently used in power plants has further complicated the situation. The IAEA has identified 1600 cases of illicit nuclear trafficking since1993[129]. The alarming thing is that the International Atomic Energy Agency (IAEA) has documented the 18 cases involved in the theft or loss of HEU or Plutonium from 1993 to 2007[130] none of the HEU that was recovered had been reported missing[131]. A survey conducted by NTI in 2014 on nuclear security conditions puts North Korea as the last country in the overall score category and Pakistan the last country in the Risk environment category, the index included 32 countries. The NTI Index, assessed countries with weapons-usable nuclear materials based on five categories mainly:- i) Quantities & Sites, ii) Security & Control Measures, iii) Global Norms, iv) Domestic Commitments& Capacity, v)Risk Environment[132].The endeavour of this organization has been to simply highlight the vulnerable conditions under which nuclear plants operate in some of these Nuclear States. Hence it is very essential for nations that are developing nuclear plants to have stringent domestic nuclear laws as well as vigilant security arrangements both in and off the nuclear plant area, since it is better to prevent the theft then to catch the offenders later on. The loss of life would be irreparable and justice might not be guaranteed since there are several land and sea transit routes available in most of the countries for them to escape.

Dirty Bombs OR Improvised Nuclear Device (IND)

A dirty bomb is a "Radioactive Dispersal Device (RDD)" or in other words a conventional bomb spiked with radioactive material. It has a mix of explosives, such as dynamite mixed with radioactive powder or pellets and when the dynamite or other explosives are set off, the blast carries radioactive material into the surrounding area.[133] The IAEA has estimates that there are between 100,000 and 1million radiological sources around the globe[134]In China, alone, there are an estimated 400,000 sources.

The common radioactive materials and the rays which they emit are: - Cobalt-60 (Co-60) Cesium-137 (Cs-137). These materials emit gamma rays whereas Iridium-192 (Ir-192) emits beta and high-energy gamma rays, Strontium-beta, low-energy gamma rays, Americium-241 (Am-241) alpha and low-energy gamma rays[135]. After Uranium, Cesium is the other material which has been high on illegal radiological trafficking. These beta and gamma emitters, unlike the alpha emitters are quite easy to detect. The use of these radioactive material vary, from being used in sterilization and food irradiation like Co-60 and Cs-137, to multi-beam teletherapyCo-60,radioisotopes and thermoelectric generators- Strontium90,etc[136].

The people are at risk because the probability of this bomb is higher than the actual nuclear bomb as the radioactive material is easily available due to its wide use in the civilian sector, mainly for sterilizing equipment, diagnostic purposes and treating illnesses in hospitals, research institutions and inspecting welding seams. The dirty bomb can also be constructed and detonated rather easily. This can often lead to radioactive hazards, causing unnecessary panic and force people to abandon the area. Often these hazards depend on the dose of radiation a person is exposed to and mostly low level radiations do not have a major impact on the population as a whole. However, being exposed to large dosages of radiations for a short period of time can cause organ function loss, nausea, hair loss, skin burns, hypothyroidism etc. If exposure is between 50-70 rem, the health effects can be Nausea, fatigue, vomiting, if more than 100rem there can be haemorrhage and above 400 possible death within two months [137]

Terrorist organizations attempt to use such devices in congested areas to create and breed fear, panic, chaos and stampedes. Enormous psychological as well as considerable local damage – involving contamination of property, could be orchestrated and if the area is an economic hub then the whole area would become inaccessible for an extended period of time, as it would require costly methods of cleaning up, thus impacting the daily life of that region. However such a severe impact of the dirty bomb would depend on a number of factors, including the size of the explosive, the amount and type of radioactive material used the means of dispersal, and weather conditions.[138] The impact of this can be mitigated substantially, if people are made aware of radioactive contaminations by educating and providing them with antidotes and safety gears.

The dirty bombs can be can be easily detected hence a difficult task for the terrorist organisations to transport but certain materials – such as the isotope used in the Litvinenko case – are effectively impossible to detect if contained within a minimal form of shielding.[139]

Nuclear Sabotage and cyber attacks

The sabotage of a civilian nuclear plant can have a massive impact not only in terms of the destruction of property, but also the possibility of starting a hazardous radioactive leak which would cause immense collateral damage. Edwin Lyman, a senior researcher with the Union of Concerned Scientists, an American nongovernmental organization says that the fact that storage pools for spent nuclear fuel are located outside the containment vessels and, therefore, may have insufficient protection and if terrorists destroy back-up functions and cut off the water and power supply, they might be able to create a whole new Fukushima crisis.[140] This facet could therefore be used by terrorist organizations for both – sabotage as well as nuclear material theft purposes. Radiation contamination would require a long-term relocation of people and businesses. Most of the nations are not equipped well enough in terms of dealing with quick response and contingency plans. Even storage depots and transit routes could be attacked. The threat or use of nuclear material as a blackmail technique or the use of nuclear threat to sabotage key public infrastructures such as transport facilities, oil fields etc are a cause of concern because a localized occurrence can have a global impact.

Cyber Attack

The technological advancement has opened up new problems for the nations. There has been a transformation in the art of warfare. The traditional warfare system is in the process of being replaced by Information Warfare (IW). More and more countries are relying on the technique of C4ISR which has led to computer hacking and cyber warfare. The most vulnerable link in the chain is the Command and Control centre of Nuclear Weapon States. Faking a nuclear attack or a command signal to launch an attack, posting false claims of responsibility on accessible government websites, disrupting or corrupting with false information emergency communications within and between governments (including on hotlines established between governments to deal with tense or ambiguous situations) are few examples[141]. Another example of weakened security is the shared connection which exists in most areas. If all the computers are connected to the internet through a common bandwidth or channel, it becomes easier for a professional hacker to hack into the accounts. Computers which operate on a closed network may also be compromised by various hacking methods, such as privilege escalation, roaming notebooks, wireless access points, embedded exploits in software and hardware, and maintenance entry points[142]. Various highly qualified engineers and computer hackers are being lured and motivated by various terrorist organisations, in the name of Ideology /Religion to participate in their warfare.

The threat to civilian nuclear plants is equally grave. Terrorists could hack systems and thereby interfere with power sources by remote control and perhaps disable cooling functions.[143].Even if the nuclear plant operators sever links between their computer networks and the outside world, terrorists can bring in USB flash drives, and can easily infect systems with viruses, as stated by Charles Ferguson, president of the Federation of American Scientists, a cyber-terrorism analyst. U.S. nuclear power industry has spent a total of $1.2 billion (about 114 billion yen) on improving its facilities[144]. Can the other nations spend so much money on the nuclear safety of civilian nuclear plants? Even the P 5 countries find it difficult to tackle such issues. If one needs to counter the threats posed by these Non State Actors, there is a need to adopt a more holistic approach and all the nuances of the safety and security issues need to be debated and discussed. Precaution is better than cure, the global community therefore needs to sit together and take a firm stand on what might easily escalate into a volatile nuclear attack. A proactive approach will help in avoiding later regret. This daunting task can be only achieved through global cooperation. The countries need to share information and help each other in executing the cyber laws rather than getting involved in stealing information through computer hacking and other such heinous acts. Nuclear Security Summit 2014 had tried to address these problems

Impact on India

The threat mentioned above can have a major impact on India because India is surrounded by nations who profess asymmetric warfare, where the core is the NSAs. India has a robust civilian nuclear programme and this makes it vulnerable to all those threat which were mentioned earlier. Hence nuclear safety and security issues are of utmost importance to India. These issues cannot be handled in isolation, hence international cooperation, tight internal security .and create opinion to Isolate these NASAs in international forum are some of the measures to control them.

This brings us to the next issue of global cooperation to combat nuclear weapons , through various international treaties and ultimately achieve the goal of "Global Zero". The possibility of a Global Zero lies in systematic planning. The first step in this arduous journey is arms control followed by disarmament and ultimately a Nuclear Weapon Free World (NWFW). Such a vision might be achieved through a series of disarmament treaties and Nuclear Weapon Free Zones (NWFZ).The next chapter deals with various ways whereby the nuclear threat could be controlled, and ultimately abolished.

Opportunities for Global Disarmament

Since the atomic bomb was first detonated, nations have debated vociferously about the necessity and relevance of nuclear weapons. UN's Conference on Disarmament has been a watchdog for the escalation of nuclear weapons. Various groups like the Campaign for Nuclear Disarmament, Greenpeace, International Physicians for the Prevention of Nuclear War, Campaign for a Nuclear Weapons Free World, Mayors for Peace, Global Zero, and the International Campaign to Abolish Nuclear Weapons[145] are testimony to the efforts adopted by citizens to make this world a better place to live in. The debate regarding "Nuclear Deterrence" verses "Total Nuclear Disarmament" still continues. Proponents of both the theories are convinced that the illusive peace can be obtained if their theory is promulgated. The dangers of mismanagement of nuclear weapons either through theft, or through nuclear accidents are becoming more and more apparent. A series of nuclear treaties have been initiated which have become a significant step in controlling if not totally eliminating nuclear weapons. In spite of these treaties there is still a substantial amount of nuclear stockpile present and there has also been an increase in the number of countries possessing nuclear weapons. In 1945 there were just 6 nuclear warheads and all of them belonged to the US. By 2002, five nations had a total of 20,190 warheads and now there are approximately 18,000 nuclear warheads distributed amongst 9 countries[146]. This depicts that after the initial boom, the nuclear arsenal has decreased substantially, especially between the two major powers mainly the USA and

Russia. However, a major cause for concern is that new entrants have come to acquire nuclear weapons. In order to have a greater impact, the present treaties should incorporate subjects which have hitherto being evaded. Rehashing past treaties is not a good method to gain signatories. Recent global developments prove that the framing of such treaties requires constant scrutiny and adequate amendment since it is very difficult to formulate new treaties and even harder to sustain them. The nuclear issues that plague most countries are deeply intertwined, and to successfully detangle or unravel them, one needs to examine the situation in a step by step manner. The first and the most important link in this process is the relationship between US and Russia, as they still retain more than 90 per cent of world's nuclear arsenal .So any process must start by analysing the disarmament issues initiated by these two countries.

US- Russia Disarmament Initiatives

In the Post-Cold War era, after the dissolution of the erstwhile USSR the two countries recognised the need to deescalate the nuclear threat. Various bilateral agreements mentioned below, were the steps taken by these two countries, to achieve this goal. Beginning with Partial Test Ban Treaty (PTBT) of 1963, to the recent New Start Treaty of 2011, both nations have tried to decrease their vertical arsenal. Despite these measures, as on 2013, "Russia has 1,480 deployed strategic warheads, the Federation of American Scientists estimates Russia has another 1,022 non -deployed strategic warheads, approximately 2,000 tactical nuclear warheads, and additional thousands are awaiting dismantlement"[147]. The US arsenal is equally matched, as in 2013 the US has approximately 5,113 nuclear warheads of which 1,654 are strategically deployed nuclear warheads, tactical nuclear arsenal numbers 500 warheads and non -deployed strategic arsenal is approximately 2,800[148]. This demonstrates that even today they have a substantial number of nuclear stockpiles between them. Various treaties signed by them are given in the table below:-

Table: 7 US- Russia Nuclear Disarmament Treaties

S. NO	Treaty	Year	Salient Feature
1	Partial Test Ban Treaty	1963	Prohibited all testing of nuclear weapons except underground.
2	Nuclear Non Proliferation Treaty	1968	Based on non-proliferation, disarmament, and the right to peacefully use nuclear technology.
3	Strategic Arms Limitation Talk 1(SALT)	1972	USSR and USA to decrease the deployment of ICBM and SLBMs
4	Anti-Ballistic Missile treaty (ABM)	1972	USSR and USA to decrease the deployment of ABM interceptors
5	SALT II	1979	Placed limits on ICBM/SLBM launchers and MIRVs
6	Intermediate Range Nuclear Forces Treaty(INF)	1987	Global ban on short- and long-range nuclear weapons systems, as well as an intrusive verification regime.
7	Strategic Arms Reduction Talk -1(START)	Signed 1991 Ratified 94	Limited the number of long range nuclear warheads and ballistic missiles between USA and USSR.
8	START-11	Signed 1993 never Ratified	Limit the deployment of warheads to 3,000 to 3,500 and prohibited MIRVs and ICBMs
9	Strategic Offensive Treaty(SORT)	Signed 2002 Force 2003	USA and USSR agreed to reduce their "strategic nuclear warheads"
10	Comprehensive Test Ban Treaty (CTBT)	Signed 1996 Not Ratified	Bans all nuclear explosions in all environments.
11	New Start Treaty	Signed 2010 Ratified 2011	Both USA and Russia agreed to decrease the deployment of nuclear warhead substantially

Source: Compiled from Arms control .organisation

Out of all the treaties mentioned above, the main treaty which will have a direct impact on the two powers is the New Start Treaty. Conversely CTBT will have a more global impact. One needs to analyse CTBT because with China's emergence as a major power the requirement from various sections is to have more multilateral treaties so that other Nuclear Weapon States especially China could be involved in the disarmament process.

If this treaty is ratified by all the NWS and put into force, then it will have a cascading effect on the other nuclear states and will consequently be a shot in the arm for global peacekeepers as they would then come much closer to achieving their goal of global nuclear disarmament.

Comprehensive Nuclear Test Ban Treaty (CTBT)

The CTBT text states[149]:-

- It makes it mandatory for all states not to carry out nuclear tests/explosions.

- The verification regime – the International Monitoring System has the right to conduct on-site inspections. This has facilities for seismological monitoring and radionuclide monitoring systems.

- All State Parties, irrespective of their technical and financial capabilities, will enjoy equal right of verification and assume equal obligation to accept these verification.

- Its International Data System has made all data available, both raw and processed, and any reporting products, to all states parties, It also says that it will coordinate to provide additional data also if the state so desired.

- Article VI also mentions ways to settle disputes arising due to the application or the interpretation of this Treaty.

This treaty should be ratified by all the countries as it is a systematic and progressive effort of the world community to first reduce nuclear weapons globally and then ultimately to eliminate those weapons through a strict and effective international control[150].

The encouraging fact is that this treaty has been signed by 183 states and ratified by 159 states. However some major and minor Nuclear Weapon States like US, China, India, Pakistan have not ratified it, and until they ratify it, this treaty's potential cannot be effectively utilized.

Shortcomings and Suggestions

This treaty was signed on 10 September 1996 and even after a decade this treaty has not been ratified by many Nuclear Weapon States mainly USA and China. The treaty cannot be effective because 6 out of 8 Nuclear Weapon States still have reservations about it and have not ratified it.

1. The treaty bans nuclear explosions but the nations can still develop Tactical Nuclear Weapon (TNW) and first generation weapons of 15 – 50 kilotons (which do not require nuclear testing) for local/ regional wars, which create instability and proliferation problems. The possibility of TNWs being acquired by Non State Actors, especially by those nations that do not have a sound command and control system makes the nuclear threat a reality. An amendment should be introduced to deal, mainly ban this class of weapons so that the threat level is not lowered which is an essential step of disarmament.

2. The major concern according to US officials is that the International Monitoring System is not a foolproof system because there is no concrete definition given of what a nuclear test is. Some nations can carry out nuclear explosions of very low yield, below few hundred tons or at times even less than one ton of nuclear yield .This becomes very difficult to detect as these can be carried out in small labs with minuscule radioactive material. Furthermore, the Americans have an apprehension that the Russian "hydro-nuclear experiments" and repeated non explosive chain reaction could be helpful in maintaining the inventory of Russian nuclear weapons and it would go undetected even by advanced U.S. Atomic Energy Detection System (AEDS)[151], Thus to remove this asymmetry, zero yield should be the criteria along with banning scaled

miniaturized nuclear experiments, for experimental proof test, of nations' stockpiled nuclear arsenals. [152]

3. The development of new weapons should be banned and efforts by countries like Russia and China employ low-yield, clean, penetrating, Electro Magnetic Pulse (EMP) nuclear weapons[153] as primary means of attack should be discouraged, since these actions will further increase the race for more sophistication and miniaturization. Thus it is essential that low yield nuclear tests also be banned.

4. It is difficult for the treaty to come into force as it requires the ratification of 44 special states which include US, China, India, Pakistan Israel etc. Amongst the P5 only three countries, namely, Russia, UK and France have ratified it. The treaty's authenticity can only be seen, if all the above mentioned countries ratify it, which at the moment seems to be a difficult task, as the countries are very staunchly divided due to their narrow domestic objectives.

5. If the states are going to continue sustaining nuclear stockpiles, it is hard to envision any substantial progress and the mutual mistrust amongst nations will hinder them from building a consensus in working together for a common cause that is Global Disarmament ultimately leading to Global Zero.

Treaty on the Non-Proliferation of Nuclear Weapons (NPT)

Nuclear weapons proliferation is the biggest challenge facing the nations today. The NPT is an approach that was supposed to tackle the horizontal proliferation of weapons. It was signed on 1st July, 1968 and came into force in 1970[154]. Since then it has achieved mixed results. On one hand, the NPT can claim that it has persuaded countries like South Africa, Ukraine, Belarus and Kazakhstan to renounce their nuclear programme, and the former soviet republics have handed over their weapons to Russia. However; on the other hand it has been unsuccessful in stopping new nuclear countries like India, Pakistan and North Korea from becoming Nuclear Weapon States. It has also failed in preventing countries like Israel and Iran, from developing their covert nuclear plans. Even countries like Japan and South Korea have the capabilities required to develop the weapon at short notice. This depicts that the treaty has been ineffective in all three departments and needs to be amended if it needs to survive and become universally accepted.

Pillars of NPT

- Articles 1 and 2 emphasise the principle of non-proliferation. This however is not followed universally. There has been vertical and horizontal nuclear proliferation by nations, and the latter is due to the covert nuclear support to non-nuclear weapon nations by the NWS, which has gone unpunished .It had stated that NPT prevents NWS from transferring nuclear weapon technology to any Non-Nuclear Weapon States and they in turn should avoid receiving the same from the former under any condition.

- Secondly Article VI of the treaty lays stress on negotiations by the NWS for effective nuclear disarmament and ultimately complete disarmament under strict effective international control. However the NWS have been unsuccessful in successfully achieving this goal

- Finally Articles IV and V give all the parties, the right to peaceful use of nuclear energy under appropriate international observations and procedures mainly through IAEA safeguards. The scientific knowledge and technology for the same could be shared by all the member – states.

India's Position

India was one of the few countries who had highlighted the discriminatory aspect of this treaty that causes a mismatch between the responsibilities of NWS and NNWS. However since the time India declared herself an NWS she acknowledges her duty as a responsible nuclear power and is even ready to join the NPT as a NWS and abide by all the articles of the treaty. It is up to the world community to amend the charter, since the global scenario has altered the power dynamics and if the world community desires that the treaty be uniformly accepted, then new Nuclear Weapon States should be encouraged to join it and the treaty must be redefined accordingly.

Weaknesses and Suggestions

- **Not a Binding Force:** It is voluntary, like any other treaty and only those nations that have abandoned or are not pursuing their nuclear weapons development programme are parties to it. Any country that wants to continue its nuclear weapon development programme is free to do so by not signing the treaty. It is the P5 countries that have the capability to pressurise non-participating countries to sign the treaty but they themselves are disunited and have their own narrow interest to achieve. The Americans ignored Pakistan's nuclear programme, China did not stop North Korea's nuclear weapon programme and both China and Russia ignored Iran's' nuclear programme. The NPT can be successful only when the P5 nations take a major interest in enforcing the objectives of the NPT without covertly supporting other nonnuclear states in their nuclear development programmes.

- **Failure to Prevent Proliferation** The treaty had failed to prevent the proliferation of nuclear weapons both vertically as well as horizontally (the latter more so). The fact that India, Pakistan and North Korea have declared themselves as Nuclear Weapon States and the presence of many threshold states illustrates that this treaty had several articles that were weak and prejudiced. It was not based on sound non – proliferation arguments and it did not have punitive measures enshrined for defaulters.

- **Failure to achieve global disarmament.** Article VI of the treaty probes the members to take effective measures relating to cessation of the nuclear arms race at an early date and to nuclear disarmament, and on a treaty on general and complete disarmament under strict and effective international control[155]. This has been a failure. Though new treaties like the NSG (Nuclear Supplier's Group), PSI (Proliferation Security Initiative), etc. are being designed to curtail this proliferation, the ground fact remains that when it comes to a collective disarmament of the P5 countries, there is no concrete effort made from their side to achieve this goal. For example, the Chinese are constantly increasing their nuclear arsenal and they believe in a zero sum game. Article VI should be amended by designing a feasible disarmament time frame with international verification agencies to monitor the procedure.

- **Amendment of Article X** This article gives nations the right to withdraw from the treaty under extraordinary conditions, but it does not specify what those extraordinary conditions are. This has been exploited by several Non-Nuclear Weapon States. Once they have availed of all the benefits of peaceful nuclear programme, they could easily divert the Uranium and Plutonium for producing their own nuclear weapons, which is exactly what North Korea and Iran did. Thus often it was seen that the Non-Nuclear Weapon States could leave the obligation of the NPT if they were caught cheating[156] .This clause leads to continual nuclear proliferation without consequences as the nations' know that they can leave the treaty at any point in time using this clause as a pretext, hence it needs to be abrogated.

- **Non-compliance of Article IV and V** Most of the P5 countries especially the US, are reluctant to share nuclear technology because this technology could be misused and used for dual purposes for example the same gas centrifuge that can be used to enrich Uranium for nuclear fuel can also be used to enrich weapons-grade Uranium. The same reactor technology used to power homes can also be used for breeding Plutonium.[157]

- **The Additional Protocol should be made Mandatory** .This protocol should be made mandatory rather than voluntary as this will ensure strict non –proliferation.

- **No Penalty for Non-compliance** NWS can continue to aid NNWS to build their nuclear programme covertly. Due to the emergence of a multipolar world the P5 nation's clandestine activities that support North Korea and Pakistan end up nullifying the basic principle of non-proliferation

Security regimes are hard to create and even harder to sustain[158] , and treaties can become more relevant and survivable if appropriate amendments are created while keeping in mind the changing trends.

National Security Summit

There has been an increase in the number of states capable of developing nuclear weapons and most of the newly developed states have fragile political institutions and poor command and control systems. This exposes the world to Nuclear Terrorism", To counter this the National Security Summit was proposed by President Obama. During his speech in Prague in 2009[159], he highlighted the need for a strategy to address international terrorism. In his three pronged approach he emphasised the need to

- Reduce and eventually eliminate nuclear weapon

- Strengthening NPT

- Preventing Terrorist from acquiring nuclear material and weapons

As of 2012 there is still an estimated 1, 380 tons of highly enriched Uranium and 495 tons of separated Plutonium around the world, (enough to make more than 55,000 simple nuclear weapons[160]) is a major cause for concern and this organisations' primary aim is to address the challenge of nuclear safety, security and terrorism. The Global Nuclear Security Summit was held in 2010 in Washington DC and 46 nations participated. The Washington summit concluded that "nuclear terrorism is one of the most challenging threats to international security, and strong nuclear security measures are the most effective means to prevent terrorists, criminals, or other unauthorised actors from acquiring nuclear materials, (and) to prevent Non State Actors from obtaining the information or technology required to use such material for malicious purposes," [161] The 2012 Seoul Nuclear Security Summit had 53 heads of state and representatives of the UN, IAEA, EU and INTERPOL in attendance. These states had 99 per cent of nuclear material holdings. This meeting, held for a common cause, makes this summit a special effort by the world community to address pressing issues which have global ramifications. The Communiqué highlighted:-

- The setting up special actions in 11 areas. Some of them involve eliminating and minimizing the use of highly enriched Uranium, Strengthening the management of spent nuclear fuels and radioactive wastes, ensuring the safety of nuclear installations etc.

- It reflects the need to address both nuclear safety and security in a coherent manner and to provide an enforceable time line for the states to announce their voluntary actions on minimising the use of HEU.

- It emphasised the need to secure nuclear spent fuel and radioactive waste in a better way

- It focused on specific measures to prevent radioactive terrorism

India's role

India has often depicted her commitment to international cooperation on safety and security issues. It supports International legal instruments, IAEA and other such global initiatives. It volunteered for capacity build up, by announcing the setting up of "Global Centre for Nuclear Energy Partnership". This centre will consist of four Schools dealing with Advanced Nuclear Energy System Studies, Nuclear Security, Radiation Safety, and the application of Radioisotopes and Radiation Technology in the areas of healthcare, agriculture and food and the centre will conduct research and development of design systems that are intrinsically safe, secure, proliferation resistant and sustainable.[162] There was a lot of rhetoric involved at the Summit, but the countries failed to take some concrete measures away from the discussion. This inability to nail down the specifics and details makes one question the success of this treaty.

Short comings and suggestions

The current nuclear security regime is not robust, adaptable, or coherent enough to adequately protect against the intensifying and evolving threats posed by nuclear terrorism in the 21st century[163]

- The summit is voluntary and there is no binding assurance from any of the nations. This is because nations consider nuclear safety a national prerogative, and they do not want their national sovereignty to be infringed on. The fact is that nations need to understand that nuclear accidents are incidents with global repercussions. They are very rarely confined to a particular regional diameter. All the nations, therefore, have an international obligation which is bigger than their national agenda .They need to cooperate and be more transparent as far as their nuclear inventory is concerned. Such a step will aid global monitoring, which would in turn become a huge aid in combating the theft of nuclear materials.

- Nations need to have better transparency and greater cohesion within their nuclear safety and security systems. The involvement of the IAEA as an independent and neutral body, to assess the safety standards is a step that should be welcomed. The IAEA's advance nuclear security centres of excellence for information sharing, can really help in bringing transparency to the system and help in achieve uniform global procedures.

- There is no database available regarding the presence of nuclear materials in the world. There is a need to develop a reporting system whereby the nations submit their nuclear inventory which would consist of the fissile material, radioactive material, spent fuel and nuclear waste. This inventory will help in creating a more transparent environment and preventing nuclear theft.

- The NSS included many cooperative issues but specific controversial issues were left unattended. There is a need to have a long term vision that includes pertinent issues with a timeframe for their implementation and review.

- There is no unified instrument for monitoring nuclear safety, one needs to build a unified and durable nuclear governance regime. [164]

- Many states have still not ratified the 2005 amendment of the Convention on the Physical Protection of Nuclear Material

(CPPNM). This should be made mandatory for all the nations who are a party to NSS.

Thus by integrating nations, through transparent systems the political will to shoulder greater global responsibility can be enhanced.

Proliferation Security Initiative

Failure of the "*So San*" incident compelled the Bush government to re-examine the policy of preventing and containing the proliferation of WMD to hostile states and terrorist organizations.

On May 31, 2003, President Bush officially proposed the PSI in his speech in Krakow[165] when he stated that "*When weapons of mass destruction or their components are in transit, we must have the means and authority to seize them. So today I announce a new effort to fight proliferation called the Proliferation Security Initiative*

The members of 10 nations formed the core group and the meeting took place in Madrid on June 12, 2003. The charter declared that measures would be taken to stop the movement of WMDs and missiles, to and from various states and Non State Actors. Thus an organization was created to strengthen international counter proliferation capabilities.

The characteristics of PSI Statement of Interdiction, Principles after its issuance in September 2003 are as follows[166]:-

- "Undertake effective measures, either alone or in concert with other states, for interdicting" proliferation transfers.

- Streamline procedures for sharing information on suspected proliferation.

- Take specific action to avoid proliferation from its own territory, interdict suspected proliferation shipments under its jurisdiction, "seriously consider" allowing others to board and search its flag vessels suspected of proliferation, interdict or deny over flight to suspected prolife rant aircraft, and inspect and seize any proliferation trans-shipment cargoes.

In simple terms this initiative aims to stop shipments of biological, chemical, and nuclear weapons, as well as missiles and goods that could be used to deliver or produce such weapons, to terrorists and countries suspected of trying to acquire WMD[167] . Initiative participants intend to carry out cargo interdictions at sea, in the air, or on land.[168] There are more than 100 countries which are its members.

India's status on PSI

India has attended the PSI exercises as an observer, but has not yet formally joined the PSI, despite U.S. encouragement. The reason for this delay is mainly because the operational effectiveness of the exercise is doubtful and it actually has an escalatory potential. India would prefer a UN backed legal multilateral formal framework to deal with the proliferation issues. There are a lot of questions that need to be answered satisfactorily, before India joins the organization. One can argue hypothetically that if India joins the exercise, does it possess the authority to interdict Pakistan's ships, if it carries WMD or nuclear material from North Korea or China? In such a tense situation will the US back India? If not, then there is really no point in joining an organization which will not serve the purpose of de-escalating nuclear proliferation from Pakistan and North Korea. Moreover, there are several legal issues which do not allow the exercise to become a universally acceptable initiative.

Limitations of PSI and Recommendations

- Lack of a formal mechanism. There is no international secretariat and no distinct formal funding. It's more of an activity rather than institutional work. It is just a cooperative measure and the charter is not legally binding for the states. A formal institution would give it more credence and sustainability.

- Lack of transparency. The Secretary of State Condoleezza Rice, on the second anniversary of PSI, announced that the PSI was responsible for 11 interdictions in the previous nine months.[169] But the interdictions themselves as well as their operational details are usually not declared publicly. This lack of publicly available information has led to questions regarding the actual success of the organization. Public information will make more countries become aware of the incidents and will encourage them to join the organization, making it more universal in nature.

- Legal Issues-Countries like China and Indonesia argue that PSI members are violating the Laws of the sea (UNCLOS) as international law guarantees freedom of the sea. Article 23 of the United Nations Convention on the Law of the Sea (UNCLOS) allows ships "carrying nuclear or other inherently dangerous or noxious substances" the right of innocent passage through territorial seas[170] as long as they "carry documents and observe special precautionary measures established for such ships by international agreements." Their right to operate on the high seas is uncontested.

The PSI has 100 members but it is often considered a "US-led" initiative that targets specific states, especially Iran and North Korea. Indonesia's Foreign Minister Hassan Wirajuda argued that the PSI "initiative was not initiated through a multilateral process, but only a group of nations that have a common goal to conduct a certain initiatives."[171] It is clear that any such initiative if backed by the UN would have more credibility and relative more acceptability.

Future trends

Nuclear Weapon free zones (NWFZ)

If the countries of a region were to voluntarily commit themselves to freeing their region from nuclear weapons by pledging not to manufacture, acquire, deploy or test nuclear weapon that region is known as the Nuclear Weapon Free Zone. These have been acknowledged and propagated in many forums. The NPT and the UN General Assembly have adopted them, as being positive steps towards nuclear disarmament. However, they have attained mixed success. On one hand, the world has witnessed the creation of five Nuclear Weapon Free Zones; on the other hand, efforts to create NWFZs in the Middle East and South Asia could not be accomplished.

The basic requirement - NWFZs require commitment and determination from all the countries residing in that region. The need to come together with a unified will to ratify and enforce the NWFZ Treaty. The treaty cannot be successful if even one of the countries of the region refuses to ratify it, for example, The Treaty of Tlatelolco was signed on February 14 1967, but it came into force only in 2002 when Cuba ratified it. Along with this there is also a protocol which should be followed by the five Nuclear Weapon States .These protocols, which are legally binding, call upon the Nuclear Weapon States to respect the status of the zones and not to use or threaten to use nuclear weapons against treaty states-parties and such declarations of non-use of nuclear weapons are referred to as Negative Security[172]. The territory mentioned in NWFZ is understood to include all land holdings, internal waters, territorial seas, and archipelagic waters.[173] There have been five Nuclear Weapon Free Zones till now .Some of them have entered in to force and some still await ratification by all the parties of that Zone. The five NWFZ are as follows :-

- The Treaty of Tlatelolco (Latin America and the Caribbean) Entered into force: October 23, 2002.

- The Treaty of Rarotonga (South Pacific) Entered into force: December 11, 1986.

- The Treaty of Bangkok (Southeast Asia) Entered into force: March 27, 1997.

- The Treaty of Pelindaba (Africa) Entered into force: July 15, 2009.

- Central Asian Nuclear-Weapon-Free Zone Treaty.

- (CANWFZ). Entered into force on March 21, 2009.

India's Position

Global, verifiable and non-discriminatory nuclear disarmament is a national security objective[174] .India's nuclear doctrine clearly mentions the policy of "No First Use" (NFU). Since the NFU of nuclear weapons is India's basic commitment, India will make every effort to persuade other states possessing nuclear weapons to join an international treaty banning first use and this entails nuclear free zones also. It further provides unqualified negative security assurances; it states that India shall work for internationally binding unconditional negative security assurances by Nuclear Weapon States to Non-Nuclear Weapon States.

Challenges faced by NWFZ

- The biggest challenge faced by the Nuclear Weapon Free Zone is the negative security assurance from the Nuclear Weapon States. The Treaty of Bangkok has still not been ratified by the NWS as they have lot of reservations. Protocol I and Protocol II (ban on nuclear testing in the Nuclear Weapon Free Zone) of The Treaty of Pelindaba has not been ratified by the US[175].

- Regional zones are left with the challenge of not only obtaining full ratification of their treaties and protocols, but also to look into the continued verification of compliance.

- The question of the transit of nuclear weapons in that region remains uncertain for most NWFZs[176] To what extent will NWFZs be able to prevent the presence of nuclear weapons in the seas before coming into conflict with the Law of the Sea needs to be seen?[177]

- It has been observed that the treaty is effective only when the nations of that region do not possess nuclear weapons and all the nations of the region have the same objective of making their region a NWFZ. If one of the nations has a separate nationalistic agenda, the free zone cannot be achieved as was seen in the case of Middle East where Israel and Iran are major roadblocks towards an NWFZ status. Hence the formulation of such a treaty is doubtful in Middle East though majority of nations in Middle East support it.

Possibility of a NWFZ in South Asia

South Asia has seen the emergence of two Nuclear Weapon States namely India and Pakistan. If the region wants to prevent further proliferation of nuclear weapons and create a NWFZ in South Asia, then it is essential for both these countries to disarm their nuclear weapons. Such a step is not possible at the moment, since both countries have different threat perceptions, and they consider nuclear weapons as potential deterrence factors that would help in maintaining the geo – strategic stability. For India, any talk of nuclear disarmament is linked to broader global nuclear disarmament. It is also important to take into consideration China's nuclear status which is an ever looming sword over the Indian peninsular. China on the other hand, is a permanent nuclear weapon state and they have already declared that any talk on disarmament is possible only when US and Russia decrease their nuclear arsenal to the Chinese level. Pakistan's nuclear programme is linked to the threat they perceive in the Indian nuclear status. The conclusion therefore is that the process of disarmament is a chain reaction, which will require a lot of Confidence Building Measures (CBM) by all the three countries before any substantial result is achieved. However, there are certain regional measures that could speed up the process, for example, both India and Pakistan can help create a South Asian Nuclear Weapon Free Zone by creating the same protocols which has been followed by the P5 nations, especially the protocol I and II of the African Nuclear Weapon Free Zone treaty, Under Article 1, each Protocol Party undertakes not to use or threaten to use a nuclear explosive device against (1) any Treaty Party[178] and Protocol II Under Article 1 states, each Party to this Protocol is obligated "not to test or assist or encourage the testing of any nuclear explosive device anywhere within the African Nuclear Weapon Free Zone."[179] .India and Pakistan as NWS can accept the above said protocol by incorporating it in the South Asian Nuclear Weapon Free Zone. Thus by creating a NWFZ in South Asia, they can dissuade other countries from going nuclear, and by giving negative assurances, they can build better relations with nations of this region and prevent further nuclear proliferation.

Global Zero

A nuclear weapon free world is a long cherished dream and Global zero is the process initiated to achieve this dream. This movement which originated in 2008 is the culmination of the collective efforts of 300 international non-partisan groups of world leaders.

They articulated that in a phased manner it is possible to destroy all nuclear devices held by official/unofficial nuclear states. Their desired comprehensive goal is to establish a complete verification and enforcement system, to strengthen safeguards on the civilian nuclear fuel cycle and to prevent diversion of materials to build weapons. They target 2030 as the year by which the proportionate dismantlement of all nuclear arsenal to zero is possible, provided the four phased targets are met with. The first phase of which has already started, it includes the START replacement accord, the new START in which Obama's latest proposal was to limit nuclear arsenal by 2018 and further if fully implemented it would reduce the stockpile by one third roughly to 1000,warheads for each country[180] . However; it still remains to be seen whether they will agree to reduce their target to 500 warheads each, since this first step is the foundation for the second phase of the multilateral framework where other nations could be asked to initiate their disarmament process. Negotiating a global zero accord is very difficult to achieve, as it requires all nuclear capable countries to come to a unanimous decision to decrease their nuclear weapon in a phased and verifiable manner to a base level. It is difficult to visualise this organisation achieving its goal because it does not have the legal authority to bind nations to work for such a goal. At the moment, all it appears to be is a grand vision or a utopian dream at best. For its implementation, it would require world leaders to display a high level of maturity and extraordinary commitment. At the current rate of progress, it will be a challenge for them to achieve this in the time frame that has been set.

Nuclear Weapon Free World (NWFW)

This is the ultimate utopian vision that the world leadership collectively hopes to achieve. How much of this is possible and how fast it can be implemented depends on the commitment of the major Nuclear Weapon States. Like the movement towards Global Zero, the success of this movement is also dependent on the decisions and actions of world leaders'. There needs to be a more compromising stance to enable universal action. World leadership needs to find the will to sacrifice their national goals for larger objectives of world peace. There have been three views adopted by various academicians to approach this goal.

- **The Idealist Approach.** The supporters of this view consider the constant tussle between total disarmament and the arms control as a worthy battle specially when seen from a larger perspective of global peace. They consider arms control as the foundation step to achieve total disarmament. The idealist approach of NWFW is though accepted universally, but they find it difficult to articulate a time-bound executable programme. The main principle of this group is therefore a position of deep reductions in nuclear weapons first, from which then; abolition can be "envisaged, mapped and navigated later on. However they have failed to chart a detailed roadmap acceptable to all the nations.

- **The realist approach** also needs to be analysed because they have based their arguments on the fact that nuclear disarmament cannot be seen in isolation. As long as a nation has their national interest they will always find means to protect and enhance those interests. Nuclear weapons are a formidable means to achieve this goal and this makes the nuclear disarmament that much more complex and nation will be deterred from even planning the necessary steps. However "Stability in low numbers "may be the desired initial goal here.

- **The Pragmatic approach** directs a bold and time –bound programme, that calls for action by both the NWS as well as the NNWS, seeks to achieve nuclear disarmament not by a series of incremental moves, but in a time-frame, through a multilaterally negotiated, universal, non-discriminatory and internationally and effectively verifiable convention or treaty. The initiative commenced by Global Zero envisages such an approach.[181]

In conclusion one can say that both the realistic and pragmatic views are not mutually exclusive. As it is, one can argue that the stage is already set since the arguments of both the sides can be accommodated. With the new START having been negotiated, significant cuts could be achieved and vertical proliferation could be controlled but to curtail horizontal proliferation China and the other NNWS needs to be involved in a multilateral treaty negotiations The starting point for which can be a universally acceptable global maximum and minimum weapons criteria, which all nations needs to follow. In recent years, the twin threats of proliferation and terrorism have led to a growing chorus of world leaders calling for the global elimination of nuclear weapons. All that is missing is the will and commitment by the world leaders to an action plan. If that can be secured, the goal of a NWFW can indeed be achieved. The path is long and arduous but the ultimate goal will make it eminently worthwhile.

Endnotes

1 Muzaffer Ercan Yllmaz, "The New World Order: An Outline of the Post-Cold War Era", in Alternatives,Volume-7,No-4,2008

2 Willrich Mason, "Guarantee to Non-Nuclear State", Foreign Affairs, July,1966

3 Global Nuclear Weapons Count ,2002 Bulletin of Atomic Scientists at http://rense.com/general47/global.htm

4 "The Manhattan Project: Making the Atomic Bomb", American archives. com at www.atomicarchive.com

5 James R Arnold &Roberta Wiener ,Editors, (2012), Cold War: The essential Reference Guide, ABC-CLIO,LLC

6 Ibid

7 History of Russian Nuclear Industry, Rosatom at http://www.rosatom.ru/en/education/history/

8 Ibid

9 History of Russian Nuclear Industry in www.rosatom.ru

10 See n, 5, Cold War

11 Ibid

12 National Archives, "Explosion of the first British Bomb", at www.nationalarchives.gov.uk

13 "British French & Chinese Nuclear Weapon" Data Book V By Robert Snorris, Andrew S Burrows and Richard W Fieldhouse

14 Ibid

15 Ibid

16 Ibid

17 Lewis Wilson John, (1991), China Builds the Bomb, Stanford University Press

18 China's First Thermonuclear test, CTBTO Preparatory Commission, at http://www.ctbto.org/specials/testing-times/17-june-1967-chinas-first-thermonuclear-test/

19 Khan Feroz, (2012), Eating Grass: The making of the Pakistani Bomb,

20 "Who has the bomb" Times, June 3, 1985.

21 Project 706 from Wikipedia at http://en.wikipedia.org/wiki/Project-706

22 William Marsden "North Korea's 60-year-old nuclear programme" at http://o.canada.com/news/north-koreas-60-yar-old-nuclear-program

23 Richard Lloyd Parry. "North Korea is fully fledged nuclear power, experts agree". The Times (London). Retrieved, December 1, 2010

24 Chronology of US-North Korea Nuclear Missile Diplomacy, Arms Control Association, at http://www.armscontrol.org/factsheets/dprkchron

25 Ibid

26 "The Third Temple's Holy of Holies: Israel's Nuclear Weapons "Warner D. Farr at http://www.informationclearinghouse.info/article26442.htm

27 Ibid

28 Ibid

29 The US Defence Intelligence Agency, The Decades Ahead :1999-2020,July 1999 Excerpt from 160-page secret DIA report, first disclosed and reproduced in Rowan Scarborough, Rumsfeld's War(Regnery, 2004),

30 See n, 26,The Third Temple's Holy

31 Reinterpreting Japan's Constitution", Forbes Asia at http://www.forbes.com/sites/sheilaasmith/2014/07/03/reinterpreting-japans-constitution/

32 Sato's "Four pillar policy" at http://en.wikipedia.org/wiki/Japan's_non-nuclear_ weapons_policy

33 Takahashi Sugio, "Changing Military Dynamics in East Asia" ,Study of Innovation and Technology in China, Policy Brief 4, 2012at http://igcc.ucsd.edu/assets/001/503564.pdf

34 Park Chung Hee ,the CIA and the bomb, NAPSNet Special Report, at http://nautilus.org/napsnet/napsnet-special-reports/park-chung-hee-the-cia-and-the-bomb/#axzz3BUR1MLCZ

35 "South Korean Special Weapons" http://www.globalsecurity.org/wmd/

world/rok/ index.html

36 *Dafna Linzer,* "S. Korea Nuclear Project Detailed Work Called Near Weapons Grade", *Washington Post,* 12 September, 2004

37 International Atomic Energy Agencies: IAEA Board Concludes Consideration of Safeguards in South Korea

38 " S. Korea, US agree to set N. Korean nuclear deterrence policy by 2014", Korean Times Oct 25, 20012

39 Roe, Sam, "An atomic threat made in America". *Chicago Tribune* Retrieved July 1, 2009.

40 Kerr, Paul, "Iran's Nuclear Programme: Status". Congressional Research Service Retrieved October 2, 2012

41 Implementation of the NPT Safeguards Agreement and relevant provision of Security Council resolution in the Islamic Republic of Iran, Report by Director General, IAEA, at https://www.iaea.org/Publications/Documents/Board/2011/gov2011-65.pdf

42 Besant, Alexander, "Iran expected to sharply increase uranium capacity, IAEA report". *Globalpost* Retrieved November 17, 2012.

43 Ibid

44 Andrew Clapham, (2009), "Non-State Actors" , Post Conflict Peace Building: A Lexicon, Oxford University Press, .

45 Raghavan B S ," Fight the War on New Terrorism to the finish," http://www.rediff.com/ news/2008/may/14guest1.htm

46 Bruce Hoffman,(2006), "Inside Terrorism" , New York, Columbia University Press

47 Jasjit Singh Air Commodore (Retd),"Why Nuclear Weapons?", Nuclear India ,(1998), New Delhi, KW Publications,

48 Global Nuclear Weapons Inventories, 2014 Center for Arms Control and Non –Proliferation at http://armscontrolcenter.org/issues/nuclearweapons/articles/fact_sheet_global_nuclear_weapons_inventories_in_2014/

49 Kishner Andrew, "US Conducts Subcritical Nuclear Test" ,Oped News ,12 September 2010 at http://www.opednews.com/articles/U-S-CONDUCTS-SUBCRITICAL-by-Andrew-Kishner-100920-795.html

50 Andrew Kishner in "Revival of Nuclear Arms Race :US conducts new underground Nuclear Tests" Global Research, 30 Sep 2012

51 ibid

52 For a detailed account see "The Voyage of the Empress of China" by John W. Swift, P. Hodgkinson and Samuel W. Woodhouse in The Pennsylvania Magazine of History and Biography Vol. 63, No. 1, Jan. 1939.

53 Section One "Current and emerging US National Security Interests" US Force Posture Strategy in Asia Pacific Region: An independent Assessment a CSIS Publication.

54 US and Japan Sign Agreement on Host Nation Support,21 January 2011,Embassy of the United State, at http://japan.usembassy.gov/e/p/tp-20110121-72.html

55 Harlan and Whitlock "US likely to scale down", Washington Post, February 8 ,2012

56 Tanguy Struye de Swielande "The Reassertion of the United States in the Asia-Pacific Region" at http://strategicstudiesinstitute.army.mil/pubs/parameters/articles/2012spring/struye_de_swielande.pdf

57 See for further information US Force Posture Strategy in the Asia Pacific Region: An Independent Assessment, Center for Strategic and International Studies,2012,

58 Lyon Rod, "Is Another Guan Doctrine Movement Approaching in Asia?', The Strategists, Australian Strategic Policy Institute,28 February 2013

59 Stephen Ranger "The Limits of Assertive Behaviour :US –China relations and the South China Sea ",East Asia Institute, EAI-US China Relation Briefing No 2 at file:///C:/Users/Roshan/Downloads/201202011891889.pdf

60 Military Balance 2014, IISS, Routledge Publications,2014

61 Division of Korea, Wikipedia at en.wikipedia.org/wiki/division of Korea

62 Ibid

63 Armistice Agreement for the Restoration of South Korea State, National Archive, at wwwarchive.govt/historical_docs

64 Bunn George and Rhinelander B John, "NPT Withdrawal: Time for the Security Council to Step In" ,Arms Control Association, May 2005

65 Duyion Kim, Fact Sheet :North Korea's Nuclear and Ballistic Missile Program, Center for Arms Control and Non Proliferation, July 2013

66 North Korean Missile,FAS at www.fas.org/nuke/guide/d_prk/missile

67 North Korea's Missile Programme, BBCs NEWS, 12 December, 2012, file:///C:/   Documents%20and%20Settings/user/Desktop/BBC%20News%20- %20North%20 Korea's%20missile%20programmeme.htm

68 Hyung Jin Kim, "North Korea Celebrates Launch of Long Range Rocket", The Washington Times ,11 December 2012

69 David E. Sanger and Choe Sang-Hun "North Korea Confirmed it conducted Third Nuclear Test", 11 February 2013, New York Times

70 Pollack Jousha, "Ballistic Trajectory the Evolution of North Korea's Ballistic Missile Market, Non Proliferation Review, Vol 18,No 2,July 2011

71 Hatf 5 (Ghauri) ,Missile Threat , at missilethrear.com/missile/hatf5

72 "Report to Congress, January – June 1999. Unclassified Report to Congress on the Acquisition of Technology Relating to Weapons of Mass Destruction and Advanced Conventional Munitions Central Intelligence Agency" Cia. gov. Retrieved March 1, 2012

73 Ronald Sieget, "The Missile Program of North Korea ,Iraq and Iran", Institute for Defense and Disarmament Studies, September 2001

74 Tom G Jel Ten, "What North Korea's Rocket Launch tells us about Iran's Role", NPR, 14 December 2012

75 Butler, D, "North Korea ranks last for nuclear weapons security". January 2012, Christian Science Monitor ,at http://www.csmonitor.com/ World/ Latest-News-Wires/2012/0112/North-Korea-ranks-last-for-nuclear-weaponssecurity

76 South Korean Presidential Election,1948, Wikipedia

77 Mutual Defense Treaty between US and Republic of Korea, The Avalon Project, 1 October 1953,

78 David J. Berteau, Guy Ben-Ari, Joachim Hofbauer, Priscilla Hermann, and Sneha Raghava, Asia Defence Spending, 2000-2011, CSIS,

79 Jayshree Bajoria, and Youkyung Lee, "The US-South Korea Alliance", Council On Foreign Relations,13 October 2011

80 US, South Korea could Tabletop Nuclear Deterrence Exercises, Strategic Defense Intelligence, 6 October 2012

81 Garamme Jin, "US, South Korea participate in Nuke Deterrence Exercise", US Department of Defense, 05 October 2012

82 " U.S. flies B-2 stealth bombers to S. Korea in extended deterrence mission, aimed at North", CBS NEWS 28 *March ,2013*

83 Ibid

84 Veress & Pomper, "Dealing with South Korea's Spent Fuel Challenges without Pyro processing", Arms Control and Association, July/August/2013

85 Taylor Brendan ,"Japan and South Korea: The limits of Alliance", Survival; Global Politics and Strategy, Oct-Nov 2012

86 North Korea has 10,000 Km range, BBC News Asia,23 December 2012

87 Vivek Kapur "Ballistic Missile Proliferation: Implications for India "IDSA Comment , 19 December 2012 at http://idsa.in/~idsa/idsacomments/ BallisticMissileProliferationImplicationsforIndia_vkapur_191212.html

88 The Six Presidents, US Institute for Peace ,at Iranpremier.USip.org/resource/ six president

89 Ehud Eilam , "A New Take on the Iranian-Israeli Conflict", Israel Journal of

Foreign Affairs II: 2 (2008).

90 Bergman Ronen, ,(2008), The Secret War With Iran, New York, Free Press

91 Weston Mark, (2008), Prophet and Princess :Saudi Arabia from Mohammed to the President, New Jersey, John Wiley & Sons

92 Dalia Dassa Kaye,Alireza Nader ,Parisa Roshan "Israel and Iran - A Dangerous Rivalry" Rand Publication 2011 at http://www.rand.org/content/dam/rand/pubs/monographs/2011/RAND_MG1143.pdf

93 Sharp MJeremy, "US Foreign Aid to Israel", Congressional Research Services,11 April 2014

94 US may leave PAC3 system in Israel, at http://www.liveleak.com/view?i=388_1254827331

95 See n , 92, Dalia Dassa

96 Abdullah Toukan and Anthony H. Cordesman, *Study on a Possible Israeli Strike on Iran's Nuclear Development Facilities*, Center for Strategic & International Studies, Washington, DC,08 March , 2009.

97 Lavette Marianne, "Iranian Undisputed Weapon: Power to Block the Strait of Hormuz", Daily News, as cited in National Geographic News,6 February 2012

98 Bruce Riedel, "The Israel-Anti Attack –Iran Brigade", The Daily Beast, Nov 7, 2011

99 Rick Gladstone, "Iran Suggests Attacks on Computer Systems Came From the U.S. and Israel", The New York Times, Dec 25, 2012

100 Frank Gardner, "Is Iran already under covert attack?", BBS NEWS Middle East , 15 Nov , 2011

101 See n, 233, Dalia Dasa Kaye,

102 Special Analysis: Israel- Iran Potential for Conflict .Executive Summary in MSA Worldview, 22 Aug, 2012

103 "First Step Understandings Regarding the Islamic Republic of Iran's Nuclear Programme, The White House, Office of the Press Secretary, 23 Nov, 2013

104 Michele Chabin, "Israel calls Iran Nuclear Deal a Historic Mistake", USA Today 24 November , 2013

105 Ibid

106 Middle East Boils, Iran Stirs the pot with Ships to Suez Canal, 21 February, Times

107 Sean O'Connor, "Strategic SAM Deployed in Iran", Air Power Australia, January 2013

108 Iran Missile Arsenal, Intelligence on Iran at www.Iranintelligence.com/arsenal

109 Saudi Nuclear Weapon on Order from Pakistan ,BBC NEWS Middle East,06 November 2013

110 Gulf State Requesting ABM Capable System, Defense Industry Daily,15 July 2014

111 Gulf Cooperation Council and Ballistic Missile Defence, Frank A. Rose, Deputy Assistant ,Secretary, Bureau of Arms Control, Verification and Compliance, Peter Huessy Breakfast Series; Capitol Hill Club, Washington, DC, May 14, 2014

112 Ibid

113 Ibid

114 Nidhi Verma, India's Jan-June Iran oil imports climb by a third –trade", 23 July 2014, Reuters.com

115 To know more read, Looking to the Future by   Mohammed ElBaradei, Statement of Director General,   September 14, 2009 ,Fifty third Regular Session of the IAEA General Conference ,2009

116 Warner Anne Cesley, "Trans Sahara Counter Terrorism Partnership", CAN Analysis and Solutions, March 2014

117 Country Report Middle East and Africa, Office of the Coordinator for Counter Terrorism, Country Report on Terrorism 2011

118 Country Reports on Terrorism 2011 United States Department of State Publication Bureau of Counterterrorism Released April 2012

119 Ibid

120 Allison Graham, "Graham Allison Commentary: Don't Underestimate Nuclear Terror Threat, Detroit News,09 October 2009

121 Bunn Mathew, "Securing the Bomb 2010:Securing all Nuclear Materials in Four Years", Project on Managing Atom, Belfer Center for Science and International Affairs, Commissioned by NTI,2010

122 " Baghdad Bomb Fatalities pass 150", BBC News,26 October 2009

123 Nuclear Power in the World Today ,Updated on November 2013,World Nuclear Association at www.**world-nuclear**.org

124 Ibid

125 Mirosolav   Gregoric, Activities in Nuclear Security, Briefing for the 23 IAEA,CEG Planery Meeting, Rome,07 October 2009

126 Eliminating Nuclear Threats by Gareth Evans and Yoriko Kawaguchi Co-Chairs ,(2009), Report of the International Commission on Nuclear Non–proliferation and Disarmament, Canberra

127 Ibid

128 Kevin Crowley, "Are Nuclear Spent Fuel Pools Secure?" Transcript of

First Roundtable on Nuclear Security Issues, Council on Foreign Relations Washington DC, June 7, 2005, http://www.cfr.org/weapons-of-mass-destruction/nuclear-spent-fuel-poolssecure/p8967.

129 Tim Andrews, "Strengthening Global Nuclear Security: The Role of the IAEA," Presentation to the Nuclear Security Conference, King's College London,18 February , 2010.

130 Mathew Bunn, "Beyond Crisis: The unending Challenge of controlling nuclear Weapons and nuclear Materials, at file:///C:/Users/Roshan/Downloads/Chapter%209_Bunn_Security%20Crises_History.pdf

131 Ibid

132 NTI Nuclear Material Security Index Building a Framework for Assurance, Accountability, and Action, January 2012

133 "What is Radiological Emergency?," IAEA.ORG, at www-ns.iaea.org/tech-areas/emergency

134 To read more, Radiation Safety, at https://www.iaea.org/Publications/Booklets/Radiation/radsafe.html

135 Langford Everett R, Introduction to Weapons of Mass Destruction, Radiological, Chemical and Biological,(2004),New Jersey, John Willeng &Sons

136 For more see Sealed Radioactive Sources ,IAEA Division of Radiation, September 2005 at http://www.iaea.org/Publications/Booklets/SealedRadio active Sources/pdfs/flyer_public.pdf

137 Radiation Protection, US Environmental Protection Agency at http://www.epa.gov/radiation/understand/health_effects.html

138 Fact sheet on Dirty bomb,USNRC, AT http://www.nrc.gov/reading-rm/doc-collections/fact-sheets/fs-dirty-bombs.html

139 See,n, 126, Gareth Evans and Yoriko KawaGuchi

140 "Attacks on nuclear sites are best prevented by abolishing the plants" The Asahi Shimbun, Asia and Japan Watch, 08 March,2013

141 See,n, 126, Gareth Evans and Yoriko KawaGuchi

142 Ibid

143 Attacks on nuclear sites are best prevented by abolishing the plants" The Asahi Shimbun, Asia and Japan Watch March 8,2013

144 Ibid

145 Nuclear Disarmament, at http://en.wikipedia.org/wiki/Nuclear_ disarmament

146 Global Nuclear Weapon Stockpile 1945-2002,Natural Resource Defense Council at www.nrdc.org/nuclear/data19.asp

147 Arms Control Association Updated: November 2013, in "Nuclear Weapon:

Who has what at a glance', Press contacts: Daryl Kimball, Executive Director, Tom Collin Research Director.

148 Ibid

149 CTBT Treaty Text at www.ctbto.org/the-treaty/treaty-text

150 Ibid

151 "The Comprehensive Test Ban Treaty: Questions and Challenges" *Ambassador C. Paul Robinson, John Foster, and Thomas Scheber in Lecture No 1218 Nov 7 2012Published by The Heritage Foundation*

152 Ibid

153 Schneider Mark Dr, "The Emerging EMP Threat to the United States", National Institute for Public Policy ,US Nuclear Strategy Forum, November 2007

154 Treaty of the Non-Proliferation of Nuclear Weapons, IAEA Information Circular, INFCIRC/140,22 April 1970

155 ibid

156 Sisodia N S ,Krishnappa V,Singh Priyanka Editors, "Proliferation and Emerging Nuclear Order- In the Twenty First Century" Academic Foundation, 2009

157 Monitors 'to See N Korea Reactor,' BBC NEWS, June 27, 2007, http://news. bbc. co.uk/2/hi/asiapacific/6243874.stm.

158 Rajesh Rajgopalan "The future of Non Proliferation Regime" in Proliferation and Emerging Nuclear Order in the Twenty –First Century, Editors: Sisodia, Krishnappa & Priyanka Sing,(2009), Academic Foundation

159 For further information see "Remarks by President Barak Obama, White House Office of the Press Secretary,05 April 2009

160 Global Fissile Material Report 2013, Seventh Annual Report of the International Panel on Fissile Material

161 Communiqué of the Washington Nuclear Security Summit, published on April 13, 2010, CFR, USA.

162 Statement by the Prime Minister of India Dr Manmohan Singh at the Nuclear Security Summit, The Hindu, April 13, 2010

163 Responsibility Beyond Rules: Leadership for a Secure Nuclear Future March 2013, a NSGEC report. At www.nsgeg.org/NSGEG_Responsibilty_**Beyond_ Rules_2013**.pdf

164 Ibid

165 George Bush , "Remark to the People of Poland in Karakov, The American Presidency Project, 31 My 2003, at www.presidency.ucs6.edu/urs

166 Proliferation Security Initiative: Statement of Interdiction Principles, The

Fact Sheet, The White House Office of the Press Secretary,04 September 2003,Washington DC

167 The Proliferation Security Initiative (PSI) At a Glance Press Contact: Kelsey Davenport, Non-proliferation Analyst; Arms Control(202) 463-8270 x102

168 Ibid

169 Secretary of State Condoleezza Rice ,at http://www.state.gov/secretary/rm/2005/46951.htm for the text of Secretary Rice's speech

170 "Chinese Realpolitik and the Proliferation Security Initiative" By William Hawkins in AFAR ,18 February2005

171 Iftekar Ahmed Chowdhary,"Non Proliferation Versus Disarmament: A Destabilizing Dichotomy", Institute Of South Asian Studies, Working Paper, National University of Singapore, 21 October 2009

172 Nuclear Weapon Free Zone at a glance .Press Contacts :Kelsey Davenport ,Non Proliferation Analyst in Arms Control Association

173 Ibid

174 India's Draft Nuclear Doctrine

175 Harvey Cole, African NWFZ Enters into Force", Arms Control Today, September 2009

176 To read more see-Nuclear Weapon Free Zone at archive.pnnd.org/issues/**NuclearWeapon**FreeZones.htm

177 Ibid.

178 Protocol I and II to the African Nuclear Weapon Free Zone Treaty at http://www.unidir.org/files/publications/pdfs/the-treaty-of-pelindaba-on-the-african-nuclear-weapon-free-zone-297.pdf.

179 Ibid

180 Cohen Tom, "Obama calls for reducing US, Russia Nukes," CNN,23 June 2013

181 Nuclear Disarmament in India and a Nuclear Weapon Free World- A Viewpoint Col GG Pamidi & Dr Roshan Khaniejo, Strategic Perspective, USI

4   The Asian Nuclear Challenge

The global security setting is undergoing a transformation. The idea of a 20th century unipolar world is being challenged, by emerging Asian powers and this transformation is defying traditional security paradigms. New strategies focusing primarily on the Asian region are emerging and this is changing the security calculus. Security is no longer spoken of in terms of the traditional sense of territorial integrity and sovereignty. 'The struggle for resources embedded in the pursuit of energy security, environmental degradation, forced migration, international terrorism, insurgency, ascendency of Non State Actors in drugs, arms money laundering and financial crime organization"[1] are other typically Asian threats which are impacting the global security environment. Asia is fast emerging as the center of gravity of the political, economic and military power in parallel with what many view as the progressive diminution of western hold and dominance over global affairs.[2] The Asian security environment will be determined by the strategic power play displayed by the key players in Asia, predominantly by China, India and Japan. The sub regional variance can be seen in South Asia (Pakistan), East Asia (both the Koreas) and West Asia (Iran and Israel), all of them playing a significant role along with the key players in maintaining the balance. The global strategic dynamics, however, are still to a large extent dominated by the United States. The United States possesses unparalleled military power both in terms of strategic assets and conventional military power. More significantly, the United States is uniquely placed as the only world power with force –projection capabilities with a global reach [3] However; a resurgent Russia, and economically strong China with its burgeoning military strength have started challenging this situation. The imprints for this opposition are already visible in China's aggressive policy in the Asia-Pacific Region.

The Asian canvas is hued with different political, social, economic and demographic pressures which makes the region highly volatile and prone to insurgencies, drug trafficking, terrorism and other violent menaces. To complicate matters, the Asian continent is home to four declared Nuclear Weapon States namely China, India, Pakistan and North Korea. This nuclear imbalance has led to an increase in the number of Nuclear Threshold States which has now become a cause of anxiety for not only the Asians but for the global security as a whole. One must remember that any nuclear stand-off will pose a universal threat and have global ramifications. In such a precarious situation, prudence necessitates the reassessment of the nuclear philosophy, nuclear capabilities and the dangers of such nuclear posturing in creating a stable Asia. The roles of Non-State Actors and the Nuclear Threshold States have already been discussed in the previous chapter entitled "the Global Nuclear Challenge". The endeavour in this chapter would be to analyse in detail the nuclear capabilities of China and Pakistan, and their collusive threat to India. The possibility of the Indian Ocean emerging as a potent war zone for India and China, due to the increased demand for energy resources, will be very briefly touched upon in the next chapter. In this age of commerce, the protection of the Sea Lanes of Communication will become an integral part of national security and a major strategy in dealing with the global power dynamics.

Asian Nuclear Challenge an Overview

After the end of Cold War, the power play has moved from Europe to Asia. Asian countries defy new challenges every day. On one hand, there are emerging markets and booming economies, whereas on the other hand there are problems like uncontrolled population growth, social inequalities, poverty and major resource crunches. Terrorism, piracy, drug trafficking and increased nuclear stockpiles have brought instability to the Asian subcontinent. While there has been a decrease in the global nuclear stockpile, (especially in the combined nuclear arsenal of US and Russia) the nuclear clout of both overt and covert nuclear powers in Asia has increased tremendously.

The traditional arms conflict has given way to asymmetric warfare. In South Asia the Non–State Actors have been propelled by Pakistan to forge a limited war on India .The unresolved boundary dispute between China and India has the potential to escalate at any given moment. The unpredictable antics of North Korea in East Asia pose threats to both South Korea and Japan. China's increased hegemony in the South China Sea has made the Southeast Asian states extremely insecure, and lastly, Iran's constant endeavour to nuclearize its arsenal has halted the efforts of nations attempting to declare the Middle East a Nuclear Weapon Free Zone. The Arab spring and the American withdrawal from Afghanistan will add to this conundrum and continue to make the nations in this region vulnerable to terrorism, drug trafficking and piracy.

There have been several debates on the nuclear safety and security standards of Asian countries. The non-transparent nuclear Command and Control (C&C) systems, increased number of nuclear power plants and possible deployment of tactical nuclear weapons tend to make these countries more vulnerable to nuclear theft and espionage. The Asian nations have turned to nuclear arsenal out of a need for nuclear deterrence, to maintain strategic balance and global prestige. If Iran chooses to declare itself as an overt Nuclear Weapons state, it will change the security calculus of the Middle East entirely. Various nations in the Middle East, especially Saudi Arabia and Turkey might feel threatened by this changing power dynamic and they might feel the need to follow suit. Asia is sitting on the precipice of a volcano waiting to erupt. One wrong move could lead to a chain reaction and once the inferno spreads, it will be nearly impossible to control the repercussions. It would therefore be prudent to analyse the situation and recommend ways and means to amend and transform this nuclear game. The nuclear genie is already out of the bottle and it is impossible to go back to a world of ignorance. What is required right now is to prevent the situation from escalating, by controlling it at the initial stage and preventing nuclear proliferation. Deterrence has played an important role in preventing war world over. What needs to be analysed now is whether the same effect can be achieved and implemented in Asia.

The Prospect of Nuclear Deterrence in Asia

The emergence of new nuclear power states has changed the geopolitical dynamics of Asia and has led to what Paul Bracken calls a Second Nuclear Age.[4] This is different from the first (Pre Cold

War Era) in terms of the drastic increase in numbers and the sheer magnitude on the threat scale. The multipolar, diverse independent nuclear power centers make this threat more widespread and dangerous. The old concepts fail to fit in with the new environment hence new concepts have been added to the traditional theory of deterrence. Since the "Global Zero" ideal has remained as elusive as it was during the Cold War era, additional efforts are being made to understand the global system of the primary and secondary nuclear powers along with the all-important Non State Actors. With the advent of the atomic age, it has been evident that as long as nuclear weapons are around, even in small numbers, deterrence is going to be the safest doctrine to deal with them[5]. Deterrence is a dynamic relationship between the nations and leaders, it has become more complex to understand it due to diversity, opaqueness and recklessness of political leadership[6] .The emergence of New Nuclear Weapon States, Non State Actors, and the growing advances in new fields such as space and cyber space are all strategically challenging the hegemonic control held by the major nations. Old concepts, which were prevalent in a bipolar world, need to be reshaped to take into account the change in polarity, and deal with the nuclear multipolar world. The emerging world structure requires new, innovative responses and a new architecture where the aspirations and objectives of all the countries, strong and weak are put together

Fundamentals of Deterrence

"Deterrence is the use of threat (explicit or not) by one party in an attempt to convince another party not to upset the status quo."[7] The threat of using force to dissuade an enemy state from attacking has been a visible aspect of deterrence. Thomas Schelling, an exponent of arms control had predicted that the capacity to hurt another state is now used as a motivating factor for other states to avoid it, and influence another state's behaviour, he further states that in order to be coercive or deter another state, violence has to be anticipated and can be avoided by accommodation, it can therefore be summarized, that the use of power to hurt becomes bargaining power and is the foundation of deterrence theory, and is most successful when it is held in reserve[8].

This deterrence method can be either direct or extended, and in Asia, both types of deterrence are visible. A direct deterrence is applied by nations in preventing an armed attack on its own territory, often adopted by antagonistic neighbours like India and Pakistan for safeguarding their territorial integrity. An extended deterrence situation arises when the threat of an armed attack on a nation is prevented by the third party that is not involved directly in the conflict. The third party usually changes the strategic balance through weapons support. In many situations, the support is often provided by the P5 nations, for example, the nuclear umbrella provided by the United States to Japan and South Korea. Another arms expert, Mr. P K Huth a political analyst further elucidates that deterrence policies may be implemented in response to a pressing short-term threat (known as immediate deterrence), they can also be used as a strategy to prevent a military conflict or short term threat from arising (known as general deterrence).[9]

The aim of deterrence is primarily to prevent war; however various alternatives to a classical theory of deterrence have been developed. Some examples would be Game theory, Perfect Deterrence theory etc. Various thinkers like Schelling, Powell, Zagare, Kilgour, etc. have worked relentlessly to evolve a workable "Deterrent Structure".

The methods used by these strategists may vary but the end product remains the same. For example, in a unilateral deterrence game, it is essential that the two nations – namely the challenger and the defender cooperate - in order to obtain a perfect equilibrium or stability. If any one of the two countries violates the status quo, then various permutations and combinations can arrive and the equilibrium is disturbed.[10] For example, if the challenging nation refuses to cooperate then the defending nation has an opportunity to respond by either conceding to the challenger's demands (in such a case the equilibrium can be restored but at certain cost) or accepting the challenge, in which case the initial challenger state has the option to withdraw. However, if both refuse to draw back, then the conflict is imminent and illustrates that deterrence has failed. Thus, in order to have or maintain perfect deterrence, it is essential for nations to understand the concept of capability and credibility.

In order to prevent any challenge, the defending nation should have the capability to thwart the challenge especially if a nation is a hard state which prefers conflict to backing down. Such scenarios are possible in conventional war games because the cost and damage is less compared to actual nuclear warfare where nuclear weapons have the potential to not only destroy their enemies but humanity itself. Hence it is often believed by non-nuclear states that nuclear deterrence is a potential tool in a nations' armoury and a compelling reason for nations opting for nuclear weapons.

Nuclear Deterrence

President Dwight D. Eisenhower was sceptical about the notion of a limited nuclear war, because he believed that each small war makes global war the more likely[11], and also that any conflict with the erstwhile USSR would have escalated the situation to a full-fledged thermonuclear war. Hence the concept of Mutual Assured Destruction or MAD emerged, which was believed to bring about elusive nuclear peace. During the Cold War era, nuclear powers avoided direct confrontation and the probability of a direct war between the two superpowers decreased drastically. Both the countries had started working through their proxies and ensuring that the minor conflicts did not escalate into major ones. Post the Cold War, the sword of limited nuclear warfare gained prominence once again due to the revival of tactical nuclear weapons and the possibility of the dissemination of nuclear weapons to Non State Actors. The consequences of latter acquiring nuclear bombs are unimaginable. With the increase in the number of Nuclear Weapon States, especially the New Nuclear Weapon and Threshold States, the concept of stability has changed. This stability–instability Paradox (SIP) is a result of low intensity conflicts. While on one hand nuclear weapons provide strategic stability and help prevent a large scale war, on the other hand they also allow more risk taking in low intensity conflicts. Thus sub-conventional low intensity wars, (which involve small- scale incursions by terrorists, counter measures by Special Forces), have become more widespread. Even the New Nuclear Weapon States have realized this theory and does not allow the low intensity conflict to escalate into a full-fledged war as could be seen in the case of the Kargil crisis of 1999 between India and Pakistan.

It can be safely stated, therefore, that the nuclear deterrence has worked but not exactly in the way it was envisioned. It has worked in a different stability paradigm with different security architecture.

Several nations are adopting nuclear weapons for various reasons. Apart from the rationale of security and prestige, a new reason for developing nuclear weapon is geo-strategic balance. If a country does not have an allied nuclear partner and is surrounded by a nuclear adversary, then to protect its national interest, it is often felt that by becoming a Nuclear Weapon State the deterrence could be maintained. Moreover, the cost of nuclear warfare is so high that it automatically dissuades the states from going in for an all-out war. China and India are classic examples of this theory. Tactical warfare becomes another reason for investing in nuclear arsenal. If the adversary has a superior conventional force, then developing a nuclear force helps thwart the adversary's advantage. India and Pakistan have fought three Wars but since the time Pakistan has developed its nuclear forces there has been a sudden shift in the strategic outlook. Asymmetric warfare continues between the two but an all-out war has successfully been avoided by both countries thus far. Iran also wants to develop her nuclear weapons because Iran knows that Israel has nuclear weapon and is conventionally also superior hence the need to maintain the strategic balance in West Asia, may have prompted it to become a covert nuclear state. Another reason why countries are investing in nuclear weapons is out of the fear that powerful allies might not always be there to provide aid. In Asia a lot of countries like Japan, South Korea, and Saudi Arabia etc have been given extended deterrence by the United States. All these states have chosen not to develop nuclear weapons because of the security provided by the American nuclear umbrella. However, if a situation arises, where Japan thinks that it will not be assisted by the US in its war against China, it will be forced to resort to the nuclear option for its own survival. South Korea is also in the same situation.

In order to have successful nuclear deterrence, it is essential for the countries to have preventive or pre-emptive strategies based on the nuclear status of its adversaries. If the nuclear programme is in its nascent stage or if the adversary does not possess nuclear weapons, in such a situation, the attacker can opt for a preventive strike and destroy the adversary's nuclear programme. This was evinced by Israel's strike on Syria and Iraq. However, if both nations have a substantial amount of nuclear weapons, a pre-emptive strike does not work .Thus a preventive strike is designed to defeat an adversary before he can develop and deploy his full potential might[12]. Secondly, dissuasion by deterrence operates on the principle of punitive counterattack. Thus deterrence is achieved through the ability of a nation to punish its attacker. It is not the defensive forces that provide deterrence, but the capability of a credible, lethal, second strike that deters the adversary from attacking. Political will and the demonstration of nuclear power also become important factors in achieving this balance. Thirdly and most importantly, the weapons must not be susceptible to accidents or theft. Hence nations should have a strong C&C system ensuring the security of their nuclear arsenal. Thus it is essential for nations to have not only a sound Nuclear Doctrine but also a nuclear force which complements and implement this doctrine.

Thus one can expect wars to become less likely when the weaponry makes conquest more difficult. Moreover, if states can only score small gains (because large ones risk retaliation), they will have little incentive left to fight.[13]Secondly, if the loss during a war is limited and bearable, (as is usually the case in conventional warfare), the frequency becomes higher as nations are willing to wield the risk for the desired gains. But, if the loss ratio leads to the annihilation of the entire human race, the frequency of such a high risk war is very limited and almost negligible as nations are unwilling to fight a war at such high stakes no matter what the gain is. New nuclear states, therefore, will be more concerned for their safety, and more mindful of dangers of such a war. Hence while nuclear weapons have spread, conventional weapons have proliferated and under these circumstances, wars have been fought not at the center but at the periphery of international politics.[14] The likelihood of war decreases as the deterrent and defensive capabilities increase and nuclear weapons makes wars hard to start, as nations that have nuclear weapons have strong incentives to use them responsibly[15]. This applies to all states irrespective of being big or small, weak or powerful.

Challenges

It cannot be denied that nuclear deterrence has prevented a war for many years but deterrence during the Cold War period had different connotations. In that era, the concept of deterrence applied to few countries as the nuclear power was mainly confined with the P5 countries. In the post-Cold War era, with the emergence of new Nuclear Weapon States and Threshold states, the nuclear power has been decentralized and proliferated. This proliferation of technology and weapons has already led the world to a vulnerable precipice with threats boiling under the surface. Apart from the inherent threat to deterrence which emerges from nuclear accidents and mishaps, the greatest challenge to nuclear deterrence right now is international "Terrorism". The ability of Non State Actors to act independently or through the backing of certain nation states can complicate the deterrence theory in the future. The safety and security of civilian nuclear plants and WMD of New NWS is already a cause for concern and conjecture. Questions are also being raised about the efficiency of the Command and Control systems of these states. There have been instances where the national police of various nations have caught people with nuclear material theft. Moreover, there were reports of Al Qaeda's attempts to obtain enriched Uranium, as some of the senior members of the group, had meetings with the Pakistani nuclear experts[16]. Though Non State Actors may find it difficult to acquire nuclear weapons, the possibility of obtaining "loose nukes" remains quite high and cannot be ruled out entirely. As already mentioned earlier, the global stock of enriched uranium and plutonium, (for military as well as civilian purposes), is gradually increasing. Apart from these fissile materials, dirty bombs or radiological weapons are easily acquirable and no amount of deterrence would be effective in such a situation.

Asia is infested with terrorist groups. Weak political systems and the Arab spring have fuelled instability, which in turn has created a perfect breeding ground for terrorist organizations. Additionally, the havoc that can be caused by cyber-attacks is unimaginable. It is a known fact that multiple attempts have been made in the past to penetrate military systems. The dispersed nuclear weapons and the nuclear C&C systems are vulnerable to hacking. Even closed networks can be compromised by adopting various methods such as privilege escalation, roaming notebook, wireless access points etc.[17] The increase in the civilian use of uranium and plutonium has further escalated the risk of theft, sabotage, blackmail etc. The challenges posed by the nuclear threat today are varied and require a collective effort from nations willing to stop it. Non-proliferation and disarmament treaties are a step in the right direction but these treaties must recognize the New Nuclear States and integrate them in the system so that they can also shoulder the responsibility of preventing nuclear proliferation. The fact is that nuclear weapons are here to stay. It is every country's right to protect its sovereignty, and in the process if a nation chooses to rely on nuclear deterrence, there is very little that the world community can do. Hence preventing nations from becoming nuclear in the first place should be the primary objective. If a nation is surrounded by non-nuclear states then it will not rely on nuclear deterrence and consequently a global Nuclear Zero might be envisioned. Secondly, providing extended deterrence would also dissuade nations from taking the nuclear path, providing negative security to Non-Nuclear States and finally creating Nuclear Weapon Free Zones would aid tremendously in decreasing the nuclear threat and ultimately bringing peace and stability to the region.

Escalatory power of Asian Nuclear Weapon and Threshold States

Any increase in the number of Nuclear Weapon States, will increase the inherent risk of accidents, miscalculations and actual use, thus making the region unstable. The distinctive feature of the second nuclear age has been the spread of civilian nuclear technology, which has had an overarching implications in the checks and balances provided by various non-proliferation organizations. Various nations have been covertly developing their nuclear weapons under the disguise of civilian nuclear programmes and this strategy is most obviously visible in Asia, which has the largest number of Threshold states. The countries in Asia are focused on the quantitative as well as qualitative aspects of their arsenal development and this can be seen from their constant attempts to improve the speed, distance and payload capacity of their conventional and nuclear weapons. The P5 or primary nuclear powers have constantly modernized their nuclear weapons and this process has had a cascading effect on the secondary nuclear powers as well. The increasing ranges covered by weapons have made geographical natural defenses irrelevant. The modernization and spread of missile technology has had an impact on both the conventional as well as the nuclear armament. As on today, an Iranian long range missile can target Israel, and the North Korean test missile can fly over Japan. Nations in Asia are competing to acquiring the latest missile technology, making the region volatile and unpredictable. North Korea is flaunting its nuclear capability and uses it to blackmail nations to negotiate deals, while Iran is aspiring to use its covert nuclear programme to play a major role in West Asia. In the bargain both the nations have disregarded the outcomes of such actions, which have led to instability, alarm and an increased arms race. The strategic capricious postures adopted by the P5 nations have heightened the arms race not only amongst themselves but also among the other nations in Asia as well. Since many countries in Asia have weak political systems and inherent insurgent movements, they become all the more vulnerable to threats like nuclear theft, sabotage and blackmail. Thus Asia is sitting on a bubbling volcano and a small spark is enough to tip it over the edge.

1 . West Asia

Americans and Israelis have declared several times that they will not accept the emergence of any new nuclear state in the Middle East. In the past, Israel (with American support), has destroyed the nuclear ambitions of many states in the region like Iraq, Syria etc. The addition of any new nuclear states may lead to a chain reaction in the area. The other states might begin considering the nuclear option as a viable mode of deterrence, thus exposing the region to competition and creating further instability. One must keep in mind the fact that many states in Middle East have started developing civilian nuclear programmes, and in such a situation, diverting the resultant nuclear fissile material towards the nuclearization of their military arsenal is highly feasible, and has been successfully conducted by other countries in the past. North Korea is the example of a nation which has surreptitiously diverted its civilian nuclear programme for developing nuclear weapons.

Nuclear Iran

The major question that emerges from this conundrum is whether or not the time has arrived for the world to witness the emergence of another nuclear state in West Asia, namely Iran. Will Iran's nuclear programme be officially legitimized or will the same fate of destruction, as was forced onto Iraq and Syria be meted out to Iran. The big debate that stems from this is whether Israel possesses the strength required to stop this nuclearization process, or whether it is already too late and the much talked about window to destroy the Iranian nuclear installations through aerial attacks has already gone by. After Iran's interim nuclear deals in 2013, there have been conflicting responses from the Americans and the Israelis. The Americans believe that the nuclear deal will curb Iran's nuclear programme whereas Israel thinks that the deal might make Iran a covert nuclear power, and hence limit its options as far as curtailing Iranian influence is concerned.

Iran's strategic installations are very complex both in terms of numbers as well as locations. Hence, massive and repeated air strikes are required to incapacitate them. Moreover, the fact that Israeli society is divided and a majority of the citizens do not favour attacking the Iranian nuclear installations makes it clear that Iran is not Syria or Iraq. The escalating dominance that Israel has enjoyed in the Middle East for so long is now finally being challenged. The fact that Iran has several options that it can use to respond, (mostly punitive – either through the Persian Gulf blockade, or an offensive attack through its missiles or through its proxies), restrains Israel from attacking Iran. Israel knows that any war will lead to oil prices skyrocketing which will impact the Israeli economy adversely. Moreover, it will also escalate violence since any blockade (either by laying mines or attacking naval ships) will invariably bring US in to the foray and will reopen the otherwise dormant dynamics. The safest option for Israel right now is to delay the procedure as much as possible through asymmetric means (Cyber-attack, sabotage, targeted kidnapping/killing etc.) and if Israel fails in this endeavour then it should work on containing Iran. Iran on its part has maintained an ambiguous position and it might be taking the same step that Israel adopted during its initial stages. Even today, Israel is not an overt Nuclear

Weapon State though unofficially the world community considers it as one.

The psyche that lies behind states wanting to become nuclear powers is to change the regional power structure. Post the disintegration of USSR and the Iraq war, Iran aspires to fill the geostrategic space. A nuclear Iran can reshape the regional and global power structure without actually going into a war, hence the urgency in developing its nuclear status. No amount of sanctions imposed by the world community will deter Iran from its objectives and the IAEA reports have exposed the Iranian nuclear programme time and again. In such a situation there are two main possibilities. Either Iran will declare itself as a Nuclear Weapon State or it will continue its covert nuclear weapons programme secretly. However at this moment, it has been conjectured by several strategists that post Iran's nuclear deal, it will continue to be a covert nuclear power and retain the leverage that it currently enjoys.

Possible Future Scenarios

Iran's nuclear programme is not at a nascent stage, but still it can be stated that it does not have the hi-end technology required to challenge the US. However; post the Iranian interim nuclear deal, Iran might like to improve its relations with the US, and therefore any future standoffs, if it occurs, it might be with Israel and not with US directly. Iran might opt for asymmetric techniques like naval swarming, supplying weapons to Hezbollah, terrorism etc. instead of getting involved in a direct confrontation. The military strategy which will be adopted will depend on the strategic posture that Iran adopts. For example, if the nature of the conflict is for defensive purposes to safeguard its territorial sovereignty, then nuclear Iran will adopt what most of the nuclear nations have adopted, which is the strategy of minimum nuclear deterrence. This strategy was first adopted by the Chinese who believed that a small but potent nuclear arsenal is also effective against larger nuclear adversaries. A small and survivable nuclear force can easily deter Israel, US and Saudi Arabia. However Israel's fear is that Iran might choose to use their nuclear arsenal for the purposes of offensive strategies like dispersing mobile missiles, providing "smart IED's (Improvised Explosive Devices) to sub-national groups, cluster bombs, missiles, anti-ship missiles[18] etc. Iran may adopt a strategy of extreme provocation, (usually adopted when a nation wants to distract attention from its domestic problems) in order to create fear and instability. Such a situation can become extremely dangerous as was seen during the escalation of the Cuban Missile crisis. Conjecture aside, keeping the nuclear debate open and using it as a political tool to expose Israel's nuclear bid as a leader in the Middle East, will benefit Iran the most and be in their best interests. Its nuclear weapons programme can even threaten the European Union as it has the missile capabilities to traverse the distance between them. Mr Gates American Defence Secretary stated "—if Iran were actually to launch a missile attack on Europe, it would be just one or two missile but it would be more likely to be a salvo kind of attack[19]--" The US has already acknowledged this possibility and made attempts to counter it by deploying missile defence system in Europe.

Israel on its part has diversified its options. Apart from its traditional aircraft and missile strength it is trying to develop its sea based forces. It already has submarines, capable of carrying cruise missile armed with nuclear weapons and also Israel has successfully modified Nuclear Weapons to fit its harpoon missile[20]. The submarines give it seaborne nuclear missile capabilities as well as second strike capabilities making it a formidable power in the region. These measures and developments make its deterrence more potent and survivable. To achieve this status, it has started developing its R&D programme a major example of which is its new satellite system. Israel's new spy satellite can transmit information to a communication satellite, and this information can immediately be downloaded in Israel. Thus any dispersal of mobile missiles can be immediately tracked and this way they are no longer dependent on the American satellite systems for information[21].

Iran's nuclear road has created misgivings amongst nations of West Asia and the possibility of new nations' traversing this road cannot be ruled out. Reports of Saudi Arabia contemplating nuclear options through Pakistani help are a worrying possibility. Gulf nations have also reassessed its security policies and its dependence on the American anti-missile systems is going to increase. Thus a security churning is taking place and until stability is attained this region might remain volatile.

On the other hand though it is too early to predict what will happen post the Iranian nuclear deal, current indications can also lean towards an improvement in the relations between the US and Iran. The former might use the Iranian influence in solving the Syrian problem while Iran may make use of American help in improving its economic conundrum. There is also the possibility that the US might put pressure on Israel to adopt a more moderate approach towards Iran, and its policy of assisting gulf nations through its missile defence systems might consequently bring a brief period of stability.

Conclusion

Missiles do not respect geography, hence the activities in the Middle East, are definitely going to impact other regions. Iran's missile development has made Europe and South Asia vulnerable to a nuclear attack. The possibility of low intensity warfare being transformed into a full-fledged war is more probable in the Middle East rather than in any other region. The widespread nuclear installations and the Iranian missile programmes are here to stay and under such conditions it is necessary for both the countries to declare their red lines. They should maintain open channels of communication, and preferably set up emergency communication systems as well to avoid confusion and mistrust. Israel needs to accept the advancements made by Iran in their nuclear programme and adopt more practical oppositional strategies instead of developing offensive confrontational plans. Iran needs to understand the dangers of nuclearization, especially with regards to the nuclear threats arising due to accidents and Non State Actors. A robust Command and Control system would be the stepping stone towards avoiding nuclear terrorism, and building confidence amongst the nations would be of utmost importance to avoid nuclear catastrophe.

2 . East Asia

In East Asia there is interplay between two of the most powerful powers in the world, namely, the United States and China. The stability in this region will be determined by the interactions of these two nations, with each other, and in congruence with the other nations in the region. Activities of a nuclear North Korea will be monitored by China to a great extent while Japan and South Korea have got the extended deterrence or the nuclear umbrella provided by the Americans. An unpredictable North Korea has created instability in this region and it has now become necessary to analyse the violent, escalating nature of this conflict.

North Korea

The armistice of 1953 may have ended the Korean War but North Korean tactics aimed at wilfully escalating the tension continue. Whether it is the sinking of the ROK Navy Ship Cheonan or the shelling of the Yeonpyeong Island, North Korea has demonstrated time and again that it possesses the political will required to risk war. The nuclear dimensions of this conflict have theoretically escalated their power despite the fact that their nuclear forces are primitive and relatively small in number.

Strategy behind the hostility

The question that arises is why Pyongyang continues to implement these hostile acts and why the alliance between US and South Korea is unwilling to meaningfully retaliate. Pyongyang has the capability to bombard Seoul, as they have kept a huge amount of their artillery close to the De Militarized Zone. Historically, in times of conflict, North Korean dynastic rulers have shown their willingness to up the ante. But there is logic to this seemingly volatile madness. They escalate the conflict situation only till a tolerable and sustainable level. For example, the choice of the Island they attacked – the civilian Yeonpyeong Island – depicts their foresight in ensuring that the casualties remain minimal due to the isolated location of the Island. This was done keeping in mind the fact that an attack on any of the mainland towns would be a major provocation, the counter retaliation to which, would be difficult to contain. North Korea wants to keep the impact of the conflict low while ensuring that its intensity is high. They are aiming for a rhetorical deterrence with propaganda and psychological warfare rather than engaging in an actual war. On the political side, the reason for this rhetorical deterrence is because the dynastic rulers are aware that the regime would face extinction in the event of war and not mere defeat, hence they use a precarious caution in their hostility, moreover, if they go in for too much reform then their tyrannical regime will collapse[22] In spite of the rampant reports about starving people, horrendous acts of cannibalism and severe poverty, the regime has managed to survive so far due to the foreign aid received overtly from China and covertly from US, South Korea and Japan in the form of humanitarian aid. Developing nuclear weapons is for deterrence purposes and to prevent a regime change, (the rumours of which have been circulated in the media off and on.) By institutionalizing hard–hitting military options comprising of nuclear and chemical weapons, North Korea wants to engage in psychological warfare. A KCNA release on April 21, 2010 states the objectives of pursuing nuclear weapons are "The mission of the nuclear armed forces of the DPRK is to deter and repulse aggression and attack of the country and the nation till the nuclear weapons are eliminated from the peninsula and the rest of the world and the DPRK has invariably maintained the policy not to use nuclear weapons against non-nuclear states or threaten them with nukes as long as they do not join nuclear weapon states in invading or attacking it"[23]. Another reason for this nuclearization is that nuclear weapons are used as bargaining tools to receive food and oil from the rest of the countries, thus it has successfully linked its national existence to those of South Korean and Japan.[24]

The Response

South Korea and the Americans do possess the capability to deter North Korea, both by punishment and by denial; they have the capability of overwhelming retaliation in the event of an invasion and also strong defences that can deny successes. [25] South Korea has time and again declared a proactive deterrence approach along with sanctions, UN pressure and alliance strength in the form of joint exercises.[26] This strategic flexibility is often challenged by the North Koreans but in a measured manner with the help of Chinese support. China has been playing an important strategic role in the survival of the North Korean regime. Historically, whenever Seoul and USA have cut back humanitarian aid, Beijing has picked up the slack. A sort of covert understanding has been developed between these three countries. The Americans understand North Korea's importance for China and while Japan has the capability to counter North Korea, they often ignore these skirmishes as they do not want to overtly antagonize China. However, while China pretends that there is no alternative to supporting North Korea, they would not allow the situation to escalate too drastically. They have a tremendous amount of control over North Korea as the latter is heavily dependent on China militarily and economically. It is also believed that China resents the American interference in East and Southeast Asia. They do not want a pro American regime within its vicinity hence they provide North Korea with the help required to secure its border. The North Korean nuclear programme has Chinese lineage and it will keep swinging from an escalatory mode to a de-escalatory mode from time to time. However, China will definitely maintain the strategic balance because it knows that it cannot match the combined onslaught of US, Japan and South Korea .At the same time all the key powers in the region, while tolerating its incursions, will not allow the situation to escalate into a full-fledged war thus this game of controlled brinkmanship will continue.

China and the Second Artillery

In order to break the nuclear monopoly of the super-powers, China created a special force called the Second Artillery Force (SAF), the power behind China's Nuclear Strategy. It was founded on 1st July, 1966 and is directly under the control of the CMC; historically its objective was to build a lean but effective nuclear missile force[27]. It is mainly responsible for deterring other countries from using nuclear weapons against China, and for conducting nuclear counterattacks and precision strikes with conventional missiles[28]. In 1983 Deng Xiaoping stated "we must have what anyone else has, and anyone who wants to destroy us will be subject to retaliation"[29]. This statement set the tenor of their nuclear doctrine. By the 1990s, China had started developing a strong conventional missile force along with nuclear weapons under the SAF for tactical deployment. This evolution was necessitated by the changed threat perceptions, as China now perceived the threat as localized and emanating from a peripheral geo strategic location. The Taiwan Strait, East China and South China Sea are potential conflict zones. Also along with this the growing economy and modernisation trends have made China take missions which are beyond its periphery like the naval projections in the Indian Ocean region and the various humanitarian assistance and disaster management plans. Thus China's nuclear policy complements its grand strategy which has been defined as "the overall strategy of a nation or an alliance of nations in which they use their combined national strengths for political goals, particularly those related to security and development " [30]

From the beginning of the 21st century, China had realized the significance of developing their information and technology sector. They changed their traditional military doctrine and approached it with an innovative concept. They called it as a warfare based on informationalisation. These C4ISR capabilities which China is developing will enable it to conduct military operations in Asia and beyond. Over the years, the PLA Second Artillery Corps (SAC) has already grown in strength. The philosophy behind China's nuclear strategy has been to acquire a land-based strategic force which would be capable of counterattacks and precision strikes, through both nuclear as well as conventional missiles. Following the principle of building a lean and effective force and going with the tide of the development of military science and technology, the Second Artillery Force strives to raise the informationization level of its weaponry and equipment, ensure their safety and reliability, and enhance its capabilities in protection, rapid reaction, penetration, damage and precision strike[31]. Undoubtedly, *the SAC is one of the most dynamic branches of an already active and rapidly modernizing PLA...It is expected that the Corps may assume new missions such as Counter-Space Operations.*[32] This chapter attempts to provide an analytical assessment of China's current capabilities and also to evaluate the path that the SAC is likely to take in future. It studies the strengths and weakness of the Second Artillery Force, especially the conventional missile force and other force multipliers (like the cruise missiles) with special reference to its threat to India. Additionally, China's Tibet policy and the impact it could have globally are also analysed in this chapter.

Nature of Warfare

Local war under conditions of "Informationalization" has become the official Military Doctrine of China[33]. The Second Artillery Force is endeavouring to form a complete system for war preparations, optimize its combat force structure, and build a missile operational system suited to informationized warfare[34].Hence its nuclear and conventional missile forces are kept at an appropriate level of readiness. Also, since the nature and method of the warfare has changed, it has become more localized and limited to China's periphery. Information in terms of advanced computer usage, information technology and communication networks to gain operational advantage over the adversary have become important milestone to achieve[35], or in other words 'high-intensity, information –centric regional military operations of short durations' is the key.[36] The method of electronic warfare, comprising of electronic jamming, reconnaissance system, anti-radiation and decoys, if used properly can neutralize the missile sensor systems. In order to counterattack its adversaries' missiles, the application of precise targeting systems through guided missiles (supported by space platforms) is essential, and so China is working to develop an advanced space sensor systems. This sophisticated technology will provide China with advanced warnings about the adversary's attacks, thus helping them build a pre-emptive counter attack strategy. This strategy is in keeping with their military doctrine of 'active defence'[37].This Active defense has for pillars, mainly China will not be the first to use the nuclear weapons, China will also not threaten to use it, the attempt will be to first deter war, however; on nuclear attack, the retaliation or the response would be offensive[38] (uses the concept of a surprise attack on enemy territory as a means of self-defence). Thus this form of active defence is a holistic strategy which incorporates both active as well as defensive measures. Keeping all these strategies in mind, China has modernized its nuclear and conventional missile capabilities, both in terms of quality as well as quantity.

Role of Second Artillery

Over the years the PLA Second Artillery Corps (SAC) have grown in strength, and the philosophy underlying this growth has been the acquirement of a triad-based strategic force capable of counterattacks and precision strikes with both nuclear as well as conventional missiles. China already has credible deterrence capabilities against conventional attacks on its mainland, and additionally, it continues to plan the use of ballistic and cruise missiles in its anti-access strategies.

SAC's Strategy

In the 1980s, China added the concept of 'Dual Deterrence and Dual Operations' to its SAC. This addition has been implemented due to the change in the nature of modern warfare. The 'conventional guided missile campaign army group' has become an integral part of the SAC. This group is considered to play the role of a rapid response force that acts as a deterrent against enemy attack. The Science of the Second Artillery Campaign emphasizes three main aspects which have changed the force structure of the SAC. Firstly, it has changed the target objective of the Second Artillery Corps campaigns from dealing with a nuclear war in the past, to a more progressive participation in a high tech local war under the conditions of nuclear deterrence in the present. Secondly, it has shifted the focus of their research, from using single nuclear tactics to accomplish the mission of nuclear counter attacks in the past, to using dual operational tactics. Thus, it embodies the perfect utilization of both nuclear and conventional missile forces, with significant importance being given to the conventional missile force. (*hechang jianbei, yi chang wei zhu*) ; Thirdly, it has changed the content of the military strategic research from focusing on strategizing in the past to focusing on a combined use of strategy and technical means.[39] In other words it has increased the focus on aggressively exploring and boldly innovating in the military/technological field (*jijitansuo, dadan chuangxin*).

The basic logic put forth through this science was that during wartime, both the conventional as well as the nuclear missile force was required to counter the adversary. This strategy is most effective for situations involving local wars. In this strategy, the conventional missile campaigns were designed to achieve battlefield effects first – that is to destroy an enemy's ability to wage war effectively – next, in the case of a nuclear attack, the second step would be to survive the attack and finally to use the nuclear weapon as an offensive-defence strategy for massive retaliation. All these strategies have been enunciated in the Chinese nuclear and conventional missile strategies.

China's Nuclear Strategy and Nuclear Modernization

China's nuclear force structure was formed, two years after its first nuclear explosion in 1964, and the SAC developed as a 'basic retaliatory force.' Since then, its role has undergone a substantial evolution and there have been several structural and technological modifications as well. China's nuclear thought process was influenced by the book entitled 'Guidelines for the development of Nuclear Weapons.[40] Furthermore, in July 2000 at the Central Military Commission's Conference, President Jiang Zemin gave his "Five Musts on Nuclear Weapons", expounding China's need to have five key basics, namely "a definitive quality and quantity of nuclear weapons to ensure national security, to ensure safety of strategic nuclear bases, to keep nuclear weapons in high degree of war preparedness, to be able to launch nuclear counterattacks and finally adjust its strategic nuclear weapon development strategy in a timely manner."[41] Most of these have been incorporated in the Chinese strategic thought process; however, the main principles that guide China's nuclear policy are summarized below.

- **A conditional 'No –First Use' (NFU)**. China unequivocally professes that they will not use or threaten to use nuclear weapons, against any Non-Nuclear Weapon States or those within any Nuclear Weapon Free Zones. They have also said that they will not employ a first use policy against USA and Russia. However many believe that the declared policy is not binding or verifiable and thus not indicative of actual Chinese operational nuclear policy, there is a fears that China may rollback it's No First Use commitment in a future crisis, if that threatens its national interest[42] . Also if the same is used for safeguarding those territories which are perceived by China as theirs, then this conditional NFU will always give an option to China to use these weapons, especially against India, as there are quite a few contentious territories between India and China. India also does not figure in the above said categories, where they have refused to use Nuclear weapons, because India is a Nuclear Weapon State, but China refuses to recognise the same. This implies that China can use or threaten to use nuclear weapons against any country and especially against India, if they find that their core interests are threatened.

- **Counter strike** Counter strike *(zhongdian Fanji)* is one of the pillars of China's policy of 'Active Defence.' It is the offensive after strike that would damage massive military and civilian targets, especially the Command and Control systems, thus reducing the enemy's war making potential so that the adversary ends the nuclear exchange. Counter attack campaign is planned to be done jointly by SA and PLAN/ PLAAF Thus her retaliatory counter value posture is in stark contrast to US's Counterforce targeting policy.

- **A Credible Minimum Deterrence** China has developed a limited, reliable, precise and effective nuclear force capable of surviving the first strike and executing a massive counter strike through its nuclear triad. In recent publications, the PLA has also been using the term 'Effective Nuclear Deterrence' *(you xiao he weishe)* and this has been interpreted as being a 'reliable, survivable delivery system, capable of penetrating an adversary's missile defences.'[43]

- **Second-Strike Retaliatory Capability** In order to achieve a potent second-strike retaliatory capability China started her modernization programme in the 1980, with a sole aim to increase the survivability, reliability, safety, and penetrating ability of her small nuclear arsenal. China's thrust area so far in following these principles have been:-

- Focus on the quality rather than the quantity of its nuclear force. The accuracy and the penetrating ability of her nuclear arsenal are important aspects, because a missiles that can hit deep and accurately, can only do colossal damage.

- Increase the survivability of her nuclear force by replacing older, liquid-fuelled missiles with solid-fuelled, road mobile ballistic missiles and constructing deep underground tunnels that can act as missile bases.

- Significantly increased the size of her conventional weapon especially its Land Attack Cruise Missiles (LACM).

- **Nuclear Command and Control.** Another important aspect is to enhance and prepare the state's capacity for nuclear coercion and limited nuclear warfare through an efficient Nuclear Command and Control (NC²).For example the limited nuclear force strategy could spiral out if value target (urban centres) were inadvertently struck instead of through a failure of NC. Under such circumstances and depending on the magnitude of hostilities, control over one's own forces could pose a substantial challenge[44].This is an on-going process and China has to streamline her Command and Control especially after she adopted the doctrine of 'Dual Deterrence and Dual Operation.'

- **Survivability of China's Nuclear Force** China follows a 'Close Defence' (yanni fanghu) and this is a 'broad catch all concept that embodies the policies and actions used to improve the survivability of China's Nuclear Forces[45].' China's policy of limited nuclear arsenal is often debated as being contradictory, because China has a vast network of underground tunnels, often referred to as China's underground great wall which is 3000 miles and could host a large number of nuclear weapons. The necessity to build such infrastructure is paradoxical, and contrary to her nuclear stance. These tunnels can withstand conventional and nuclear attacks as they are hidden in deep mountainous areas and hundreds of meter under the ground, they are well connected with the rail system as a result the missile along with its paraphernalia can be transported to any location when required. Chinese are also converting their land based missile system into tunnel based system[46]

No First Use Controversy

On April 16, 2013, the Chinese Ministry of Defence released the eighth edition of China's bi-annual white paper on defence[47]. However this defence White paper did not include the long standing traditional Chinese policy of No First Use. The absence of this NFU policy led to several debates and conjectures about the reasons underlying this glaring omission. There were concerns that China had abandoned its No-First Use policy which had been a major Chinese nuclear strategy from the time China declared itself a Nuclear Weapons State. Colonel Yang Yujun, a spokesman for China's Ministry of Defence, however clarified that "China's National Defence" were comprehensive (zonghe xing), and further elaborated that China's nuclear policy was detailed in sections on "national defence policy" and "arms control." However, he further reiterated that this edition of the white paper adopts a "thematic" model (zhuanti xing) for the first time and focuses specifically on the deployment of China's armed forces, it does not address nuclear policy in detail"[48], which is why the No First Use policy statement was missing. This white paper however continues that the SAF is "primarily responsible for deterring other countries from using nuclear weapons against China, and carrying out nuclear counterattack." It further states that "[China] keeps an appropriate level of readiness in peacetime... If China comes under a nuclear attack, the nuclear missile force of the PLASAF will use nuclear missiles to launch a resolute counterattack either independently or together with the nuclear forces of other services." .This seems to be a continuation of the line of thought adopted by its previous policies. However; according to a study undertaken by Prof. Phillip Karber, China's long network of underground tunnels (ranging up to 3000 miles) have the capability to hide a large number of missiles. This statement is criticised by thinkers like Jeffery Lewis[49] but the fact remains that the information given by the Chinese cannot be verified The Russian analyst, Hramchihin Alexander, deputy director of the Institute of Political and Military Analysis, also believes that China has a large arsenal of nuclear missiles and that it could be the largest in the world. While the view may be exaggerated, the fact remains that the number of weapons China possesses is much more then what SIPRI had predicted earlier (250-300 nuclear weapons). The fact that underground tunnels do exist in China demonstrate that China might be covertly changing their nuclear policy. The previous Chinese premiers had also emphasized the need for China to adapt its strategic policy according to the changing geopolitical situation. Considering Chinese are master of "Denial and Deception", hence these tunnels can be considered as protecting the missile from surveillance and targeting.

Since its economic boom, China has started projecting itself as a major global power. It has challenged the US, as well as the ideology of a unipolar world. This transition towards becoming a major global power has been depicted by the usefulness of such long underground tunnels which can be used for hiding these strategic missile forces. Keeping in mind these attempts to project themselves as a major power, it becomes increasingly difficult to believe in the applicability of China's No First Use Policy. Apart from the nuclear doctrine, China has subsequently developed its conventional strategy as well.

The Characteristics of this doctrine are given below.

China's Conventional Missile Strategy

This doctrine is the dynamic leg of the SAC and is different from the nuclear doctrine in number of ways.

- Firstly it is an offensive doctrine and unlike nuclear doctrine, not for deterrence purposes, but is based on the philosophy of strike first, strike hard, precise and rapidly. Basically to seize the initiative and quickly gain campaign control[50].

- It is an important part of a joint operation, which is to be conducted in collaboration with PLA Army/Navy/Air force.

- The numbers of conventional weapons are large and are constantly increasing.

- Perfectly suited to the concept of local wars.

Main Tasks

The main goal is to "smash or weaken the enemy's military strength, to politically shock the enemy, to shake the [enemy's] willpower [to wage] war, to check the escalation of war, and to speed up the progress of war."[51] However the basic operational task is:

- To prevent and discourage the adversary from attacking;

- To conduct "missile firepower blockade" (low-intensity missile attacks on the key targets upon which the enemy relies- land, air, and sea mobility that are intended to block or inhibit the mobility of enemy troops and supplies)[52]

- To attack on the civilian targets to get a psychological advantage;

- To attack on enemies troop movement in order to disrupt the adversaries Command and Control system[53].

To achieve the goals set in both these doctrines. China has developed a missile infrastructure which fairly complements its nuclear and conventional strategies.

Conventional and Nuclear Missile System

Second Artillery has diversified, developed and deployed various missile systems representing different theatres. The conventional arena is dominated by three main weapon systems mainly the SRBMS, MRBMs and GLCMs - the highly lethal cruise missiles. China has developed various conventional variants of her nuclear MRBM DF21, the conventional DF-21C which has a range of 2500kms. What is further alarming is the sheer rate at which the SRBMs are growing .From a mere 350 in 2002 it has increased to 1100 by 2012[54]. The quantity is amply matched by the quality as the new missile's precision and lethality have been amplified .The latest naval version JL-2 has been developed to counter the US edge in Taiwan theatre .The land and Air force vector has been deployed in the Tibetan sector to thwart any attack from India. Further in order to hit large distances it has developed its long range ballistic missiles the ICBMs and IRBMs .Thus there is a mix of ICBM, IRBM SRBM and GLCM. As of 2012 the numerical strength of Chinese missiles are as follows:

Table: 8 Chinese Missile Force in 2012

System	Missile	Launcher	Range
ICBM	50-75	50-75	5,500+Kms
IRBM	5-20	5-20	3,000-5,500Kms
MRBM	75-100	75-100	1,000-3,000Kms
SRBM	1,000-1,200	200-250	<1000Kms
GLCM	200-500	40-55	1,500+Kms

Source: Office of the Secretary of Defence, Report to Congress on Military and Security Development involving the People's Republic of China 2012, Department of Defence, May 2012

Force Structure of Second Artillery Corps

The chain of command runs from the CMC, the Second Artillery Force and missile bases to missile brigades[55]. The Second Artillery Force is mainly composed of the nuclear missile force, the conventional missile force, the support force, educational institutions, research institutes and the headquarter organizations[56]. The missile force is organized into missile bases, missile brigades and launch battalions and the support force is organized into technical and specialized support units such as reconnaissance, intelligence, signal, ECM, engineering, logistics and equipment units[57]. China has a total of six missile brigades, located in the six regions of China, and each Brigade has either 3-3 or 4-4 subordinate entities[58]. Along with this it has training and storage brigade and testing sites. It has worked to create an integrated data bases for field support and informationized management platforms for logistic materials, and improved support systems for the survival of combatants in operational positions. As a result, its integrated logistical support capabilities in case of actual combat have been markedly enhanced.

Table: 9 Chinese Nuclear Bases

Name of Base	Brigade	Weapons
51st Base (Shenyang, Liaoning)	1. 806th Brigade, Hancheng, Shaanxi 2. 810th Brigade, Dalian, Dengshahe. 3. 816th Brigade, Tonghua. 4. 822nd Brigade, Laiwu. 5. U/I Brigade, U/I missile, Fengrun. 6. U/I Brigade, U/I missile, Jingyu.	DF-21 DF-3A& DF-21 DF-15, DF-21,

Name of Base	Brigade	Weapons
52nd BASE (Qimen, Anhui)	1. 807th & 811thBrigades, Lianxiwang/Jingdezhen. 2. 815th Brigade, Leping. 3. 815th Brigade, Shangrao. 4. 815th Brigade, Xindian. 5. 817th Brigade, Yong An 6. 818th Brigade, Meizhou. 7. 819th Brigade, Gangzhou. 8. 820th Brigade, Jinhua. 9. U/I Brigade, Jiangshan. 10. U/I Brigade, Nanping. 11. U/I Brigade, , Xianyou . 12. U/I Brigade, U/I missile, Ningbo.	DF-3A& DF-15 DF-15C DF-11 & DF-15 DF-15, DF-11A, DF-15 DF-15, DF-15 DF-11 & DF-15 DF-15 DF-11A
53rd BASE (Kunming)	1. 802nd Brigade, , Jianshui. 2. 802nd Brigade, , Kunming. 3. 808th Brigade, , Chuxiong. 4. 821st Brigade, Luorong.	DF-21 DF-21 DF-21 CJ-10,
54th BASE (Luoyang, Henan)	1. 801st Brigade,Lushi. 2. 804th Brigade, Luoning/ Luoyang. 3. 813th Brigade, , Nanyang. 4. U/I Brigade, , Sundian. 5. U/I Brigade, , Xixia. 6. U/I Brigade, U/I missile, Sanmenxia.	DF-5A DF-5A, DF-31 DF-4 DF-31

Name of Base	Brigade	Weapons
55TH BASE (Huaihua, Hunan)	1. 803rd and 814th Brigades, Jingxian. 2. 805th Brigade, Tongdao.	DF-5A, DF-4,
56TH BASE (Xining, Qinghai)	1. 809th Brigade, Datong. 2. 812th Brigade, Beidao/ Tawanli. 3. 823rd Brigade, Korla. 4. U/I Brigade, Da Qaidam. 5. U/I Brigade, Delingha. 6. U/I Brigade, Liuqingkou. 7. U/I Brigade, Mahai. 8. U/I Brigade, Xining.	DF-21, DF-31A, DF-21 DF-11&DF-15, DF-4,DF-11, DF-15, DF-21, and DF-31, DF-21 DF-11 & DF-15 DF-21 and DF-31

Source: Compiled from Air power Australia

Training facilities are at The Delingha, Linyi, Dongkoug, and Luoyang. An important training school is the SAC Engineering School in Xian[59]. Seven Test Facilities are also present. Six of these locations are equipped with facilities to launch various types of ballistic missiles, the seventh facility is an impact range equipped with mock targets used to assess missile accuracy.[60] They are at Wuzhai, Shuangchengzi, Bayan Hot, Huludao, Jinzhou, Songlin, and seventh one an impact zone located 100km northwest of Dunhuang. It actively conducts specialized training, integrated training and operational training exercises where specialized training mainly involves the study of basic and specialized missile theories, and the training in operating skills of weapons and equipment; integrated training mainly consists of whole-process coordinated training of all elements within a combat formation and Operational training exercises refer to comprehensive training and exercises by missile brigades and support units in conditions similar to actual combat[61]. It enhances on-base, simulated, web-based and realistic training, explores the characteristics and laws of training in complex electromagnetic environments and integrated training of missile bases, and is conducting R&D of a new generation of web-based simulated training systems.[62] Significant progress has been made in building the "Informationized Blue Force" and battle laboratories.[63]

Figure: 11 Missile Force Structure

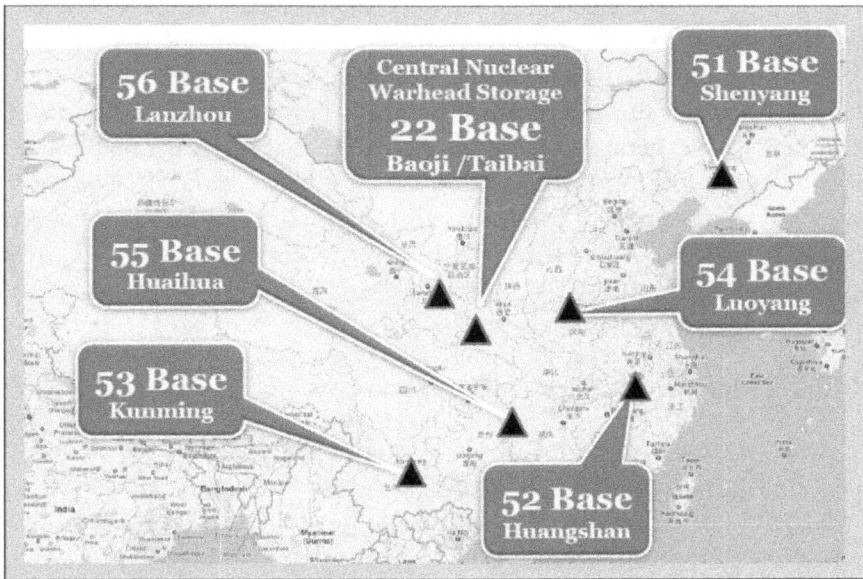

Source: The Project 2049 Institute

Missile Force Structure

It consists of six Army level bases in1 in Shenjang and Beijing Military Region (MR),1 IN Jinan MR 1 in Nanjing MR,2 in Guangzhou MR and 1 in Lanzhou MR[64]. They have six departments under them being headquarters, political, logistics, technical and equipment, missile storage, and launch battalions. Both the conventional and the nuclear missile brigades have this structure .The missile storage department consists of a central depot, and a missile/warhead transfer section.

Operational Hierarchy and Deployment

Units fielding armed nuclear weapons, most notably the ICBM brigades, report directly to the Chinese national command center west of Beijing. A regional command cell, called a "war front" command, would assume control of relevant conventionally-armed ballistic missile units as part of a conventional missile corps. This missile corps would be subordinate to the war front command, acting as part of a total force package consisting of air, land, sea, and missile elements. Beijing's leadership and SAC commanders would be able to communicate directly with the war front command, and would retain the ability to directly control assigned missile brigades should the need arise or the situation warrant it. At the brigade level, individual firing battalions would be assigned operating areas consisting of pre surveyed and/or prepared launch positions.[65]Further China is modernizing and deploying new capabilities for its C&C so that it can control multiple units in the field, China's ICBM units now have better access to battlefield information and uninterrupted communications connecting all command echelons, and unit commanders are now able to issue orders to multiple subordinates at once, instead of serially, via voice commands[66]

China's Missile Brigades and Implications

The strategic implications of missiles like the DF3, DF-21 based in the Northern Region are to counter the threat emerging from Russia, Mongolia and to some extent the Far East regions. In South East China, the 52 Base at Huangshan, Anhui has DF-11/DF-15, which is short-range, road-mobile, solid propellant ballistic missile. These are tactical weapons meant for the Taiwan and the South China Sea theatre. These are for offensive purposes as they can be quickly transported and launched and it is difficult for the adversary to target and destroy them in time. The Southern Unit or the 53rd Base is at Kunming, Yunnan and has DF-3s/DF-21s. The DF-3s have mainly been deployed in border areas and once China has a sufficient number of DF-21s they might remove the DF-3s altogether. This DF-21 is what India needs to be worried about as these MRBMs have been placed all along the Indian border. These missiles have been specially developed for the Indian theatre. The MRBM is a solid road mobile tactical weapon capable of hitting all the important cities in India and can be used as a nuclear deterrent as well. The weapon serves a dual purpose and can be used as a nuclear as well as conventional weapon to target Indian nuclear facilities. According to sources, over 100 DF-21 missiles have been built, some of them being reconfigured with conventional warheads that can be put to use along China's southern and north-western borders, making them capable of striking targets throughout northern India.[67] The 54th Base in China is located in the South Central region at Luoyang, Henan and the 55th Base is Huaihua and Hunan, both of which have DF-4s and DF-5s.

These are the bases for Chinese ICBMs. The old ICBM DF-4 and DF-5 have been replaced by the advanced DF31 and DF-31A. The latest version is the DF41 (which is an MIRV with the capability of 10 warheads that has a range of 14,000 km) which is supposed to be inducted by July 2013[68]. The 56th Base which is in the North Region at Xining, Qinghai has DF-3s/DF-21s and DF-4s. Also China's DF-31 ICBM has a range of 8,000 km and the advanced version of this missile, the DF-31A, possesses a strike capability ranging anywhere between 10,000 and 14,000 km[69] Thus it is developing a "Global Precession Strike Capability"

However; China like India, also suffers from the threat of a two front War, but the missile brigades of all the regions have the flexibility to move their brigades and relocate themselves to the required areas in the case of emergencies. Through its modernization process, China has worked towards attaining better logistical connectivity through an excellent system of roads and railways. So the brigade from the central and eastern sectors could easily be mobilised in a short time to the all-important western sector of Tibet in case of any eventuality. The two basic sectors for China are:-

Taiwan Sector – The 52nd Base generally has weapons which will be used for the Taiwan Theater. These include a large number of DF-3A, DF-11, DF-11A, DF-15, and DF-15 C ballistic missiles. The DF-3A is to be used in the Pacific Ocean.

Indian Sector – The southern Missile Base 53 has 3 brigades of DF-21 at Jianshu, Kunming and Chuxiong and one brigade of CJ-10 at Luorong, also the 55 Base has a Df-5A and DF-4 at Jingxian, and

Tongdao[70] .All these missile brigades are probably for the Indian Theatre.

China's Nuclear and Conventional Missile Force Modernization

China has significantly expanded her size and quality of her nuclear as well as conventional missile force and the modernization has mainly been based on the following criteria.

- **Diversification of Nuclear Missiles** This was mainly to shift the missile system from the Silo base liquid missile system to road mobile solid fuel missile system. A great deal of efforts were put in to develop the road mobile solid fuel missiles system as it was considered that this would enhances the survivability of deployed assets and also make it harder for the adversary to target them. Simultaneously exercise was conducted to reduce the readiness time. They worked to increase the range and accuracy of these missiles.

- **Triad Capabilities** China has strengthened her triad capacity by inducting sea based nuclear missiles. It has 4 SNBN, 1 Xia (type-092) with 12 JL-1 (1000+ KM) three Jin (type-094) with 12 JL 2 SLBM[71] (7400+ KM), and has inducted an anti-ship ballistic missile (ASBM) the DF-21-D which is a variant of DF-21. The DF-21 D has a manoeuvrable warhead with a range of 1500km which they believe can hit even an aircraft carrier.

- **Re-loadable Launchers** They have moved away from single use launchers to re-loadable launchers thus increasing their stockpile. If ICBM is primarily retaliatory in nature, developing Short Range Ballistic Missile (with an arsenal of 1200 missiles) and 100 MRBMs force is for the purpose of surprise attack that is pre-empting enemy's attack and this strategy is especially meant to be used in a regional war scenario.[72]

- **Largest Conventional Missile Force in Asia –Pacific** In the conventional field, the SAC, which had no conventional missiles till 1985, now has the largest conventional missile arsenal in the Asia- Pacific.[73] They also have 350 GLCMs[74.]

This is basically meant to destroy the adversary's political and economic centres as well as military bases, depots, communication and network centres thus paralysing the enemy and winning the war without actually using their own potential strengths.

This approach of using concentrated ballistic and cruise missile can be used not only against Taiwan but also against India.

If one sees the ballistic missile development from 1985 as seen from the chart given below, one finds that there has been tremendous growth in the development of SRBMs .The number has increased from a mere 60 in 2000 to a phenomenal 216 in 2012, similarly the MRBMs have increased from mere 50 in 1985 to 122 in 2012. A drastic decrease was found to be in the stockpile of IRBMs from 60 in 1985 to just 2 in 2012. This is due to the nature of threat perception being changed from a global to a more localized one. Also new variants like the DF-21 series and the lethal cruise missile the GLCM were developed to suit this concept of Local Wars.

Table: 10 China's Transition of Missile Forces

Type of Launcher	1985	1990	1995	2000	2005	2010	2012
LACM	0	0	0	0	0	54	54
ICBM	6	0	17	40	46	66	66
IRBM	60	80	60	30	2	2	2
MRBM	50	0	10	50	33	116	122
SRBM	0			60		204	216

Source : IISS, Military Balance 1985-2012 as cited in Chinese Military Modernisation, A Western Perspective, Cordesman & Yarosh, Revised CSIS, 30 July 2012

Trends in Force Structure

Since 1985 the PLA concept of winning local wars under condition of Informationization has made the SAC gradually change her nuclear force structure from non-mobile liquid fuelled missile with a nuclear warhead to a road mobile solid fuelled missile having dual capability of carrying a nuclear as well as conventional warhead. Also there is a shift in the range and type of missile from medium –intermediate range nuclear missile to a divided force comprising an exponential number of conventional short /medium range missiles. The number of nuclear missile launcher has remained more or less static since the past two years. In 2011 and 2012 the SRBMs had remained-225, MRBM-88, IRBM-13,ICBM-63 and GLCM-48[75] but SAC has increased her conventional missile force by 60 per cent and cruise missile by 10 per cent .

Importance is also being given to Electronic Warfare; the aim is to counter the U.S. technological advantage. Chinese EW doctrine emphasizes using electromagnetic spectrum weapons to suppress or deceive enemy electronic equipment and PLA EW strategy focuses on radio, radar, optical, infrared, and microwave frequencies, in addition to computer and information systems.[76] EW weapons include jamming equipment against multiple communication and radar systems and GPS.[77] EW systems are also being deployed with other sea and air-based platforms intended for both offensive and defensive operations and this had been possible as they have been conducting force-on-force, real-equipment confrontation operations in simulated EW environments[78]

Trends. The following trends can be discerned.

- Firstly the force structure has a phenomenal number of conventional short/ medium range missiles with an equally potent nuclear force of medium and long ranges ICBMs. The local war concept has made China increase her near precision SRBMS and LACM which constitutes nearly 11 per cent of the SAC Strength[79].

- Second there is not only an increase in the size of ICBMs but also they are being modernized in to new version of DF-31 and DF-31A. The DF-31 is available in three variants road mobile DF-31, road mobile DF-31A with extended range, and submarine launched JL-2 SLBM (Submarine Launched Ballistic Missile) The DF-31A is believed to have three warheads per missile and a range of about 7,000 miles, which allows China to target even the U.S, The DF-31A is portable and can be launched from the back of a tank, train, or a truck. [80]

- Thirdly India should be concerned about the SRBMs and LACM as they are not only mobile, solid fuelled but also the range and precision has been improved .These launchers are given more number of missiles per launcher thus the adversaries can face multiple salvos per SRBM or GLCM[81] in a rapid regional strikes. The trend is to develop advanced variants of these missiles with an eye on constantly increasing the range and payload capacity. By the end of 2013 China had more than 1000 SRBMs and the PLA continues to field air- and ground-launched LACMs for stand-off, precision strikes and air-launched cruise missiles include the YJ-63, KD88, and the CJ-20. China recently revealed the CM-802AKG LACM.[82]

- Fourthly the Chinese DF-21 is also a cause of concern for India. All the variants of this class are solid propelled and road mobile .All its land based variants are operational. DF-21 A is the improved version and has larger range and accuracy, they can be used as conventional as well as nuclear strike weapons.DF-21-C is employing terminal guidance for increased accuracy and have off-road mobility not present in the original towed launchers used by the DF-21 and DF21A.[83]The latest variant to join is the DF-21D an ASBM (Anti-Ship Ballistic Missile) variant employing a terminally guided MARV (Manoeuvring Re-entry Vehicle) and the MARV may be equipped with a RADAC system similar to that found on the MGM-31, Pershing II IRBM[84].DF-21 variants serve as the basis for the KT-1 space launch vehicle and the SC-19 direct-ascent ASAT weapon system.[85]

- Finally China is carrying out various land based mid-course missile interception test thus coming near to building a shield for China's air defence by intercepting incoming warheads such as ballistic missile in space. China's constellation of satellites is transitioning from the limited ability to collect general strategic information, into a new era in which it will be able to support tactical operations as they happen.[86]

Anti-Ship Ballistic Missile Capability (ASBM)

In order to become a global power and to support sovereignty claims in South China Sea .It is imperative for China to be seen as a major naval power .She has already graduated to a blue water navy by acquiring its first aircraft carrier. China is now developing ASBM capabilities. Her phased plan was to have a rudimentary 2000km range ASBM by 2010, followed by an increased range of 8000 by 2020 and a global precision strike capability by 2025 and to have a more advanced solid motor and a "boost-glide" trajectory that would complicate mid-course missile defences.[87] American strategists are closely watching China's experimental anti-ship ballistic missile with a manoeuvrable warhead, which could make it hard for American fleets to approach the Chinese shore. [88] At some stage they can think of using this missile in the Indian Ocean theatre also. Annual Report to Congress (2010) depicts in detail the total size of the Chinese inventory:-

Table: 11 China's Nuclear Force 2010

Type	NATO designation	Number	Range	Number of War heads
Land Based Ballistic Missile				
DF-3A	CSS-2	15-20	3100	5-10
DF-4	CSS-3	-15-20	5,400+	10-15
DF-5A	CSS-4	-20	13,000+	-20
DF-21	CSS-5	85-95	1750	75-85
	CSS-6	350-400	600KM	90-110
	CSS-7	700-750	300KM	120-140
DF-31	CSS-10 MOD 1	<10	7,200	<10

| DF-31 A | CSS-10 Mod 2 | -10-15 | 11,200 | 10-15 |
| DH-10 | | 200-500 | 1,500+ | 45-55 |

Source-Annual Report to Congress ,Military and Security Developments involving People's Republic of China,2010

Submarine Launched Ballistic Missile

Name	NATO Designation	Range	Number of Launchers
JL-1	CSS-NX-3	1000	12
JL-2	CSS-NX-4	7400+	36

Source: Compiled from IISS 2014

China's Force Multiplier

- **The SRBM's** The introduction of SRBMs and LACMs has increased the lethality of China's attack .The SRBMs count has increased from being just 30 per cent in 2000 to now nearly constituting 50 per cent of SAF's missile system.

- **Cruise Missiles** China has rapidly developed her cruise missiles; she has one of the largest arsenals of cruise missiles now. The missile per launch has also increased for both the SRBMs and the GLCMs thus ultimately increasing their stockpile.

- **ICBM Variants** The ICBM size has increased from 5 per cent to nearly 14 per cent and may further grow as they are constantly bringing out new variants like the DF 31/31A and DF-41.Thus constantly increasing the range and manoeuvrability.

- **The MRBMs** The IRBM may have decreased but the 21C and 21D MRBMs have increased phenomenally and large number of these are being deployed in Tibet All these indicators reflect that though China is concentrating on her periphery but She has kept the larger picture of becoming a major power (through nuclear coercion) also open.

Future Projections

- Increase in counterforce and counter attack capabilities.

- To increase the range and survivability of her nuclear forces new variants of DF-31 like the DF 31-A and DF -41 and an offload TEL is being developed so that the weapons can be deployed from garrisons whose launch area would be difficult to identify .This will give her a counter force as well as counter attack capability

- To improve anti carrier strike capability using precision guided nuclear as well as conventional ballistic missile capability.

- To efficiently operationalize the dual deterrent system

- With the integration of a higher range ICBM along with accurate conventional theatre weapon system the SAF will become a strategic deterrent along with dangerous regional force to reckon with.

Second Artillery Force as Leverage

The SAC is a potent strategic deterrence tool against its adversaries mainly India, USA and the nations of the Southeast Asia. China has realized that the threat stems more from the regional countries and not so much from Russia or from US and as a result China has changed her strategy once again to include the use of conventional weapons. The concept of dual operation stems from the belief, that with the development of precision-guided munitions, the utility and strategic importance of conventional missiles has drastically increased. Hence a conventional missile attack campaign becomes an important part of a joint campaign to inflict maximum damage. This has in turn increased the lethality of the Chinese attack in the local war scenario. Furthermore, in order to consolidate this strategy they have developed a phenomenal amount of cruise missiles both ground and sea based, such as the GLCM and ASBM along with SRBMs, thus giving China a superior tactical – strategic option. China has deployed SLBMs/MRBMs throughout the Indian border in Tibet and also backed this up with DF-4s, the longer range ICBMs. China's ASBMs are specially developed for striking US aircraft carriers in a conflict scenario against Taiwan, but they can also be used and deployed in the Indian Ocean Region in the future. China's DF-31/As, DF-41s and their submarine launched JL-2, SLBMs work with their cruise missiles and altogether, these missiles have increased the range and intensity of the warfare, thereby allowing China to target all their adversaries. China continues to test its offensive missiles and is currently developing the world's most diverse ballistic missile programme.

The Tibet Dilemma

China considers Tibet as its core national interest and all its energies are currently concentrated on the infrastructural development of this region. China has an edge as far as the construction of road and rail connectivity is concerned and the missiles deployed here have ranges which can hit all the major cities in India. The infrastructure has developed to the extent that China can now mobilize major military regions within few months. They are also regularly conducting joint exercises to test the adaptability of their manpower and the ability of their weaponry system to function in such adverse conditions. India needs to monitor China's railway and airfield development programmes constantly, mainly for the purpose of assessing their capabilities and subsequently to counter them effectively if the need arises. Some programmes that should be looked into with extra caution are:

- **Lhasa-Shigatse Railway Route** China has built a 1000km railway line to link Lhasa with the mainland. The closest railhead is at Golmud in Qinghai province. 'The 253 kms long Lhasa- Shigatse railway line which was undertaken as a national key project has completed the track-laying. According to the Ministry of Railways[89]. This is a cause of concern to India as it would be used to transport combat weapons especially ballistic missiles. Since 2010 the Tibetan military region has already started using extensively the rail routes.

- **Highway Network Up-gradation** China is upgrading their network of highways, especially the one stretching from Jianshui-Kunming-Yunan, and Chengdu-Lhasa-HaiyanDatong highway. This is designed to take heavy mobile missiles, with suitably surveyed and constructed launch sites all along the route[90].

- **The ancient 'Silk Route'** This ancient route has been revived .China is trying to connect the Southern Xinjiang railway to central Asian Republics, and also constructing a parallel route from Kunming through Southern Yunnan into Indo China up till Singapore.

- **Rail and Operational Airfields** According to Defence Minister, A K Antony had said "The total road network in TAR is assessed at 58,000 km in 2010. Extension of Qinghai Tibet Railway to Xigaze is in progress. Another railway line from Kashgar to Hotan in Xinjiang Uighur Autonmous Region is under construction[91]" and have 14 airbases of which five operational airfields are at Gongar, Pangta, Linchi, Hoping and Gar Gunsa from where Chinese Sukhoi-27UBK and Sukhoi-30MKK fighters have practised operations in recent times[92].

- **Nuclear weapons Deployment** China has deployed Nuclear Ballistic missile in Tibet, DF-4 are in Tsaidam sites, also southern Amado bordering Sichuan has four DF-5A missiles. It is estimated that 8 ICBMS, 70 MRBMs and 20 IRBM are concentrating in and around this area.

- The testing site for China's First Nuclear test was close to the Ninth Academy ,since then all documented test have been have been carried out at the north west of Tibet at Lop Nor in Xinjiang, province[93].

These crisscrossed roads, railway links and airfields allow the Chinese military leaders to deploy, concentrate and relocate any brigade from their Military Regions, especially from the Lanzhou and Chengdu Military Regions because they are responsible for the security of Western China. Also with extensive road-rail links in TAR, PLA can amass upwards of two divisions (30,000 soldiers) at their "launch pads" along the border in just 20 days now compared to the over 90 days it took earlier[94]. Thus for China, Tibet shall always remain part of its core national interest along with Taiwan. However; due to their vulnerability, they will continue to protect and fortify them with lethal weapons and ammunitions.

China's Competitive Edge

- Ballistic Missile Inventory. China has a clear edge over India; in fact there is no competition as far as China's missiles are concerned, both in terms of number and their variation .As of now China out powers India in all departments more so in her long range ICBMs and MRBMs.

- China's strategic Missile strength is nearly 458 whereas the same for India is 54[95].China has 66 ICBM and has a clear edge over India though India's Agni V has cleared the launch test but it will still take some time before it can be successfully inducted.

- China's strategic MRBMs/IRBMS strength is 140 where as India it is just 24+ Similarly China has 252 SRBM compared to Indian 30 + (that includes Prithvi I, and II and Dhanush) and further China has 54 LACM whereas India's Nirbhay under development[96].

- The biggest advantage that China has right now is that most of its missile development programme is indigenously built, and China is therefore not majorly dependent on any other country for access or spare parts. India needs to learn from this example and utilize the private sector better in order to enhance the production of specialized weapons and armament.

Shortcomings

As far as doctrines are concerned, amalgamating conventional weapons with nuclear weapons is still a challenge, especially in terms of the sections dealing with the Command and Control system. China's sea based capabilities, while advancing at a rapid rate, still have scope for development. For example, the Jia Dong SLBM is still experiencing developmental hic-cups and is not operationally deployable[97]. Streamlining the operational hazards of the Carrier Battle group will still take a few years. "The PLA has only a limited capacity to communicate with submarines at sea, and [the PLA navy] has no experience in managing a [submarine] fleet that performs strategic patrols with live nuclear warheads mated to missiles," as stated by the US Defence Department in 2010[98]. The airborne vector is another area that needs serious improvements, especially in the development of the engines and the improvement of the stealth technology.

New Missions for the SAC

Apart from the diversification of missiles, the SAC is also trying to develop its nuclear triad. For this tri-pronged attack to be successful enabling independent modes of authorization and communication become extremely important and satellites, therefore become the next major development in the programme. The Chinese are taking this development a step further by programming their satellites and missiles to engage in and deal with anti-satellite warfare as well.

Anti-satellite weapons

In 2007, China successfully conducted a test aimed at destroying the weather satellite by using a ballistic missile with a kinetic kill vehicle. This was an effort to develop anti-satellite weapon technology in the low orbit region. However, the Chinese are now planning to extend their field of attack, and operate the anti-satellite weapon in the mid and high orbit regions as well, thereby threatening the American GPS systems (which are placed at heights of 20,000km), and the military intelligence and missile defence satellites (which are situated approximately 36,000km above the equator) as well.[99] Rumours state that the Chinese have also developed a new anti-satellite missile, called the Dong Ning-2, or DN-2, which is considerably more advanced in its capabilities, as it can go further in to the space when compared to the ASAT missile launched in 2007. The DN-2 is said to be able to hit several types of navigation, communication and intelligence satellites, by colliding with them at high speeds. This is a particular threat to the U.S. intelligence because it relies heavily on satellites, as does the American military.[100]

The People's Liberation Army, in addition to directly attacking satellites, could interfere with GPS and communication satellites in mid to high orbit. Such ability means a Chinese counterattack would deliver a fatal blow to any US blitz warfare plan. Russia's Air & Space magazine reported that the PLA is developing nuclear-powered satellites as attack platform, equipped with signal interference capabilities, it will complete ground experiments in 2015, and is expected to launch its first nuclear-powered satellite in 2025, the report said.[101] China's Academy of Space Technology has successfully developed land and station based laser weapons to attack satellites. China can now send their astronauts to their space station and return them safely to Earth. Once their astronauts can directly operate laser weapons conduct attacks on enemy communication, radar, reconnaissance and GPS satellites, space-based anti-satellite warfare will far exceed ground based laser weapons.[102] China is thus transforming and evolving its satellite capabilities. They have progressed from the relatively limited initial ability whereby the satellite was used only to collect strategic information, towards a more advanced usage of it in the tactical operations sector. They have combined space technology with military power and thus enhanced their warfare capabilities exponentially.

The Chinese are also enhancing their computer network attack capabilities as they consider information warfare and offensive computer network operations critical for any crisis[103] China is trying to develop Radio Frequency (RF) and Laser weapons. RF is generally used to impede carrier battle groups, guided missile and the C4ISR capabilities. China is trying to develop advanced weapon systems based on laser technology[104].

Thus the key deductions can be that Principle of Dual Deterrence and Dual operations' reflects the amalgamation of the nuclear with the conventional force .An offensive defense strategy for her local war construct.

- **Doctrinal strength:** China's nuclear /conventional doctrine complements her force structure .Capable of an offensive first strike followed by a punitive second strike. Further it aims to have a global precision strike capability by 2025

- **Diversification of Nuclear Missiles:** Modernization process has transformed her nuclear and conventional forces .Nuclear forces has diversified from liquid silo based missile to solid road mobile to improve the survivability . By 2025 China's nuclear forces would be larger and more sophisticated .She might double her ICBM capabilities by 2025 especially her DF-31 A.

- **Increase in counterforce and counter attack capabilities:** To increase the range and survivability of her nuclear forces new variants of DF-31 like the DF 31-A and DF -41 and an offload TEL is being developed so that the weapons can be deployed from garrisons whose launch area would be difficult to identify

- **China's force multipliers:** They are her SRBMS and the Cruise missiles .which are bound to increase substantially by 2025

- **Re-loadable Launchers:** They have moved away from single-use launchers to re-loadable launchers thus increasing their stockpile.

- **Largest Conventional Missile Force:** China already has nearly 200-500 GLCMs. By 2025 this force will increase substantially and will be a force to reckon with.

- **Missile Interception test:** China's various land based midcourse missile interception test will enable her to develop a shield for China's air defense by intercepting incoming warheads such as ballistic missile in space

- **Defence Indigenization Programme:** China has indigenized her defence industry to a large extend, thus decrease dependence on foreign powers.

- **China Pakistan Nexus:** China by supporting and aligning with Pakistan both politically and militarily has made India's western sector vulnerable to attack from, state as well as Non State Actors and also the possibility of a two front attack a reality.

- **Supplying Military Hardware.** China is supplying military hardware and setting up Pakistan's defence infrastructure. She is also Pakistan's largest arms supplier mainly tanks, M11-missiles, advanced J-10 fighter jets, submarine up gradation etc

Conclusion

Thus China is supporting and enhancing its military doctrine of local war under Informationization by adding conventional missiles to its nuclear arsenal. "The Guided missile forces become trump cards *(sa shou jian)* in achieving victory in limited high technology warfare."[105] This force, aided through the maintenance of a survivable nuclear force that can ride out any nuclear attack, as well as inflict a lethal counterattack on the enemy is in keeping with the philosophy of nuclear deterrence whereby any adversary of China will be forced to think twice before attacking them.

In the past decade, China has changed its force structure from a purely nuclear force to a mix of nuclear and conventional forces. They have also increased the survivability of their missiles by constructing long tunnels ranging up to 3000 km, equipped with Command and Controls well as transportation facilities. Further SAF is constantly modernising its artillery with new precision variants. China is focussing on dual function missiles in order to retain its edge as far as local warfare is concerned. China has one of the largest land based missile forces comprising of 38 operational missile units spread across the country, heavily oriented towards short and theatre range missile with only 8 facilities supporting ICBMS.[106] The greatest advantage of their current missile force, as mentioned earlier is the dual nature of the attack capability. The improved mobility and the frequent exercises which are conducted are constantly aimed at reducing the requisite readiness time in any combat situation. Most of their missiles have been changed from liquid fuel silo based missiles to road mobile solid fuel missiles. Their SRBMS and LACMs along with a large number of their reserve missile per missile launcher are her rapid reaction forces, having the capacity to sustain long combat operations. The new force of DF 21-Cs, DF-21 Ds and ASBMs along with their modernised variants, depict a focussed development of the force structure aimed at dealing with the concept of local warfare. The increase in the number of missiles and the escalating range of land based ICBMs such as DF-3/4/5 and the DF- 31 series in tandem with the development of SLBMs such as the JL-2, all point to the fact that China is steadily working to fulfil their quest of achieving triad capabilities. Their greatest advantage right now, is their indigenous defence industry, and the modernization of their missile defence technology.

Nuclear Challenge from Pakistan

From the time Pakistan declared itself a Nuclear Weapon State, nuclear weapons, have become an intrinsic part of Pakistan's military strategy. To understand their posture, it is essential to first analyse Pakistan's psychological mind set, its anxieties, the motives underlying the framing of its nuclear doctrine and finally, the role played by its civilian and military leaders in the development of its nuclear programme. Pakistan and India has strained relationship, the baggage of partition, that both the countries are jostling with even today. Pakistan's reasons for viewing India as a threat stem mainly from India's geographical largeness, its inherent religious diversity, economic and military strength and its democratic principles. These apprehensions have in turn created insecurity within Pakistan, which they have attempted to hide under a veneer of overt aggressiveness. Moreover, the defeat of Pakistan in the 1971 war and the subsequent creation of Bangladesh have cumulatively scarred the Pakistani army. Their key objective since then has been to regain their lost esteem and attain parity with India. When their use of overt aggressiveness failed, they adopted strategies of terrorism and insurgency, which led to the emergence of covert wars. This was chiefly aimed at what they termed as "bleeding India through thousand cuts[107]".

Pakistani political leaders had been debating the nuclear options. Before India's peaceful nuclear explosion in 1974, Pakistan's Prime Minister Zulfiqar Ali Bhutto had openly announced their intention of acquiring nuclear weapons. Pokhran became a mere pretext which rationalized their intent. Bhutto cloaked the more insidious agenda under the guise of religious sentiment, and declared that an Islamic bomb needed to be created. He used Islamic faith inappropriately as a smokescreen to develop Pakistan's nuclear ambition, thereby generating the requisite resources, (especially the financial assistance required for developing the nuclear bomb), from Islamic countries, especially Saudi Arabia. Bhutto has stated "We know that Israel and South Africa have full nuclear capability, The Christian, Jewish and Hindu civilizations have this capability. The communist powers also possess it. Only the Islamic civilizations was without it; but that position was about to change."[108] The fundamental principle behind this was Pakistan's assumption that any threat or inequality could be countered through nuclear weapons. They believed that the weapons would give them the leverage required to maintain a balance and attempt to achieve dominance in its relation with India. The development of tactical nuclear weapons is the ultimate tool on their path to complete this strategy, which they adopted from the NATO countries. This strategy was used by the NATO countries against erstwhile Soviet Union during the Cold War. The Russians have also adopted this as a part of their military strategy. Pakistan is convinced, that nuclear weapons, (especially the tactical nuclear weapons) can be used as counter measure against India's conventional forces. G Parthasarthy, the former Indian Ambassador to Pakistan also states that "Pakistan decided to acquire nuclear weapons, not because India had nuclear weapons but because its ruling elite believed that after the dismemberment of the country during the Bangladesh conflict, it needed such weapons because of India's size and conventional superiority."[109]

Role of Army and Religion

The Army plays a central role in Pakistani politics. Unlike India, where the army's role is restricted to maintaining territorial integrity and upholding the sovereignty of the country, the Pakistani army's role is multifarious and supreme. The army is involved in maintaining its traditional function of preventing external aggression, but it also considers nation building as part of its primary duty. The Army Chiefs, especially Gen Zia-ul Haq, considered religion a necessary cohesive force that could be used to achieve internal stability. In his first speech as Chief Martial Law Administrator, Zia described himself as a "Soldier of Islam" and stressed his commitments to build a new political, economic and social order based on religion.[110] Under Zia's leadership, Pakistan saw the Islamisation of its army, as well as its civilian population. Since then, religious ideology has become an extremely important part of its domestic culture. The Army has exploited this ideology time and again in order to achieve its ends. Whether it is Afghanistan or India, the army's imprints are all too visible, especially in the civilian strategies that Pakistan adopts.

Pakistan's threat perception is India centric and its military strategies have revolved around the following three principles:-

- To acquire advanced technologies to seek a competitive edge.

- To align with major powers mainly US and China to acquire this technology.

- To continue and strengthen its asymmetric warfare through nuclear blackmail.

Offensiveness and surprise attacks have been trademarks of the Pakistani military strategy. To strengthen this strategy, Pakistan has worked to develop its infrastructure and amalgamate its policies with a larger vision to achieve its goals. The Pakistani nuclear programme is fundamental to this objective and all its strategies revolve around the implementation of this nuclearization policy.

Nuclear Doctrine

The doctrines adopted by different nations highlight their varying strategies and their overall world vision. The nuclear doctrine, as Brigadier Naeem Salik (Ret.) has said, "is the principle of belief or bedrock on which organizational and force structures are built. It provides the guidelines for force configuration and the nature, type and number of weapons and delivery systems that would be needed to implement the doctrine."[111] Unlike India, which has a well-documented written nuclear doctrine, Pakistan is conspicuous by the absence of such a written doctrine. They believe that ambiguity in their nuclear policy serves as a useful tool since it becomes a threat and a source of leverage. Therefore, there is no officially declared nuclear doctrine, but various policy makers and military Generals have outlined the basic nuclear policies, based on which, the Pakistani nuclear policy can be described as follows:-

First Use

Pakistan has often claimed that it will not hesitate to use nuclear weapons, even in the initial stages of a war. In 1998, Foreign secretary Shamshad Ahmad that "Pakistan's policy implies that it will not only use nuclear weapons in a retaliatory strike, it is also ready to take the lead and use nuclear weapons first to counter Indian conventional aggression[112]." This stems from the theory that the possibility of the first use of nuclear weapons will act as a deterrent against enemies and the power manoeuvrability will remain with the country that maintains the policy of first use. Such a policy becomes especially useful for weaker states and in conditions where the adversary's conventional weapon superiority has been reinforced time and again. This has been clearly described by Lt Gen Lodhi in the Pakistan Defence, Journal where he has said that "In a deteriorating military situation when an Indian conventional attack is likely to break through our defence or has already breached the main defence line causing a major setback to the defenses which cannot be restored by conventional means at our disposal, the government would be left with no option except to use nuclear weapons to stabilize the situation. Further he states that India's superiority in conventional arms and man power would have to be offset by nuclear weapons, Pakistan's nuclear doctrine would, therefore, essentially revolve around the first strike option. In other words, we will use nuclear weapons if attacked by India even if the attack is with conventional weapons "[113]

He elaborates further about how this can be used by stating "In other words we will use nuclear weapons if attacked by India even if the attack is with conventional weapons." With his American experience of a graduated nuclear response Professor Stephen P. Cohen feels that Pakistan would use what he calls an 'option-enhancing policy' for a possible use of nuclear weapons. This would entail a stage-by stage approach in which the nuclear threat is increased at each step to deter India from attack, the first step could be a public or private warning, the second a demonstration explosion of a small nuclear weapon on its own soil, the third step would be the use of a few nuclear weapons on its own soil against Indian attacking forces and finally it would be used against critical but purely military targets in India across the border from Pakistan, probably in thinly populated areas in the desert or semi-desert, causing least collateral damage.[114] This may prevent Indian retaliation against cities in Pakistan and some weapon systems would be in reserve for the counter-value role and these weapons would be safe from Indian attack as some would be airborne while the ground based ones are mobile and could be moved around the country.[115]

The civilian rulers also agreed with this view, as Mr. Abdul Sattar (former Pakistani foreign minister), Mr. Agha Shahi and Mr. Zulfiqar Ali Khan jointly authored an article on October 5, 1999 which states that "The exigency under which Pakistan may use nuclear weapons is spelt out as: Although the precise contingencies in which Pakistan may use nuclear weapons have not been articulated or even defined by the government, the assumption has been that if the enemy launches a war and undertakes a piercing attack to occupy large territories or communications junctions, the weapon of last resort would have to be invoked."[116] This particular tenet of the nuclear policy was not malleable initially and the Pakistanis refused to accept the Indian proposal of signing a joint No-First Use Policy, as the felt that nuclear "First – Use" gave them the option of a pre-emptive nuclear strike, which could disrupt India's nuclear retaliatory capabilities and thus unsettle the Indian C&C system. However; with time certain sections in Pakistani society have understood the futility of this intent and have started debating the possibility of adopting a more moderate view. Lt. Gen Khalid Kidwai, the head of the strategic Planning Division in Pakistan commented in an interview that "nuclear weapons would be used only if the very existence of Pakistan as a state is at Stake"[117] and for the first time a few red lines or thresholds under which nuclear weapons could be used were elaborated by him. They being:-

(a) Space Threshold. If India attacks Pakistan and conquers a large part of its territory;

(b) Military Threshold. India destroys a large part of Pakistan's land or air forces;

(c) Economic Threshold. India Proceeds to the economical strangulation of Pakistan;

(d) Stability Threshold. If India pushes Pakistan into political destabilisation or creates a large scale internal subversion in Pakistan.[118]

Many analysts also believe that another red line that should not be violated is the Indus River Water Treaty (with the Indus water or its vital arteries) which forms the *"lifeline"* of Pakistan. The Indus and its tributaries originate in India and so Pakistan has an apprehension that India being an upper riparian in the Indus treaty can use water as a leverage to trouble Pakistan. Pakistan would prefer to continue with the Indus water treaty but some sections in India want to renegotiate it .They believe that due to demographic changes in Jammu and Kashmir, the demand for water has increased and they believe that the water is given to Pakistan at the cost of the Kashmiri people hence the treaty should be renegotiated. Another red line is if any of the nuclear installations in Pakistan is attacked, or if there is a chemical or biological weapons attack against Pakistan, then it would be responded by massive retaliation. The economic threshold may also refer to a blockade of the Sindh[119] province and the coastal cities of the Baluchistan province, which the Pakistanis think that if Pakistan navy is unable to safeguard effectively, then it can use its nuclear weapons.

Minimum Credible Nuclear Deterrence

In 1999 PM Nawaz Sharif had said that "Nuclear restraint, stabilisation and minimum credible deterrence constitute the basic elements of Pakistan's nuclear Policy"[120]. "Minimal" numbers for credible deterrence in Pakistan depend on Rawalpindi's targeting strategy, which remains deliberately opaque. Consequently, important aspects of this analysis are conjectural.[121] Initially the op-ed by Agha Shahi, Zulfiqar Ali Khan and Abdul Sattar had stated "Of course, minimum [credible deterrence] cannot be defined in static numbers. In the absence of mutual restraints, the size of Pakistan's arsenal and its deployment pattern have to be adjusted to ward off dangers of pre-emption and interception."[122] He further mentioned that "Obviously our deterrence force will have to be upgraded in proportion to the heightened threat of pre-emption and interception."[123] This can be summed up in the statement of Mr. Zafar Nawaz Jaspal "...parity between opponents is not based on numerical equality of the numbers of nuclear delivery systems, or of the number of warheads or in the yield of megatons available to each opponent .Parity requires assured destruction capability."[124] Thus Pakistan's credible minimum deterrence is mainly India centric. Therefore, they are constantly increasing their number in a bid to speed up its trajectory towards achieving triad capability. Indian think tanks have often debated about the fact that a situation that involves Pakistan going in for a first strike without a capable retaliatory arsenal is suicidal. Therefore, the assumption that emerges is that the Pakistani Army has realistically worked towards achieving counter strike capabilities. The details of this counter strike capability will be discussed later on

The Minimum Credible deterrence that has evolved as a result of these strategies has four main objectives as stated by Mr Durani:-

a) deterrence of all forms of external aggression;

b) building an effective combination of conventional and strategic forces;

c) avoiding a pre-emptive strike through protection and the threat of nuclear retaliation; and

d) stabilizing strategic deterrence in South Asia[125]

Nuclear Force structure

Pakistan's initial nuclear programme was influenced by the erstwhile US President, Eisenhower's "Atom for peace" programme. However post the 1971 war, the focus shifted towards the military use of nuclear energy. This shift in specialization led to the beginning of the missile programme in the early 1980s. Since Pakistan did not have any intrinsic nuclear technological expertise, they began attempting to form alliances with nations like China and US, with the hope that these nations would aid Pakistan in their nuclearization process. While the US remained wary of overt commitment, China did not hesitate to aid Pakistan, since a Sino – Pak nexus worked to effectively undercut India's superiority in the peninsula. In fact it can be stated that without China's help, Pakistan would never have developed its missile programme so efficiently. They have already developed short and medium range missiles along with the requisite delivery systems.

Pakistan's main aim has always been, to compete with India and achieve parity in the nuclear weapons sector, the parity that it has failed to achieve in the conventional arena thus far. The development of nuclear weapons is considered extremely important by them due to the escalated threat potential of the weapons and therefore, Pakistan is not keen on conventional parity. Their focus has moved towards the development of their nuclear triad. After developing their strategic air and land vectors they are now trying to develop naval nuclear capabilities in order to complete the triad and consequently achieve counter strike capabilities. Triad will help in enhancing their first strike capabilities and their by achieve a potent nuclear deterrence

Ballistic missile programme

As mentioned earlier Pakistan's nuclear missile programme has been developed through Chinese support. When China's nuclear assistance was exposed and after Beijing suppressed the prodemocracy demonstrations in 1989,the United States imposed sanctions and suspended arms sale and military to military contact[126]. However; the assistance continued covertly through North Korea. China's short range Ballistic missiles (SRBM), especially the M series mainly M - 9 and M -11, have been given to Pakistan. The two nations had begun discussions regarding the transfer of M – 11 missiles to Pakistan in the early 1990s. "In the same period, the National Development Complex (NDC) reportedly acquired complete unassembled M-11s and possibly an undisclosed number of M-9 SRBMs from Beijing."[127] "The M-9 missile is of dual use and has a range of 600 km and M-11 is road mobile single staged solid fuel missile. Pakistani Shaheen missile series are of Chinese M-11 and M-18 lineage, whereas the Ghauri series were built from North Korean Nodong designs."[128] Since then, the growth of Pakistan's nuclear arsenal has been phenomenal. The quantity of weapons has increased from merely two in 1998 to over a hundred nuclear weapons in 2013. The weapons since then have undergone a transformation both quantitatively as well as qualitatively. The liquid fuelled silo based systems have been changed into solid –fuelled road mobile missile systems. The current nuclear system of Pakistan consists of:

- Hatf-1 and Hatf-2 (Abdali) both resemble Chinese N series and are SRBMS The former has a single staged solid propellant system with a payload of 500kg, and could be conventional or High Explosive (HE) chemical or sub munitions [129]. The latter has a range of less than 200km with a payload of 500kg and Pakistan 's Chairman of the Joint Chiefs Of Staff Committee described it as providing "operational level capability ,addition to the strategic level capability ,Which Pakistan already possess."[130]

- Hatf-3 (Ghaznavi)-A single warhead with a payload of 700 kg and a range of 280 km. This warhead closely matches with the Chinese M-11 hence there are views that its actual range has to be 350 kms and this can carry a longer nuclear warhead and a shorter conventional warhead [131]

- Hatf-4 (Shaheen) Single stage solid propelled missile with an inertial guided system and a maximum range of 750km [132]

- Hatf-5 (Ghauri)-A single stage liquid propelled with a range of 1200km based on the North Korean Nodong missile system .Ghauri -2 has 1800km range. Ghauri-3 is supposed to have range of 3000km and is still under the development stage[133].

- Hatf-6 (Shaheen II) a 2000km range solid propelled two stage missile whose range has been increased to 2500 km.[134]

- Hatf-9 (Nasr) Test fired in 2011 is Pakistan's battle field short range (60km) surface-to-surface multi tube nuclear missile. This has been developed to add deterrence value. Pakistan's Strategic Weapons Development Programme at short ranges, NASR, with a range of 60 km, carries nuclear warheads of appropriate yield with high accuracy, [and] shoot and scoot attributes, this quick response system addresses the need to deter evolving threats.[135]

- Hatf-7 (Babur) and Hatf-8 (Ra'ad) are the cruise missiles. The former is all purpose short range turbojet powered cruise missile with single warhead and a range of 600km. It is believed that the two Tomahawk which was captured by Pakistan may have been reversed engineered to make this missile[136] .The latter has a payload of 400kg and range of 350 km meant to be launched from aerial platforms and this is believed to have stealth capabilities and is a low altitude terrain following missile with high manoeuvrability and can deliver all types of warheads ,with high accuracy[137]

Apart from these systems, Pakistan has also improved the prowess of its Air force through the acquisition of the Chinese JF-10s and JF-17s, the latter being a fourth generation Chinese fighter aircraft and a low cost, multi-role combat aircraft aimed at meeting the tactical and the strategic requirements of the Pakistani Air force, co-developed by Pakistan and China.[138] The co-production of sub-assemblies and structural parts has commenced and Pakistan is expected to join the exclusive club of the few nations manufacturing fighter aircrafts.[139] Apart from these, they also have American F-16s and the Chinese A-5s along with French Mirage, the Ra'ad missile could be deployed on this irage Vs.

Table: 12 Pakistan Nuclear Delivery System, 2012

Delivery System	Range	Deployment
	Aircraft	
Aircraft F-16A/B	1,600	1998
Mirage V	2,100	1998
	Ballistic missiles	
Abdali (Hatf-2)	180	(2012)
Ghaznavi (Hatf-3)	400	2004

Delivery System	Range	Deployment
Shaheen-1 (Hatf-4)	>450	2003
Shaheen -2(Hatf-6)	2500	2011
Shaheen-1A	2500-3000	2012 test fired
Ghauri (Hatf-5)	1200	2003
Nasr (Hatf-9)	60	(2014)
	Cruise missiles	
Babur (Hatf-7)	600	(2011)
Ra'ad (Hatf-8)	350	(2013)

Source: *Updated and as cited in Hans Kristensen and Robert S. Norris, "Pakistan Nuclear Forces 2011,"* Bulletin of the Atomic Scientists, *Volume 67, No. 4, pp. 91-99*

Fissile Material

Pakistan has built an extensive nuclear infrastructure comprising facilities for uranium mining, uranium enrichment, reactor fuel fabrication and spent fuel reprocessing units, thereby allowing it to produce not only Highly Enriched Uranium but also Plutonium .As on 2011; it was believed to have produced 2–3.5 tonnes of HEU.[140] At this rate it must be producing 120-180 kg per year which is enough to produce 10-15 warheads. The Kahuta plant is believed to have a capacity of 15 000–45 000 separative work units per year.[141]

Plutonium stockpile

Pakistan has recently started diversifying its fissile material production and constant efforts are being made to increase the production of Plutonium. "At Khushab, two reactors are operating and two others are being built, new reprocessing facilities are also being constructed at Nilore and probably at Chashma."[142] *Khushab-I* has a capacity of 40–50 MWT, the *Khushab-II* reactor became operant towards the end of 2009 and the beginning of 2010, the third reactor is nearly complete and the construction of the fourth began earlier in 2011[143]. All these reactors function with similar power calibre and are capable of producing 6–12 kg of weapons grade plutonium per year depending on how efficiently they are operated.[144] As of the start of 2012, Pakistan is estimated to have produced a total of about 140 kg of plutonium.[145] At this rate, (assuming hypothetically that 5 kg weapons grade plutonium is required for each warhead), Pakistan's reactors would be producing the amount of plutonium sufficient for creating 30 warheads. Moreover, Pakistan also reprocesses the spent fuel from its *Khushab* reactors at the Rawalpindi New Labs facility, which has two reprocessing plants, each with an estimated capacity of 10–20 tons per year of spent fuel[146]. While the location of the varied fissile material types have not been disclosed openly, the information that is available from open sources states that Pakistan has a very elaborate nuclear fissile infrastructure, and is continually diversifying it. The increase in the production of HEU and Plutonium is a cause of concern .Reports further state that they have an infant tritium production plant also.

The table below depicts a detailed analysis of this nuclearization process.

Table: 13 Pakistan's Fissile Material Facilities

Location	Facility Type	Material
Dera Ghazi Khan	Uranium mine, ore concentration plant, conversion plant	Uranium
Kahuta	Enrichment (Khan Research Laboratories)	HEU
Gadwal (Wah)	Enrichment (secondary plant)	HEU
Chaklala	Enrichment (pilot plant)	HEU
Sihala	Enrichment (pilot plant)	HEU
Golra	Enrichment (pilot plant)	HEU
Khushab–I	Heavy-water reactor 40–50MWt	Plutonium
Khushab–II	Heavy-water reactor 40–50MWt	Plutonium

Location	Facility Type	Material
Khushab–III	Heavy-water reactor 40–50MWt (under construction)	Plutonium
Khushab–IV	Heavy-water reactor 40–50MWt (under construction)	Plutonium
Chashma (Khushab)	Reprocessing facility (under construction)	Plutonium
Rawalpindi	Reprocessing facility–I (New Laboratories)	Plutonium
Rawalpindi	Reprocessing facility–II (New Laboratories))	Plutonium
Khushab–I and II	Tritium production	Tritium
Chashma (Kundian)	Reactor fuel-fabrication plant	
Multan	Heavy-water production facility	
Khushab	Heavy-water production facility	

Source: *Adapted and updated from* Nuclear Black Markets: Pakistan, A.Q. Khan and the Rise of Proliferation Networks, *International Institute of Strategic Studies, London, 2007.*

The National Engineering and Scientific Commission of Pakistan looks after the three main bodies that are responsible for Uranium and Plutonium production, namely :-

- The A.Q. Khan Research Laboratory (Kahuta) producing enriched uranium;

- the Pakistan Atomic Energy Commission is responsible for uranium mining, fuel fabrication, reactor construction and operation, and spent fuel reprocessing to produce plutonium; and

- the National Development Complex is responsible for weapons and delivery system research and production[147]

Nuclear Command and Control (NCC)

As mentioned earlier, Pakistan's nuclear arsenal is increasing at a phenomenal pace and it is estimated, that the upsurge in the nuclear weapons will be close to 10-15 warheads per year. It has been predicted that Pakistan will have more than 200 nuclear warheads by 2020[148]. The fact that Pakistan has diversified its fissile material by developing plutonium plants and reprocessing units has amplified the security and safety threats both internally as well as externally. Pakistan is vulnerable to instability and terrorist attacks both within its subcontinent and from outside as well. Bruce Riedel, a South Asia expert and co-chair of the Obama Administration's Afghanistan Pakistan strategy review describes Pakistan by saying "It has more terrorists per square mile than anyplace else on earth, and it has a nuclear weapons programme that is growing faster than anyplace else on earth."[149] In such volatile conditions, it becomes important to understand and analyse the Pakistan Nuclear Command and Control (PNCC) system. Pakistan's NCC was revamped in 1998 after Pakistan conducted its first nuclear test in the month of May 1998[150]. Major General Khalid Kidwai was given the task of providing recommendations for the nuclear Command and Control system. Soon, a National Command Authority (NCA) was created and Kidwai was made the head of the Strategic Plans Division, or the SPD. The National Command Authority is headed by the Prime Minister and the details for the same are given in Figure 12. This is the first tier that supervises the functions and administration of all the organizations working on the research, development, and employment of nuclear weapons and the military services that operate the strategic forces[151]. The ECC is the main policy making organ and functions as a politico-military committee [152]

The DCA is responsible for ensuring that the development of the strategic weapons programme progresses as per the approved development strategy.[153]

Figure: 12 Pakistan's National Command Authority[154]

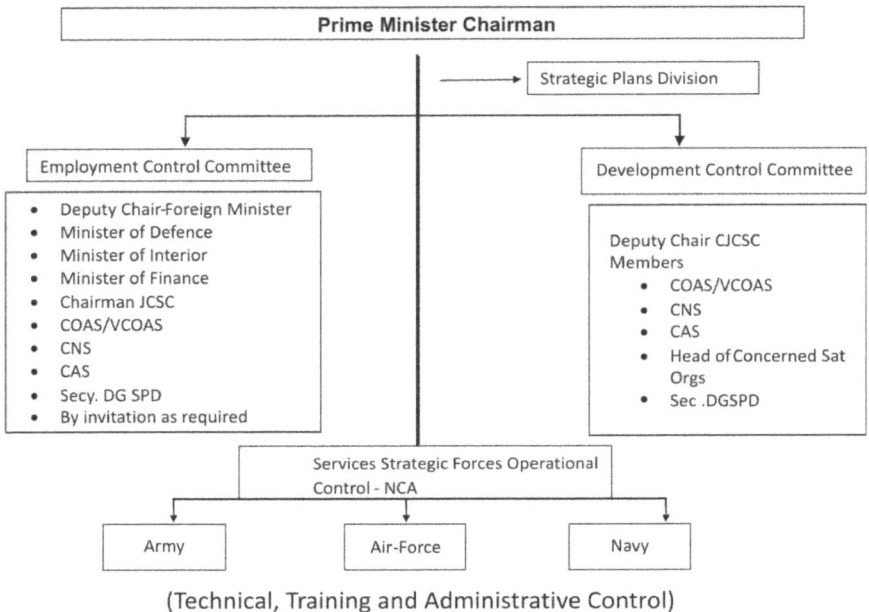

Prime Minister Chairman

Strategic Plans Division

Employment Control Committee
- Deputy Chair-Foreign Minister
- Minister of Defence
- Minister of Interior
- Minister of Finance
- Chairman JCSC
- COAS/VCOAS
- CNS
- CAS
- Secy. DG SPD
- By invitation as required

Development Control Committee

Deputy Chair CJCSC
Members
- COAS/VCOAS
- CNS
- CAS
- Head of Concerned Sat Orgs
- Sec .DGSPD

Services Strategic Forces Operational Control - NCA

Army	Air-Force	Navy

(Technical, Training and Administrative Control)

The most important tier in this hierarchy is the SPD and the entire nuclear strategy is formulated by them. This level is headed by the Director General of the Army. During peacetime, the SPD is responsible for protecting Pakistan's strategic programmes from insider and outsider threats, most importantly from theft or loss of nuclear material and against infiltration of the Strategic organizations by ill-intentioned actors.[155] The SPD maintains a high level of secrecy as far as the nuclear weapons and their delivery systems are concerned. These systems are firmly controlled by the SPD and the information is not shared by any other organization, not even with the military and the ISI. The service's Strategic Force Command (SFC) also reports directly to the NCA. "The primary responsibility of these commands is to exercise technical, training, and administrative control over the strategic delivery systems. The operational control, however, rests with the NCA[156] Following the A.Q. Khan scandal, Pakistan identified Khan's oversight of Khan Research Laboratory security staff as a key deficiency and SPD's security division overtook responsibility for the inner perimeter. A second-rung consists of fencing, electronic sensors, cameras, and security personnel, finally, counter-intelligence teams work on identifying threats.[157]

The details Organization of SPD could be seen in Figure 13

Figure: 13 Pakistan's Strategic Plans

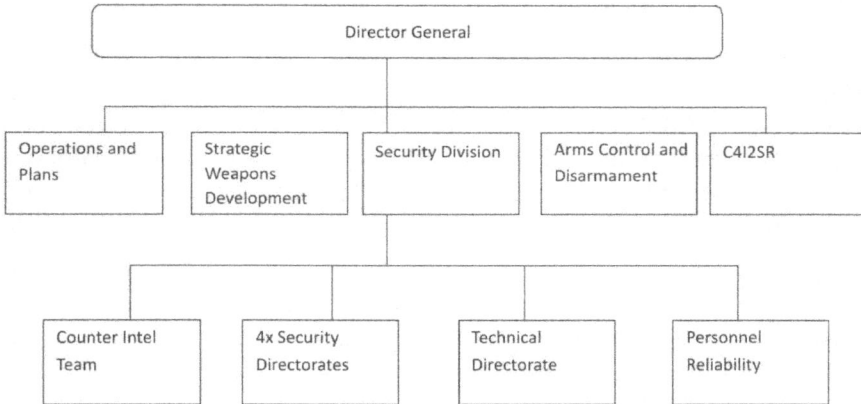

Source: Christopher Clary" Thinking about Pakistan's Nuclear Security in Peacetime,Crisis and War

Strategic Force Command

This is the final tier of the Command and Control system. The service's Strategic Force Command also reports directly to the NCA. "The primary responsibility of these commands is to exercise technical, training, and administrative control over the strategic delivery systems. The operational control, however, rests with the NCA"[158]

Safety and Security of Nuclear Weapon and Fissile Material

Pakistan has diversified and expanded its nuclear weapons along with its fissile extraction and reprocessing plants. Its strategy of acquiring tactical nuclear weapons exposes the civilian population to nuclear threat. The Pakistani government has repeatedly claimed that they have taken exhaustive measure to make its nuclear programme safe and secure.

Firstly it states that nuclear warheads have been stored partially disassembled and de-mated, as the nuclear core is removed from the detonators. These are widely dispersed with several nuclear weapon storage sites in the country and not centrally localized. The 2001 US Defence Department report on Proliferation, Threat and Response states that "Islamabad's nuclear weapons are probably stored in component form and "Pakistan probably could assemble the weapons fairly quickly...."[159]

Secondly, all the weapons are fitted with permissive action links (PALs). Air Commodore Khalid Banuri and Adil Sultan, serving and recently retired SPD officials state "To preclude any possibility of inadvertent or unauthorized use of nuclear weapons, Pakistan has developed physical safety mechanisms and firewalls both in the weapon systems themselves and in the chain of command. No single individual can operate a weapons system, nor can one individual issue the command for nuclear weapons use"[160] and the Pakistanis have worked with the Americans to strengthen their nuclear security. Admiral Mullen commented on May 2009 saying that "The United States, have invested fairly significantly over the last three years, to work with them, to improve that security. And we're satisfied, very satisfied with that progress"[161]. Since then, US has provided 100 million dollars' worth tinning equipment to them.

Thirdly, Pakistan claims to have placed detailed screening procedures that include a "Human Reliability Programme" for civilian personnel and a "Personnel Reliability Programme" for military personnel[162], to ensure secrecy and loyalty as nearly 10,000 personnel are working and have access to sensitive information which could become a major threat if leaked[163].

Fourthly, the Pakistan Nuclear Regulatory Authority (PNRA), which was created in 2001 and consists of 200 experts, is in charge of the physical security of fissile material and radioactive sources. It is stated that all known sources have reportedly been registered, orphan sources have been recovered and two secure storage sites have been set up.[164]Four of the civilian nuclear power plants namely Karanchi Nuclear Power Plant and Chasma-I power Reactor and the Pakistan Atomic Research Reactor I and II in Rawalpindi are under IAEA safeguards however the plutonium and weapon grade uranium plants along with Khushab and Kahuta plant are not under safeguards[165].

Apart from all these measures, Pakistan's biggest security challenge would be to safeguard its arsenal from Jihadist intervention. This includes terrorist organizations within the country and those coming from outside. Post the withdrawal of US troops from Afghanistan; the chances of Pakistan's internal dynamics becoming volatile and unstable are quiet high. A number of terrorist attacks have already taken place in the region, and some have been dangerously close to the nuclear installations. For example, Pakistan Aeronautical Complex at Kamra was hit in 2007 and 2009[166]. Another prominent attack was executed on the Mehran Nuclear Base, "In May 2011 the Pakistani Taliban attacked the Mehran Nuclear Base in Karachi, about 15 miles away from a suspected nuclear storage facility is another glaring example of insider collaboration"[167]

While the Pakistani leadership maintains that they are confident that they can tackle any eventuality, the ground reality remains that a survey conducted by the NTI on Nuclear Security conditions places Pakistan and North Korea as the last two countries in an index comprising of 32 countries in the "Risk Environment" category. These unsafe conditions can further precipitate once the US withdraws from Afghanistan.

Nuclear Strategy

Pakistan's nuclear strategy, as mentioned earlier, is mainly India centric, and its principal aim is to deter all forms of aggression from India. One of the major reasons for Pakistan's development of nuclear weapons was their defeat in 1970 and the subsequent dismembered of Pakistan and the creation of Bangladesh. This had happened when they were still members of CENTO and SEATO. After this war, they realized the importance of building a strong militarily with advanced nuclear capabilities in order to prevent any vulnerability in future. They opted for nuclear weapons since they believed that it would provide them with the required security against India. In other words, they understood the Waltz theory of Balance of Power that "states exist in an anarchical international system and must therefore rely on self-help to protect their sovereignty and national security."[168] From that time onwards efforts were made to develop a nuclear Pakistan. At that point they were financially as well as technologically incapable of building nuclear weapons and therefore they opted to align with US and China. Pakistani strategists accept the fact that without China's help, it would have been difficult for them to build their nuclear arsenal.

Once Pakistan gained nuclear capability, they began using the nuclear weapon as a shield to pursue their grand strategy of proxy/covert wars. The constant threat that they could use them in the Kargil war and in operation Parakram depicts their aggressive mind-set, where they would not hesitate to destabilize the situation using any means possible. In its nuclear policy during its earlier years, Pakistani strategists had clearly mentioned their willingness to use nuclear weapons in the beginning of the warfare, even if the warfare was conventional in nature. They believed that India's conventional superiority denies them the dominance that they so ardently desire. Hence, the use of nuclear weapons and their First Use policy, became a strategy to achieve this goal for dominance and was aimed at maintaining the deterrence and balance of power. However according to them the Indians in their Cold Start Doctrine (CSD) exposed the gaps of Pakistan's strategic thinking. The CSD envisages reorganizing strike corps into at least eight smaller division-sized Integrated Battle Groups (IBGs) that combine mechanized infantry, artillery, and armour on the pattern of Soviet Union's operational manoeuvre groups[169]. Within a short period of time these IBGs would ingress 50 – 80 kms deep in to the Pakistani territory.

Pakistanis debated about plugging these apparent gaps at the operational and tactical levels and hence developed tactical nuclear weapons to deny India the space to launch limited military operations. Pakistan perceives "Nasr" as giving its National Command Authority (NCA) an important option in the times of crisis, apart from the usual retaliation with full nuclear and conventional force.

Keeping this policy in mind, Pakistan had started developing plutonium and working on its strategy to expand its reprocessing plant. As of now, Pakistan is the nation with the fastest growing nuclear arsenal[170]. Pakistan has gradually changed its strategic posture as well, from an all-out war to a more flexible response option. This is mainly due to its development of the tactical nuclear weapon. It feels that through Nasr it has developed the ability to have a credible layered deterrence. It already possessed strategic deterrence as far as its various short and medium range ballistic missiles were concerned and the Nasr has given it the tactical deterrence required to counter India's CSD. This is often described as "the Strategy of Assured Deterrence" as exhibited by the figure below. In order to make it more potent, however, Pakistan is developing and enhancing its triad capabilities.

Figure: 14 Pakistani Missile Range

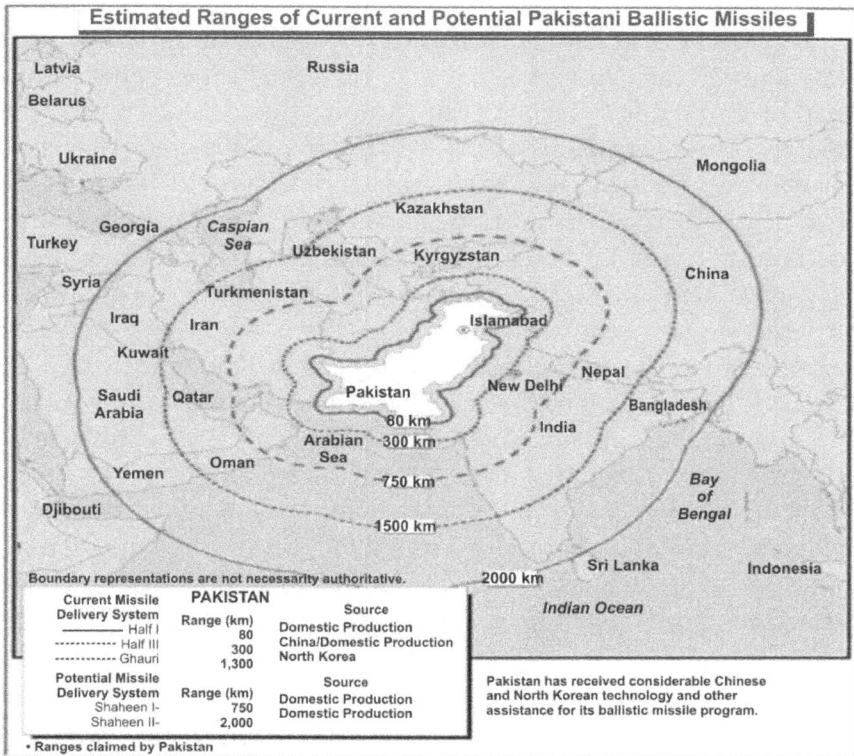

Source: - www.intellectualtakeout.org

Pakistan and Nuclear Triad

In the last few years, Pakistan has realized that they lacked second strike capability and in such a scenario, the use of its "First Strike policy" will be detrimental for their survival, as India has clearly mentioned in its nuclear doctrine that any attack on its territory or on its soldiers would amount to a punitive retaliation and Pakistan would not be able to deal with such retaliation.

Hence its next agenda has been aimed at developing a credible nuclear triad that would increase the survival rate of its nuclear weapons as well as function as a potent second strike strategy. Pakistan already has a varied ballistic arsenal and its Shaheen series has the range to hit any city in India. It has also started building its Air Force. It already has the American F-16s and Mirage V and it has also acquired the Chinese J-10s and J- 17s, the former being an all-weather multi-role fighter aircraft. Amongst its defence forces, the Pakistani Navy is considered the weakest link in the chain. Pakistan has started understanding the importance of the sea as a source of strategic depth. It is working towards increasing its maritime strength by trying to increase the number of its submarines. It has decided to field tactical nuclear weapons aboard their small flotillas of diesel-electric submarines and ships, as it is also believed that Pakistan would be stationing nuclear weaponry aboard its surface ships and maritime-patrol aircrafts and they sought to make Hatf 7 Cruise missile compatible with naval platforms[171] Not only would this provide the country with greater strategic depth, it would also extend some of the more dysfunctional elements of the Indo-Pakistani nuclear interactions from land to sea. By threatening first nuclear use against an advancing Indian aircraft carrier strike force, Islamabad can hope to acquire escalation dominance and considerably dilute its larger neighbour's coercive naval power.[172] For Pakistani planners, acquiring nuclear-armed cruise missile submarines would provide an opportunity to skew its existing power relationship with India in Pakistan's favour, primarily by injecting a sizable degree of uncertainty and ambiguity in India's tactical calculus, but also by preventing the Indian Navy from concentrating the bulk of its power projection platforms in one specific location.[173] Thus they are trying to "reaffirm credibility of deterrence at sea[174]"

Pakistan may have developed its nuclear tipped Submarine Launched Cruise missile (SLCMs), if it has plutonium and tritium available from its Khushab Nuclear Complex then it can develop the boosted –fission warhead for its SLCMs- Babur, its naval version and such warheads can also be deployed on conventional attack submarines (SSKs) such as the Pakistani Air Independent Propulsion (AIP) equipped Agosta 90-Bs in the future.[175] Pakistan will also be acquiring six Chinese Qing-class AIP SSKs which can launch anti-ship and land-attack cruise missiles from its torpedo tubes, and this does come close to a reliable, if not assured second strike capability.[176]

What remains to be seen is whether or not Pakistan has developed its warhead miniaturization capability. If it has, then the next logical step would be for it to develop MIRVs (Multiple Independently Targetable Re–entry vehicles). The conjunction of this capability on medium and long range ballistic missiles would challenge and hinder India's Ballistic Missile Development programme.

Pakistan's Satellite Programme

With Chinese help, Pakistan had successfully launched its communications satellite, PAKSAT-IR in 2011. This satellite has a design life of 15 years and provides TV broadcasting, internet and data communication services across South and Central Asia, Eastern Europe, East Africa and the Far East[177].

The country's space agency, Pakistan Space and Upper Atmosphere Research Commission (SUPARCO), is all set to launch an advanced high resolution Remote Sensing Satellite System (RSSS) technology in 2014, to meet the national and international user requirements in the field of satellite imagery and under the Pakistani Space Programme, "vision 2040" many more satellites will be launched.[178] These satellite developments will increase the Pakistani air intelligence capabilities which will in turn enable them to target and track India's nuclear arsenal. The weapons delivery systems, such as the air bases and the ballistic missile units will become more vulnerable to attacks, since in a warlike scenario, Pakistan's main objective will be to target Indian cities, and to neutralise and block their satellite based communication systems thus unsettling the Indian Command and Control systems.

Conclusion

India's growing economic development and its increasing military expenditure will amplify the asymmetries between the two nations and a cornered Pakistan, consequently, is going to turn towards its nuclear arsenal. Pakistan believes that its nuclear weapons have increased the deterrence value within the region and it will continue to blackmail India through its First Use policy in order to covertly carry out its proxy war of terrorism. Pakistan also believes that its tactical nuclear weapons have outmoded the Indian CSD. They believe that Nasr has given them the requisite tactical edge and this miniaturization technique will further help Pakistan in developing their MIRV capabilities culminating in the establishment of its nuclear triad. Pakistan believes that through its land and sea based nuclear tipped cruise missiles, it can achieve greater depth in the Indian Ocean Region (IOR). Pakistan will continue to expand and diversify its nuclear fissile material in order to develop both tactical as well as strategic nuclear weapons and thereby fulfil its nuclear policy requirements of "First Use" and consequently ensure the development of a credible second strike capability as well. Lastly it is also trying to enhance and develop its conventional capabilities by concentrating on the modernization of its air power and developing maritime strike capabilities through its nuclear tipped missiles and SLCMs. It has already realized the important role that satellite technology can play as far as local warfare is concerned, and it is gradually working towards increasing its presence in this field as well.

India's Nuclear Challenge

The necessity for India's nuclear programme is based on a number of security concerns that emerged due to the changing strategic environment. Chinese action in Tibet, the 1962 war, the 1964 nuclear explosion by China, and importantly, the triangular US-Pakistan China nexus initially, completely altered the security calculus in Asia. Pakistan's persistent efforts to acquire nuclear weapons, and the constant Chinese support provided to them in this endeavour along with the China's increasingly aggressive ballistic missile development programme compelled India to transform its Peaceful Nuclear

Programme (PNP) into a militarized one. India's Integrated Guided Missile Programme began in the 80s, and with its second nuclear explosion in 1998, India emerged as an overt Nuclear Weapon State. Since then, India has maintained its nuclear capabilities solely for the purposes of deterrence. In order to understand a nation's defence strategy, it is essential to start by first analysing its doctrines and policies. In examining India's Nuclear Doctrine, one needs to reassess its main tenets, inspect its temporal adaptability, and its eventual compatibility with the development of its weapons programme.

Nuclear Doctrine of India

A nuclear doctrine is an indicator, of the mind-set and psychology of a nation. In a broader sense, it "is critical to any consideration of how [its] nuclear ... weapons will be used and how the presence of these weapons might affect [its] international relations generally."[179] It essentially enunciates the strategy adopted by a particular nation with regard to the subject matter and proscribes the methods and goals through which the nation state plans to develop its weaponry to achieve its strategic objectives. India's Nuclear Doctrine was first created in the form of a Draft Report in 1999. Although it has had its share of controversies over time, (the key concern being whether it was just a draft or the BJP's official policy), the draft still remains the foundation on which the future report was based.

Nuclear Draft Report[180]

While the draft on the nuclear doctrine was very comprehensive, some analysts believe that it serves more of a rhetorical function instead of a practical purpose.

- **Preamble** The doctrine begins with a preamble that highlights the reasons underlying India's decision to opt for nuclear weapons which was basically due to the appalling lack of global disarmament. Moreover, the NPT had legitimized the vertical proliferation of nuclear material among the NWS but curbed the horizontal proliferation of information and materials. This discrimination, along with the aggressive doctrines adopted by some nations that legalized the first use of nuclear weapons even against non-nuclear states, has been considered a universal threat to peace and stability. Hence, the document outlines the broad principles for the development, deployment and issues related to nuclear forces.

- **Objectives** The second paragraph deals with the objectives of developing effective, credible nuclear deterrence with adequate retaliatory capabilities – a strategy aimed at providing a level of capability which is consistent with maximum credibility, survivability, effectiveness, safety and security.[181] It also added the dynamic concept of minimum nuclear deterrence that works fundamentally to prevent or deter the use and threat of the use of nuclear weapons against India. To ensure this deterrence, this part of the doctrine stated that India will have a sufficient, survivable and operationally prepared nuclear force along with a robust Command and Control system and effective early warning capabilities. It also states the No-First Use of nuclear weapons policy and also provides the non – nuclear states with negative security by stating that it will not resort to using nuclear weapons as threats against them.

- **Nuclear Forces** The doctrine further states that the nuclear forces will be based on a triad of aircraft, mobile land based missiles and sea based assets thereby ensuring the assured capability of effective retaliation.

- **Credibility and Survivability** The credibility to retaliate with effectiveness in case of a nuclear attack by maximizing synergy among all the elements is another important aspect, along with survivability of nuclear forces after a surprise attack so that a punitive response could be given.

- **Command and Control** The nuclear weapon was to be tightly controlled at the political level. The highest authority to take the nuclear decision lies with Prime Minister of the country .It also states the unity of C&C of nuclear forces including dual capable delivery system. It also deals with having a survivable C4I2 systems

- **Security and safety** Security of nuclear weapons along

with the entire nuclear paraphernalia will be fully guarded
.Full proof procedures and system to be instituted and an
appropriate disaster control system to be developed.

- **Research and Development** In order to keep up with the
technological advancements India will take steps to increase
its efforts on research and development

- **Disarmament and Arms Control** Having a global, verifiable
and non-discriminatory nuclear disarmament is a national
security objective and India shall continue with its efforts to
create a Nuclear Weapon Free World at an early date[182].

Cabinet Committee on Security (CCS)

In 2003, the Cabinet Committee on Security Review[183] Progress
operationalized India's Nuclear Doctrine. It incorporated most of the
key issues discussed in the previous draft except for a few marginal
changes, for example: 1) in case of first strike the retaliation would
be massive instead of punitive and 2) likewise an attack by nuclear
weapons was introduced in case of a biological or chemical attack on
India or its soldiers. It further reviewed the Command and Control
system and approved the appointment of a Commander-in Chief,
Strategic force command, to manage and administer its strategic
forces.

Doctrine Analysis

The objective of developing nuclear weapons is to maintain deterrence,
so that a nuclear war can be avoided. This deterrence then needs to
be constantly examined and evolved, since "deterrence" is a relative
term, and the changing geopolitical environment must influence
and define any evolution in the doctrine. Therefore, a good doctrine
aims to bridge the gap between the theorization of a concept and
its actual operation, through a crisp strategic plan. It is a two way
process that requires the amalgamation of political thought with
military strategies. Hence, both the political as well as the military
leaders need to be in sync, which unfortunately is often deemed
implausible in a democracy. The constant debate between political
will and military might deters the efficient development of the nuclear
doctrine. This political tug of war notwithstanding, however, India

has turned to a middle course where strong personalities from both fields have charted historical moments. It is the art of conviction, more so in the case of the latter, that can bring results and keep the nation's deterrence effective and reliable.

No-First Use

India's strategic problem in the deterrence field has been complicated due to its two different nuclear adversaries. If India has an edge due to its conventional and nuclear superiority over Pakistan, it is still struggling to unravel its nuclear predicament in terms of China. A few issues of the nuclear doctrine have been constantly debated over time, for example questions have been asked regarding the efficacy of the NFU. Pakistan has declared its First Use policy and China a conditional NFU option. Between the aggressiveness of its two adversaries, India's NFU declaration becomes a weak response unlikely to deter Pakistan, redundant Vis-à-vis China, and irrelevant against India's non-nuclear neighbours, so what strategic value does it possess then?[184] Questions are raised regarding the judiciousness of NFU, for example India by adopting NFU is cautious in using nuclear weapons but in case the adversary is not being sensible then in that case should one give the NFU the go-by? The Indian government has often said that nuclear weapons are political instruments and not meant for war –fighting [185] so if that is the case, then it becomes imperative to keep ones options open. As Admiral Arun Prakash (Retd) states "As political instrument the best use of our nuclear weaponry would be to persuade, compel or coerce a recalcitrant adversary" he further reiterates that "The threat of use of nuclear weapons, no matter how subtle, subliminal or understated, has to be held out by forswearing First use, we obviously cannot hold out such a threat."[186] Ambassador Chari also believes that the "serious problem arising from India's NFU pledge; India must be prepared to absorb multiple strikes before launching its retaliatory forces... Could it be ensured that Command and Control arrangements would remain in the event of a nuclear multiple attacks?"[187]

All these views are relevant in their own right and certain caveats can be relooked. This will only be possible if politicians decide, whether nuclear weapons are for political rhetoric or the purpose is to have credible nuclear deterrence, because for credibility three things are essential, firstly the capability of a nation in terms of comprehensive force structure, secondly the resolve to use the nuclear weapon if situation demands and lastly most importantly to communicate the same to the adversary. Proper communication can strengthen nuclear deterrence because a nuclear war is the failure of deterrence. Deterrence can be successful only if the adversary recognizes the opponent's lethal capabilities. If India does not adapt its doctrine accordingly then, the covert proxy war of Pakistan will continue unabated, and also China's impetuous border incursions. India lacks parity against one adversary and the other has increased its nuclear arsenal to improper proportions and is working to improve its conventional strength .Moreover India's nuclear doctrine does not specify the course of action which the country will adopt if India's nuclear installations were hit by conventional weapons. Considering all this, a review of nuclear doctrine is advisable .However; India should continue with its NFU, as it validates India's stance that nuclear weapons are for deterrence, India is also genuine as far as nuclear disarmament is concerned and importantly it depicts the maturity of the nation in de-escalate conflicts, however; appropriate nuclear signalling (based on comprehensive force structure) by the political leaders is absolutely essential. Also nuclear doctrine should be considered as guidelines; hence ambiguity is essential (the specifics should be implicit and not written). After all keeping all your cards on the table is not a wise move .Too much transparency defeats one's manoeuvring capabilities.

Credible Minimum Deterrence

India has kept this aspect of its doctrine dynamic and avoided quantification of its minimum nuclear deterrence. Therefore, it is believed that the credible minimum force will be in proportion and keeping in mind the qualitative and quantitative increase of the nuclear arsenal of our adversaries. The National Security Adviser, Brijesh Mishra has stated that we have adopted a policy of minimum deterrence as the basic building block of our nuclear thinking. Minimum but credible deterrence is the watchword of our nuclear doctrine[188]. He had also elaborated that the force size quality and mix can change, these changes can happen any time and it is left to the government of the day to decide what to do and how to define minimum credible deterrence. The problem here stems from bureaucratic obfuscation, political insensitivity coupled with technical ignorance – a cumulative meld of all the banes of democracy. While military rule can accelerate the strategic decisions as well as the follow-ups required such as procurement, testing, etc., this democratic weakness can undermine the deterrence capabilities. The usability of a nuclear weapon is dependent on its technical advancements, preparedness and its support systems. The indigenization process should cater to military requirements and the Indian triad needs to be operationalized in a structured and timely manner. For such an efficient process, a great amount of synergy is required between the scientists and the military leaders. Secondly, deterrence should be made available at all levels, strategic as well as tactical. Some strategists believe that India should adopt the NATO concept of tactical nuclear weapons. According to this concept, India would need to develop, demonstrate and then deploy its tactical nuclear weapons against China in the eastern theatre. An example of this strategy can be seen in the Russians refusal of letting go of their tactical nuclear weapons and even today, a large number of these weapons are deployed near the Russia–China border. Daryl Kimbal Executive Director of Arms Control Association said "Russians see Tactical Nuclear Weapons (TNW) as a way to counter –balance China's large number of conventional forces on the eastern border, so Russians have retained --- a large number of deployed TNW than the US"[189]

It is stated that flexible response is essential part of war strategy and if used efficiently, it can increase the deterrence capabilities exponentially. Lastly, while one may talk about the possibility of a Credible Minimum Deterrence, the actual cost required to maintain this deterrence is phenomenal since one need to first survive an attack in order to guarantee retaliation and for that one requires a large amount of nuclear arsenal. As mentioned earlier, the concept of deterrence is a relative term and it varies with the degree of motivation which the enemy feels for our destruction in other words if deterrence fails, one needs to fight total war effectively [190]The failure of deterrence in any case depicts that one's deterrence was not credible and in that case it is very essential to have a retaliatory force which can strike first and is overwhelming to the enemy's retaliatory force and for this the nuclear force needs to be maintained at a very high pitch of efficiency and readiness [which should be] constantly improving.[191]

Triad of Nuclear Force

India has rightly declared in its doctrine the need to develop a triad of aircraft, mobile land based missiles and sea based assets. This is extremely important to counter nations that have a NFU policy and a declared massive retaliation policy. According to Ambassador Chari (Retd) to develop a triad facility nuclear and missile test would be unavoidable .The issue gains salience because India declared a moratorium on nuclear testing [192] Even if this issue of the triad is addressed through computer simulations, the political delays and slow indigenization process remains detrimental towards deterrence capabilities. The Sagarika SLBM had been initiated in the 1990s and it is still not inducted in the navy. One of the reasons for this delay can be that building sea based nuclear missiles is more complicated and expensive when compared to land based capabilities.

Developing an effective SSBN force is a major challenge for a nation's technological skill and operational ability. Though India's 30 year induction programme is a step in the right direction, it has been constantly marred by political, technical and financial delays. It is as Admiral Sushil Kumar (Retd) said in the *Times of India* that "while going for our own home grown strategic nuclear submarine capability has certainly been a major achievement…, the diversion of resources and added thrust to the induction of Arihant, with others to follow may have taken a toll on the navy's submarine arm, it has drastically delayed the induction of conventional submarine by almost a decade."[193] To ensure effective deterrence capability, it is essential to have a sound technological base as well as a steady flow of replacements for a nation's aging weaponry. A desired level of combat capability can be achieved only when there is a balanced mix of both the above mentioned principles.

Command and Control

In India, nuclear weapons are believed to be kept in a de-mated state and there is no central authority directly dealing with strategic weapons. The warheads remain with the scientists and the delivery vehicles are manned by the armed forces. This often creates complexities in efficient execution since deterrence is about the dual function of the precision of the missiles as well as the efficacy of the extended paraphernalia namely – the Command and Control system. The quality of an organization's C&C system determines the efficiency of its eventual war based mission. However; once India operationalises its nuclear triad then this de-matted state will also change and this will bring changes in the Command and Control structure also. In India, while the executive decision to launch a nuclear weapon lies with the Prime Minister, the major development of nuclear hardware lies with the Defence Ministry. The Defence Minister however, does not have any credible power as far as the development and production of nuclear weapon systems is concerned. This in turn may impact the efficiency of the applicability of the nuclear warheads. The DRDO (which is the sole body for developing the hardware) is an autonomous centre of power and the Defence Ministry has to share the responsibility with them. It is essential that a synergy should be implemented between the DRDO officials and the military. As General Ved Prakash Malik, former Chief of the Army Staff, points out that "the armed forces of India are kept out of the national security loop and were not adequately consulted by the government on operational and strategic matters, and this can result in large communication gaps between what is politically desirable and what is being planned by the military."[194] While things have changed marginally, major gaps and lacunas still remain. Another area where it is equally important to establish an efficient synergy would be the three wings of the armed forces. "In every major country there is a CDS or a CGS to bring synergy in military planning and operations."[195] "Today there is no unified command post in the capital from where the three service chiefs can jointly monitor and conduct conventional operations."[196] In India it is believed that the COSC is ineffective in performing the requisite coordination among the three pillars. Vice Admiral Verghese Koithara, states that "SFC which is considered accountable for the success of the military level nuclear deterrence in all its dimensions is over looking too many functions. He further reiterates that apart from training of personnel and units; ensuring appropriate material state of weapons and equipment...

and ensuring operational readiness at all times …it also includes strategic planning and creation of infrastructure; ensuring the quality of weapons and equipment inducted ;…and looking out for nuclear risks in conventional military operations."[197] Furthermore, the officers in the SFC are deployed on deputation basis and once their tenure is completed, they return to their respective units. This arbitrary deployment causes a lack of continuity that leads to security threats such as the risk of information leaks etc. Pakistan has developed a system whereby the men involved with nuclear issues are professionally trained and psychologically prepared to remain in the cadre until it is time for them to retire as mentioned in the Pakistan chapter. With this closed door policy, surveillance becomes easier and chances of information leaking out less likely. In order to ensure the efficacy of the C&C system, fundamental changes are required beginning with the Defence Ministry, which needs to be made more proactive, responsible and accountable. A lack of will amongst the politicians, coupled with the turf war amongst the three services tend to make the process of implementing planned systematic changes that much more difficult.

Research and Development

India needs to streamline the functioning of the DRDO. The fact that India has been the largest arms importer from 2009-2013 questions the success of the DRDO[198]. The targets set by the organizations are often unachievable due to basic infrastructural loopholes. As a result, most of its major projects are behind schedule. In fact Defence Minister, Mr Antony had pointed out to the frequent delays in weapons systems and singled out the LCA Tejas fighter project.[199] Moreover, it needs to be capable enough to compete globally. In continuing with the privatization policy of the country, certain sections of the defence industries are being opened up to private sector. The DRDO's monopoly in this field therefore will be challenged, and this healthy competition will therefore lead to an efficient technological advancement of the indigenization process. An efficient and accountable DRDO is a necessity, since the ground reality remains that no other institution in India can match the amount of advanced technological innovations and research conducted by the DRDO. Informational and Technological availability has increased of late due to the liberal policies adopted by the government and the increasing collaboration between India and the United States. The opportunities have increased after the Indo-US nuclear deal and the DRDO should make use of this available window. Additionally, the willingness of Indian and foreign corporate houses to invest in defence industries provides an added impetus to increase the efficiency of our Indigenisation process. The DRDO needs to oversee the working of their facility as well as these other agencies in order to ensure a wholesome developmental environment.

Conclusion

India's nuclear Doctrine was an exhaustive doctrine at the time it was formed. There are fundamental issues and questions regarding its relevance and applicability that still need to be answered. The doctrine should be more than a mere political tool, and the usability of nuclear arsenal needs to be authenticated in case of conventional threats to nuclear installations. The power of India's nuclear arsenal needs to be demonstrated so that tangible deterrence can be achieved. A few red lines also need to be incorporated especially keeping Pakistan's proxy war in mind, so that the adversary is cautious about attacking India due to the lethality of the countermeasures that would be employed. To ensure this applicability, it is essential to have crisp R&D organization, and well-structured procurement policies. The DRDO needs to be aware of emerging technological innovations and trends while simultaneously focusing on the timelines that need to be adhered to. The timelines become especially important in order to ensure that the weapons do not become obsolete by the time they have been inducted into the military. The conventional and nuclear weapon systems necessitate quick replacements. The aberrations in the C&C system need rectification, where greater stress is laid on synergy between the civil and military as well as between the three services of the armed forces.

India- China A comparative Analysis

China poses a multi-layered threat against India. India currently shares a 4200 km long unresolved border with China and to add to this, China's strategic partnership with Pakistan and its increased presence in the Indian Ocean Region is a challenge that needs to be carefully analysed. The difference between the two countries stems from culture and political governance and manifests itself in antagonistic ideology. Indians believe that peace begets security whereas for China it is strength that ensures stability. Therefore China's constant endeavour has been to display power and intimidate its adversaries. India needs to understand this philosophy and it is even more essential now for India to build its deterrence by enhancing the country's military and economic assets. Currently, China has a clear edge over India in both these departments, and as far as the defence sector is concerned, India lags behind China, more so in the nuclear field. China outnumbers India quantitatively as well as qualitatively in terms of its nuclear missiles. China has a dual doctrine that emphasizes the merger of its conventional strategy with its nuclear strategy ensuring that both the doctrines complement its force structure. It has developed this force structure on the principle of a local warfare construct with an assured punitive counter-strike as already mentioned in previous sub chapters. It also has an offensive conventional doctrine complemented by a retaliatory nuclear arsenal which has the dual capability to pursue counter value as well as counter force targets in Asia. China has the flexibility to respond to an attack through any of the three platforms as it has an extremely potent, functional triad as far as the Asian construct is concerned. Its missiles are qualitatively as well as quantitatively superior, its cruise missiles are the largest in Asia and it has transformed its navy to a blue water navy after the acquisition of the aircraft carrier. Moreover, its nuclear submarines are constantly displaying their presence in the Indian Ocean Region (IOR). It has a progressive cyber programme and cyber espionage is a cause of concern even for the Americans. China is, therefore, superior to India in all the departments, especially in terms of their long range ICBMs and MRBMs. China has 458 strategic missiles comprising 66ICBM, 6-IRBM,134- MRBM, 252-SRBM and 54-LACM compared to India's 54 Strategic missiles ,ICBM (Test Phase), 24-IRBM and 30SRBM[200]. China has a clear edge in her ICBMs, though India's Agni V has cleared the launch test but it will still take some time before it can be successfully inducted. The biggest advantage that China has is most of her missile development programme is indigenously built and is not dependent on other nations for the spare parts.

China also has developed an extensive logistic support in the Tibetan regions as described in the China chapter .The extensive road and rail route connects the mainland with the Tibetan plateau on one side and on the other side the infrastructural development till the LOC in India's eastern sector of Arunachal Pradesh and also in the Ladakh region has ensured a smooth supply chain, thus enhancing the mobility of its troops.

India needs to drastically improve its nuclear capability. If India can develop counter-strike capabilities by increasing the quantitative as well as qualitative potential of its nuclear warheads to ensure that all the important Chinese cities remain within the coverage of India's nuclear radar, then a genuine deterrence can be generated and sustained. India has already demonstrated its long range missile capabilities through the Agni series, especially Agni V. India is also working towards developing its nuclear triad. However, the key issue right now is the need to enhance the production, operationalization and efficient replacements of its nuclear assets to ensure that credible minimum deterrence is achieved at all times.

Like India, China also has to consider the possibility of a two front war. As long as Taiwan exists, as an independent identity, India has room to develop its military strength since China's military strength will also remain divided. Moreover, China also has certain major fault lines. Its heavy militarization of the Tibetan plateau depicts its insecurities concerning that region. It has often violently pacified its western provinces, Tibet and Xinjiang, with strike hard campaigns ruthlessly to end Tibetan and Uyghur Muslim dissent and eviscerate their freedom movement. The rebalancing policy of the US and its power projection in the Asia-Pacific region is an important geopolitical restraint for China. The United States has engaged in economic cooperation with Asian countries such as Japan, South Korea and India and it is also the security provider for countries like South Korea, Japan and Taiwan. The nuclear deal signed between US and India has been an irritant for China. China's misadventure in South China Sea has not gone unnoticed and several Asian nations have grown increasingly wary of China. Therefore, in spite of having established economic relations, China's neighbours remain cautious when dealing with China. This cautiousness and the security umbrella that is being provided by the US has constrained China despite its geopolitical claims regarding the setting up of the first and second Island Chains. China's economic progress has also made China succumb to what is commonly called the "middle income trap", and with time, due to its one Child policy, there will be an impact on China's skilled labour, and its inherent advantage of having cheap labour will diminish, hence to counter this China is trying to graduate to a more technology-intensive and innovation based path. Any decrease in the economic growth will intensify the internal fissures within China, and if China is unable to contain them, then it might opt for an ultra-nationalist approach which might lead to China choosing an aggressive stance against India. If India is able to build and demonstrate its deterrence capabilities then a balance of power between the two countries might be achieved. However, if India opts for an appeasement policy and the economy and military preparedness is compromised, then the low intensity border standoffs with an offensive Chinese posture will continue. There is always the chance that this low intensity warfare may get blown out of proportion, due to the high nationalist streak that is present in both the countries. Moreover, if China feels that India's force structure has weakened or the geopolitical trends have been compromised in India's favour, then it might choose to adopt an aggressive attitude under the pretext of teaching India a lesson and thwarting India's aspirations of becoming a major power. In terms of global politics, India and China are often competing for the same ends such as energy, raw materials etc, because both the countries constitute developing economies that are growing. China might also find the southern push more viable than its eastern and western sectors since the south can provide China with the added advantage of controlling the SLOCs thereby securing the energy corridors as well. According to the situation, China may opt for either Asymmetric warfare – the proxy war – or the coercive muscle flexing or may continue the limited war with high intensity. The possibility of a full scale war is very remote but it cannot be completely ruled out. Thus it has now become imperative for India to maintain its conventional strength backed by a credible counter value nuclear strike. In both the scenarios, cruise missiles have the potential to play a very important role. Currently, China has the fastest growing cruise missile inventory in Asia whereas India has collaborated with Russia to develop the supersonic Brahmos. However, India needs to increase the range of its cruise missiles and also increase the variability and the feasibility of its multi-platform weapons. Due to limitations of aircraft endurance; strategic depth; air defenses, expensive missile defense system along with the precision and counter force operations being difficult to achieve [201]Cruise missiles are considered the appropriate platform to fill these deterrent gap, in other words cruise missiles' high on affordability, flexible in deployment and provides an offensive counter to missile defence due to its low radar cross- section and minimal infrared signature. [202]

In the future, nations might use unmanned combat air vehicle (UCAV), or combat Drones, as they have been used by the US in the gulf war and in the war against terrorism. The X-47B is a strike fighter-sized prototype drone developed as part of the United States Navy's UCAS-D (Unmanned Combat Air System Demonstration) programme, this is supposed to demonstrate reconnaissance and strike capabilities ...and is designed to fly autonomously, with just the occasional click of a mouse.[203] China has also developed its UCAV and is the third country to have a stealth drone the Lijian ('sharp sword') ,which made a test flight for around 20 minutes in Chengdu region of China[204]. It would be used by PLA Navy and PLA Air Force for combat purposes. China has thus transformed its military doctrines based on global transformations of warfare. Its doctrine amply stresses on informationalisation and Hi-Tech warfare.

India's Shortcomings and Recommendations

India's nuclear doctrine needs to be compatible with its force structure. The massive retaliation that the doctrine professes requires a deterrent counter force as well as counter value system. India has a potent ballistic missile system, but it is not adequate as far as China is concerned. India needs to increase the number of warheads, their respective ranges as well as the fast and efficient induction of new missiles. Agni V has given India the necessary credibility to target any city in China but it is still in its testing phase and will require a few years before it can be inducted into the strategic forces. Thus, there remains a gap in the long range missile section (ICBMs) as far as the two countries are concerned. In the conventional field India needs to bridge the gap between Grad Bm21 and Smirch also the range between the Smirch and Prithvi SSM also needs to be bridged with a suitable weapon system .The range of the present Brahmos and Kh35 cruise missile is inadequate and also the induction of Nirbhaya should be expedited as it is still in the testing phase. India has made the right decision in opting for the nuclear Triad and with the induction of the SSNs; the power of the naval wing has increased drastically. However, the development of SSBNs still needs to be facilitated and the Sagarika missile is still under the testing stage; its induction needs to be hastened. The Chinese navy has re-established its dominance with its Jin class of SSBNs and its aircraft carrier. India may be ahead as far as the operational aspect of the aircraft carrier is concerned, and the Indian navy also possesses the requisite wherewithal to control the choke points despite China's "String of Pearls" theory. However; the Chinese advances in the production of submarines is phenomenal. As of 2014, according to Jess Karotkin of the Office of Naval Intelligence, China has five nuclear attack submarines, four nuclear ballistic missile submarines, and 53 diesel attack submarines[205]. In October 2013, Chinese state media also for the first time showed images of the country's nuclear powered submarines, touting it as a "credible second-strike nuclear capability[206]. The American head of US Pacific Command, Admiral Samuel Locklear, has stated that "the latest class of Chinese subs would be armed with a new ballistic missile with an estimated range of 4,000 nautical miles (7,500 kilometres). This will give China its first credible sea-based nuclear deterrent, probably before the end of 2014,"[207] However, India is still lagging behind as far as the numbers of conventional and nuclear submarines are concerned. China's ICBM capabilities are far superior to India and with the modernization process, all the old missiles along with the advanced new long and medium range missiles can be used effectively against India, since China has not really made any claims about decommissioning its old weaponry. Thus China has a potent number of ICBMs for prompt response, SLBMs for "survivability" and bombers that provide it with the much needed flexibility. All this is indigenously built and additionally China has also focused on its infrastructural development, connecting Tibet through rail, road and helipads. They also have a massive terrain advantage in Tibet. Conversely, India lacks the requisite infrastructure to ensure such development. The absences of a railroad network connecting rear areas to the forward posts makes it impossible logistically to support sustained action, speedy mobilization and... rapid reinforcement of the forward line in operations.[208] The delayed Indian Government sanctions to raise a "strike Corps" and the other strategic reserves are measures that are too little too late. China has a very efficient well trained mobile Rapid Reaction Force, whereas India's Special Frontier Force (SFF) has been relegated to performing guard duties. Even the ITBP (Indo-Tibetan Border Police) needs to be proactive and efficient to ensure that they perform the role for which they were created. India's ISR also should have the intrusive precision engagement with dominant manoeuvrable capability. Thus India needs to enhance its defensive as well as offensive capability in a major way.

Dealing with Pakistan

Geopolitically, India is surrounded by nuclear neighbours and the intimidating fact is that both the adversaries are bound together by strong ties. This can be seen by the fact that Pakistan has ceded Shaksgam Valley to China[209] and has allowed Chinese troops to make use of the Gilgit –Baltistan region of the Pak Occupied Kashmir. China in turn, has helped Pakistan in building and enhancing its conventional arsenal as well as its nuclear programme. More recently, China has been helping Pakistan with the construction of new nuclear plants. China has committed to provide $6.5 billion in financing for the construction of Pakistan's nuclear power plant in Karachi[210]. However, India remains confident about its ability to neutralize Pakistan. Pakistan had initially preferred a nuclear strategy of First Use to counter the conventional superiority of India. Its grand strategy was to weaken India through proxy wars and Kargil, the Parliament attack, etc. are examples of proxy wars. India's response in the form of coercive diplomacy backed by the threat of a military showdown, and its readiness to consider nuclear action in a situation where the adversary destabilizes the situation further, has forced Pakistan to rethink its first use strategy. India's nuclear doctrine that declares massive retaliation and its Cold Start strategy has made Pakistan wary and defensive. India's Cold Start strategy has left Pakistan with difficult choices at every turn, leaving it to escalate the hostilities to the nuclear realm, confident that India has the upper hand.[211] In order to counter the Indian strategy, Pakistan has come up with a counter strategy that is aimed at deploying tactical nuclear weapons strategically. Nasr has been developed by them primarily for this purpose. However, Pakistan's tactical strategy that was to initially use nuclear weapons on Indian soldiers and tanks may not be viable due to geographical proximity of the two countries and the fact that there are no limited wars when nuclear weapons are involved. The sheer range and magnitude of the weapons would act as a cautionary measure whereby any attacking country would have to think twice before deploying it within its vicinity. The purpose of nuclear weapons therefore, is to create deterrence. However, if a situation arises where the deterrence fails and the weapons are used, the war will invariably be converted in to a full-fledged nuclear war and have far reaching global consequences.(Generally nuclear bomb is considered as a political weapon when it is used as a deterrent, but the same weapon becomes a lethal weapon of war if deterrence fails) It has been widely accepted that if Pakistan responds to India's conventional strike with nuclear weapons, then the magnitude of India's nuclear counter strike would devastate Pakistan. In such a situation, India would be faced with two options, either to engage in massive retaliation or execute a controlled attack. The survivability of India's nuclear forces have been reinforced after the development of its triad capabilities. According to Air Chief Marshal Krishnaswamy (Retd) "we will be able to swamp the Pakistani air defenses and strategic forces."[212] The geographical contours in conjunction with its credible second strike capability will support the survivability of the Indian forces. The premise that applies here is that the bigger country with larger forces can absorb and, therefore; survive nuclear damage better than a smaller state and that this fact ultimately will deter the smaller state from committing suicide just because it fears that –suicide being the core belief of the "massive destruction" school of nuclear deterrence "[213] Hence the aftermath of a policy of nuclear first use, especially in the case of Pakistan would lead to utter destruction. The Pakistani generals understand this complexity and hence they have attempted to effect a change in their strategy. They now propagate the policy of minimum credible deterrence instead of force to force parity, increase second strike capability and maximize their nuclear weapons survivability as well. Pakistan is, therefore; planning to diversify and convert its nuclear dyad to a more lethal and effective nuclear triad. It was publicly declared that Pakistan's Navy considered the deployment of nuclear weapons aboard its submarine and surface ships[214]. They have already started developing their plutonium plants along with the requisite reprocessing facilities. Their increased production of this fissile material is a major cause of global concern. Pakistan already has a dual purpose cruise missile that they obtained from China earlier. Pakistani strategists also plan to increase and develop their conventional arsenal as these forces are essential to defend and destroy aggression. India on its part needs to prevent complacency. The political leaders need to come together with consummate political will in order to expedite the defence procurements and the indigenous ballistic missile development projects through a competitive and responsible DRDO. India has shifted its interests to the eastern sector but it should remember that a collusive threat from Pakistan and China remains a possible threat. Therefore, it needs to strengthen its eastern border as well as its western border to maintain territorial sovereignty and integrity. Post the US withdrawal from Afghanistan, it has been predicted that there will be an increase in the terrorist activities in the Kashmir region. India needs to reassess its strategy to prevent Pakistan's proxy wars from succeeding while simultaneously working towards nullifying any Chinese challenge that could crop upon the eastern front.

China Pakistan Nexus

China-Pakistan relationship has become stronger as years have gone by. In their parlance it is higher than the mountains and deeper than the sea. This has become possible because their primary interests have converged as far as India is concerned, which is mainly to weaken India. China is trying to achieve this goal by strengthening Pakistan through various military and infrastructural developmental policies. Pakistan on its part also values this all-weather friendship as this could be best understood from the quote of Husain Haqqani, a former Pakistani ambassador to the US ,in 2006 "For China, Pakistan is a low-cost secondary deterrent to India," while "for Pakistan, China is a high-value guarantor of security against India[215]."

China by supporting and aligning with Pakistan both politically and militarily has made India's western sector vulnerable to attack from, state as well as non-state actors. By opening this flank China has ensured that India's energies will be dissipated and the threat of a two front war will weaken her forces. Since India's military logistics will now be divided and spread across these two fronts. This military alliance between the two countries is escalating arms race and instability in South Asia. China's assistance to Pakistan can be seen in various fields:-

- **Supplying Military Hardware.** China is supplying military hardware and setting up Pakistan's Defence infrastructure. She is also Pakistan's largest arms supplier mainly T-59MBTs, M11-missiles, advanced J-10 fighter jets, submarine up gradation etc. are supplied by China .China has supplied nearly 65 per cent of Pakistan's aircraft and roughly 75 per cent of its tanks.[216]

- **Joint Military Ventures.** She is responsible for the joint military ventures. This is to enhance efficiency of the weaponry system mainly the JF-17 Thunder fighter aircraft, K-8, Karakorum advance training aircraft, space tech, AWACS, Al-Khalid tank, Babur cruise missile[217].

- **Pakistan's Infrastructural development.** China has helped Pakistan to build the Gwadar Port and now Pakistan has already given the operational and management control to a Chinese company[218]. The port of Pasni will also allow China an access to Strait of Hormuz which is an important SLOC for securing China's energy imports.

- **China's Nuclear Support.** Pakistan would have found it very difficult to become a Nuclear Weapon State had it not been for China's nuclear support, right from technology to fissile material to the launch vehicles. Mr Gary Milhollin the nuclear proliferation analyst commented that "If you subtract Chinese help, there wouldn't be a Pakistani programme"[219] China is also assisting in constructing nuclear reactor at

Khushab and the civilian reactors at Chashma. Shaheen II is based on the Chinese M-18 technology. China sold her M11 ballistic missiles to Pakistan and Americans had infect imposed sanctions on China[220].

It is not only Pakistan which has benefitted from this relationship but China too has benefitted. The various add-ons' which China has acquired are:-

- **Territorial Expansion** She has expanded her territory, as she acquired Shaksgam Valley from Pakistan .China has deployed her troops informally in the areas of Gilgit –Baltistan in Pak occupied Kashmir. Army Chief Gen V K Singh confirmed some 4000, Chinese including troops belonging to PLA in POK[221] .

- **Karakoram Highway.** China has upgraded Karakoram highway .China has built roads and railway tracks - 800 Km long railway link has been constructed from Havellian to Khunjerab Pass. An infantry battalion has also been stationed in the Khujerab Pass. Work is also being done on the transKarakorum highway to connect northern areas of Pakistan with Xinjiang province of China[222]

- **Asymmetric Warfare.** China covertly supports Pakistan in her Jihadi terrorist movements thus continuing the asymmetric warfare against India.

Thus this threat requires a multilevel response. More asymmetric strategies than pure military response will be effective. Diplomatic manoeuvring, building partnerships and exploiting the fault lines of both China and Pakistan are required. Both the nations are also vulnerable to a two front war and both have to tackle the problem of insurgency. Pakistan has substantial number of freedom fighters in Baluchistan and Sind who are unhappy with the Punjabi politics. The Baluch people have never been integrated into the mainland. FATA is beseeched with insurgency where militant organisations follow their own rule of law. China is also facing Uyghur insurgency in its Xinjiang Province and Tibet will remain a sore area for some time to come. Adopting strategic game plan by developing strong partnerships with the neighbouring nations where the interest coalesces is an important diplomatic endeavour. The details of which are given in chapter five. However; if the countries of Asia desire peace and stability than they need to respect each other's territorial integrity and sovereignty and realise that terrorist only understand one language and that is the language of violence. Any fuelling their ideology is going to backfire at some point of time and engulf the host nation eventually.

Recommendations

Firstly it is very essential to develop cordial relations with the Chinese government. The relations could be built starting from unofficial Track II level interactions to full-fledged diplomatic initiatives, so that an environment of mutual trust and confidence could be built up.

Secondly nuclear and military CBMs should be started at the political level and subsequently involvement of the higher military officials in the form of exchange programmes and joint exercises should be encouraged.

Thirdly economic cooperation should be encouraged as it can transport the relationship to a higher level. This was amply demonstrated during the Chinese premier's visit to India in 2013 .where it was decided to increase the trade further, and to striving to realize the trade turnover target of US$ 100 billion by 2015[223]. However it is equally true that the economic cooperation does not guarantee peace and stability as was seen between the two countries in the past, though the trade has prospered and China has become the biggest trading partner of India ,it did not stop China from intruding in the Indian territories. This is because China understands and respects the language of power .A realist deterrence could be achieved only from the power of strength .For that India needs to and build her nuclear triad at a faster pace. The strategic gaps discussed in the previous chapters need to be rectified through modernization and indigenization. India's long range ballistic missile is still in the testing phase. The time taken between the production and its induction into the forces needs to be shortened. She needs to enhance her production and deployment of missiles especially Agni

VI and V to achieve credible nuclear deterrence with China .India should also have sufficient number of ballistics and cruise missiles along with precision targeting .This will help India in building a credible nuclear deterrence. India needs to develop the infrastructure especially all along the border mainly roads and helipads along with economic development of the sates which border China especially Arunachal Pradesh. The lessons to be learnt, is one can continue with the track one and two dialogues, but ultimately it is the military power which is going to create the deterrence required, to maintain the balance of power . A display of credible conventional and nuclear arsenal can deter the adversary from its misadventures.

Fourthly this can be done by re-examining India's Nuclear Doctrine. Gaps between nuclear doctrine and actual missile force needs to be rectified India needs to develop her conventional missile doctrine to get more clarity in the use of her conventional weapons. India's nuclear force structure should have both offensive as well as defensive capabilities. India needs to enhance her counter attack strategy. India as far as China is concerned does not have at present an effective nuclear triad force which can sustain the first attack and then through a punitive attack destroys enemy's nuclear and conventional strength. India needs to improve her nuclear and conventional strategic capabilities by increasing the number as well as the range of her missile force. India should also try to integrate the conventional weapon with the nuclear ones and bring clarity in the strategic war concepts, which can help in streamlining the forces. India has the potential to achieve all this, what is required is a strong political will .Tough decisions need to be taken by the policy makers to prevent the defence gap from getting widened.

Lastly the defence industry needs to be more indigenized with impetus on private sector companies to get involved in the construction of weapons and armaments preferably joint collaborations with leading foreign companies. Greater budget need to be allocated for space research. India needs to develop her defence satellites, preferably for all the services separately, so that India's C⁴ISR capabilities are enhanced. The strategic forces should be synergized with the other three forces and joint exercises should be conducted in the war zone areas of northern and eastern sectors so that the soldiers get acclimatize and the weapons are tested in the extreme conditions as the Chinese forces are doing in the Tibetan area.

It is essential to have credible leverages so that China's weakness of multi theatre warfare could be exploited and for this it is essential for India to have partnerships with nations in China's periphery. India can develop closer partnership with the US, Vietnam, Japan and this aspect is dealt with in the next chapter.

Pakistan

As far as Pakistan is concerned India needs to take a mix of military and diplomatic initiatives. Active posturing of the military is required to send an effective signal .The low intensity warfare needs to be dealt with firmness. An effective counter measures to tackle Asymmetric warfare can be developed by building strong intelligence network, safeguarding the border from infiltrations and declaring certain red lines in the nuclear doctrine which will help in countering low conflict situation . A formal discussion with the policy makers and the think tanks is a must to formulate the requisite red lines. Control of Islamic extremism, along with economic and infrastructural development of the border areas like Jammu and Kashmir, Sikkim etc. needs to be prioritized. Certain leverages should also be developed as far as Pakistan is concerned. The so called Pakistan's strategic depth in Afghanistan needs to be neutralized by developing cordial relations with the pro Indian factions in Afghanistan through systematic diplomatic endeavours. Civil capacity building in the war torn areas of Afghanistan by providing economic packages, infrastructural developments and training of security officials are important non-military options. Moreover, maintaining a cordial and friendly relation with Iran provides India with strategic leverage and finally a coercive diplomacy to expose the terrorist links in Pakistan at various international forums is an important tool to create global opinion on terrorism.

Conclusion

Asia is currently undergoing a transition. The presence of an increasing number of nuclear and non-nuclear threshold states is making Asia unstable. The nuclear deterrence doctrine is also gaining salience in Asia. Due to an increase in the number of nations embracing civilian nuclear programme, the proliferation and diversion of enriched uranium for making weapons covertly has increased security concerns. Terrorism is making Asia vulnerable to nuclear volatility. In the coming years all this will change the security dynamics of Asia. Due to its geostrategic location, India is encircled by two nuclear states and it shares a hostile history with them. Hence, it is imperative for India to build and enhancing its credible deterrence capabilities, and at the same time it also needs to forge alliances and partnerships with those nations where its interests converge, because in the coming years it would be difficult for nations to deal with a hostile China independently. In order to take a holistic approach there has to be a balance between its diplomatic endeavours and its military strength. These two parameters need to complement each other to create a realistically applicable deterrence. Weakness on any of these two fronts will make India vulnerable to Chinese aggression. Such a policy can only be developed when there is greater synergy between the political and the military units of a nation. A greater interaction between the two in terms of understanding the requirements and implementing the policies will be the key for safeguarding India's core interests. The next Chapter Future Prospects-India's Road Ahead, tries to delve on some of these issues.

Endnotes

1   Banerjee Dipankar, (2000) "Security Studies in South Asia: Change and Challenge", New Delhi: Manohar Publication ,

2   Dr. Subhash Kapilla "Asian security environment and choices for India", in IntelliBriefs, 03 April,2010

3   ibid

4   Bracken Paul , (2012) "The second Nuclear Age: Strategy, Danger Power and The New Power Politics", Macmillan Publishers

5   Therese Delpech , (2012), "Nuclear Deterrence in the 21st century" , A Rand Publication

6   Ibid

7   Quackenbush Stephen L, "General Deterrence and International Conflict: Testing Perfect Deterrence Theory In International Interactions: Empirical and Theoretical research in International Relations, Vol 36,Issue 01 ,2010

8   Schelling, T. C, (1966), *"The Diplomacy of Violence,* New Haven: Yale University Press,

9   Huth, P. K. (1999), "Deterrence and International Conflict: Empirical Findings and Theoretical Debate", *Annual Review of Political Science* 2

10   See n, 7, Quackenbush Stephen L

11   National Security Policy, Arms Control and Disarmament, Foreign Relations of the US 1958-1960,Volume III,FAS , at fas.org/spp/starwars/offdocs/like

12   Waltz Kenneth "The Spread of Nuclear Weapons : More may be better", in Adelphi Papers, Number 171(London: International Institute For Strategic Studies,1981)

13   Ibid

14   ibid

15   ibid

16   Gareth Evans and Yoriko Kawaguchi "Eliminating Nuclear Threats: A Practical agenda for Global Policymakers", Report of the International Commission of Nuclear Non Proliferation and Disarmament.

17   Ibid

18   See n,4,Paul Bracken

19   "Europe could face hundreds of missile in Iran attack," Mail Foreign Service, 18 June 2010

20   Israeli Submarine Capabilities, NTI, 29 July 2013 at www.nti.org/analysis/article/israel-submarine-capabilities

21   Zoren EL, , (1991) Israeli Quest for Satellite Intelligence, Central Intelligence Agency,

22   See n, 4 Paul Braken

23   "Foreign ministry Issues Memorandum on Nuclear-Issues ", Korean Central News Agency, 21 April 2010, at www.KCNA.co.jp/index-e.htm.

24   See n, 4, Paul Bracken.

25   Michael McDevitt " Deterring North Korean Provocations' ",Brookings Northeast Asia Commentary ,February ,2011

26   ibid

27   The Second Artillery Force of the PLA, Second Artillery, Ministry of

National Defence, The People's Republic of China   at http://eng.mod.gov. cn/ArmedForces/second.htm

28   Ibid

29   Nair K Vijai ,"China's Evolving strategic capabilities :Doctrine, Concept, Force- Structure", South Asia Strategic Forum ,25 May 2013

30   Cleary, Christine A, "Culture, Strategy and Security", in China's Nuclear Future, Bolt P. and Willner A (Eds), (2006), Lynne,Rienner,

31   See n 27,China's Second artillery

32   Evan S Medeiros, 'Minding the Gap : Assessing the Trajectory of the PLA's Second Artillery, Chapter-4, p-143, Rightsizing the PLA: Exploring the Contours of China's Military, Strategic Studies Institute, US Army War College, Carlisle, Sep 2007.

33   Anthony H Cordesman ,Hess Ashley &Yarosh S Nicholas, Chinese Military Modernization and Force Development, A western Perspective,CSIS,23 August 2013,

34   See n 27, China Second Artillery

35   Annual Report to Congress, Military and Security Development Involving the People's Republic of China, Department Of Defence .2013

36   Ibid

37   Scobell Andrew, "China's Use of Military Force: Beyond the Great Wall and the Long March ", Pacific Affairs, Vol 77,No -4(Winter -2004-2005)

38   See n 33,Cordesman

39   Science of Second Artillery Campaigns, (English Translation; Beijing, PRC:PLA Press 2004).

40   Chongn Lin, (1988), "China's Nuclear Weapon Strategy: Tradition within Evolution", Lexington books,

41   See n 29, Nair

42   Stephanie Spier, "China's nuclear Policy: No First Use", Center for Strategic and International Studies, 20 October 2011

43   See, n, 32, Evan S Medeiros, .

44   Stephen Polk, "China's Nuclear Command and Control", in China's Nuclear Force Modernisation, Goldstein with Erickson ,Naval War College, (2005)

45   See, n,32, Evan S Medeiros

46   Hui Zhang, 'China's Nuclear Weapons Modernization: Intentions, Drivers, and Trends', Belfer Center for Science and International Affairs, July 15, 2012

47   Diversified Employment of China's Armed Forces, Information Office of

the State Council, The People's Republic of China, April 2013 Beijing

48   Hui Zang, "China's No-First Use Policy Promotes Nuclear Disarmament" The Diplomat, 22 May 2013.

49   Jeffery Lewis, "Collected Thought on Phil Karber", Arms Control Wonk,07 Dec 2011

50   Evan S Medeiros, 'Minding the Gap : Assessing the Trajectory of the PLA's Second Artillery, Chapter-4, p-143, Rightsizing the PLA: Exploring the Contours of China's Military, Strategic Studies Institute, US Army War College, Carlisle, Sep 2007.

51   Xue Xinglin, *Zhanyi Lilun Xuexi Zhinan*, Guidebook on the Study of Campaign Theory] (Beijing: Guofang Daxue Chubanshe, 2002, p. 394

52   Implementing PLA Second Artillery Doctrinal Reforms *By Kenneth Allen and Maryanne Kivlehan-Wise, at* www.defensegroupinc.com/cira/pdf/doctrinebook

53   Ibid

54   Cordesman & Yarosh, Chinese Military Modernisation and Force Development, A western Perspective, Center for Strategic and International Studies,Revised 30 July 2012

55   See n, 27,China's Second Artillery

56   Ibid

57   Ibid

58   Zhongguo Junshi Baike Quanshu [Chinese Military Encyclopedia], Beijing: Academy of Military Science Publishers, July 1997, Volume 2.

59   Air Power Australia, PLA Second Artillery Corps, Technical Report APA-TR-2009-1204 Sean O'Connor, BA, MS (AMU),December 2009,Updated April, 2012

60   ibid

61   See n, 27, China Second Artillery

62   Ibid

63   Ibid

64   Military Balance ,IISS,2014

65   See n, 27, China's Second Artillery

66   Annual Report to Congress , Military and Security Developments, Involving the People's Republic of China 2014 ,Office of the Secretary of Defense ,

67   Chansoria Monica, Agni V bolsters India's Deterrence, The Sunday Guardian, 28 August 2014

68 Perspective on China 'Nuclear complexities in the third nuclear age'. Oct,9,2012 at ,cewces. wordpress.com

69 See n 67 Chansoria

70 See n, 59, Air Power Australia

71 Military Balance, IISS,2014

72 Implementing PLA Second Artillery Doctrinal Reforms By Kenneth Allen and Maryanne Kivlehan-Wise at www.defensegroupinc.com/cira/pdf/ **doctrine**book_ch6.pdf

73 IISS, Military Balance 2012,

74 Ibid

75 Chinese Military Modernisation, A Western Perspective, Cordesman &Yarosh,23 August 2013

76 See n, 66, Annual Report

77 Ibid

78 Ibid

79 See n, 75, Chinese Military Modernisation

80 Johnson Robert "China's New MIRV Ballistic Missiles A Big Deal", Business Insider 11.December 2012.

81 "A Question of Balance: Political Context and Military Aspects of the China- Taiwan Dispute", Schlapak, David A., David T. Orletsky, Toy I. Reid, Murray Scot Tanner and Barry Wilson. Santa Monica, CA: RAND Cooperation 2009

82 See,n, 66,Annual Report

83 'PLA Ballistic Missiles', Australian Air Power, Technical Report APA-TR-2010-0802.Sean O'Connor, (AMU)August 2010,updated 2012

84 Ibid

85 Ibid

86 Ben Blanchard, "China developing new military satellites", China Post, Reuters, 13 July, 2011

87 Mark Stokes , "China's Evolving Conventional Strategic Strike Capability" project2049, at .net/documents/**chinese**_anti_ship_ballistic_missile_asbm

88 'China's Missiles', The Economists, 06 Dec 2010

89 "Lhasa-Shigatse railway to complete track-laying' In People's Daily Online, 22 January,2013 at chinatibet.**people**.com.cn/8101821.html

90 Nair K Vijai, "China's Evolving Strategic Capabilities: Doctrine, Concept, Force-Structure", South Asia Strategic Forum,25 May 2013

91   Pandit Rajat, "China have five airbases, extensive rail-road networks in Tibet : Anthony",08 March 2011,The Times of India

92   Ibid

93   Chitkara M G , "Toxic Tibet under Nuclear China",(1996), New Delhi, APH publishing

94   Ibid

95   Compiled from data obtained from Military Balance ,IISS,2014

96   Ibid

97   Ibid

98   Shortcomings Persist in China's Submarine-Based Nuke Force: NTI Report , 04 June 2012

99   Tseng Fu-sheng, "PLA Anti-Satellite Weapons Pose Challenge to US", Missile Threat, 01 February 1, 2013

100   Michelle FlorCruz   "Anti-Satellite Missiles, Planes And Submarines: China As A Military Threat", International Business times, 11January 2013

101   Ibid

102   ibid

103   Evan S Medeiros, 'Minding the Gap : Assessing the Trajectory of the PLA's Second Artillery, Chapter-4, p-143, Rightsizing the PLA: Exploring the Contours of China's Military, Strategic Studies Institute, US Army War College, Carlisle, Sep 2007

104   ibid

105   Ge Xinliu, Mao Guanghong, and Yu Bo in Military Science Editorial Group, WoJun Xixi Zhan Wenti Yanjiu,

106   PLA Second Artillery Corps, Australian Air Power,Technical Report APA-TR-2009-1204, Sean O' Connor (AMU)Updated 2012

107   Kukreja Veena, (2003), Contemporary Pakistan: Political Process, Conflicts and Crisis, Sage Publications, New Delhi

108   Transcription of Testimony Before the Supreme Court Of Pakistan ,in reply to Pakistan Government White Papers, as cited in- " From Surprise to Reckoning : The Kargil Review Committee Report", (New Delhi Sage ,1999)

109   G Parthasarthy, "The Nuclear Doctrine –For Ensuring Global Security", Business Line , 22 September 2005

110   Chawala Shalini Dr, "Nuclear Pakistan By " as cited in Lt Gen Jahan Dad Khan, "Pakistan: Leadership Challenges", (Karachi: Oxford University Press,1999)

111 Naeem Salik,,(2010), The Genesis of South Asian Nuclear Deterrence: Pakistan Perspective, New York ,Oxford University Press , p. 219.

112 Lodhi, Lieutenant-General, (April 1999), "Pakistan's Nuclear Doctrine" at http://www.defencejournal.com/apr99/pak-nuclear-doctrine.htm

113 Lieutenant General Sardar F.S. Lodhi (Retd), "Pakistan Nuclear Doctrine", *Pakistan Defence Journal ,*1999

114 Pakistan Background Information Overview at www.du.edu/korbel/cenex/media/ documents/Pakistan_Background_Document.pdf

115 Ibid

116 As quoted by *Colonel Gurmeet Kanwal,* India's Nuclear Doctrine and Policy at http://www.idsa-india.org/an-feb-1.01.htm

117 Dr Shalini Chawala , Nuclear Pakistan ,KW, Publishers, New Delhi.

118 As cited in Landau Report on "Nuclear Safety, Nuclear Stability and Nuclear Strategy in Pakistan", Prof Paolo Cotta-Ramuniso and Prof Maurizio Matellini.

119 Ibid

120 "Remarks of the Prime Minister of Pakistan ,Nawaz Sharif ,on Nuclear Policies and the CTBT" ,National Defence College ,Islamabad, 20 May 1999

121 Krepon Michael, "Pakistan's Nuclear Strategy And Deterrence Stability", in http://www. stimson.org/images/uploads/research-pdfs/krepon-Pakistan Nuclear Strategy and Deterrence Stability.pdf

122 Agha Shahi, Zulfiqar, Ali Khan and Abdul Sattar, "Securing Nuclear peace," The News, 05 October 1990.

123 ibid

124 Zafar Nawaz Jaspal, "Requiring Pakistan's nuclear Strategy" , Defence Journal, at http://www.defencejournal.com/2001/july/reassessing.htm

125 Durrani, M. A., 'Pakistan's strategic thinking and the role of nuclear weapons', Cooperative Monitoring Center Occasional Paper 37, Sandia National Laboratories, Sand July 2004, at <http://www.cmc.sandia.gov/cmc-papers/sand2004-3375p.pdf>

126 Weeks Jenifer, "Sino-US Nuclear Cooperation at a Crossroads", American Control Association at https://www.armscontrol.org/print/224

127 "Missile Overview", NTI at http://www.nti.org/e_research/profiles/Pakistan/missile/ index_3066.html

128 "Pakistan Missile", NTI in http://www.nti.org/country-profiles/pakistan/deliverysystems/

129 Duncan Lennox, ed., "Hatf 1,, Jane's Strategic Weapon System, Issue

Fortyeight, January 2008

130   Zia Mian , "Pakistan" as cited in   Press Release no PR62/2011-ISPR,Pakistan Inter Service-Public Relation Directorate,Rawalpindi,11 March 2011

131   Chandrashekhar S, Arvind Kumar and Rajaram Nagappa, "An Assessment of Pakistan's Ballistic Missile Programme:Technical and Strategic Capability", NIAS Study,2006

132   Ibid

133   Stockholm International Peace Research Institute (SIPRI), *SIPRI Yearbook 2011: Armaments, Disarmament and International Security* (Oxford University Press

134   Military Spending and Armaments, SIPRI, 2008 at www.sipri.org/research/amament/nbc/nuclear /Pakistan

135   Rodney W. Jones, "Pakistan's Answer to Cold Start?", The Friday Times at http://www. thefridattimes.com/13052011/page7.shtml

136   Iftikar A.Khan "Cruise Missile Fired from Aerial Platform", Dawn, 09 May 2008

137   Ibid

138   Dr Shalini Chawala , Nuclear Pakistan ,KW, Publishers, New Delhi.

139   Ibid

140   Stockholm International Peace Research Institute (SIPRI), *SIPRI Yearbook 2011: Armaments, Disarmament and International Security* (Oxford University Press: Oxford, 2011) and the International Panel on Fissile Materials (IPFM), *Global Fissile Material Report 2011* (IPFM: Princeton, NJ, 2011)

141   Bruno Tertrais "Pakistan's nuclear and WMD Programme: status, evolution and risks", EU Non-Proliferation Consortium, No 19 July 2012

142   Ibid

143   Ibid

144   Ibid

145   *Global Fissile Material Report 2011: Nuclear Weapon and Fissile Material Stockpiles and Production*, International Panel on Fissile Materials, January 2012.

146   *Global Fissile Material Report 2010: Balancing the Books,* International Panel on Fissile Materials, December, 2010.

147   Key facilities in Pakistan's nuclear weapons programme infrastructure are described in *Nuclear Black Markets: Pakistan, A.Q. Khanand the Rise of Proliferation Networks,,* International Institute of Strategic Studies,

London, 2007

148   Kriestein & Norris, "Pakistan Nuclear Force 2011", Bulletin of Atomic Scientiest, Vol 67,No 4(July/Aug/2011)

149   David E. Sanger, "Pakistan Overshadows Afghanistan on US Agenda," New York Times, 06 May 2009. Also for further reading, see Riedel his vision of the likely consequences of a jihadist controlled Pakistani state in Bruce Riedel, "Armageddon in Islamabad," The National Interest, July-August 2009.

150   " Pakistan Nuclear Weapon Programme,1998,the Year of Testing", at nuclear weapon archive .org/Pakistan/Paktest.html

151   Christopher Clary " Thinking about Pakistan's Nuclear Security in Peacetime, Crisis and War" in IDSA ,Occasional Paper

152   Kenneth Luongo and Naeem Salik "Building Confidence in Pakistan's nuclear Security", Arms Control Today, 01 December 2007.

153   See n, 151,Clary

154   Ibid

155   Ibid

156   Ibid

157   Ibid

158   Ibid

159   Office of the Secretary of Defence, "Proliferation: Threat and Response", GPO, Washington, DC, January 2001.

160   Khalid Banuri and Adil Sultan, "Managing and Securing the Bomb," DailyTimes, 13 May 2008 at http://www.dailytimes.com.pk/default. asp?page=2008\ 05 \30\ story_30-5-2008_pg3_6.

161   Boon, Huq &Lovelace, (2011), Catastrophic Possibilities threatening US Security, Terrorism ,Vol 119 ,Oxford University Press

162   "Pakistan Nuclear Program: A Net Assessment", Foundation Pour La Recherche Strategique,13 June 2012

163   ibid

164   Bruno Tertaris,Pakistan Nuclear and WMD Programme Status: Evolution and Risks, EU – Non Proliferation Consortium, July 2012 at http:// www.sipri.org/research/disarmament/eu-consortium/publications/ Nonproliferation-paper-19

165   Kenneth Luongo and Naeem Salik,"Building Confidence in Pakistan's Nuclear Security", Arms Control Today ,01 December 2007,As cited in Shalini Chawla, Nuclear Pakistan , (2012) KW Publication

166   Militants Attack Pakistan Nuclear Air Base, The Telegraph,16 August 2012

167 "Insiders Helped Militants Plot PNS Mehran Naval Base Attack :Experts," The Nation ,23 May 2011

168 Kenneth Waltz, (1979), *Theory of International Politics*, New York: Random House,

169 Y.I. Patel, "Dig Vijay to Divya Astra: A Paradigm Shift in the Indian Army's Doctrine," *Bharat Rakshak Monitor,* Vol. 6, No. 6

170 Pakistan has the Fastest growing Nuclear Stockpile, Times of India, 18 Jan 2013

171 Deterrence Stability: Escalation Control in South Asia, Edited by Michael Krepon & Julia Thompson, 2013, The Stimson Center

172 Recipe for Disaster: Israel & Pakistan's sea based nukes" Iskander Rehman in The Diplomat, MAY 31, 2013

173 Ibid

174 Ibid

175 Mansoor Ahmed," Security Doctrines, Technologies and Escalation Ladders: A Pakistani Perspective" at www.hsdl.org

176 Ibid

177 Salman Siddique, "PAKSTAR-1R;China launches Pakistan's first Communication Satellite" ,The Express Tribune,12 August 2012

178 " Pakistan to launch third satellite in 2014" Pakistan Today, 19 Aug ,2013

179 Peter R. Lavoy, Scott D. Sagan, and James J. Wirtz (eds.), (, 2000,), "*Planning the Unthinkable*, "Ithaca: Cornell University Press

180 Draft Report of National Security Advisory Board On Indian Nuclear Doctrine 17 August 1999

181 Draft Report of National Security Advisory Board on Indian Nuclear Doctrine, August 17,1999

182 Ibid

183 Cabinet Committee On Security Review Progress in Operationalizing India's Nuclear Doctrine

184 Chari,P.R , " India's Nuclear Doctrine :confused Ambitions" , The Non-proliferation Review/Fall-Winter 2000

185 Bharat Karnard, (2008), "India's Nuclear Policy", Pentagon Press

186 ibid

187 See n,184,Chari

188 Opening Remarks by National Security Adviser Mr. Brajesh Mishra at the Release of the Draft Report at http://mea.gov.in/in-focus-article. htm?18916/Draft+Report+of+National+Security+Advisory+Board+on+I

ndian+Nuclear+Doctrine

189 "Next Arms Talk between US, Russia might involve Tactical Weapons", Voice of America, 01 April 2012

190 Bernard Brodie, "Strategy in the Missile Age," Princeton, University Press.

191 Ibid

192 See n,184, Chari

193 Admiral Sushil Kumar "Struggling to stay Afloat " Times of India.,23 Wednesday August,2013

194 Rahul Bedi, "A Credible Nuclear Deterrent," Frontline, at www. hinduonnet.com/fline/ fl2007/stories/20030411003009700.htm

195 Verghese Koithara, (2012), "Managing India's Nuclear Forces", ,Routledge Publications

196 Ibid

197 ibid

198 Trends in International Arms Transfer ,2013, SIPRI Fact Sheet , at http:// books.sipri.org/files/FS/SIPRIFS1403.pdf

199 "Weak Defence", The Indian Express, 29 Mar 2013

200 Military Balance 2014 ,IISS

201 Kalyan M Kemburi, "China India and Cruise Missiles", Monterey Institute of International Studies, at https://csis.org/images/stories/poni/110707_ Kemburi.pdf .

202 Ibid.

203 Sharon Weinberger ,X-47B stealth drone targets new frontiers, BBC, 19 December 2012

204 China Flies First Stealth Drone,22 November 2013, BBE NEWS China at http://www.bbc.com/news/world-asia-china-25033155

205 China Will soon place Long Ranged Nuclear Missiles on Submarines,, Business Insider, 25 March 2014 at http://www.businessinsider.in/Top-US-Official-China-Will-Soon-Place-Long-Range-Nuclear-Missiles-On-Submarines/articleshow/32682401.cms

206 "China to have nuclear missile on subs soon: US Admiral ", Yahoo News ,25 March 2014,Yahoo. News

207 China will place long range nuclear missiles on Submarines,27 May 2014 ,in http://beforeitsnews.com/alternative/2014/03/china-will-soon-place-long-range-nuclear-missiles-on-submarines-2927394.html

208 Chitkara M G ,(1996), Kashmir Imbroglio:Diagnosis and Remegy,New Delhi APH Publications Corporations

209   Ibid

210   Shannon Tiezzi, China Financing Pakistan Nuclear Power Plant, The Diplomat, 25 December 2013

211   ibid

212   Bharat Karnard , (2008), " India's Nuclear Policy, Pentagon Press

213   Morgan Patrick M, ,(2003), "Deterrence Now" , Cambridge University Press

214   "Pakistan may install nuclear missile ",Los Angel Times,23 February 2001

215   Jamal Afridi & Jayshree Bajoria, "China Pakistan Relations", Council Of Foreign Relations, 06 July 2010

216   Pervez Iqbal Cheema, (2002), "The Armed Forces of Pakistan", Oxford: Oxford University Press,

217   "Das A k Col, Sino-Pak Collusion and US Policy ", Asia Publication House, Mumbai.

218   Pakistan's Gwadar Port may get special China Status, Mail On Line India, 31 August 2013

219   Gordon Corera ,interview with Gary Milhollin, Washington D.C, December 14 2005,as cited in Shalini Chawla in ,Nuclear Pakistan

220   Weeks Jenifer, " Sino-US Nuclear Cooperation at a crossroad", Arms Control Association, June/July 1997,at https://www.armscontrol.org/act/1997_06-07/weeks

221   Chinese Troops in Pakistan Occupied Kashmir, Economic Times,06 October 2011,as cited in POK NEWS Digest,Vol-4 No 11 2011,IDSA

222   See n 219,Corera

223   Joint Statement on the State Visit of of Chinese Premier Li Keqiang to India, Document Ministry Of External Affairs, Government of India,20 May 2013

5   Future Prospects: India's Road Ahead

In the 21st century, the geo-strategic space of Asia has transformed. The rise of China and India are challenging the traditional security architecture. China is flaunting its new found confidence based on economic dominance by trying to actively participate and manoeuvre the affairs of global commons. India on its part, is still struggling to respond. While it has achieved an impressive economic growth rate, India is still a decade behind China in most of the developmental yardsticks. Another important development is that security is no longer considered in isolation. A more holistic security approach is emerging where traditional issues are getting merged with non-traditional ones. Terrorism, cyber warfare, space warfare are evolving trends, which along with the regular conventional, sub – conventional and nuclear threats have emerged as important limbs of security. The external factors also greatly impact a nation's security environment. In today's global age of interdependence, low intensity conflicts will take precedence over a full-fledged war. In a country's foreign policy, alliances and partnerships will become significant indicators aimed at maintaining balance, hence to achieve a strong security environment, it is essential to understand the global power swing and adapt accordingly.

The rise of China has been remarkable as well as worrisome. China's aggressive approach towards the South China Sea, Tibet and Taiwan is a major cause of concern. In the coming years if China is able to sustain its economic growth rate and uphold its internal stability then it will be difficult to challenge China's supremacy. In such a scenario, it is imperative for India to have a two pronged policy. Externally, it needs to build partnerships, and internally the prerequisite would be working towards indigenization through developing its technological prowess, both scientific and industrial.

India has a very small window of opportunity to develop this because it has been predicted that by 2025 China would be one of the world's largest military powers. To make this opportunity work, it is imperative to enforce effective policy decisions. A healthy economic growth rate, an efficient administration, an astute political leadership, and robust democratic institutions are essential ingredients to achieve this aim. Globalization has linked India's economy with the outside world and this has opened new challenges which are very diverse. These may vary from providing security to Indian investments, to developing, modernizing and innovating technologies in order to compete with other nations. In today's age economics and security are interrelated, hence when economy is better, the defence budgets become larger, and stronger the defence, greater is the leverage to project power. So India needs to develop a more comprehensive mode of national power and this is a complex process. The complexity lies in the choices that need to be made because each choice will impact the result in totality. Since the time for achieving political supremacy in this window of opportunity is very small, it becomes even more essential to analyse and make the right decision at the right time since these decisions will determine India's road ahead.

Unlike the Cold War era, the world is no longer bipolar. The weakening US economy has eroded the illusion of unipolarity which the Americans enjoyed for a substantial period of time. In an emergent multipolar world, USA and China may remain major powers, but they may not have the total control or the global dominance that the superpowers had during the Cold War period. This gives the other powers the leverage to negotiate and swing the power away from the adversary's direction; hence the major powers would always like to keep the swing states in their pool.

Alliances and Partnerships

Indo-US Partnership

In Asia there has been a mounting competition between US and China. The US policy of rebalancing its forces in Asia is considered by many Chinese as restricting and threatening China's peaceful rise as a global power. The Americans have adopted a policy of alliances and partnerships to covertly challenge China. In its "Sustaining Global priorities for 21 Century" India has been given a significant place as a strategic partner, and Secretary of State, Leon Panetta, called India as a "Linchpin" in its rebalancing Asia-pivot[1] policy. India's relation with US has improved since President' Bush's period. Post the demise of the Soviet Union, India has reached out to the US in a more open manner. Bush had reciprocated by refusing to see India through a Pakistani prism for the first time, and he delineated Jammu and Kashmir from bilateral talks and considered India as a rising power in Asia[2]. He implemented a conscious strategy of projecting India as a counter weight to China. This was further strengthened through the Indo-US civil nuclear deal which made it easier for India to build a working relationship with the US. Though India is not ready to become a US linchpin completely, the camaraderie between the two has definitely increased since the Bush tenure. However; President Obama's policy has been like a sea saw, fluctuating between continuing the Bush legacy, to having bouts of overt cooperation with China. India should keep all these factors in mind and choose its strategic options intelligently. Currently, the relationship with the US largely depends on US perception. If US believes that it needs to build new partnerships to balance China; it will capitalize on the Indo-US partnership and dissuade others from developing overt China centric policies. But if the US makes China the interlocutor in Asia then India's strategic choices would be severely limited. In today's globalised world US and China's economies are intertwined and since the US economy is in duress it may not want to overtly provoke China. However lately, Americans have started refocusing on providing greater responsibility to its alliances and partners. It would be difficult for the US to just abandon its allies and partners, hence India should use the American belief that rising China could be countered through a policy of containment[3] - balancing it through supporting the growth of other countries along China's border namely India Japan etc. This provided the regional system the best of both worlds: an opportunity to limit Beijing's capacity for malevolence without sacrificing the common prosperity arising from trade and interdependence.[4] The question which needs to be considered however; is whether India would be able to progress as required, in order to become a power in the Asian strategic perspective. It is in India's interest to accept the strategy, as India would not like to have an aggressive China in its periphery. The solution lies in the rapid economic development of India through "second-generation reforms"; which would include holistic measures to rationalize subsidies, labour laws, manufacturing policy; agriculture, expanding public infrastructure, restructuring inefficient public enterprises, improving financial sector and rectifying India's increasingly dangerous fiscal imbalances.[5]. Former Foreign Secretary, Shyam Saran phrased it, as openly embracing economic reforms rather than resorting to "reform through stealth" or "reform through crisis."[6] Providing increased opportunities for foreign investors across the board remains the single quickest way for India to overcome its vast development deficits with the lowest risks to state, while simultaneously incurring benefits of improved technology levels, increased revenues, and better management.[7] India has got the opportunity to cooperate with the US in sectors such as defence technology, and this has included seeking access to critical technologies in an attempt to overcome and outpace asymmetry with China. Presently, India does not possess "access to R&D capabilities with advanced technology infrastructure and laboratories supported by a robust policy to systematically pursue the task of acquiring critical technologies[8]. The answer is a mix of imported products and indigenous production. India needs to specialize at a faster pace in the indigenous sectors where there is a comparative advantage, while continuing to rely on trade to provide the commodities in areas where India lacks such benefits. In sectors where the indigenous technology isn't sufficient, state-of-the-art weapons and armament can be imported through the US and this bilateral trade will benefit both countries, and USA and India could work together in areas of common interest like disaster response, humanitarian assistance, counter-piracy, and peacekeeping."[9] US help, in the arenas of maritime domain awareness, space security, cyber warfare, electronic warfare, and ballistic missile defence, promise a dramatic increase in India's own military effectiveness— which cannot be secured currently by autonomous Indian efforts."[10] India should re-examine its policy on operational cooperation with the United States in light of its own larger strategic interests.[11]However, there are challenges in this relationship and the foundation, therefore, should be made on hard choices. The leaders have shown the requisite resolve to move forward despite US financial assistance to Pakistan (which often undermines India's security) and the ambiguous inconsistencies in the Sino-US relations which confront Indian policy makers, as the relation can cause Sino-US collusion or confrontation.[12] The Iranian problem should also get streamlined in due course of time since Iran has been successful in negotiating a nuclear deal for an interim period of six months in 2013. This will ease the Indian pressure as far as Indo-Iran relationship is concerned which had been adversely impacted thus far due to the US pressure to impose sanctions on Iran The possibility of permanence in this deal, will further aid and enhance the US-Iran relation and thereby reduce the pressure on India to impose sanctions on Iran.

However, there remain structural problems in the Indo-US defence relationship. US has been insisting that India should sign foundational agreements on defence cooperation – like the Communications and Information Security Memorandum of Agreement (CISMOA), Logistic Support Agreement (LSA) and Basic Exchange and Cooperation Agreement[13] for Geo-Spatial Cooperation, nevertheless, this has not deterred the two sides from doing some big business on arms deals. India has already signed a big contract for the purchase of 10 C-17 Globemaster - III super heavy transporter and six more C-130 J Super Hercules Special Forces aircraft, and the IAF has already acquired six C-130 J Super Hercules.[14]

The future of Asia will depend largely on the triangular relationship between these three nations and the strategic relationship between India and US is greatly driven by the centrality of India in Asia's future balance of power.[15] The way Indo-US relations develop in the future will be of major strategic significance for China also. Both India and the US, working in tandem, have the capability of upsetting the Chinese power calculus. China is also increasingly concerned about the growing military co-operation between India and the US and moreover, Chinese strategists have noticed that the quality of US arms sales to India have shown a marked improvement. It is in India's interests to isolate the competitors and work with friends who would help India in achieving the status of a major power.

Indo-Russian Partnership

Post the demise of the Soviet Union, both nations have undergone a substantial shift in their policies. India has opened her doors to the US, and Russian economic dependence on China has increased, to the extent that they cannot afford to antagonize China. Russian maps also depict a disturbing duality as the Pakistan-occupied Kashmir region is shown as a part of India, but the Aksai-chin region is shown as a part of China and this reflects deeper geo-political thinking and approach.[16] Although Russia had initiated the "strategic triangle" between Russia, China and India to counter US predominance, India did not see any merit in it. Moreover the global scenario has changed since then and each country has been trying to reassess the global trend to suit its own needs. Russia has had to readjust its global goals after the Soviet Union debacle and since then, they have been exploring the idea of diversifying the energy markets to strengthen their economy. Russia's ambition to create energy and transport corridors in the Eurasian region has had far reaching geopolitical implications. They wanted to expand their supply routes and Pakistan's geo strategic position became an important link for the energy corridor traversing through south, central and west Asia. The Russians have been trying to build relations with Pakistan with a new prism. Hence the stability and integration of Afghanistan became important factors in the equation as well, since a stable South Asia can help the Russian economy. Russia started viewing India as a privileged strategic partner, Afghanistan as an important neighbour and Pakistan as an emerging regional power.[17] The railroad transport corridor from Tajikistan to Pakistan, cutting across Wakhan Corridor, will ensure Russia and CAR countries getting access to Arabian Sea and Indian Ocean through Gwadar[18]. Though it is still in an infant stage, the possibility cannot be ruled out. Post the American withdrawal from Afghanistan, the regional powers will be affected the most. They will also have the potential to shape the future of Afghanistan, and, Russia, also being a major geo strategic power, will be forced to play a greater role in the region. Her relations with Pakistan will also be shaped largely by how Pakistan acts post US withdrawal. If it continues to support terrorism then Russia Pak relations will deteriorate but if Pakistan adopts a constructive approach then Pakistan might become an important link in a system of trade and transport routes and gas and oil pipelines running across Central Asia to the Arabian Sea ports and onwards to the large Indian market.[19] One needs to remember that a pro Pakistan Russia is not in India's interest. Hence India needs to increase its area of convergence by highlighting and working with Russia to combat terrorism and diversifying the bilateral trade.

Outwardly Indo-Russian relations continue to be friendly and this was substantiated by the Russian President's' visit to India in 2012 when he said "For Russia, Deepening friendship with India is a top foreign policy priority[20]"; however statements notwithstanding, fissures have appeared in this relationship. The main reason being that this "strategic partnership" is largely limited to the arms trade and energy projects (especially nuclear power). Russian military hardware is still the best value for money in the global arms market.

Last year India's purchases of defence equipment from Russia were close to 11 billion dollars. However any downturn in the arms trade and the defence industry will have an extremely adverse impact on the bilateral relations. According to SIPRI during last five years from 2007-11 India has spent $12.7 billion in arms and 80 per cent of that comes from Russia, major purchase being 120 Sukhoi's, 16 Mig 29 Jet fighter planes, but in coming years this might change as US has bagged defence orders worth $ 9 billion in the last seven years and France and Israel have emerged as major defence supplier.[21]

Russia is also diversifying its arms trade. The countries of South and Southeast Asia are allocating large funds to buy Russian armaments. The demand for Russian combat aircraft has increased and especially Russian arms export in the Asia-Pacific region has increased, Malaysia, Indonesia Singapore and Philippines have shown great interest in Russian weaponry [22]

The Indo–Russian bilateral trade ratio, however, is abysmal. There is a serious imbalance in co-operation between the government-led Russian front and the private sector in India. The Indian Ministry of Trade statistics, in April-November 2012 states that Russia ranked 27th on imports from India, and 35th on exports[23]. Bilateral trade was just $11 billion, India's export being just $8 billion and imports at $3 billion. In coming years it will be essential for India to diversify her relations with Russia. There are various sectors where both the countries can cooperate successfully. India has an opportunity to make a start by investing in Russia's proposed $33 billion privatization programme and Russia can concomitantly reaffirm that partnership by investing in India's $3 trillion infrastructural programme.[24]

India's attempts to strengthen ties with the Central Asian Republics can benefit significantly from Russian support. A beginning has been made towards a Comprehensive Economic Cooperation Agreement (CECA) between India and the Customs Union of Belarus, Kazakhstan and the Russian Federation for creating a platform for a free trade agreement with them[25]. But in order to rectify the dwindling bilateral trade more participation is required from the private sector of both the countries especially in the sectors like oil, gas, minerals, metals, pharmaceuticals, IT etc. It is essential to bolster the relations on a firm footing by investing in the above said areas over and above the defence agreements. Defence is one area where Russia has been a dependable source. They have provided India with almost everything that was required including all the advanced technologies, the classic example being "Arihant" the nuclear powered submarine. India already has an advantage since both the nations have been great friends through history. The next step now would be to cement this relationship.

In conclusion, India is one of the largest importers of Russian arms. In order to use this as leverage, India, as mentioned above, needs to build and increase bilateral trade in other sectors, over and above the arms import in order to ensure a more reliable economic dependence. The Central Asian region and the mutual goals that both countries hold becomes another area where they can work together for each other's benefit. Highlighting the evils of terrorism and jointly working on Afghanistan can help increase stability in South Asia.

Indo-Japan Relation

India and Japan had its own share of highs and lows. When India had conducted her nuclear test in 1974, Japan imposed economic sanctions and CTBT, NPT and arms control, became significant deterrents in their relations. However; soon the relationship changed,

American change in perception due to President Bush's foresight saw a change in relation with Japan also, because Japan's Prime minister Kiozumi's and Bush 's view converged as far as creating a new balance of power in Asia was concerned [26]. For Japan, India can become counterbalance to China. The Japanese believed that IOR is the space where Japan's strategic interests coalesce with US and India because Japan relies heavily on the import of oil and 80 per cent of its energy requirements are met through imports of oil from the gulf region. Hence it is vital for Japan to have the Sea Lanes of Communications (SLOCs) safe and open. This strategic aim can be achieved, by building a partnership with India because India has a formidable naval strength which makes it an important player in the Indian Ocean Region Also both the countries share common liberal-democratic values. The fact that India remains one of the few powerful states in the Indo-Pacific arc without historical grievances against the Japanese helped in building the relations. In fact PM Nehru had helped Japan in the post war political rehabilitation[27]. The ascendance of Chinese power, regionally and globally have strategically converged the goals of these two nations, and this alignment will have important consequences in the region, and certainly in any power transition involving the United States and China.[28]. Japan has aspired to be a major economic power and with the emergence of an economically and militarily strong China there has been a clash of interest between the two countries. Both the countries have divergent views as far as Senkaku Island was concerned. The Japanese government acquiring three of the disputed islands from their private owner created problems between Japan and China as the latter did not recognize this endeavour. This in turn, prompted large-scale protests in China and deteriorated the relations between the two countries. Chinese declaration of Air Defence Identification Zone (ADIZ) in the East China Sea further precipitated the relations between the two. Japan has hastened its efforts to build alliances and partnerships with various nations in an effort to counter Chinese aggression. This development is in congruence with the Indian interests too. The ascendance of Chinese power, regionally and globally has strategically converged these two nations, and this alignment will have important consequences in the region, and certainly in any power transition involving the United States and China.[29].

India and Japan are strategically global partners and have concluded a Joint Declaration on Security Cooperation, the two states enjoy a Comprehensive Economic Partnership Agreement that liberalizes bilateral economic activity and since 2006, India and Japan have held annual Prime Ministerial level talks—a privilege afforded by each to no other state in Japan's case, even the United States[30]. In 2011 both the countries signed Comprehensive Economic Partnership Agreement (CEPA) which is a milestone in their relationship, as it covers more the 90 per cent of trade, investments, IPR[31] etc. Japan is likely to increase its share of investments in the Delhi- Mumbai-Infrastructural development corridor. There were proposals for "quadrilateral initiative" consisting of Japan, the United States, Australia, and India as a force for structural stability and peace in Asia which did not materialize, nonetheless these four democratic states conduct joint military exercises and security consultations leading to a *de facto* bloc poised against China.[32]The naval Malabar exercise is an important event where Navies of five countries mainly US, Japan, India, Australia and Singapore participated which included apart from non-conventional maritime activities, anti-submarine operations, maritime interdiction, and aerial combat exercises as well.[33] Japan and India both have extensive economic relations with China especially Japan and so both nations play down the possibility of any overt build-up of multilateral partnerships. However both nations continue with covert hedging strategies in the economic as well as military fields. This can be seen from the joint strategic exercises conducted in the Indian Ocean as well as in the coast of Tokyo. These are indicators that this partnership has the potential to grow and become an alternative power structure in Asia. Provided that both nations are bold enough to adopt progressive policies. An important pointer in this direction is the rapid defence modernization done by Japan and the economic reforms initiated by the Indian government.

Sino –Indian clash in South Asia and Indian Ocean

China's Challenge China's rise has been phenomenal, and its emergence as a major power creates complexities and challenges for India, because both the countries have become rivals in several fields due to their geographical proximity. The current economic resurgence has compelled both the nations to experiment and explore different ways to sustain their growth rate. The quest for increasingly limited natural resources required to sustain this growth makes them competitors. There is a change in the security paradigm and threat perception in the region. Each country hence is trying to protect their assets and balance its internal power dynamics. The traditional deterrents like the unresolved border dispute and the growing Sino-Pak nexus, in tandem with increasing Chinese aggressiveness continue to build mistrust amongst the two countries. It is often believed that economic cooperation may help in bridging the hostility between the two but this has not been the case with China. In fact, trade itself has become a source of friction between the two countries as India's trade deficit with China has soared from $1 billion in 2002 to $40 billion in 2013.[34] Chinese incursions in the Depsong valley, staple visa and the disputed LAC (Line of Actual Control) in an attempt to establish new territorial claims (Army recorded nearly 600 incursions over the last 3 years)[35] are a cause for concern and cannot be downplayed. The American policy of containing China has been diluted as China's economic resurgence has given it a new found economic and geopolitical power which China fully understands and flaunts. Territorial claims (both land and sea) on the pretext of historical claims continue to create tensions in Asia. China's foray into the Indian Ocean is a cause of concern for India. Their transformation of warfare from land to sea can be seen as a prelude to becoming a great power and like all great powers China is also trying to make their own rules and create a world order which is compatible with the Chinese interest. China's aspirations to rekindle the "Middle Kingdom Syndrome" are often visible in their revival of a "Sino-Centric" mentality among the Chinese ruling elite. This is amply visible in Asia and can be evinced by the Chinese provocations in the South China Sea .Also the Chinese claim of the Senkaku Island along with the Sino-Indian border standoffs are classic example of this hangover. Even in South Asia it is expanding its area of influence.

China's South Asian and Indian Ocean Policy

Continuing with its Sino centric policy, China is trying to woo the nations of South Asia and in the bargain curtailing India's growing influence in South Asia. Just as China is central to Southeast Asia, India has been central to South Asia. The rise of India has impacted Chinese ambition and China therefore wants to contain India within the South Asian region. They have resorted, therefore to the encirclement of India through the String of Pearls and by adopting new strategies of asymmetric warfare. Chinese strategic moves in South Asia are aimed at:

1. Isolating India in South Asia and denying her any traditional strategic space;

2. Exploiting India's neighbours view of India as a hegemonic 'big brother';

3. Providing economic and infrastructural largesse in India's periphery, thus pulling countries to the Chinese influence

4. Developing military links aimed at strategic partnerships/ alliances with India's immediate neighbours for strategic objectives against India and IOR;

5. Building ports and pipelines to meet growing energy demands, embedded along the Indian Ocean seaboard.

6. Investing in island nations in IORs such as Sri Lanka, Maldives and Seychelles, aimed at a future China led alliance in IOR; China is also building land based energy and transportation corridors to avoid Straits of Malacca.

China's economic largesse is all too evident in South Asia. Whether it is Pakistan, Bangladesh, Nepal or Sri Lanka, Chinese investments have been large and often in the form of easy interest free loans and grants. The defence deals have varied from supplying the Military tanks, frigates and combat aircraft (Bangladesh and Pakistan) to modernizing military training establishments (Sri Lankan). Some of China's major infrastructural developments include: developing the deep water port in Chittagong, the strategic Hambantota Port in Sri Lanka and developing ports and naval facilities at Hainggyi, Coco, Sittwe, Zadetkyi Kyun, Myeik and Kyaukphyu[36] The strategic motive behind all this is to decrease China's dependency on Malacca Strait and gain strategic access to

IOR. China understands the significance of the Indian Ocean hence they have inducted the aircraft carrier in an attempt to convert its navy to a blue water navy. There has been an increase in the number of submarines sighted in the Indian Ocean Region. Its diplomatic endeavour to befriend South Asian and Indian Ocean Littoral states is seen by strategists as an encirclement of India. Its String of pearls strategic moves can be seen in:-

1. *Hainan Island*: The Island of China with its upgraded military facilities.

2. *Woody Island*: The Island located in South China Sea, near Vietnam.

3. *Chittagong*: The port at Bangladesh with container shipping facilities.

4. *Sittwe*: Deep water port in Myanmar. 5. *Gwadar*: Port of Pakistan a dual purpose base.

6. *Hambantota*: Port developed in Sri Lanka.

7. *Coco Islands Seychelles Islands.*

Figure: 16 String of Pearls

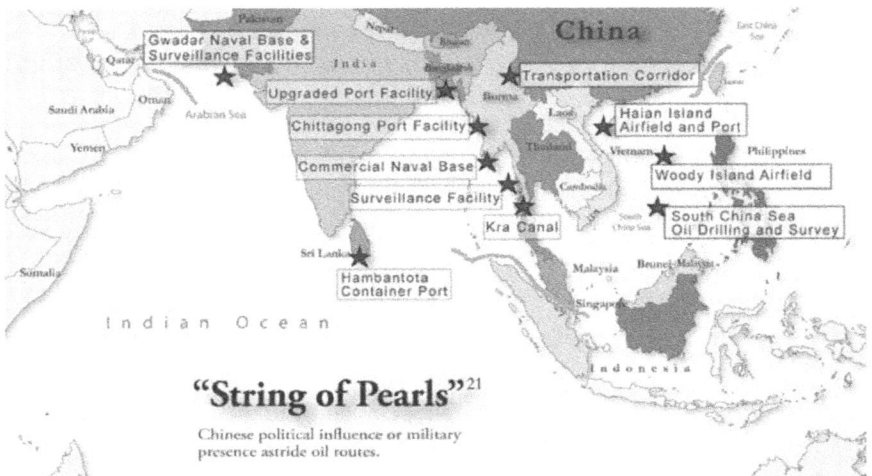

"String of Pearls"[21]

Chinese political influence or military presence astride oil routes.

Source: "Sunday Leader" at startrisks.com/geostrat/13282

The String of Pearls though often commented as a commercial endeavour by China and it may not be an overt military threat to India but the fact that China is involved in the development of these ports gives it a leverage, which it can use in future against India.

India's response

The question that arises now is what choices India has with respect to China. An overtly nationalist approach is not the solution since India is too far behind China as far as the most important yardsticks such as economy and defence modernization are concerned. Hence a three pronged approach needs to be adopted.

Economic co-operation

India should continue its economic rendezvous with China along with bilateral dialogues on sensitive issues. Positive engagement with China is a constructive method to build peace, and in Chinese terminology, to buy time until a nation develops its full potential.

Cordial relationship with the Neighbours

Secondly, India should build cordial relations with its neighbours and extended neighbours. India's "Look East Policy" is already attempting to deal with the latter and has consequently increased its geostrategic power. The Indo-Pacific allied arc has taken a distinct form. The Indian ambassador to the United States and the former foreign secretary, Ambassador Nirupama Rao, spoke about the potentialities of this region in a speech at Brown University: "The earlier concept of the Asia-Pacific had sought to exclude India—today the term Indo-Pacific encompasses the subcontinent as an integral part of this eastern world. We are glad that the mental map of the Asia Pacific has changed and that the centre of gravity has moved westward to include India[37]". After this change in global perception, the opportunities have also increased and India truly has an important role to play in the emerging geostrategic picture. It has become an important maritime power and its economy is rising, thus providing ASEAN with a better platform to collaborate and bring in economic resurgence.

Rigorous diplomatic initiatives have augmented India's economic partnership and enhanced greater participation by both, the state and the private sector. This greater economic integration can also help in creating inter–societal linkages including better connectivity through road and rail – thus integrating Southeast Asia with India and subtly changing the Asian security architecture. Maritime security, humanitarian efforts, disaster relief, and counterterrorism are common global problems which can be more efficiently solved through greater collaboration. Additionally, the strategic relationship with ASEAN and other likeminded nations such as US, and Japan is of paramount importance in order to keep the energy supply lines the Sea Lanes of Communication open and secure. China is central to Southeast Asia hence any effort to contain China might not work. On the other hand, if Japan and India were to accommodate China, it would ensure greater economic integration in ASEAN and would also prevent China from becoming a challenger to the alliance. Economic incentives will be the best method to lure China, because at heart they are a mercantile and trade driven nation. Regional Cooperative Economic Partnership (RCEP) would be a good first step in the right direction.

Apart from this, India also needs to make extra efforts when dealing with its immediate neighbours. The neglect of these potential allies has provided the means for China to creep in and encircle India. Dealing with South Asia is a huge challenge for India primarily due to India's size and the porous nature of its borders with neighbouring countries. But, one must remember that if there are challenges, there are also opportunities. The similarity of cultural heritage can become a good entry point into a fruitful partnership. Pakistan has already been dealt with in detail, during the previous chapters but as far as the other South Asian neighbours are concerned, India needs to develop a comprehensive plan whereby the sensitive and problematic issues are addressed in a cordial, beneficial manner.

In Nepal, the growing Chinese influence – stemming from economic dependence and anti-Indian sentiments – needs to be mitigated and dealt with. It is important to use Nepal as a buffer zone and for this it is essential to provide Nepal with meaningful economic packages with special focus on investing in the energy sector by developing energy related infrastructural projects.

As far as Bangladesh and Sri Lanka are concerned, the acerbic statements made by the Indian regional parties need to be balanced out. India needs to employ a mix of hard and soft policies to mitigate China's hold over the South Asian nations. Investing in their infrastructural sector with special focus on energy, railways, port development, telecommunication etc will be more beneficial than merely providing soft loans.

The opening up of Myanmar and its economy has provided India an opportunity and India should take advantage of this opening and improve its relations with Myanmar by aiding and investing in their economic reforms. The private sector should be encouraged to invest in Myanmar. India needs to increase bilateral trade, develop better rail and road connectivity to augment border trade, expand trade boundaries with Myanmar-Thailand, and help Myanmar exploit natural resources for mutual benefit. Myanmar's fascination for "made in India" goods should be used by Indian traders.[38] The Mekong-India Economic Corridor (MIEC) and India-Myanmar-Thailand Trilateral Highway can become crucial factors in integrating India with Southeast Asia. India can also help with Myanmar's democratization process by providing assistance in drafting their Constitution. India needs to adopt a holistic approach to influence Myanmar's politico-economic and strategic framework. The Dawei deep-sea port, for example will link North East India to Myanmar and Thailand. The Dawei deep sea port of Myanmar will serve Thailand by connecting Bangkok with Andaman Sea through road and rail link across Myanmar and will have no impact on Bangladesh whatsoever[39]. India also needs to develop its infrastructural arrangements in the north eastern sector. A good rail and road network will not only improve the connectivity but also bring about economic development in this region. Thus India needs to formulate sharp policies and more importantly ensure their efficient execution. An efficient and proactive administration, therefore, is the foundation stone for this approach.

Defence Indigenization

The third step essential in the strategic evaluation of the Chinese situation is "Defence Indigenization". In the three pronged approach, this last step dealing with defence indigenization is the most important one. This is the area where India needs to work the most and this is also the toughest target to achieve at the moment. The difficulty does not lie in the lack of skill or entrepreneurship but in the inadequate and inefficient implementation of government policies. Currently, there is too much dependence on the public sector which tends to have a lackadaisical approach towards things as it is not accountable. However in 2001, the government opened up the defence production unit to private sector. This has been a ground breaking decision as it has ensured that the Indian private sector in collaboration with foreign firms can bid for any defence items, provided the FDI (Foreign Direct Investment) remains up to 26 per cent[40]. India has a big Defence Industrial Complex (DIC) consisting of 39 OFs (Ordnance Factories), nine DPSUs (Defence Public Sector Undertakings), 50-odd R&D (Research and Development) laboratories under Defence Research and Development[41] (DRDO). The DRDO is an important government organization which is responsible for developing armament for defence forces. The defence production thus far, has been very unsystematic. While India has done remarkably well as far as developing ballistic missiles, main battle tanks, submarines etc are concerned but nearly 80 per cent of its armament continues to be imported from other countries. If one is to re-examine the SRI (Self Reliance Index), in 1992 it was nearly 30 per cent[42] and it continues to remain the same after more than a decade, in spite of implementing policies to involve the private sector. The DRDO officials revised the index and in 2013 the SRI was revised to 55 per cent[43]. There may be discrepancies but the fact remains that India has replaced China as far as the largest arms importing country in the world is concerned. According to SIPRI, from 2007-20011 India has spent nearly $ 12.7billion in purchasing arms while during the same time China has imported arms worth 6.3 billion$ only. Moreover, it has also started exporting arms and in 2013 China became the fifth largest exporter of arms.

This depicts that the defence industry has had some systemic weaknesses right from the beginning .Historically, the Blackett report[44] in 1948 was the first informed effort made to address this problem and the suggestions given by this committee were valuable, but it was not revised or implemented efficiently with time. For example, Mr. Blackett suggested that the defence budget be increased to nearly two per cent of the GDP. While this was a good decision at the time, it needs to be revised to ensure it does not become an obsolete percentage keeping in mind the global economic picture. Today, even after six decades, India continues to spend a mere two per cent of the GDP on the defence budget. If the pre 60s era was characterized by the lack of an industrial base and a poor economy, the era post the 60s saw an increased/excessive dependence on the Soviets. 'Most defence production in India was under licensee, which neither led to capacities to design nor develop advanced manufacturing techniques; licenses for assembly of weapon systems simply followed one another in boring succession.[45]It was only in 1980 when the Integrated Guided Missile Programme (IGMP) was developed, that the Government started spending more on R&D. This infusion in defence research and development boosted India's defence production and as a result joint defence collaborations began. BrahMos, the Russo-Indian alliance is a classic example of this collaborative development. Apart from this, there have been other countries such as Israel and France, with whom India has enjoyed joint cooperation.

Since the private sector has not been involved in the defence sector from the beginning, the foundation of the programme has remained weak and not developed as it should have. Corrective measures have been taken subsequently though, and one can say that private sector participation is at present in its infancy stage. It will still take India a few years to develop a solid indigenous base for defence production. The process has already started and the last decade has seen an increase in the participation of the private sector especially after the comprehensive offset guidelines under which, foreign companies winning MoD contracts valued at Rs 300 crores or more are required to plough back 30 per cent of the foreign exchange component of the contract into the Indian industry[46]. Additionally, the foreign companies have the freedom to choose their Indian partners and in the 'Buy and Make (Indian)' category,

MoD contracts are to be given to Indian industries, including capable private companies, which may form joint ventures with foreign companies to deliver the final product.[47]

These basic measures need to be followed and implemented since India already is slowly developing its defence industrial base. What it requires now is the infrastructural and technical specialization. The DRDO needs to begin developing niche technology while leaving basic technology to the private sector. Such a division will ensure that constant progress is made as both simple and intricate weapons will be built indigenously. In order to develop advanced technology it is essential that India increases the defence budget and ensures its judicious utilization. To implement such a goal, the defence sector requires comprehensive planning at every stage of development, keeping in mind the eventual users – the armed forces. Hence more synergy is required between the production unit and the defence forces. Post the Kargil conflict, a lot of reports were written and one of the key reports, which focused on the recommendations of a Group of Ministers (GOM) in 2000, made several valid points such as laying down "broad objectives of long term equipment policies and planning on production [and the] simplification of procedures to facilitate the participation of the domestic industry.[48] Moreover, the Kelkar report, the Sisodia Committee report, the Rama Rao Committee etc provided several valid analytical recommendations about the programme. The implementation of these recommendations, however, has been haphazard and disorganized at best.

A distinct Defence Item Description List (DIDL) should include: Quick licensing procedures, easing procurement procedures, fixing the accountability, quickly identifying the Raksha Udyog Ratnas (RURs), increasing the FDI and also clearing it on a priority basis. These are few of the suggestions made in the above reports which need to be examined. With respect to the FDI problem, the Finance Minister stated in the Economic *Survey 2008-09* that the FDI should be increased to 49 per cent across the board, and 'up to 100 per cent, on a case by case basis, in high technology, strategic defence goods, services and systems that can help eliminate import dependence.[49]

In conclusion, if India desires to be seen as a major power, it is imperative for the policy makers to perform a holistic reassessment of the situation and implement the requisite measures efficiently. Any negligence in any of the sectors would be highly detrimental and would eventually dampen the progress of the country. Efficient implementation through astute administration and a farsighted approach would bring rich dividends.

India and Disarmament / Arms Control

"I know not with what weapons World War III will be fought, but World War IV will be fought with sticks and stones."

Albert Einstein.

This adage completely tells the story of weapons and their tryst with mankind. If nuclear issues are not addressed in a comprehensive manner, the world will be annihilated. To negate this scenario, disarmament and arms control need to be projected as the sole potent antidote

These two also remains the most important characteristic feature of the security architecture post World War II. Disarmament has had a longer history by comparison but its inability to achieve the desired result has led to the conceptualization of "Arms Control". This change in strategy has been implemented in the hope that if a consensus is achieved in controlling the arms race, a gradual reduction could be enforced leading to the total elimination of nuclear weapons. Disarmament is generally spoken in terms of total elimination of nuclear weapons. Nations have realized that conventional and nuclear armament has been the major cause for conflict, instability and insecurity. Hence the reduction of arms through both bilateral as well as multilateral treaties has now become a globally desired universal objective of nations. In fact, the United Nations had spoken about the need for the elimination of nuclear weapons in its first General Assembly meeting in 1946. Since then subsequent Conferences on Disarmament have vehemently pursued the issue of disarmament, arms control and nuclear proliferation.

India has been committed to this cause right from the beginning. This can be seen in its call for the peaceful use of nuclear energy as early as 1948. In 1954, India was the first country to call for a ban on nuclear testing. In 1988, India proposed the Rajiv Gandhi "Action

Plan for Ushering in a nuclear weapon –Free and Non-Violent World Order". Further in 1996 India was the member of the Group of 21 which presented to CD the "Programme of Action", as contained in document CD/1419, for the elimination of nuclear weapons with a specified timeframe.[50]. In the Global Zero Summit held in June 2011, the Indian Prime Minister stated that "India has been steadfast in its support for global, non-discriminatory verifiable nuclear disarmament[51]. India is also a party to the Biological and Toxic Weapons Convention (BTWC) and Chemical Weapons Convention (CWC). It remains strongly committed to the Convention on Certain Conventional Weapons (CCW) and has contributed actively to UN efforts made towards strengthening regulations of small arms and light weapons as it believed that it was necessary to break the nexus between small arms proliferation and terrorism and organized crime.[52] Thus Nuclear disarmament was and continues to remain a high priority as far as India's global nuclear strategy is concerned.

However the security architecture post the Cold War has seen a distinct transformation in its paradigms. A different nuclear structure with its own unique characteristics has emerged and it has made what Mr. Paul Bracken rightly calls "The Second Nuclear Age"[53] very complicated. This has created new challenges for India too and therefore requires different contemporary solutions.

Firstly, the emergence of new Nuclear Weapon States has decentralized nuclear power; the nuclear power is no longer under the influence of the P5 nations. This multipolarity makes controlling conflicts that much more difficult, as there is no centralized authority or group of nations (like USA and USSR during Cold War) to put pressure on countries to moderate their actions. The NPT which was created to prevent the horizontal proliferation has failed to prevent the emergence of new nuclear nations, the reasons for its failures can range from, being discriminatory in nature to verification, compliance and enforcement problems. It has refused to amend its charter to incorporate new players like India thus denying the country to play a responsible role in the global non-proliferation struggle.

Secondly the rivalry within the P5 nation, to modernize their nuclear weapons continues, though measures have been taken by US and Russia to curtail their nuclear arsenal but China has increased its nuclear modernization programme. This has created strategic imbalance and has impacted Asia and particularly India adversely. India can no longer think of total elimination of nuclear weapons, because its neighbours' are trying to increase their arsenal, hence per force it has to abandon its dream of global zero and work towards arms control. Moreover, none of the P5 countries are seriously contemplating the possibility of disarming their arsenal to level zero. Even today, the world witnesses the presence of nearly 17,000 nuclear weapons.

Thirdly, nuclear terrorism has made the entire world susceptible to violence, the classical definition of war zones have vanished and no country is entirely safe from this menace. Africa has now become the new hub of terrorist activities. The acquisition of nuclear capabilities is still a zealous objective of terrorist organizations. The fact that Nuclear Weapon States like North Korea and Pakistan have volatile and insecure internal conditions further precipitates this danger and dirty bombs merged with conventional and radioactive materials becoming accessible options for the NSAs is a threatening proposition.

The so called peaceful use of nuclear energy has further complicated the situation. The proliferation risk associated with civilian nuclear plants can be seen in the case of the nuclear programme developed by North Korea, Iran and Pakistan. As of May 2013, more than 30 countries were involved in generating electricity through the civilian nuclear plants. A total of 2346 TWh of electricity is generated by 33 countries all around the world[54]. Many of these nations are Asian which complicates the situation since the safety and security standards of these countries are not adequate to deal with a possible crisis and in the absence of uniform standard safety procedures, the risk of nuclear terrorism and nuclear accidents is accentuated.

The Debate

Various proposals have been made from time to time by various countries in an attempt to totally eliminate nuclear weapons. India in its Rajiv Gandhi action plan had also proposed a plan for eliminating nuclear weapon. A report of the International Commission on Nuclear Non-Proliferation and Disarmament[55] also formulates various policy responses keeping in mind its disarmament objective. It lays stress on treating "Nuclear Zero" as a plausible option by adopting a two phased strategy towards its fulfilment. The two phases refer to the minimization phase and the elimination phase where through short and medium term objectives one tries to first minimize the nuclear weapons and through long term goals (some of which are aimed beyond 2025), attempts to achieve the illusive zero figure[56].

However, while all these studies are well intentioned, the major problem that remains is that the concept of "Global Zero" is utopian, unrealistic and is not achievable – at least not in this century. It can also be stated that disarmament and arms control are relative terms and often one leads to another, but the speed at which the development of weapons has taken place is unprecedented and this has made the debate more complex. Arms control is the first step along the ladder and whether it remains a sole alternative or is transformed into something more substantial depends on the motives of global players involved. Sincerity, indiscrimination, transparency and universally verifiable laws are key issues which will determine the future of nuclear disarmament.

One needs to understand, that history has legitimized the presence of nuclear weapons, but one must also observe that the efficacy of nuclear deterrence has been proved in both, the pre and post-Cold War era. The increase in Nuclear Weapon States from five to eight and the future possibility of a substantial increase in this number proves that the efforts to delegitimize and change the centrality of nuclear weapons has not been successful. This perception of the marginalization of nuclear weapons and the questioning of their utility is often considered an American concept since nations (especially in Asia) that do not possess a modernized conventional armoury consider nuclear weapon as essential arsenal to maintain regional and global balance. While the followers of the programme demanding the de legitimization of nuclear weapons argue that even if a state acquires nuclear weapons, it does not provide them with the assurance that there will be no conflict – as was clearly seen in the Kargil conflict between India and Pakistan and the low intensity conflict which continues even today. These, question the legitimacy of nuclear weapons while also questioning its practical utility. Conversely, however, in the same scenario, the counter argument that arises is that, since both nations possessed nuclear weapons, a full-fledged war/crisis was successfully averted, since both nations understood the far reaching implications of using such a destructive weapon. Moreover, both nations attempted to manage the conflict at a low intensity without allowing it to escalate into a high intensity one. The arguments can work both ways but the truth that remains is that nuclear weapons do create an unstable environment especially during stages of conflict. The solution to this problem, therefore, is complex to say the least. As globalization has intertwined the economies of nations worldwide, the proliferation of nuclear weapons has entangled the security architecture. The situation has now become similar to global economics where the appreciation or depreciation of any individual currency tends to have a cascading effect. Similarly, the amassing of nuclear weapons by even a single nation has far reaching repercussions. If the entire world was moving along the path towards nuclear elimination, only then would the concept of nuclear disarmament be successful. In the case of a global tug of war, the dichotomy between the NWS and NNWS would make the path that much more difficult. The only way out now lies in stabilizing the environment through an unbiased, universal rule of law.

Managing the Nuclear Environment

In this new scenario it is very essential to perceive the situation through a realistic lens. One needs to reassess the dangers and establish a reasonable, workable solution avoiding the dangers of mere rhetoric at all costs. The emergence of a multipolar world has not only amplified threat levels, but also made most regions vulnerable to proliferation, an increasing arms race and nuclear terrorism. The safety and security standards of nuclear installations are also becoming a cause for concern. It has been repeatedly stated that the nuclear installations of P5 nations are considered to be the safest and since there are no standardized norms for monitoring the safety and security standards of these installations, the pressing issue remains that the nuclear installations of New Nuclear Weapon States– such as North Korea and Pakistan are vulnerable to nuclear accidents, attack and sabotage.

To tackle all this, it is essential to formulate a policy where by the thrust area remains focused on managing nuclear issues first and working towards total disarmament later. This management of nuclear issues can be monitored and implemented through arms control. The idea of "Arms Control" was conceived in the 1950s due to global disillusionment with the policy of disarmament but somehow in the 1980s, even arms control lost its sheen. It is a possibility that the present multipolar environment requires the arms control policy more than the erstwhile bipolar world and therefore it might actually be useful in this age. Efforts in this direction are already being made and the New START Treaty, signed between US and Russia in 2010 (which came into force in 2011) has already set targets aimed at limiting accountable deployed strategic nuclear warheads and bombs to 1,550, which would bring it down approximately 30 percent from the 2,200 limit set by SORT and down 74 percent from the START-accountable limit of 6,000.[57] The time has come to transform such bilateral treaties into multilateral forums by inviting other P5 nations and New Nuclear Weapon States to join this effort and shoulder more individual as well as collective responsibility. It is a fact that the P5- nation along with India (P5+1) have the potential to reshape the global scenario. India can be considered important for several reasons, firstly, it is a declared Nuclear Weapon State. Secondly, it has an impeccable record as far as nuclear proliferation is concern and finally, it has a sensible nuclear doctrine which speaks of "No First Use" as an implemented policy. India considers nuclear weapons through the prism of deterrence and not necessarily for war or fighting. If India is pushed to a corner, however, due to an attack by nuclear weapons then it will not hesitate to use its option of massive retaliation to protect its territorial sovereignty. But the careless usage of nuclear weapons as an attack possibility is not its first option. In conclusion, therefore if the P5 nations can sort out their regional rivalries and think above their narrow objectives they can come together and help in containing and monitoring the nuclear menace before it gets out of hand.

Doctrinal Changes

If the nuclear weapon nations can reach an agreement to declare NFU in their nuclear doctrines it would help in building mutual trust and consequently push the nuclear issue to a backburner since by then nuclear weapons would only be considered tools of deterrence and not applicable as offensive strategies. China and India have already declared their intentions about the NFU clause and the US declaration will bring other nations to the negotiating table as well. The promising sign currently is that the nuclear arsenal of most of the nations is kept in a de-matted stage which helps in preventing accidents and miscalculations. This indicates that most nations are beginning to consider nuclear weapons for deterrence purposes rather than attack; however what is required is a treaty whereby this change can be universally adopted, implemented and enforced. Similarly most of the nations have officially supported CTBT, but major Nuclear Weapon States like US, China, India, and Pakistan have not ratified it and again, the moratorium on nuclear testing has been supported by most, but it remains essential to legally endorse it.

Multilateral Arms Control

As mentioned earlier, it is essential to have multilateral treaties to reduce the number of nuclear weapons. In a multipolar world, all the nuclear nations from the highest to the lowest are tied together by the nuclear chain. Hence the minimization and maximization points can be achieved only through mutual consent. The old concept of MAD has already become obsolete. What is now required is to debate and discuss the number and the quality of nuclear weapons required to be reduced. There is also the need for a treaty to limit the ICBMS and MRBMS while constantly attempting to totally eliminate tactical nuclear weapons. There needs to be special focus on the tactical nuclear weapons since the past has proved that tactical nuclear weapons have made the nuclear environment highly unstable, not merely for the adversary but also for the host countries. Several European nations are also apprehensive of holding these weapons on their soil. These reasons could provide a start for the NATO countries to denounce and eliminate its tactical nuclear weapons. Germany Belgium and Netherland, home to bases containing Tactical Nuclear Weapons, have indicated some interest in doing their part and advance to a world free of nuclear weapon by removing the warheads from their siol[58] Once these countries set an example, it will become easier to push other nations to follow suit. Arms control can thus help in limiting the nuclear arsenal and should, therefore; be considered the first step in the long march to achieve global zero. For this it is essential to discuss the nuclear force structure in terms of numbers as well as the type of delivery weapons, the operational and storage numbers etc. A global maximum and minimum need to be debated and arrived at and all the nations should explicitly commit to adhere to these numerical limits. A strategic dialogue between all the Nuclear Weapon States is the next logical step required on the path towards reaching a nuclear zero. These measures should not be limited to strategic weapons but should be extended to conventional and small arms. For a more comprehensive approach, the numbers of both the deployed warheads as well as the stored warheads should be considered for reduction and the dismantlement of nuclear warheads should be hastened. Secondly, the Negative Security Assurance given by the Nuclear Weapon States needs to be legalized. All the P5 nations need to ratify the Nuclear Weapon Free Zone treaties as well. Such ratification will put a good precedent and also encourage other zones to adopt similar endeavours.

Fissile Material Cut off Treaty

The global stockpile of HEU is supposed to be shrinking but even at the end of 2012, it was still 1380 tons, which is sufficient to make nearly 55,000 first generation fissile weapons, and 98 per cent of this material was held by the nuclear weapon states.[59] Though the production of fissile material, especially highly enriched Uranium, has been stopped by most of the P5 nations, the progress in this reduction plan has been slow and obscure. Similarly, the reduction of Plutonium suffers from the same inefficiency and obscurity. Its stockpiles during 2012 were 495 tons, and the cause for concern is that, half of these stockpiles have been produced in the civilian nuclear programme and the other half was for producing weapons[60]. There has been a drastic increase in the Plutonium reprocessing programme. It is essential to have a global consensus on the need for reduction if the production of fissile materials is to be stopped and for this, it is vital to involve the remaining Nuclear Weapon States and take into account their fears and concerns as well. Once a global standard for a maximum and minimum is set, it will become easier to control the nuclear fissile material. The Fissile Missile Cut off Treaty (FMCT) should be broad based, controlling not only the current and future fissile materials, but also the pre –existing stockpiles. As on 2013, a substantial amount of nuclear warheads (nearly 3000 American and 4000 Russian) await dismantlement[61]. Most of the P5 nations have stopped the production of Plutonium and Uranium but the clandestine production of these materials amongst the other Nuclear Weapon States continues. Any ambiguities in this regard should be addressed too, because if the treaty is to be adopted universally, then the concern of all the Nuclear Weapon States should be looked into. Isolated cases should be examined with firmness because a single nation cannot be allowed to jeopardize the global objectives and the implementation of these regulations. To achieve this a greater solidarity between the Nuclear Weapon States is required.

Transparency and Verification

Increasing the transparency of nuclear warheads and fissile materials is the demand of the Non-Nuclear Weapon States. This is a demand that they have been flagging in various NPT Review Conferences. In fact, the Action Plan on Nuclear Disarmament at the 2010 NPT Review Conference agreed that "nuclear disarmament and achieving the peace and security of a world without a nuclear weapon will require openness and cooperation, and …enhanced cooperation through increased transparency and effective verification". Disarmament initiatives cannot be successful if there is even a smidgen of distrust between the Nuclear Weapon States. Amongst the P5 nations China continues to be opaque as far as warheads and production of fissile materials are concerned. There is no official declaration by the Chinese government about the number of nuclear weapons they possess or an official moratorium on fissile material production. It is only through indirect sources that one can conjecture that China has nearly 250 nuclear weapons and that it had ceased production of HEU in 1987 and Plutonium in 1991[62]. This opacity in the size and composition of China's nuclear arsenal is having a cascading effect in Asia. The CTBT is also stuck because important nuclear nations are unable to ratify the treaty. The transparency and verification shown by a majority of the NNWS is laudable but it will not help in eliminating the nuclear menace. What is required is the equal participation of all the NWS in an attempt to counter this menacing situation. Here the concept of nuclear deterrence needs to be enhanced because if nuclear weapons are required for deterrence then each nation can declare their force structure. It is understandable that the nations cannot divulge the placement of its nuclear warhead but at least the base line numbers and type can be intimated. The latter information can actually help in preventing war. In fact, a "Standard Reporting Form" was proposed by the ten members of the Non-Proliferation and Disarmament Initiative Group. This required nations to report on the number type, and the status of the nuclear warhead, delivery vehicles and the amount of fissile material produced for military purposes.[63] .There is another group which is working on these issues as well, like the New Agenda Coalition, and all of them have given valuable suggestions for achieving better transparency. In nutshell, what is required is a universal verification system where the grievances of both P5 nations as well as the other Nuclear Weapon States are addressed and implemented to ensure that the treaties can be universally adopted.

Amend Nuclear Non-Proliferation Treaty (NPT)

This treaty was formulated in 1968 and came into force in 1970 and in 1995 in accordance with article X, paragraph 2, the Review and Extension Conference of the Parties to the treaty decided to extend it indefinitely. The strategic environment at the time was quite different – the Cold War was about to end but the nuclear control was mainly kept with the two superpowers. Initially the treaty was adopted by only three P5 nations mainly US, UK, and the erstwhile USSR. However; gradually, it found its own share of admirers and critiques. The NPT has achieved mixed results. It can boast of having 190 nation states as its members but at the same time North Korea and Iran are examples of where it has failed to execute its obligations. Most importantly, the era post the Cold War saw the emergence of new nuclear security architecture, which was characterized by multi polarity. Since nuclear power is no longer concentrated with the erstwhile powers it is essential to understand the process of decentralization and the possible threat it can generate. Since its extension, new nuclear players have emerged on the scene. Israel has developed its nuclear power clandestinely; India and Pakistan have declared themselves as Nuclear Weapon States. In these altered circumstances it is imperative for the NPT to bring the participation of these countries in its gambit. The formation of a new treaty is not a viable option because the paraphernalia required to achieve that is quite cumbersome, hence the best solution is to review the relevant article and carry out amendments accordingly. If the declared Nuclear Weapon States are included in this treaty, it would make them feel more responsible and will make the treaty more authentic. Some analysts believe that instead of amending the treaty, parallel structures should be created around the NPT whereby the participation of these non- members can be achieved. However, the latter suggestion will not have the same effect because the NPT is recognized as the foundation of the disarmament and non-proliferation movement. Formulating new structures may not carry the kind of authenticity that the NPT has. Moreover it is often easier to debate and amend issues in the review conferences rather than formulating entirely new organizations. A treaty's success also depends on how efficiently it can adopt itself to the changing environment. Pragmatic approaches by political leaders will shape the strategic space and survivability of legal organizations.

Conclusion

Globally there are number of efforts being made by the world community to tackle the nuclear issue but a consensus on many issues is still lacking. As a result, the progress on these treaties has been slow and the major concerns like nuclear proliferation and nuclear terrorism continue to grow. The Arms Control Association Report 2010-2013 highlights that countries like North Korea, Iran and Pakistan continue to challenge the world because they refuse to cease the production of nuclear fissile material. As far as banning nuclear tests are concerned, except for Russia, UK and France, all the other nuclear nations are yet to ratify the CTBT. This is why even though it is signed by a mammoth 183 nations it is still not legally enforceable. Similarly, in 1995 the Geneva based Conference on Disarmament reached a consensus on negotiating a mandate for a FMCT (the so-called Shannon Mandate), but procedural and substantive divisions within the 65-member body have prevented progress in negotiating such a treaty.[64]

As far as nuclear weapon alert levels are concerned, Israel, USA and Russia still maintain nuclear weapons on high alert. There were reports in 2012 that Israel may have fitted its Dolphin class Submarine with nuclear tipped Submarine Launched Cruise missiles.[65] Though the Nuclear Weapon States have agreed to give negative security assurance to Non-Nuclear Weapon States but none of them have ratified the Nuclear Weapon Free Zone treaty in Southeast Asia. Pakistan and India refuse the concept of South Asia Nuclear Free Zone Treaty. Moreover as far as nuclear proliferation is concerned certain nations still continue to proliferate clandestinely the nuclear technology. The chart given below grade nations on important nuclear issues:-

Table: 14 Nuclear Grades

Standard	China	France	Russia	UK	US	India	Israel	Pakistan	DPRK	IRAN
Banning Nuclear Test	B	A	A	A	B	D+	C	D+	F	B-
Ending Fissile Material Production	B	A	A	A	A	F	F	F	F	NA
Reducing Nuclear Weapon Alert Levels	A	B	C+	B	C	A	D+	A	D	NA
Nuclear Force Reduction	D	D+	B+	C+	B	F	D	F	D	NA
Negative Security Assurances	B+	C	C	C	C	B+	D+	B	F	NA

Standard	China	France	Russia	UK	US	India	Israel	Pakistan	DPRK	IRAN
Nuclear Weapon Free Zone	B	B	B	B	C	C-	D-	C-	F	C
IAEA Standards	NA	NA	NA	NA	NA	C	C	C	F	F
Nuclear Weapon Related Export Control	F	A	C	A	A	A-	A	C-	F	F
Multilateral Nuclear Security commitments	A	A	A+	A	B+	A	A	B+	D	D+
Criminalization and Illicit Trafficking	A	B+	A	A	B+	A	B+	B	F	C
Overall Grade	B-	B	B	B+	B-	C+	C-	C-	F	D+

Source: An Arms Control Association Report 2013[66]

Grade	A	A-	B+	B	B-	C+	C	C-	D+	D	D-	F
Value	4.0	3.7	3.3	3.0	2.7	2.3	2.0	1.7	1.3	1.0	.7	.0

It is amply clear that a lot needs to be done both by the P5 nations as well as the non NPT states. To achieve a consensus, it is important to amend the NPT treaty. The NPT also needs to look into the aspirations and grievances of the non NPT nuclear states These states need to be included under the specifications of the treaty because until they ratify, the objective of complete nuclear disarmament cannot be achieved and any number of suggestions or drafts put forward by NPT review conferences to deal with this will be pointless. All the nations need to be responsible and to achieve this aim of a global nuclear ground zero, greater participation of those nations which disagree with the measures need to be ensured. Until that is achieved, stability in Asia cannot be achieved and keeping in mind the changing power structures, if Asia is not stable can the world remain stable?

Endnotes

1   Koshy Ninan, "India Linchpin of the Pivot?",Foreign Policy in Focus, 20 September2012 at fpil.org/india_linchpin_of thepivot

2   For details see C. Raja Mohan's "Managing Multipolarity: India's security Strategy in a Changing world" NBR Special Report, May 2012

3   "Policy of Containment: Comparing Cold War Containment with China Containment"   at   http://southasianthinkers.wordpress.com/2012/12/23/ policy-of-containment-comparing-cold-war-containment-with-china-containment/

4   Tellis Ashley, "Opportunities Unbound .Sustaining the transformation in US-Indian Relations", Carnegie Endownment.2013

5   Ibid

6   Shyam Saran, "The Perils of India's Arbitrage Economy," *Business Standard*, 21 November , 2012

7   Tellis Ashley "Opportunities Unbound .Sustaining the transformation in US-Indian Relations by, Carnegie Endownment.2013.

8   Ravinder Pal Singh, *Recommendations on Arms Procurement Reforms in India*, ORF Policy Paper No. 1, Observer Research Foundation, New Delhi, September 2012, 4–5.

9   S. Amer Latif, *U.S.-India Defense Trade: Opportunities for Deepening the Partnership*, Centre for Strategic and International Studies, Washington, D.C., June 2012,

10 See n,4,Tellis

11 Ibid

12 Ibid

13 Gautam Dutt, "Arming a Friendship: Despite differences in level of Military Ties, India and US going great guns as far as Arms deal go", Mail On Line ,India, 06 June 2012

14 Datt Gautam "Arming a friendship: Despite differences in level of military

ties, India and the U.S. are going great guns as far as arms deals go" Mail Online India, 5 June 2012

15 See n, 2, C.Raja.Mohan

16 Ibid

17 Petr Topychkanov "Russian policy on India and South Asia", 27 Feb 2013 OP-ED Moscow Defence Brief.

18 Radyuhin V, "Changing face of Russia-Pakistan Ties", The Hindu, September 9, 2010

19 *Bakshi Jyotsna,* "Russian Policy Towards South Asia" , *IDSA at http://www. idsa-india.org/an-nov9-9.html*

20 "For Russia ,deepening friendship with India is a top priority", The Hindu,24 December 2012

21 India-Russia Relations by Amb Kanwal Sibbal in AGNI,Volume XV.NO II

22 New trends in Indo-Russian Relations, Edited by V D Chopra,(2003),Kalpaz Publications

23 Petr Topychkanov, Russian Policy on India and South Asia, OP-ED, Moscow Defense Brief,Carnegiee Endownment ,at http://carnegieendowment. org/2013/02/27/russian-policy-on-india-and-south-asia/ftdb?reloadFlag=1

24 See n, 21,India-Russia Relation

25 "India agrees free trade with Belarus, Kazakhstan, and Russia." The Hindu, ,23 October 2013

26 See n, 2 ,C Raja.Mohan

27 Raja Mohan C "Talking Tokyo", The Indian Express, 27 May 2013.

28 Panda Ankit " India and Japan come together", The Diplomat, ,1 Oct 2012

29 Ibid

30 Ibid

31 Dasgupta Pinaki Dr, India and East Asia: Towards a Regional Economic Integration, at https://www.kkc.or.jp/english/activities/indianscholars/KKC_FINAL_PAPER_PDG_.pdf

32 See n, 28, Panda Ankit

33 Ibid

34 Malik Mohan "Victory Without Bloodshed": China's India Strategy , The Diplomat ,August 20, 2013

35 Ibid

36 China's Myanmar Dilemma international crisis group, Asia Report, 14 September 2009

37   "America's Asia Pivot :The view from India", Lecture by Honorable Nirupama Rao, India's Ambassador to United States, Brown India Initiative, Brown University,04 February 2013

38   Ibid.

39   Shafiqullah A K M "Deep Sea Port in Sonadia: A Unique Opportunity for Bangladesh, The Daily Star,20 March 2013

40   Press Note No. 4 (2001 Series) also see Department of Industrial Policy and Promotion, Ministry of Commerce, Government of India, http://dipp.nic.in/English/Policies/FDI_ Circular_01_2012.pdf

41   Behera L K , "India's Defence Industries: Issues of Self Reliance", IDSA Monogram Series, NO 21July 2013

42   Ibid

43   Ibid

44   Blackett's Report as quoted in Ramdas P. Shenoy, Defence Research and Development Organisation 1958-1982 (DRDO:New Delhi 2006)

45   Ravinder Pal Singh, ' Arms Procurement Decision Making: China, India, Israel, Japan, South Korea and Thailand (Oxford University Press and SIPRI: Oxford, 1998),as quoted in India's Defense Industry Issues of Self Reliance by Laxman Kumar Behera, IDSA Monograph Series No 21 July 2013

46   See n, 41,Behera

47   Ibid

48   Ibid

49   Ministry of Finance, Government of India, *Economic Survey 2008-09*

50   India and Disarmament, at meaindia.nic.in/pmicd.geneva

51   Prime Minister Man Mohan Sing's Message to Global Zero Summit ,Press Information Bureau , Prime Minister's Office, Government of India, 22 July 2011

52   Ibid

53   Bracken Paul "The Second Nuclear Age Strategy, Danger and the new power politics"

54   Nuclear figures, May 2013 in World Nuclear Associations, http://www.world-nuclear.org

55   Evans and Yoriko Kawaguchi, "Eliminating Nuclear Threats-A practical Agenda for Global Policymakers" Gareth. Report of The International Commission On Nuclear Non –Proliferation and Disarmament, 2009

56   Ibid

57   "New START At A Glance", Tom Z. Collina, Research Director, August

2012, in Arms Control Association ,for further see www.**armscontrol**.org/factsheets/NewSTART

58 Grant Scneider, "Tactical Nuclear Weapons NATO and Russia", at CSIS.org/images/stories/poni//111007_schneider.pdf

59 Global Fissile Material Report 2013, Seventh Annual Report of the International Panel On Fissile Material at www.fissilematerial.org

60 Ibid

61 "Armament, Disarmament and International Security", SIPRI Year Book ,2013,

62 David Albright and Coery Hinderstein ,"Chinese Military Plutonium and Highly Enriched Uranium Inventories" Institute of Science and International Studies (ISIS) 30 June ,2005

63 Global Fissile Material Report 2013, Seventh Annual Report of the International Panel On Fissile Material.

64 Assessing Progress On Nuclear Non-proliferation and Disarmament – Updated Report Card 2010-2013,April 2013 by Kelsey Davenport and Marcus Taylor.An Arms Control Association Report.

65 Ronen Bergman et al., "Operation Samson: Israel's Deployment of Nuclear Missiles on Subs From Germany," Der Speigel, June 4, 2012, http://www.spiegel.de/international/ world/israel-deploysnuclear-weapons-on-german-uilt-submarines-a-836784.html.

66 See n, 64, Kelsey Davenport and Marcus Taylor.

Bibliography

Books

Angelo A Joseph Jr, "Nuclear Technology", Greenwood Press, 2005

Avnet Cohen, "Israel and the bomb", New York: Columbia University Press, 1998

Banerjee Dipankar, "Security Studies in South Asia: Change and Challenge", New Delhi: Manohar Publication, 2000

Bracken Paul, "The Second Nuclear Age", Times Book, Hennery Holt and Company, New York

Brodie Bernard, in "The Absolute Weapon", New York: Harcourt, 1946,

Bruce Hoffman, "Inside Terrorism", New York: Columbia University Press, 2006

Cohen P Stephen, "The Pakistan Army", Himalaya Books, New Delhi, 1984

Chongn Lin, "China's Nuclear Weapon Strategy: Tradition within

Evolution", Lexington Books, 1988

Chawla Shalini Dr., "Nuclear Pakistan", K W Publications, 2012

Dennis J Blasko, "The Chinese Army Today, Tradition and transformation for the 21st Century", Routledge, New York, 2006

Ferguson D Charles, "Nuclear Energy", Oxford, 2011

Frey Karsten, "India's Nuclear Bomb and National Security", Routledge, 2006

Gupta Arvind, Kapur K D, "Emerging Asian Nuclear Environment", Indian Pugwash Society (2012)

Gupta Arvind, "India in a Changing Global Nuclear Order", IDSA India, Pugwash Publications 2009

Guangqian Peng and Youzhi Yao, Ed, "Strategic Guidance of High-Tech Local War,

The Science of Military Strategy", Academy of Military Science, Beijing, Jun 2005

Herman Kahn, "Thinking about the Unthinkable in the 1980s", Touchstone Publishers.

Iyengar, P K, "Briefing on Nuclear Technology in India," Rupa and Co 2010

Jasjit Singh Air Commodore (Retd), "Why Nuclear Weapons?", Nuclear India, Delhi: Institute for Defence Studies Analysis, KW Publication. 1998

Karnard Bharat, "Nuclear Weapon and Indian Security", Bharat Karnard, Macmillan 2002

Karnard Bharat, "India's Nuclear Policy", Praeger Security International 2008

Koithara Verghese, "Managing India's Nuclear Forces" Routledge Publishers 2012

Kapur Ashok, "Pakistan's Nuclear Development", London Croom Helm 1987

Kenneth Waltz, *Theory of International Politics*, New York: Random House, 1979.

Poulouse T T, "CTBT and the Risk of Nuclear Nationalism in India", Lancer Publication 1996

Pervez Iqbal Cheema, "The Armed Forces of Pakistan", Oxford: Oxford University Press, 2002

Roy Kamphausen, Andrew Scobell, "Right Sizing the People's Liberation Army: Exploring the Contours of China's Military",

Strategic Studies

Institute, U.S. Army War College," Jan-2007

Saalman Lora "The China India Nuclear Crossroads", Carnegie Endowment, 2012

Saran N, Banerjee B, "Nuclear Power In India-A Critical History", Rupa and Co (2008)

Salik Naeem," The Genesis of South Asian Nuclear Deterrence: Pakistan's Perspective", Oxford University Press, 2009

Sisodia N S, Krishnappa V, Singh Priyanka Editors, "Proliferation and Emerging Nuclear Order- In the Twenty First Century", Academic Foundation, 2009

Schelling, T. C, "*The Diplomacy of Violence*", New Haven: Yale University Press, 1966

Sethi Manpreet, "Nuclear Power in the Wake of Fukishima", K W Publications 2012

Singh Jasjit Air Commodore (Retd) "Nuclear India ", KW Publishers, 2007

Tellis J Ashley, "India's Emerging Nuclear Posture: Between Recessed Deterrent and Ready Arsenal", Rand Publication, 2001

Virnave S N, "Atomic Energy and India's Nuclear Capability", Anmol Publication, 2001

Wilson Ward, "Five Myths about Nuclear Weapons", Houghton Mifflin Harcourt, Boston New York (2013)

Wiesman Stieve and Herbert Krosney, "The Islamic Bomb", New York: Times Book, 1981

Zulfikar Ali Bhutto, "If I am Assassinated...", New Delhi: Vikas Publishing House ,1979

Therese Delpech, "Nuclear Deterrence in the 21st century", A Rand Publication

IISS, Military Balance 2012

Stockholm International Peace Research Institute SIPRI Year Book, 2011, 2012 , 2013

Articles

Abdullah Toukan and Anthony H. Cordesman, "Study on a Possible Israeli Strike on Iran's Nuclear Development Facilities", Center for Strategic & International Studies, Washington, DC, 08 March, 2009.

Ahmed Ali "Reviewing India's Nuclear Doctrine", Institute for Defence and Strategic Analysis (IDSA), 2009

Andrews Tim, "Strengthening Global Nuclear Security: The Role of the IAEA," Presentation to the Nuclear Security Conference, King's College London, 18 February, 2010.

Bernard Brodie in "Nuclear Weapons: Strategic or Tactical?", Foreign Affairs, January 1954

Baruah Pranamita, "India-ROK Nuclear Cooperation: Is it a Win-Win Situation?", Institute of Peace and Conflict Studies, 16August, 2011

Bakshi Jyotsna, "Russian Policy towards South Asia", *IDSA*

Bruno Tertrais "Pakistan's nuclear and WMD programmes: status, evolution and risks", EU Non-Proliferation Consortium, No 19 July 2012

Collina Z. Tom, "New Start at a Glance", August 2012, Arms Control Association

Chaitinya Ravi "The Nuclear Safety Culture in India, Past Present and Future", Institute of Peace and Conflict Studies, Special Report

Chandrashekhar S, Arvind Kumar and Rajaram Nagappa, "An Assessment of Pakistan's Ballistic Missile Program: Technical and Strategic Capability", NIAS Study, 2006

Chari,P.R , "India's Nuclear Doctrine :confused Ambitions" , The Nonproliferation Review/Fall-Winter 2000

Christopher Clary "Thinking about Pakistan's Nuclear Security in Peacetime, Crisis and War", IDSA, Occasional Paper No 12

David Albright and Coery Hinderstein, "Chinese Military Plutonium and Highly Enriched Uranium Inventories", Institute of Science and International Studies (ISIS), 2005

Dafna Linzer, "S. Korea Nuclear Project Detailed Work Called Near Weapons Grade", Washington Post Staff Writer Sunday, 12September, 2004

Dalia Dassa Kaye,Alireza Nader ,Parisa Roshan, "Israel and Iran - A Dangerous Rivalry" ,Rand Publication

Gopalakrishnan A, "Issues of nuclear safety" in Frontline, retrieved 12 November, 2012

Hui Zhang, "China's Nuclear Weapons Modernization: Intentions, Drivers, and Trends", Belfer Center for Science and International Affairs, 2012

Huth, P. K. (1999), "Deterrence and International Conflict: Empirical Findings and Theoretical Debate", *Annual Review of Political Science*

Jain S. K Dr, "Nuclear Power – An Alternative" at http://www.npcil.nic.in/ pdf/nuclear%20power-%20an%20alternative.pdf

Jasjit Singh, "Nuclear Command and Control", Strategic Analysis, May 2001 , Vol XXV

Kelsey Davenport, "The Proliferation Security Initiative (PSI) At a Glance", Press Contact, Non-proliferation Analyst, Arms Control

Kapur Vivek, "Ballistic Missile Proliferation: Implications for India", IDSA Comment

Kapilla Subhash Dr, "Asian security environment and choices for India", IntelliBriefs, April, 2010

Kalyan M Kemburi, "China India and Cruise Missiles", Monetary Institute of International Studies https://csis.org/images/stories/poni/110707_ Kemburi.pdf

Kerr, Paul, "Iran's Nuclear Program: Status", Congressional Research Service Retrieved 02 October, 2012

Kenneth Allen Maryanne Kivlehan-Wise, "Implementing PLA

Second Artillery Doctrinal Reforms"

Krepon Michael, "Pakistan's Nuclear Strategy and Deterrence Stability" http://www.stimson.org/images/uploads/research-pdfs/kreponPakistan Nuclear Strategy and Deterrence Stability. pdf

Kenneth Luongo and Naeem Salik" Building Confidence in Pakistan's nuclear Security ", Arms Control Today, December, 2007.

Latif S. Amer, "*U.S.-India Defense Trade: Opportunities for Deepening the Partnership*", Center for Strategic and International Studies, Washington, D.C., June 2012,

Lodhi FS Sardar; Lieutenant General (Retd), "Pakistan Nuclear Doctrine", *Pakistan Defence Journal, 1999*

Murphy H Charles, "Mainland China's Evolving Nuclear Deterrent," Bulletin of the Atomic Scientists, January 1972

Malik Mohan, "Victory without Bloodshed": China's India Strategy", The Diplomat, August 20, 2013

Michael McDevitt, "Deterring North Korean Provocations", Brookings Northeast Asia Commentary, February, 2011

Nair K Vijai ,"China's Evolving strategic capabilities :Doctrine, Concept, Force- Structure", in South Asia Strategic Forum ,25 May 2013

Patel Y I, "Dig Vijay to Divya Astra: A Paradigm Shift in the Indian Army's Doctrine," *Bharat Rakshak Monitor,* Vol. 6, No. 6

Peter R. Lavoy, Scott D. Sagan, and James J. Wirtz (eds.), "*Planning the Unthinkable*", Ithaca: Cornell University Press, 2000,

Quackenbush Stephen L, "General Deterrence and International Conflict: Testing Perfect Deterrence Theory", .In International interactions: Empirical and Theoretical research in International Relations

Rajesh Rajgopalan "The future of Non Proliferation Regime" , Proliferation and Emerging Nuclear Order in the Twenty First Century

Ramana, M V, "India's Changing Nuclear Policy", Peace Magazine, Jan-Feb 1998

Roe, Sam,(28January, 2007). "An atomic threat made in America". *Chicago Tribune* Retrieved 01July, 2009.

Ramana,M.V and Ashwin Kumar, "Safety First? Kaiga and Other Nuclear Stories", 2010, Economic and Political Weekly xlv no. 747:51

Ravinder Pal Singh, *"Recommendations on Arms Procurement Reforms in India"*, ORF Policy Paper, no. 1, Observer Research Foundation, New Delhi, September 2012,

S. Korea, US agree to set N. Korean nuclear deterrence policy, 2014 Korean Times 25 Oct, 20012

Shyam Saran, "The Perils of India's Arbitrage Economy," *Business Standard*, 21 November, 2012

Sibbal Kanwal Ambassador (Retd), "India-Russia Relations", AGNI, Volume XV.NO II

Scobell Andrew, "China's Use of Military Force: Beyond the Great Wall and the Long March", Pacific Affairs, Vol 77, No -4(Winter -2004-2005)

Stokes Mark, "China's Evolving Conventional Strategic Strike Capability" project2049.net/documents/chinese_anti_ship_ballistic_missile_asbm

Stephen Polk, "China's Nuclear Command and Control", AIR POWER, Journal Vol. 2 No. 4 (WINTER 2005, October-December)

Subramanian T S, "Total self-sufficiency in PHWR programme", Volume 24 - Issue 08, Mumbai: Frontline

Waltz Kenneth "The Spread of Nuclear Weapons: More may be better ", in Adelphi Papers, Number 171(London: International Institute For Strategic Studies, 1981)

World Nuclear Association, "Plans for New Reactors Worldwide", *(Updated March 2013),*

Tellis Ashley "Opportunities Unbound .Sustaining the transformation in US-Indian Relations", Carnegie Endownment.2013

Petr Topychkanov, "Russian policy on India and South Asia", 27Feb,2013 OP-ED Moscow Defence Brief

Zhongguo Junshi Baike Quanshu [Chinese Military Encyclopedia], Beijing: Academy of Military Science Publishers, July 1997, Volume 2-330.

Zafar Nawaz Jaspal, "Requiring Pakistan's nuclear Strategy ", Defence Journal, at HTTP://www.defencejournal.com/2001/july/reassessing. htm

Reports/Speeches/Testimonies

AERB Annual Report, 2012-1013

Ambassador C. Paul Robinson, John Foster, and Thomas Scheber, "The Comprehensive Test Ban Treaty: Questions and Challenges", Lecture No 1218, The Heritage Foundation, 07 Nov 2012

Bucher.R.G, "India's Baseline plan for nuclear energy self-sufficiency stage", Prepared for: National Nuclear Security Administration Office of International Regimes and Agreements, 2009

Country Reports on Terrorism 2011 United States Department of State Publication Bureau of Counterterrorism Released April 2012

Draft Report of National Security Advisory Board on Indian Nuclear Doctrine, 17 August, 1999

DOD, Military and Security Development Involving the People's Republic of China .2013

Declaration of the Government of the People's Republic of China],"*Renmin Ribao*, 16 October 1964

Dirty bomb USNRC Fact sheet

Eliminating Nuclear Threats, By Gareth Evans and Yoriko Kawaguchi, Report of the International Commission on Nuclear Non-Proliferation and Disarmament (2009)

Global Fissile Material Report 2011: Nuclear Weapon and Fissile Material Stockpiles and Production, International Panel on Fissile Materials, January 2012.

Global Fissile Material Report 2013, Seventh Annual Report of the

International Panel on Fissile Material

Ministry of Finance, Government of India, Economic Survey 2008-09

Responsibility Beyond Rules: Leadership for a Secure Nuclear Future

March 2013, a NSGEC report

Raja Mohan C. "Managing Multipolarity: India's security Strategy in a Changing world " NBR Special Report, May 2012

"Remarks of the Prime Minister of Pakistan, Nawaz Sharif, on Nuclear Policies and the CTBT", National Defence College, Islamabad, 20 May, 1999

Nuclear Weapons: The state of Play, Center for Nuclear Non-Proliferation and Disarmament, Australian National University (2013)

Thorium Fuel Cycle –Potential Benefits and Challenges" IAEATECDOC-1450

Statement by the Prime Minister of India Dr. Manmohan Singh at the Nuclear Security Summit 13 April, 2010

Journals

1. Arms Control

2. Annual Review of Political Science

3. Bulletin of the Atomic Scientists

4. Foreign Affairs

5. Jane's weekly

6. Pacific Affairs

7. Pakistan Defence Journal

8. Center For Strategic and International Studies(CSIS) Publications

9. International Institute of Strategic Studies (IISS) Publications

10. Rand Publications

11. Strategic Analysis

12. Strategic Digest

Newspaper /Magazines

1. Asia Report

2. The Asahi Shimbun, Asia and Japan Watch

3. The Diplomat

4. The Dawn

5. The China Times

6. Chicago Tribune

7. Economic and Political Weekly

8. The Economist

9. Frontline

10. Peace Magazine

11. International Energy Outlook

12. Peace Magazine

13. The Indian Express

14. The Hindu

15. The Hindustan Times

16. The Nation

17. Korean Central News Agency(KCNA)

18. The Korean Times

19. People's Daily

20. Stratfor Geopolitical Weekly

21. The Times ,New York

22. Washington Post

UN REPORTS/ WHITE PAPERS

1. Australian Defence White Paper 2013

2. The Diversified Employment of China's Armed Forces, The People's Republic of China April 2013, Beijing

3. Japan Defence White Paper 2012

4. CTBT Text

5. NPT Text

6. Nuclear Threat Initiative(NTI)

7. Nuclear Supplier's Group(NSG)

8. Seoul Communiqué-Nuclear Security Summit

9. Convention on the Physical Protection of Nuclear Materials, 2005(CPNM)

10. International Convention for the Suppression of Acts of Nuclear Terrorism (ICSANT)

Index